CHILDREN'S RIGHTS AND THE MINIMUM AGE OF CRIMINAL RESPONSIBILITY

Advances in Criminology
Series Editor: David Nelken

Recent titles in the series

Hate on the Net
Extremist Sites, Neo-fascism On-line, Electronic Jihad
Antonio Roversi

Decisions to Imprison:
Court Decision-Making Inside and Outside the Law
Rasmus H. Wandall

The Policing of Transnational Protest
Edited by Donatella della Porta, Abby Peterson and Herbert Reiter

Migration, Culture Conflict, Crime and Terrorism
Edited by Joshua D. Freilich and Rob T. Guerette

Re-Thinking the Political Economy of Punishment:
Perspectives on Post-Fordism and Penal Politics
Alessandro De Giorgi

Deleuze and Environmental Damage:
Violence of the Text
Mark Halsey

Globalization and Regulatory Character:
Regulatory Reform after the Kader Toy Factory Fire
Fiona Haines

Family Violence and Police Response:
Learning From Research, Policy and Practice in European Countries
Edited by Wilma Smeenk and Marijke Malsch

Crime and Culture:
An Historical Perspective
Edited by Amy Gilman Srebnick and René Lévy

Power, Discourse and Resistance:
A Genealogy of the Strangeways Prison Riot
Eamonn Carrabine

The full list of series titles can be found at the back of the book

Children's Rights and the Minimum Age of Criminal Responsibility
A Global Perspective

DON CIPRIANI

ASHGATE

© Don Cipriani 2009

All rights reserved. No part of this publication may be reproduced, stored in a retrieval system or transmitted in any form or by any means, electronic, mechanical, photocopying, recording or otherwise without the prior permission of the publisher.

Don Cipriani has asserted his right under the Copyright, Designs and Patents Act, 1988, to be identified as the author of this work.

Published by
Ashgate Publishing Limited
Wey Court East
Union Road
Farnham
Surrey, GU9 7PT
England

Ashgate Publishing Company
Suite 420
101 Cherry Street
Burlington
VT 05401-4405
USA

www.ashgate.com

British Library Cataloguing in Publication Data
Cipriani, Don
   Children's rights and the minimum age of criminal responsibility : a global perspective. - (Advances in criminology)
   1. Criminal liability 2. Children's rights
   I. Title
   345'.04

Library of Congress Cataloging-in-Publication Data
Cipriani, Don.
   Children's rights and the minimum age of criminal responsibility : a global perspective / by Don Cipriani.
      p. cm. -- (Advances in criminology)
   Includes bibliographical references and index.
   ISBN 978-0-7546-7730-7 -- ISBN 978-0-7546-9447-2 (ebook)
   1. Criminal liability. 2. Capacity and disability. 3. Age (Law) 4. Children--Legal status, laws, etc. 5. Children (International law) I. Title.

K5076.C48 2009
345'.04--dc22
                                                                                                2008053460

ISBN: 978-0-7546-7730-7 (Hb)
ISBN: 978-0-7546-9447-2 (eBook)

Printed and bound in Great Britain by
MPG Books Ltd, Bodmin, Cornwall.

Contents

List of Figures and Tables	vii
Foreword	ix
Nigel Cantwell and Jaap E. Doek	
Preface	xiii
Acknowledgements	xvii

1 Shifting Perspectives on Children, Shifting Rights and Criminal Responsibility in Juvenile Justice   **1**
Rights, Competence, and Competing Constructions of Childhood   1
Welfare Approach and the Postponement of Criminal Responsibility   4
Criminal Responsibility and the Justice Approach   8
Conclusion   16

2 Children's Rights' Mediation of Welfare–Justice Tensions   **19**
Progression of Rights from Welfare to Justice   20
The Best Interests of the Child and Due Process Guarantees   24
Respect for the Views of the Child and Effective Participation at Trial   26
The Evolving Capacities of the Child   29
Reintegration into Society   36
Conclusion   37

3 MACRs and States' Obligations under Regional and International Law Instruments   **41**
International Covenant on Civil and Political Rights   41
International Covenant on Economic, Social and Cultural Rights   43
American Convention on Human Rights   43
Protocol I Additional to the Geneva Conventions of 12 August 1949   44
Convention against Torture   49
United Nations Standard Minimum Rules for the Administration of Juvenile Justice   50
Convention on the Rights of the Child   53
African Charter on the Rights and Welfare of the Child   65
European Social Charter   65
European Convention on Human Rights   66
Conclusion   67

4	**Historical Influences on MACRs**	71
	Roman Law, European Law, and European Colonial Law	71
	Islamic Law	77
	Soviet Law	84
	Customary, Traditional, and Religious Law Systems	87
	Conclusion	90
5	**Current MACRs Worldwide and Modern Trends**	93
	Making Sense of MACRs and Punishment: Methodological Considerations	93
	Current MACRs Worldwide	97
	Scrutiny under the CRC and Rising MACRs	111
	Downward Pressures: Isolated Crimes and Widespread Hype	114
	The MACR as a General Principle of International Law	126
	Conclusion	128
6	**Practical Implications and Challenges of MACR Implementation**	131
	No Proof of Age or Reliable Age Estimates	131
	Problematic State Responses to Children Younger than MACRs	136
	No Effective Response to Children Younger than MACRs	139
	MACRs that Threaten Children's Right to Effective Participation at Trial	144
	Undermining of *Doli Incapax* and Similar Presumptions	148
	Instrumental Use of Young Children by Adults for Crimes	151
	Courts' Disregard for MACRs, and Extrajudicial Acts Against Children	153
	Conclusion	155
7	**Making MACRs Work for Children's Rights**	157
	Defining a More Meaningful MACR	157
	MACR Provisions: Establishment, Implementation, and Monitoring	159

Annex 1: United Nations Convention on the Rights of the Child   *165*

Annex 2: Worldwide MACR Provisions and Statutory Sources by Country   *187*

Index   *225*

List of Figures and Tables

Figure

5.1   Current MACR distribution worldwide   109

Tables

4.1   Selected Islamic school age ranges (in years) for individual
       determinations of puberty   79

5.1   Summary of worldwide MACR provisions by country   98
5.2   MACR trends since adoption of the CRC (1989)   112

Foreword

States Parties to the United Nations Convention on the Rights of the Child (CRC) are urged—though not obligated—to promote the establishment of a minimum age below which children are presumed not to have the capacity to infringe the penal law (CRC Art. 40(3) under (a)). The United Nations Standard Minimum Rules for the Administration of Juvenile Justice (Beijing Rules) recommend setting this minimum age, better known as the minimum age of criminal responsibility (MACR), at not too low a level (Rule 4.1). But the question of what might constitute "low," and what the most appropriate age level for the criminal responsibility of children should be, remains unanswered and is one of the most controversial aspects of juvenile justice policy. The issues are complex, and this book provides an unprecedented global insight into their nature and their ramifications.

The backdrop to the controversy is the extremity of the variations in current MACRs throughout the world: some countries have an age of 0 by default, whereas others have set 16 years. This first of all demonstrates the lack of agreed criteria on which minimum age determination is to be based. Even the fact that the great majority of MACR levels fall between 7 and 14 does nothing to dispel the justified perception of total discord in this regard. Rather, it leads to the inevitable conclusion that age determination has had little or nothing to do with child development considerations. This backdrop, however, is only symptomatic of the basic problem to be addressed: it reflects fundamental disagreement about what the setting of an MACR is intended to achieve, rather than simply indicating the existence of differing views about how to achieve an acknowledged objective. In other words, there is very little common ground on which to build consensus on the MACR as a children's right issue. There are two main opposing viewpoints.

On the one hand are those seeking to ensure that the highest possible age is set—some even advocate for 18, which would to all intents and purposes abolish "juvenile justice" as such. They look on contact with the formal (criminal) justice system—even when it is specially conceived for dealing with young offenders and comprises not only a special court procedure, but also diversionary measures—as inherently undesirable for young people. A relatively low MACR is then viewed as reflecting a repressive, punitive approach to juvenile offending. Undeniably this is so in some cases. At the same time, however, certain systems where MACRs are low have only the most exceptional recourse to deprivation of liberty for juvenile offenders of whatever age. Similarly, others divert most young offenders from the court process, save for the most serious (violent) crimes, in cases of persistent recidivism and, importantly, in any instance where the young person denies the alleged offence or salient aspects of the case. In other words, the level of MACR is not necessarily dictated by overall policy towards juvenile offenders.

The other approach looks on juvenile justice systems as not being, a priori, inherently negative mechanisms for responding to young people who are "suspected of, charged with or recognised as having infringed the penal law." If they operate in accordance with the principles and perspectives set out in the Beijing Rules and the CRC, including having at their disposal a range of constructive measures with which to respond, there is no reason to suppose that juvenile courts, alongside diversionary procedures for as many offenders as possible, constitute a means for denying the human rights of the young people concerned. On the contrary, only children above the MACR may be heard by a court and thus have access inter alia to due process, enabling them to be considered "innocent until proven guilty." Many systems with relatively high MACRs rely on administrative proceedings to deal with younger offenders where the latter may not be able to contest the alleged facts of the case effectively. Such proceedings also too frequently result in the imposition of forms of deprivation of liberty in the guise of educational or protective measures, often for lengthy periods that may be neither pre-determined nor properly monitored and reviewed. Thus, in turn, a high MACR does not automatically denote more effective protection of children's rights.

The debates on the question of the most appropriate MACR have indeed often suffered from a combination of sensationalism, misinterpretation, over-simplification and myth:

- Sensationalism—the relatively rare cases of younger children committing the most serious of crimes are used by some to demand the lowering of the MACR, claiming that this would provide the answer to ensuring adequate and dissuasive responses.
- Misinterpretation—the purposes and goals of the juvenile justice system are inadvertently or deliberately misconstrued: courts are portrayed by some as the purveyors of punishment whereas others view diversion and other non-judicial responses as forms of "leniency." Juvenile justice systems are in fact to be based neither on punishment nor "leniency," however; their mission is to secure appropriate, effective and above all constructive outcomes for young offenders.
- Over-simplification—such as the contention that a higher or lower MACR determines the kind of measure that will be imposed on young offenders.
- Myth—that, for example, the grounds for setting an MACR reflect the point at which "society" understands that its children know the difference between "right" and "wrong."

This study by Don Cipriani is by far the most comprehensive and analytical presentation to date of the many aspects of the establishment of a minimum age of criminal responsibility for children. It provides an exhaustive overview of current MACRs worldwide but also elaborates on states' obligations with regard to the establishment of an MACR under the CRC and other international and regional instruments. It also discusses the practical implications and challenges of the implementation of MACRs, and, finally, presents ideas on how we can make MACRs work for children's rights. It is thus a very welcome and major contribution to a well-informed discussion on the most appropriate minimum age of criminal responsibility.

We very much encourage governments and others involved in the development of a juvenile justice system that is in full accordance with the CRC to benefit from this landmark study.

Nigel Cantwell[1]
Jaap E. Doek[2]

---

1 Founder, Defence for Children International.
2 Former Member (1999–2007) and Chairperson (2001–2007), United Nations Committee on the Rights of the Child.

Preface

This study presents a worldwide analysis of minimum ages of criminal responsibility (MACRs) as they relate to international children's rights. In brief, the MACR is the lowest age limit for juvenile justice delinquency jurisdiction—the youngest age at which children may potentially be held liable for infringements of a given country's penal laws. Terminology varies widely across countries, legal families, and languages, yet the underlying concept is relatively stable: before some stipulated age, children may never face criminal responsibility, procedures, or punishments. Basic tenets of criminal law and various international legal obligations hold that all countries must establish respective MACRs. When children younger than the stipulated age are suspected of committing illegal acts, civil law measures of welfare, care, assistance, and protection may be triggered. When they reach the MACR and allegedly break the law, the possibility exists for the first time for penal procedures and sanctions. This does not mean to say that *all* such children should face criminal law procedures or criminal punishment, as alternative procedures and measures are often available. Even though the MACR seems fairly straightforward at this level, it proves to be surprisingly complex in theory and practice.

Due to common confusion, a clear distinction between the MACR and the minimum age of penal majority must be emphasized. The minimum age of penal majority is the lowest age at which children may be held responsible specifically in adult criminal courts. As explored later in this study, international standards consistently hold that national minimum ages of penal majority must be 18 years of age or higher—that is, that children should only be subject to juvenile justice court proceedings. Contrary to such standards, many countries' adult criminal courts still have jurisdiction over some children, and at times the minimum age of penal majority even coincides with the MACR (i.e., the very youngest age for criminal responsibility may signify responsibility in adult courts).

International children's rights have a great deal to say about such issues. As enunciated most visibly in the United Nations Convention on the Rights of the Child (CRC)—ratified or acceded to by 190 of 192 countries in the world—international children's rights set out all children's civil, political, economic, social, and cultural rights, as well as a comprehensive framework for their implementation.[1] An international body of experts under the CRC, the Committee on the Rights of

---

1 Beyond 190 of 192 UN Member States, Cook Islands, the Holy See, and Niue increase the total number of CRC States Parties to 193. See Annex 1 for the full text of the CRC.

the Child, periodically reviews national-level progress. In other words, children's rights offer a shared and principled approach to addressing children's issues, based on a nearly universal consensus, which international law further validates and supports. In particular, international children's rights also bring a mandate for countries to establish respective MACRs, as well as certain restrictions on how they are established and applied. The CRC and international children's rights form the explicit basis for the current study because of, inter alia, this international legitimacy and legal weight, their broad and balanced framework, their orientation towards practical implementation, and their intrinsic link to the MACR.

MACRs are not the greatest challenge in juvenile justice or for children's rights around the world, but they are consistently salient and controversial. When the Committee on the Rights of the Child considered issuing a General Comment specifically on MACRs in 2002, consensus proved impossible. As the Committee drafted its 2008 General Comment on juvenile justice overall, the MACR was still the aspect most commented upon. Given such prominence, detailed analysis of MACRs inherently risks overstating their relative significance, or the significance of specific age levels. This is not the intention of the current study, nor is there any intention to downplay other common problems in juvenile justice systems worldwide, such as the vast over-reliance on the deprivation of liberty; general conditions and violence in places of confinement; trial and/or punishment of children as adults; and application of criminal law procedures and punishments for status offenses.[2]

However, the substantial body of research on juvenile justice, including from an explicit children's rights perspective, tends to address primarily such problems and the children older than MACRs affected by them. At the same time, it tends to overlook the MACR and its implications, or to make simplistic assumptions about the MACR's implications for children's rights—particularly when it comes to preferred MACR age levels, respective governments' claims about their MACRs, and children younger than MACRs.

Thus, a narrow focus on MACRs seems justified, if for no other reason, because no thorough children's rights analysis of MACRs has ever been undertaken. Indeed, the absence of a modern foundational analysis reflects a historical lack of clarity on how MACRs fit into the children's rights framework. When applied in practice, such gaps can lead to very real consequences for children and, unexpectedly, for the broader prospects for children's rights. In this sense, stepping up very closely to scrutinize the MACR brings not only a richer understanding of the MACR itself, but upon turning around again, it also seems to offer useful insights for the larger children's rights context and some of its fundamental principles. This much is indeed intentional—to attempt to contribute to the ongoing debate on

---

2   Status offenses are acts that are not offenses if committed by adults, such as truancy and running away. For an overview of juvenile justice challenges, see Meuwese, Stan, ed., *KIDS BEHIND BARS: A study on children in conflict with the law*, Amsterdam, Defence for Children International The Netherlands, 2003.

the substance and application of children's rights. This study's examination of MACRs seeks to uncover how MACRs—as one small but important piece of a larger puzzle—can best be integrated with and reinforce children's rights.

Therefore, more succinctly, this study's scope is a worldwide analysis of MACRs and their key intersections as they ultimately relate to children's rights. The nature of this endeavor unfortunately precludes examination of the full context of any given country's criminal justice system, society, culture, and history, although crucial aspects are addressed thematically and case studies are employed to illustrate common issues. There are other unavoidable simplifications. Several closely related topics are discussed summarily or omitted entirely, such as children's lessened culpability in terms of sentence mitigation, and criminal responsibility in the context of military conflict, international crimes, extradition, and refugee law.[3] Despite such limitations, the current study seeks to offer useful contributions for such research as well.

With these caveats in mind, the seven chapters of this study are structured to peel away in succession a series of key perspectives on the MACR:

- Chapter 1 introduces basic notions about rights, explains how perceptions of children's competence largely determine which rights children are permitted to exercise for themselves, and illustrates how juvenile justice history has swung around two predominant models as such—with the MACR precisely in the middle.
- Chapter 2 directly introduces international children's rights, as well as the international juvenile justice standards derived from them, and probes how these standards mediate the classic juvenile justice tensions that hover around the MACR.
- Chapter 3 documents the precise obligations regarding MACRs under regional and international law instruments, and under their formal interpretations, in order to identify the current international consensus guidance on MACRs and their application.
- Chapter 4 explores the main historical influences that broadly explain national MACRs in force today.
- Chapter 5 presents current MACRs country-by-country—including key related provisions, statutory citations, and excerpts in most cases—and summarizes the evidence and arguments that a general principle of international law exists with respect to MACRs. It also highlights the modern trends in MACR age levels and the dynamics of national debates on MACRs.

---

3   For excellent discussions of such issues, see respectively Scott, Elizabeth S., and Laurence Steinberg, "Blaming Youth," 81 *Texas Law Review* 799, 2003; and Happold, Matthew, *Child Soldiers in International Law*, Manchester, Manchester University Press, 2005.

- Chapter 6 identifies and analyzes the main recurring challenges and implications of applying MACRs in practice.
- Finally, Chapter 7 draws from all of the preceding viewpoints in order to encapsulate the principal theoretical and practical considerations necessary to make MACRs work for children's rights.

Don Cipriani

Acknowledgements

An incalculable number of people helped lay the path to the printing of this ink on these pages. I would like to thank a few of them in particular. First, the dedicated support of Nigel Cantwell and Jaap Doek has been truly fundamental, and Sharon Detrick and Bernardine Dohrn have been constant sources of insight and encouragement. Among others, the following people also offered discerning comments and suggestions on various drafts: an Ashgate anonymous reviewer, Gerard de Jonge, Josine Junger-Tas, Ashgate's Publisher for Law and Legal Studies Alison Kirk, Gerison Lansdown, Ton Liefaard, Advances in Criminology Series Editor David Nelken, Elies van Sliedregt, Paul Vlaardingerbroek, and Nevena Vuckovic-Sahovic. Scores of UNICEF offices, NGOs, lawyers, and scholars across continents have shared with me precious sources, translations, and explanations on challenging research questions. This study would not have been possible without their expertise and generosity.

Special thanks go to Gabriela Fabiani and Anders Hopperstead for their careful reading and advice; to all of my wonderful colleagues from the Vrije Universiteit Amsterdam Faculty of Law, especially Finette Lips and Mila Volf; and to Jacqueline Rogers at the University of Maryland School of Public Policy. I am exceptionally grateful for the patience, understanding, and love of *mugghier 'm* Tiziana Lemma, my parents Alfred and Aida Cipriani, my brother David Cipriani, and the rest of my family and friends.

The John D. and Catherine T. MacArthur Foundation, the Netherland–America Foundation, and the United States Fulbright Program provided critical financial support for this study.

Para mis queridos alumnos Adrián y Elmer

Chapter 1
Shifting Perspectives on Children, Shifting Rights and Criminal Responsibility in Juvenile Justice

This chapter begins by presenting a series of basic concepts about rights, who exercises different rights, and the role of competence in describing rights. As explored thereafter, these ideas are tightly linked to the ways in which adult society interprets and constructs the meaning of childhood, and confers certain legal rights to children or not, based on assumptions about children's competencies.

The central themes in juvenile justice history offer a case study of such dynamics. Classic welfare and justice approaches were built around different ideas about children, which led to dramatically divergent roles for rights and criminal responsibility. The sliding scale from the welfare approach to the justice approach, with competency and responsibility as the central tipping points, is in reality vastly more nuanced than the account offered in the present study. However, as this chapter highlights, its history and elements present the basic dilemmas that virtually every country faces to some extent, stemming from the inherent flaws of each approach. This common narrative is part of the essential background for understanding children, age, and criminal responsibility.

Rights, Competence, and Competing Constructions of Childhood

The very meaning of "rights," even in summary form, proves to bear very real consequences in the lives of children and their families. In the broadest sense, rights are a special or justified type of claim, or a "claim against someone whose recognition as valid is called for by some set of governing rules or moral principles."[1] Such recognition both justifies and distinguishes rights from other types of claims.

Based on their properties, philosophers often divide rights into the categories of liberty rights and protection rights. Liberty rights affirm people's prerogative to act with freedom in specific contexts—in the sense that there is no restriction

---

1 Feinberg, Joel, "The Nature and Value of Rights," in *Rights, Justice, and the Bounds of Liberty: Essays in Social Philosophy*, Princeton, Princeton University Press, 1980, at 155.

on them—by triggering the duty for others to not interfere.[2] Specific liberty rights include, for example, the rights to free speech, to freedom of religion, and to vote. Depending on the context, it is possible for children not to have the requisite capacities to exercise various liberty rights on their own behalf. This does not imply that children are deprived of rights per se, but that responsible adults assist children in asserting relevant interests as protection rights.

Indeed, protection rights are claims that other people owe some duty to protect important interests of the right-holder.[3] For instance, the rights to education, health, and physical safety are protection rights, which refer to fundamental interests of all people. Right-holders see these rights fulfilled by others on their behalf— protecting the right-holders' interests. In contrast to liberty rights, protection rights may exist wherever there are such core interests at stake, and as such all children may possess them without regard to their abilities to exercise their own rights.

The majority viewpoint is that children enjoy protection rights, but that they may or may not be able to exercise liberty rights for themselves depending on the exact context and their capacity in that context. Competence thus takes a central role in the predominant rights discourse; an individual generally must have relevant competence to assert a given liberty right for himself or herself. Even though protection and liberty are both framed in terms of rights, there is an inverse relationship between the two, with competency as the pivot point. With less competency, protection rights come to the fore and liberty rights drift to the rear; yet with greater competency, liberty rights take greater prominence.[4] Thus, among other contested questions in rights discourses, the role of competence is highly controversial.

Just as competence has a decisive place for rights, it is influential in the constantly changing ideas about children and childhood. More broadly, the notion and meaning of childhood is not itself a natural phenomenon or scientific fact, even though it is certainly related to the natural, biological realities of children.[5] Childhood is a concept that bundles together ideas and expectations about young people and their roles in societies.[6] As such, its meaning is socially constructed and varies over time within and across cultures, with no one universal

---

2 Ekman Ladd, Rosalind, "Rights of the Child: A Philosophical Approach," in Alaimo, Kathleen, and Brian Klug, eds, *Children as Equals: Exploring the Rights of the Child*, Lanham (Maryland), University Press of America, 2002; and Fagan, Andrew, "Human Rights," in *The Internet Encyclopedia of Philosophy*, 2005, http://www.iep.utm.edu/h/hum-rts.htm.

3 Fagan, *ibid.*

4 See Ekman Ladd, *supra* note 2.

5 Freeman, Michael, *The Moral Status of Children: Essays on the Rights of the Child*, The Hague, Kluwer Law International, 1997.

6 Goldson, Barry, "'Childhood': An Introduction to Historical and Theoretical Analyses," in Scraton, Phil, ed., *'Childhood' in "Crisis"?*, London, University College London Press, 1997.

meaning.[7] Different conceptions of childhood then predispose people to understand, interpret, and address children's issues from distinct vantage points, including through the creation of legal norms and standards about children.[8]

With specific regard to competence, dominant ideas about children's competence are translated into precise legal age limits that mark the boundaries of childhood and adolescence.[9] This age–competency connection reduces the dynamic social construction processes in the background down to fixed age limits, and forces the difficult link between competency and rights. When law prescribes a given age limit denoting the beginning of children's legal competence in a specific area (e.g., to make medical decisions for themselves), regardless of the mix of ideas and assumptions justifying that age, it demarcates the onset of a specific liberty right. Children younger than the prescribed age are assumed legally incompetent in that context. They still enjoy protection rights for their relevant interests, but not liberty rights to assert their interests on their own behalf. In the end, the extent of justification for protection rights versus liberty rights—and thus the amount of control that the adult world has in deciding and protecting children's interests—is in effect negotiable based on predominant images of children and their competencies.[10] Competency is thus a central aspect among notions about childhood's meaning.

In most countries, children progressively acquire liberty rights as they pass successive age limits, each denoting legal competency and responsibility in different areas. Examples include legal and medical counseling without parental consent, the end of compulsory education, marriage, sexual consent, and the minimum age of criminal responsibility (MACR). For instance, Germany has reported a series of over 25 such age limits tied to 11 different age brackets.[11] Typically, the age of majority in a given country is the final or nearly final age limit, bringing adult rights and responsibilities in most contexts. This approach is broadly reflected in the United Nations Convention on the Rights of the Child (CRC), which is introduced more fully in Chapter 2. CRC Article 1 designates 18

---

7 Franklin, Bob, "Children's rights and media wrongs: changing representations of children and the developing rights agenda," in Franklin, Bob, ed., *The New Handbook of Children's Rights: Comparative Policy and Practice*, London, Routledge, 2002.

8 Boyden, Jo, "Childhood and the Policy Makers: A Comparative Perspective on the Globalization of Childhood," in James, Allison, and Alan Prout, eds, *Constructing and Reconstructing Childhood: Contemporary Issues in the Sociological Study of Childhood*, London, Falmer Press, 1997.

9 *Ibid.* James, Allison, and Alan Prout, "Re-presenting Childhood: Time and Transition in the Study of Childhood," in James, Allison, and Alan Prout, eds, *Constructing and Reconstructing Childhood: Contemporary Issues in the Sociological Study of Childhood*, London, Falmer Press, 1997.

10 Asquith, Stewart, "When Children Kill Children: The Search for Justice," 3 *Childhood* 99, 1996.

11 Committee on the Rights of the Child, *Initial reports of States parties due in 1994: Germany*, CRC/C/11/Add.5, 16 Sept 1994.

as the general age of majority, defining as children all human beings younger than this age.

In consideration of related information submitted under the CRC, it is safe to say that age limits vary extremely widely, both by the same limit among different countries and by diverse limits within countries. Apart from international norms, this seems a natural consequence of different political, historical, cultural, and other factors across countries that feed into the construction of childhood and designation of age limits. Within individual countries, however, the principle of consistency holds more strongly that the reasons underlying different age limits should roughly correspond across legal contexts.[12] Despite variations in the minimum competencies held necessary for various liberty rights, it is generally incoherent to argue that children at a given age are mature and responsible in one domain, yet unready to exercise rights on their own behalf in a comparable domain. Indeed, disparate national age limits often suggest an inconsistent narrative of children and their legal status. This is a further indication that children's age limits—plus the notions of competence behind them, and the liberty rights to which they are the gateway—depend most heavily upon fluctuating social constructions of childhood, and not on children themselves.

Welfare Approach and the Postponement of Criminal Responsibility

Contemporary juvenile justice debates exemplify the foregoing discussions on rights, competence, and children. In the simplest terms, the central continuum plays out from the welfare approach—which essentially dismisses the competence and criminal responsibility of children—to the justice approach—which relies upon criminal responsibility and children's alleged competence as its very foundation. The modern notion of a juvenile justice system as distinct from adult criminal justice began with a strong welfare orientation, but recent decades have seen clear shifts towards justice models. Although descriptions in terms of a welfare–justice continuum are simplified for the purposes of this study, an historical overview of the welfare approach and the founding of modern juvenile justice systems begins to bring relevant issues to light.

Origins of Dubious Rescue and Aid

In general terms, juvenile justice finds its origins in earlier pauper laws, criminal justice systems, child protection systems, and other elements. Towards the end of feudal England, authorities developed a range of policies to cope with poverty, which by the 1500s and 1600s included statutory authority to remove children

---

12   See, inter alia, Archard, David, *Children: rights and childhood*, 2nd ed., London, Routledge, 2004.

from the custody of their pauper parents.[13] Children were placed as apprentices with others until the age of majority, in order to ensure their proper upbringing. American colonies imported English poor laws, including a prominent role for the forced apprenticeship system, and took these laws west as Europeans settled further into North America. In their apprenticeships, children's labor was intended to offset the costs of care and education, but the quality of care provided was questionable.

The industrial revolution changed the very nature of children's labor, care, and education. In the United States, as in other countries, the family-based economy and children's role in it diminished, thus propelling new ideas about children's proper place in the family and society.[14] From pre-industrial ideas about children as small adults integrated in work and family life, society increasingly saw children as distinct from infants and adults, as a class that was both innocent and impressionable.[15] Social reformers sought to protect and isolate children from any wayward influences, especially in the context of burgeoning industrial centers. While this movement led to historic developments such as public education systems and child labor laws, many argue that its presumably benevolent spirit concealed the larger motivation of social control over the children of urban poor, minority, and immigrant families.

In terms of social policies for the poor, by the 1800s the United States saw an increasing focus on almshouses, work houses, and poor houses—in effect, institutionalization of the poor and pooling of their labor. These adult-oriented centers came to be seen as inappropriate for children. At the same time, the forced break-up of families and apprenticeship of children continued, and dedicated children's institutions arose to accommodate these practices. Houses of refuge, reformatories, and training schools assumed custody of poor children, and took charge of their education, upbringing, and vocational training. Delinquent children were also taken in, but were in the minority. More importantly, the definition of poor or unsuitable parents—from which children were to be removed—grew alongside social reformers' beliefs about the environments that endangered children.

Reformers also found new legal justification to intervene. First, in this time and context, the concept of *parens patriae* began to accrue particular importance.[16] *Parens patriae* jurisprudence had evolved since feudal England in chancery courts—originally the courts of the lord chancellor, an official delegate of the king. The doctrine generally signified the state's authority to act in place of parents for the resolution of individual cases, which often involved questions of property or guardianship, but never criminal

---

13   Rendleman, Douglas R., "Parens Patriae: From Chancery to the Juvenile Court," 23 *South Carolina Law Review* 205, 1971.

14   Feld, Barry C., "Race, Politics, and Juvenile Justice: The Warren Court and the Conservative 'Backlash'," 87 *Minnesota Law Review* 1447, 2003.

15   In general, see Cipriani, Don, *The Minimum Age of What? Criminal Responsibility, Juvenile Justice, and Children's Rights*, unpublished draft, Florence, UNICEF Innocenti Research Centre, 2002.

16   *Ibid.*

law intervention for delinquent children.[17] In the 1800s, for the first time, the notion of *parens patriae* was grafted onto a branch of the poor laws, becoming the justification for government as the ultimate custodian of children. The state could directly assume parental control when parents or guardians were unable or unwilling—as deemed by the state itself—to provide acceptable care.

Also in the late 1800s, positivist legal and criminological theory gained prominence, aiming its focus in criminal law upon human character and the influences on it. In its view, the origins of crime lay in biological, social, environmental, and other factors, not in individuals' choices to break the law. Rather than the crimes actually committed, attention turned to offenders, their personalities, and their needs for rehabilitation.

In summary, reformers were equipped by the late 1800s with their expansive vision of children needing state assistance, the long history of poor laws in intervening in families' lives, a modified *parens patriae* concept to justify broader interventions, as well as a positivist theory framework. They sought a distinct system for children separate in spirit and reality from the adult criminal justice system: a paternalistic system that would protect based upon the individualized interventions of judges.[18] The convergence of these and other elements led to the creation of the world's first juvenile court, and the advent of juvenile justice as a modern institution, in Chicago, Illinois, in 1899. As many of its components already enjoyed great influence internationally—child protection and juvenile reform systems, legal positivism, and so on—juvenile justice systems spread quickly across the United States, Canada, and Europe, leading to new laws to carry out this mission. Primarily from Europe, juvenile courts spread to Latin America and many European colonies around the world.

Nonetheless, juvenile justice was not predestined to follow this historical trajectory.[19] Tanenhaus documents how the abolition of slavery in the United States led by the late 1800s to a sophisticated discourse on children's rights, which carefully weighed the balance between liberty and protection rights. Social reformers initially included due process guarantees in the early administration of dependency cases, but their understanding of rights soon shifted towards children's needs and protection rights, and to states' obligations to ensure those rights. What might have been an entirely different starting point for juvenile justice was reverted to a classic welfare approach with little focus on procedural rights. Moreover, juvenile justice systems evolved and diversified from their very beginning and into the present—pragmatically adapting structures, rules, and institutional identity to meet local challenges—such that pure welfare approach systems may have always been rare.[20]

---

17 Cogan, Neil Howard, "Juvenile Law, Before and After the Entrance of 'Parens Patriae'," 22 *South Carolina Law Review* 147, 1970.

18 In general, see Cipriani, *supra* note 15.

19 Tanenhaus, David S., "Between Dependency and Liberty: The Conundrum of Children's Rights in the Gilded Age," 23 *Law and History Review* 351, 2005.

20 *Id.*, *Juvenile Justice in the Making*, New York, Oxford University Press, 2004.

Running Out the Course of Inherent Flaws

Although specific models varied widely, the basic justification and characteristics in this early period were quite similar across countries, with major implications for criminal responsibility. *Parens patriae*'s assumption that children are aided by the state, rather than tried and punished as criminals, means "there is no need to determine whether the child had the capacity to act in a culpable fashion."[21] The very notions of competence and criminal responsibility—and therefore the MACR—are essentially irrelevant under the welfare approach, as in early juvenile justice systems. A child's lack of maturity, and parallel lack of criminal responsibility, only highlighted the need for intervention. These underpinnings turned proceedings into civil matters, and rejected the obligations of criminal law. Fact-finding, adversarial processes to prove guilt, and criminal defenses were superfluous.

In such systems, the child became an object, without liberty rights or power, on whose behalf benevolent decisions were made by state authorities.[22] Even though there were occasional efforts to involve children in hearings, their active participation or even ability to understand processes was secondary. Instead, at all points along the way, decision-makers' discretion was maximized to allow them to meet children's presumed needs. At the same time, underlying structural problems went unnoticed and unaddressed, particularly those arising from the growth of industrial capitalism.[23]

The thinking behind the 1912 Belgian Child Protection Act, a model for legislation in many countries, further illustrates relevant assumptions as well as practical consequences.[24] The Act's presumption that children acted without discernment did not intend to suggest inability to discern—only that discernment was irrelevant to determining the best treatment for children.[25] This enables countries to set high MACRs as a question of social policy and, in theory, to treat youth less as criminals and more as children in need of services. In this view, countries fix their MACRs beyond the ages at which children are generally assumed capable of bearing responsibility.

Belgium's juvenile justice system is still based largely upon the 1912 Child Protection Act, maintaining a central role for welfare approach responses. However, mounting criticisms over recent decades have led to the formal introduction of

---

21 Walkover, Andrew, "The Infancy Defense in the New Juvenile Court," 31 *UCLA Law Review* 503, 1984, at 516.

22 In general, see Cipriani, *supra* note 15.

23 Tanenhaus, David S., "Book Review: Victoria Getis, 'The Juvenile Court and the Progressives'," 21 *Law and History Review* 240, 2003.

24 In general, see Cipriani, *supra* note 15.

25 Tulkens, F., "Les impasses du discours de la responsablité dans la repénalisation de la protection de la jeunesse," in *La criminologie au prétoire*, Gand, Editions Story-Scientia, 1985.

justice approach and criminal law components.[26] For example, critics had claimed that supposedly non-punitive care, custodial, prevention, and educational measures concealed effectively punitive responses without procedural guarantees.[27]

In Latin America, the same model inspired the former *situación irregular* doctrine, which exemplifies such problems and abuses on a wide scale.[28] The defining trend in Latin American juvenile justice is the predominance of *situación irregular* through the 20th century, and ongoing efforts to fully implement national laws that have replaced it. Argentina's 1919 Agote Law—abrogated only in 2005— was the first and model law of *situación irregular*; virtually every other Latin American country adopted the doctrine within 20 years of its passing. In essence, *situación irregular* referred to the broad and vague category of children in an "irregular situation" who needed state intervention and assistance. It was a direct application and outgrowth of the welfare approach *in extremis*: the state should step in as necessary to assist—theoretically through welfare care and protection measures—all *situación irregular* children.

In practice, judges typically ordered children to indeterminate sentences in juvenile correctional institutions, with almost no rights, safeguards, or treatment. State protection of children's interests paradoxically justified the entire scheme. *Situación irregular* assumed children's lack of competence to commit crimes, and accordingly, criminal responsibility and the MACR were technically postponed to coincide with the beginning of adult criminal court jurisdiction. The cornerstone of wide discretion to meet children's needs—historically the path to discrimination by socio-economic status and race—enabled much of the burden of *situación irregular* to fall upon children from lower socio-economic backgrounds.[29] Chapter 6 further highlights modern trends in punitive procedures and treatment for children younger than MACRs, which are frequently related to the welfare approach and its inherent weaknesses.

Criminal Responsibility and the Justice Approach

Regardless of recent trends in Belgium, Latin America, and other countries, support for the welfare approach quietly eroded in the mid-1900s, and the model's pre-

---

26 See, inter alia, Delens-Ravier, Isabelle, "La justice juvénile en Belgique: nouvelles pratiques et évolution d'un modèle," presented at the II International Conference, International Juvenile Justice Observatory, *Juvenile Justice in Europe: A framework for integration*, Brussels, 24–25 October 2006.

27 Walgrave, Lode, "Restorative Juvenile Justice: A Way to Restore Justice in Western European Systems?," in Asquith, Stewart, ed., *Children and Young People in Conflict with the Law*, London, Jessica Kingsley Publishers, 1996.

28 In general, see Cipriani, *supra* note 15.

29 Feld, Barry C., *Bad Kids: Race and the Transformation of the Juvenile Court*, New York, Oxford University Press, 1999.

eminence ended with three United States Supreme Court decisions between 1966 and 1970. The Supreme Court's decisions forced a pivotal reassessment of welfare-based juvenile justice, and prompted legal reform around the world that surged toward the justice approach and placed criminal responsibility at the center of juvenile justice.

Particularly with changing post-World War II social conditions, larger disillusionment ate away at the bases of the welfare approach.[30] Positivism in general faced criticisms for its lack of clarity between two unstated yet contradicting aims: did rehabilitation truly seek to benefit offenders, or to isolate and remove them to protect society?[31] Across the political spectrum, complaints were lobbed against the juvenile justice system: unwarranted social control; excessive discretion leading to unequal treatment among offenders; and lack of explicit punishments.[32] At the same time, almost any intervention came to be easily labeled as rehabilitative, and by the early 1970s research findings showed treatment to have little effect. As these elements coalesced for the first time into a compelling broad-based critique of welfare-oriented juvenile justice, 1960s United States Supreme Court decisions strongly advanced due process rights. Largely following the spirit and legal reasoning of key 1950s civil rights decisions, the Supreme Court further developed its interpretations of individual liberties and limitations on state authority in criminal justice.[33]

The growing debate came to a head in *Kent v. United States* (1966), *In re Gault* (1967), and *In re Winship* (1970), wherein the United States Supreme Court brusquely rejected many assumptions of the welfare model and "formally placed the concept of criminal culpability at the heart of the juvenile proceedings."[34] In essence, the Supreme Court examined the treatment and conditions in juvenile justice, and found that any proceedings that could lead to similar dispositions required the minimum guarantees for a fair trial. Welfare approach rhetoric and its *parens patriae* rationale did not justify such treatment, and certainly provided no foundation for claims that the state acted as a benevolent parent. Judges' discretion was limited in welfare-approach juvenile justice in the United States, and open-ended treatment orders were curtailed and eliminated.

Many of the criticisms that contributed to the welfare approach's fall from grace also played a role in the general decline of positivism and in the shifting debates in criminal law theory. The consensus view, by the early 1970s, supported the restoration of classic criminal law principles, in particular with desert or just deserts theory.[35]

---

30 Tanenhaus, David S., "Book Review: Christopher P. Manfredi, 'The Supreme Court and Juvenile Justice'," 17 *Law and History Review* 415, 1999.

31 Von Hirsch, Andrew, *Past or Future Crimes: Deservedness and Dangerousness in the Sentencing of Criminals*, Manchester, Manchester University Press, 1986.

32 Feld, *supra* note 14.

33 *Ibid.*

34 *Kent v. United States*, 383 U.S. 541, 1966; *In re Gault*, 387 U.S. 1, 1967; *In re Winship*, 397 U.S. 358, 1970; and Walkover, *supra* note 21, at 521.

35 Feld, *supra* note 14.

Borrowing from moral philosophy, this theory holds that people should only face punishment proportionate to the acts they commit, and to the extent that they are responsible for them. The core considerations became the actual offenses committed; evidentiary proof and procedural safeguards; determinate sentences commensurate to the gravity of the acts committed; and an overall central role for equity and justice.[36] However, as discussed further below, the fortification of due process safeguards would plant the seed of justification for increasingly punitive penalties and retribution.[37]

With the Supreme Court's historic decisions and the ascendancy of just deserts theory, new legislation around the world provided due process rights for children: a decisive step from the welfare approach towards the justice approach in juvenile justice.[38] In harmony with those broader changes, the justice approach's foundations are accountability, due process, and punishment, and juvenile proceedings that are more directly subsidiary to the criminal justice system than the child protection and welfare system.[39] Courts typically hold formal and adversarial legal proceedings, frequently with prosecution and defense attorneys, where the charges against the defendant must be proven. Offenders, once proven guilty, are held personally accountable for their actions. As such, there is significantly less focus on treatment and protection, while penal intervention becomes central. This feature was particularly true for retributive tendencies in the 1980s and 1990s in the United States, Canada, and later, Europe.

Moral and Criminal Responsibility, Liberty Rights, and the MACR

As noted, desert theory and the justice approach place individual criminal responsibility at the heart of all considerations. Relevant legal systems borrow the notion of moral agents—in simple terms, those who may be held morally responsible for the actions that they have performed—and limit criminal responsibility to those meeting an adapted definition of it. These systems view human action as governed by reason, assuming that individuals are capable of some minimal level of rationality and that they act accordingly.[40] Likewise, this outlook finds that people have some appropriate degree of ownership, causation, and control of their choices and actions; that is, the supposition is that people act with free will.[41]

---

36 Von Hirsch, *supra* note 31.
37 Feld, *supra* note 14.
38 In general, see Cipriani, *supra* note 15.
39 Muncie, John, "The globalization of crime control – the case of youth and juvenile justice: Neo-liberalism, policy convergence and international conventions," 9 *Theoretical Criminology* 35, 2005.
40 Morse, Stephen J., "Immaturity and Irresponsibility," 88 *Journal of Criminal Law and Criminology* 15, 1997.
41 O'Connor, Timothy, "Free Will," in Zalta, Edward N., ed., *Stanford Encyclopedia of Philosophy*, Stanford, Stanford University Center for the Study of Language and Information, 2002, http://plato.stanford.edu/entries/freewill.

These assumptions are abandoned for children younger than a given MACR; the conclusive presumption is that such children do not possess these various capacities to a sufficient degree, such that they can never bear criminal responsibility. For all others, who are presumed to have the capacities to follow the law, responsibility follows free autonomous choices and actions.[42] In the absence of such conditions, it is morally wrong to hold a person criminally responsible, on the basis of arguments that "'he could not have helped it' or 'he could not have done otherwise' or 'he had no real choice'."[43]

Up to this point, the basic characteristics of criminal responsibility broadly coincide with the boundaries of moral agency and responsibility, although as discussed in the next section they are not coterminous. The direct link to underlying conceptions of rights has special importance. Only those who bear the capacity for autonomy and choice—or to self-determination—may hold and exercise certain liberty rights. Where capacities are insufficient in a given context, children still enjoy the right to protection of their interests by others. Where the baseline competencies for liberty rights exist, both these rights and their correlative responsibilities accrue. The justified claims of liberty rights—to respect and protect a competent individual's choices—necessarily assign responsibility for choices and actions back to the individual who makes them.

The similarity here to both moral and criminal responsibility is no accident. Rough parallels exist between the capacities necessary for liberty rights and those necessary for moral agency. Indeed, when the respective threshold level of capacities is met, responsibility, moral responsibility, and even criminal responsibility may generally follow. Thus, when a person is held criminally responsible for his or her actions, society conveys its moral reprobation of those actions through the mechanisms of criminal justice—it operates on the premise that the person is indeed morally responsible for those actions.

Consequently, legal systems under the justice approach face the task of assessing children's normative moral competencies and assigning one age level as the onset of their potential criminal responsibility. This exemplifies an age limit set according to notions of childhood and competency. Children at and above the specified age—as a general class and as a question of legal status—are assumed to have the necessary attributes to act intentionally, and may bear criminal responsibility for their acts. Before criminal responsibility is confirmed, a court of law must still determine whether or not an individual child has intentionally committed a given offense. Age, maturity, and related factors may subsequently be re-examined as mitigating factors for the degree of criminal liability and the sanctions imposed.

The central features of the justice approach become even clearer in this light. The approach promises a fundamental respect and concern for liberty, autonomy,

---

42 Hart, H.L.A., *Punishment and Responsibility: Essays in the Philosophy of Law*, Oxford, Clarendon Press, 1968.

43 *Ibid.*, at 152.

and the individual, which also tends to support human rights and children's rights. Government intrusion into the lives of individuals, and social control through criminal justice mechanisms, is only permitted insofar as it is a proportional response to the free choices of individuals. When people do not have the ability or the chance to act freely, penal sanctions can not apply.

As such, criminal responsibility is essential for the moral legitimacy of the criminal and juvenile justice system. The burden of potential criminal responsibility, and submission to a criminal procedure, triggers the provision of certain rights in part to ensure that legitimacy. In this sense, the MACR is an important basis for children's rights in criminal proceedings; as with adults, children's potential responsibility limits the ability of government to intervene in their lives.[44] Where children's responsibility is deemed irrelevant, or where children are assumed to be free from it, wider discretion falls to governments. As explored in Chapter 2, children younger than MACRs do enjoy an important series of rights and considerations, but available rights are more extensive and context-specific for children upon the MACR who are accused of, alleged as, or recognized as having infringed the penal law.

Morality Bait-and-Switch, and the Easing of the Social Conscience

Despite the strengths of the justice approach, there are complications. For current purposes the central critique is that the theoretical reliance upon free will, and the working assumption that people act on the basis of their own free will, may be based more on a myth than reality. Most philosophers accept that it is easy to imagine examples of choices that are not free, and that the very concept of free will remains inconsistent on some level.[45] While fundamental respect for individuals and their choices may remain an important value, it may be simplistic to claim that individuals decide and act strictly based on their own deliberations and decisions. Such claims ignore the array of factors that may limit the choices available to individuals and that predispose the decisions they will ultimately make. According to such arguments, law cannot efficiently or fairly take account of such broad—and perhaps innumerable—influences in its mechanisms:

> The idea of free will in relation to conduct is not, in the legal system, a statement of fact, but rather a value preference having very little to do with the metaphysics of determinism or free will. ... Very simply, the law treats man's conduct as autonomous and willed, not because it is, but because it is desirable to proceed as if it were.[46]

---

44 In general, see Cipriani, *supra* note 15.
45 O'Connor, *supra* note 41.
46 Packer, Herbert L., *The Limits of the Criminal Sanction*, Stanford, Stanford University Press, 1968, at 74–75.

Even among scholars who support only the most limited excuses from criminal responsibility, there is an admission that "the law rests, of necessity, on a convenient fiction, that of free will, and could not operate if it did not embrace that myth."[47]

How the criminal law embraces such a myth moves quickly to the differences between moral and criminal responsibility. In effect, the legal system imposes its own processes in determining its own criminal responsibility threshold, as it effectively "truncates the inquiry into moral responsibility, deforming the generally accepted concept of moral responsibility itself."[48] For example, in transcribing one pillar of moral responsibility, "the common law employs a very low cognitive threshold—knowledge of 'right from wrong'—to establish criminal guilt"—a standard that "entails only minimally rational understanding."[49] While a moral inquiry might seek to consider whatever circumstances bear relevance and provide context for a given act, classic criminal law actively eliminates such context.[50] The law cannot easily admit more subjective, psychological, and difficult-to-prove considerations.[51] It simplifies concepts of moral responsibility and free will into easily manageable terms for courts.

These observations are particularly true with respect to children.[52] In the justice approach, criminal law conceives of, seeks, and admits knowledge about children in very limited ways. Where the criminal law appears to broaden its inquiry, for example in considering medical and socio-psychological science perspectives, it may be just as much a pro forma exercise. This exploits the appearance of broader authority and legitimacy to satisfy the needs of its own logic.[53] In contrast, children's moral competency—and thus their moral agency and responsibility—develops dynamically over time via relationships with the people that surround them.[54] While many factors are important in understanding to what extent children make decisions and act freely as individuals, a strict justice approach may downplay or ignore them entirely.

---

47 Wilson, James Q., *Moral Judgment: Does the Abuse Excuse Threaten Our Legal System?*, New York, BasicBooks, 1997, at 40.

48 Wright, R. George, "The Progressive Logic of Criminal Responsibility and the Circumstances of the Most Deprived," 43 *Catholic University Law Review* 459, 1994, at 463.

49 Feld, Barry C., "Abolish the Juvenile Court: Youthfulness, Criminal Responsibility, and Sentencing Policy," 88 *Journal of Criminal Law and Criminology* 68, at 98.

50 Armour, Jody, "Just Deserts: Narrative, Perspective, Choice, and Blame," 57 *University of Pittsburgh Law Review* 525, 1996.

51 Hart, *supra* note 42.

52 King, Michael, and Christine Piper, *How the Law Thinks about Children*, Aldershot (England), Gower, 1990.

53 King, Michael, *A Better World for Children? Explorations in Morality and Authority*, London, Routledge, 1997.

54 Fagan, Jeffrey, "Context and Culpability in Adolescent Crime," 6 *Virginia Journal of Social Policy and the Law* 507, 1999.

Reliance upon a myth assumption is, of course, vastly problematic for the justice approach on various levels. Fundamentally, it subverts the approach's centerpiece—respect for the autonomy and choices of individuals:

> We do not enhance the dignity of those deprived of the capacity for morally responsible choice by simply pretending, through the judicial system, that they do bear such responsibility. It is essentially backwards to imagine that a judicial system promotes dignity by falsely ascribing moral responsibility to any group of persons.[55]

A just legal system—as defined in the same rhetoric that led to and sustains the justice approach—requires that people be truly free if they are to be held responsible.

In practical terms, the criminal processes that embody these inconsistencies ultimately justify social control and punishment.[56] In its extreme, a sort of institutional bait-and-switch transpires. The law proclaims that only the morally responsible will be held responsible and punished, and criminal conviction and punishment indeed bear heavy moral condemnation. Yet a diluted test for criminal responsibility opens the back door to punishment. In this way, criminal law consistently assigns moral responsibility to and punishes the group of the "most deprived"—who may bear no responsibility for the greater circumstances that led to their crimes—while it refuses to recognize the contradictions of its moral accounting in doing so.[57] Given the state's stakes in maintaining social order, its own criminal courts are a poor forum to make proper judgments about moral responsibility.[58]

These legal schemes enable the public-at-large to maintain its faith in the individual acting freely; to focus almost exclusively on the role of individuals in crime; and to tell itself that the punished are morally responsible for their actions and receive only what they deserve.[59] Nowhere is there space for a candid appraisal of broader factors, beyond children's actions, that may limit their choices and drive crime trends:

> strategies of social control locate the 'causes' of delinquency in the individual offender. ... [while] juvenile courts' individualized justice focuses on [youths'] personal circumstances and real needs. While young people certainly can and do make 'choices' about their behavior, social structural conditions and economic opportunities mediate the quality of their choices. Ultimately, juvenile and

---

55 Wright, *supra* note 48, at 501.
56 Arenella, Peter, "Convicting the Morally Blameless: Reassessing the Relationship Between Legal and Moral Accountability," 39 *UCLA Law Review* 1511, 1992.
57 Wright, *supra* note 48.
58 Arenella, *supra* note 56.
59 *Ibid.*

criminal justice policies can do very little to alter the social structural forces that impel some youths to 'choose' crime and others to 'choose' college.[60]

Once such broader factors are recognized, it becomes clearer that the core issue is general societal problems, for which there is a burden of collective responsibility.[61] Thus, the criminal law serves as an anodyne for the collective social conscience: if the criminal is morally responsible, then the public is not, and any underlying collective moral responsibility remains out of sight.[62] The criminal law accentuates the blaming and moral condemnation of children who commit crimes:

> What the law has done is to choose from among the characteristics of certain children, not their lack of a decent education (through no fault of their own), or their location in dilapidated slum housing (through no fault of their own), or their unattended to health problems (through no fault of their own), *etc.*, but the instance of conduct in which they violated the penal law. So long as the legal system thus isolates and highlights that aspect of the child which rationally calls for the least sympathy, and ignores the conditions of his life that would evoke a desire to help, the law simply serves to reinforce the severity of public attitudes.[63]

True justice for children—moral and not strictly legal justice—"must surely be based as much on a concern with the effects of social and economic inequalities and injustice as on the rules and standards set by criminal law."[64] As mentioned in the previous section, juvenile court founders also focused extensively on the problems of individual children and their families—rather than appraising or addressing the underlying structural problems at hand. Yet the welfare approach omits any moral condemnation, whereas the justice approach packs one of its most powerful punches in that very condemnation.

The stakes are high in the meaning and uses of criminal and moral responsibility, so it is no surprise that they are matters of complex social construction, just as the meaning of childhood is. Political power and ideological struggle loom large in such tensions and in how responsibility is ultimately assigned.[65] Government acceptance and enforcement legitimate control over others by the group that defines responsibility. Where responsibility can be assigned, social control can be extended via the criminal law, attention and moral blame can be diverted, and

---

60 Feld, *supra* note 29, at 285.
61 Feld, *supra* note 29; and Tulkens, *supra* note 25.
62 Armour, *supra* note 50; and Tulkens, *ibid.*
63 Fox, Sanford J., "Responsibility in the Juvenile Court," 11 *William and Mary Law Review* 659, 1969–1970, at 674.
64 Asquith, *supra* note 10, at 114.
65 Wright, *supra* note 48.

broader societal responsibility is ignored. Given these dynamics, it would be surprising if a strictly moral interpretation of responsibility were to prevail.[66]

Similarly, justice approach MACRs are not based in reality upon children's normative moral agency and responsibility. Powerful forces of social construction intervene, leaving little relation to criminal law's standards for criminal responsibility, which may rest upon the myth assumptions of free will anyway. Lawmakers ultimately encapsulate in one age, at one point in time, in a specific socio-political-cultural context, some batch of ideas about children's capabilities and society's expectations about children's appropriate role. Upon that age, children may potentially bear criminal responsibility for their actions, and the state can first legitimately levy—in legal terms—criminal sanctions against them.

The calculus for designating MACRs may thus vary in extremes among countries, or even in the same country at different times. Chapter 4 outlines the major historical influences, while Chapter 5 examines modern trends in MACR changes, including the wide impact of the CRC reporting process. Chapter 5 also surveys how legal reform following the logic of the justice approach often embodies the conflicts described above, and suggests that the approach's increasing predominance places such conflicts in a central role in juvenile justice debates. As detailed there, many countries have assimilated the paradigm that delinquency is strictly a matter of individual children's decisions to offend, and have followed that paradigm's closed loop.

Conclusion

Societies' understandings of childhood do not arise because of some innate nature of children themselves. Instead, childhood is a constructed notion that is hotly contested and subject to constant revision in any given era or place. Predominant conceptions of childhood in large part determine questions of rights, legal status, parental authority, and governments' power to intervene—including which legal rights children may or may not be able to assert for themselves. In particular, children's competence—or how adults interpret and depict children's competence—proves to be an exceptionally political question that determines rights and policies for children.

Juvenile justice history reflects the influence of divergent portrayals of children's competence. The origins of juvenile justice along the welfare approach are based upon the belief in children's incompetence and lack of criminal responsibility. This foundation lends itself to broad state authority to intervene in children's lives, which in reality has often proven disastrous for children. Partly in response to such problems, juvenile justice shifted towards the justice approach, thus inserting a construction of childhood based around competence and criminal responsibility. Here the MACR symbolizes the tipping point among competing notions about

---

66   Balkin, J.M., "The Rhetoric of Responsibility," 76 *Virginia Law Review* 197, 1990.

childhood; competencies; liberty and protection rights; and the welfare–justice continuum.

Yet the notion of responsibility in the justice approach often serves as a trap door rather than the safeguard for which it is intended. Instead of ensuring freedom from state intrusion, its meaning can become distorted and may legitimize social control over children whose true responsibility is questionable. The effects of moral condemnation and punishment follow even where underlying moral responsibility is missing. At the cost of individual liberty, moral legitimacy, and justice, the public's conscience is relieved and authorities' effective social control is consolidated. Paradoxically, the welfare approach shares some of the same troublesome consequences. The two approaches may appeal to different conceptions of rights for children, but neither communicates a clear role for society-at-large, and both bring the weight of problems down upon individual children and families. Such inherent flaws leave both the justice approach and the welfare approach as problematic models.

Chapter 2
Children's Rights' Mediation of Welfare–Justice Tensions

The unanimous adoption of the 1948 Universal Declaration of Human Rights by the United Nations General Assembly was a milestone event in bringing international prominence to human rights. It enshrined the belief that all people, due to their very nature as human beings, merit certain moral considerations. As one of the nine core international human rights treaties adopted since the Universal Declaration, the 1989 Convention on the Rights of the Child (CRC) is the cornerstone for children's rights in the world, detailing the moral claims to which children are entitled both as people and because of their special status.[1] The CRC is "the most widely ratified treaty in history"—with Somalia and the United States as the only steps remaining before full worldwide ratification.[2]

The CRC addresses juvenile justice at length, while an array of non-binding international instruments offer even greater detail on how rights should apply to all people under the age of 18 involved in justice systems.[3] The CRC and related instruments compose international juvenile justice standards whose framework addresses the systemic flaws in both the welfare and justice approaches. In the most basic sense, these standards help mediate but not resolve conflicts along the welfare–justice continuum, including the fulcrum issues of children's criminal responsibility and the minimum age of criminal responsibility (MACR). This

---

1 Adopted by the UN General Assembly, Resolution 44/25, 20 Nov 1989. See Annex 1 for the full CRC text. The other core treaties are the 1965 International Convention on the Elimination of All Forms of Racial Discrimination; the 1966 International Covenant on Civil and Political Rights; the 1966 International Covenant on Economic, Social and Cultural Rights; the 1979 Convention on the Elimination of All Forms of Discrimination against Women; the 1984 Convention against Torture and Other Cruel, Inhuman or Degrading Treatment or Punishment; the 1990 International Convention on the Protection of the Rights of All Migrant Workers and Members of Their Families; the 2006 International Convention for the Protection of All Persons from Enforced Disappearance; and the 2006 Convention on the Rights of Persons with Disabilities.

2 Alston, Philip, and John Tobin, *Laying the Foundations for Children's Rights: An Independent Study of Some Key Legal and Institutional Aspects of the Impact of the Convention on the Rights of the Child*, Florence, UNICEF Innocenti Research Centre, 2005, at ix.

3 See, inter alia, the 1985 UN Standard Minimum Rules for the Administration of Juvenile Justice, the 1990 UN Guidelines for the Prevention of Juvenile Delinquency, and the 1990 UN Rules for the Protection of Juveniles Deprived of their Liberty.

chapter successively examines key themes in this mediation, including the rights of children younger than MACRs; the best interests of the child and due process guarantees; respect for the views of the child and effective participation at trial; children's evolving capacities; and the principle of reintegration into society.

Progression of Rights from Welfare to Justice

International children's rights affirm children's legal status across many contexts, and children enjoy a generally expanding range of rights and protections as circumstances shift towards justice in the welfare–justice continuum. In the case of very young children who commit crimes, referrals to family, school, and community programs and services are often the primary means to address their behavior. Many countries direct such services through local welfare, care, protection, administrative, and related civil law proceedings. International children's rights entitle children to important rights and considerations in the course of all such proceedings, actions, and measures. In exceptional cases where such welfare-oriented proceedings may contemplate the deprivation of liberty, children have right to a further set of guarantees and protections. This section highlights the main rights of children younger than MACRs who are involved in such proceedings, both generally and in those rare cases where the deprivation of liberty may be permitted.

Following this section, the remainder of this chapter focuses largely on rights as the continuum lies even closer to justice: the rights of children implicated directly in juvenile justice systems, who among other things have attained the MACR. By definition, only children who have reached the MACR may be "alleged as, accused of, or recognized as having infringed the penal law."[4] Although some rights apply both above and below MACRs, such allegation, accusation, or recognition triggers the wider range of rights and protections discussed further below for older children.[5]

Rights in Welfare-Based Responses to Young Children's Behavior

The best interests of the child are a primary consideration for all actions concerning children, both younger and older than MACRs. The CRC's monitoring body—the Committee on the Rights of the Child—considers them one of four

---

  4 When the Committee on the Rights of the Child has described children younger than MACRs facing such allegation, accusation, or recognition, it apparently understood a broad characterization of children in conflict with the law but younger than MACRs, who are not subject to judicial (delinquency) proceedings. See *General Comment No. 10: Children's rights in juvenile justice*, CRC/C/GC/10, 25 Apr 2007, par. 33.

  5 CRC Art. 40(1).

"general principles" of the convention.[6] Of special relevance for children younger than MACRs, best interests are the guiding tenet in protection-oriented actions, proceedings, and measures prompted by children's own behavior.[7] CRC Articles 3(1)–(2) give the most complete statement of this concept:

> 1. In all actions concerning children, whether undertaken by public or private social welfare institutions, courts of law, administrative authorities or legislative bodies, the best interests of the child shall be a primary consideration.
> 2. States Parties undertake to ensure the child such protection and care as is necessary for his or her well-being, taking into account the rights and duties of his or her parents, legal guardians, or other individuals legally responsible for him or her, and, to this end, shall take all appropriate legislative and administrative measures.

Article 3(2)'s concern for the rights and duties of parents and legal guardians suggests the primary means for meeting children's best interests in this context—through appropriate assistance to families in addressing their young children's behavior. CRC Article 5 reinforces the respect due to responsible adults in providing appropriate direction and guidance to children, while Article 18 specifies countries' roles in rendering child-rearing assistance to parents and guardians and in developing relevant services. Likewise, Article 10(1) of the International Covenant on Economic, Social and Cultural Rights stresses the "widest possible protection and assistance" to families in the care and education of children.

Beyond these general principles, the 1990 United Nations Guidelines for the Prevention of Juvenile Delinquency provide specific guidance to create and implement comprehensive policies in this respect, focusing extensively on measures for the family, schools, and communities. The guidelines overlap with overwhelming evidence that the most effective delinquency prevention and early intervention programs are non-punitive and home- and school-based. Chapter 6 addresses this research in greater detail.

International juvenile justice standards strongly encourage the use of such approaches with all children presenting problematic behavior, including those who have reached the MACR and are in conflict with the law, as well as in other circumstances. However, they bear special importance to children younger than MACRs, for whom responses may consist almost entirely of such programs. Although generally non-coercive, there are limited circumstances under which judicial and administrative bodies may order the mandatory participation of families and children in certain activities (e.g., parenting skills classes, community

---

6 Committee on the Rights of the Child, *General Comment No. 5: General measures of implementation of the Convention on the Rights of the Child*, CRC/GC/2003/5, 27 Nov 2003.

7 This discussion does not address welfare proceedings initiated for other reasons, e.g., abuse or neglect.

service learning). In the rarest of cases, civil law orders may imply children's deprivation of liberty, which is addressed below.

In this context of protection-oriented responses to children younger than MACRs, the advantages of international children's rights are strong. Children's best interests drive policy and practice; respect for the role of parents and guardians is stressed; and responses consist almost exclusively of assistance to families, communities, and schools. In contrast, the classic welfare approach to juvenile justice tends to arrogate critical decisions about young children's lives, and to impose state authority upon children and their families.

Rights in the Context of Deprivation of Liberty

As in the case of the best interests of the child, rights in the context of deprivation of liberty are applicable to all children, regardless of involvement in the juvenile justice system, for those both younger and older than MACRs. However, the extensive guidance and limitations on the deprivation of liberty are especially important for children younger than MACRs. Since they cannot technically be alleged as, accused of, or recognized as having committed crimes, the broader range of juvenile justice protections is rarely made available to them. Nonetheless, extensive safeguards are required whenever deprivation of liberty is at stake, through juvenile justice, child welfare, protection, medical, educational, training, and any other measures or settings whatsoever. The non-binding 1990 United Nations Rules for the Protection of Juveniles Deprived of their Liberty clarify this broad understanding of the deprivation of liberty: "The deprivation of liberty means *any form of detention or imprisonment or* the placement of a person in a public or private *custodial setting, from which this person is not permitted to leave at will*, by order of any judicial, administrative or other public authority" (emphasis added).[8] This definition includes arrest as well as the holding and/or detaining of children younger than MACRs who are not formally arrested.[9]

As a starting point, CRC Article 37(b) dictates that the deprivation of liberty "shall be used only as a measure of last resort and for the shortest appropriate period of time." In addition, children enjoy an array of additional rights and legal guarantees, including the following:

- Deprivation of liberty must be in conformity with the law and not arbitrary (Art. 37(b)).
- Right to prompt access to legal and other assistance (Art. 37(d)).
- Right to challenge legality of the deprivation of liberty before a court or other competent, independent and impartial authority, and to a prompt decision (Art. 37(d)).

---

8 Rule 11(b).
9 UN Rules for the Protection of Juveniles Deprived of their Liberty, sect. III.

- Right to a periodic review of treatment provided and all other circumstances relevant to placement, where deprivation of liberty is on the basis of care, protection or treatment of physical or mental health (Art. 25).
- Children will be separated from adults unless not in their best interest (Art. 37(c)).
- Right to maintain contact with family (Art. 37(c)).
- Treatment with humanity and respect for the inherent dignity of the human person, and in a manner which takes into account the needs of persons of the child's age (Art. 37(c)).

Parents bear additional rights that further limit the potential deprivation of liberty of their children. For example, CRC Article 9(1) holds that "States Parties shall ensure that a child shall not be separated from his or her parents against their will, except when competent authorities subject to judicial review determine, in accordance with applicable law and procedures, that such separation is necessary for the best interests of the child." Moreover, all interested parties must given the opportunity to participate in such proceedings and to make their views known.[10]

Therefore, international children's rights do grant that the deprivation of liberty may potentially be an appropriate step, but only as a measure of last resort, for the shortest appropriate period of time, and when overcoming a long series of restrictions, conditions, and mandatory reviews. The burden on state officials who would order the deprivation of liberty of children is justifiably high. With particular regard to welfare proceedings triggered by the actions of children younger than MACRs, as compared to older children in juvenile justice systems, the permissible uses of the deprivation of liberty are even more limited. Deprivation of liberty is entirely excluded as a form of punishment or penalty against them. Generally, there would seem to be only two potential categories for the deprivation of liberty of such children, still subject to the limitations noted above: (1) the temporary holding by law enforcement officials of a child apprehended *in flagrante*; and (2) cases where a child's behavior represents a serious physical danger to him- or herself or to others, and specialized services in a family setting cannot adequately address such risks.[11] For children who have reached the MACR and are in conflict with the law, all general restrictions on the deprivation of liberty continue to apply, and dispositions cannot be strictly punitive, yet the deprivation of liberty may potentially be considered as a sanction in extreme cases.[12]

States Parties to the CRC are directed to provide related information to the Committee on the Rights of the Child when they formally report on their implementation of the convention. The information requested demonstrates a high level of scrutiny, which corresponds to the heavy burden against the deprivation

---

[10] Art. 9(2).
[11] See, e.g., the 1990 UN Guidelines for the Prevention of Juvenile Delinquency, Guideline 46.
[12] See Committee on the Rights of the Child, *supra* note 4, par. 71.

of liberty on a welfare basis. For example, countries should report on how the best interests of the child are reflected—legislatively, judicially, administratively, or otherwise—in addressing the separation of children from their parents and in the periodic review of their placements.[13] Reporting guidelines also request information on measures to protect children deprived of their liberty, as well as disaggregated data on children separated from their parents, the duration of their placements, and the frequency of review of their placements.[14] Likewise, disaggregated data is requested on the number of relevant institutions, the number of spaces available in them, and the ratio of caregivers to children.[15]

Children's rights in the context of deprivation of liberty thus offer further strengths compared to the classic welfare approach, notably for responses to the problematic behavior of children younger than MACRs. International juvenile justice standards dedicate a comprehensive array of protections to children's right to liberty, and rule out the deprivation of liberty in virtually all cases regarding children younger than MACRs. The classic welfare approach instead justified systems that methodically responded to young children, who were nominally free from criminal responsibility, by depriving them of their liberty indefinitely. Parents were generally assumed to contribute to delinquency problems, and the state peremptorily intervened in spite of them, whereas international standards uphold parents' rights as a further check against state power.

The Best Interests of the Child and Due Process Guarantees

While the previous section focuses on the rights of young children in welfare proceedings, both generally and when deprivation of liberty is at stake, this section and the remainder of this chapter turn greater attention to the rights of children who have reached MACRs and are involved in juvenile justice processes. Many children's rights apply equally to children younger and older than MACRs, regardless of the setting, yet the nature of justice proceedings and trials requires a broader range of protections for children who have reached MACRs.

However, international juvenile justice standards do not simply fall into line with the justice approach, as the tensions of the welfare–justice continuum are mediated in various ways. The international standards are colored by both the best interests of the child and due process guarantees—reflecting to some extent both welfare and justice approaches. The interplay between children's best interests and their procedural guarantees is dynamic, deriving from the indivisible and mutually reinforcing nature of children's human rights. Even though isolated provisions

---

13 *Id., General Guidelines Regarding the Form and Content of Periodic Reports to be Submitted by States Parties under Article 44, Paragraph 1 (B), of the Convention,* CRC/C/58/Rev.1, 29 Nov 2005, par. 28.

14 *Ibid.,* par. 38 and Annex, par. 12.

15 *Ibid.,* Annex, par. 12.

may tend to support one approach or another in juvenile justice, all relevant rights must be considered in their fullest context. As described in the preceding section, the best interests of the child are the basis for welfare approaches in international standards, yet they are only one part of the puzzle: "[i]nterpretations of the best interests of children cannot trump or override any of the other rights guaranteed by other articles in the Convention."[16]

The principle of the best interests of the child means that children's well-being and best interests will be a primary consideration in all actions concerning them. Such consideration provides, in theory, an immediate limitation to the excesses of both the classic welfare and justice approaches, whose practices frequently run counter to the well-being of children. At the same time, children's best interests are ultimately interpreted by adults, thus exemplifying the broader category of protection rights as explored in Chapter 1.[17] State intervention in families' and children's lives based upon the perceived best interests of children—coupled with the perceived incompetence, innocence, and lack of criminal responsibility of children—was a defining feature of early juvenile courts.[18] That pre-CRC history includes a "massive legacy of misuse and abuse of the concept" of the best interests of the child; despite advances, "the ramifications of this legacy still abound, and often contribute substantially to violations of the rights of the child today."[19] The best interests of the child, in and of themselves, cannot be a complete guide to rights-based juvenile justice.

For such reasons, international juvenile justice standards also reflect in part the historic shifts towards the justice approach. The standards "reject the unfettered discretion of authorities to rehabilitate children in their best interests," while "exclusive reliance on *parens patriae* has been discarded."[20] The concept of the best interests of the child remains important, but it is moderated by the repeated emphasis within the same standards on the need for clear procedural guarantees.[21] Among many international instruments, CRC Article 40 includes a detailed series of due process guarantees in juvenile justice, including in summary terms the following:

---

16   Hodgkin, Rachel, and Peter Newell, *Implementation Handbook for the Convention on the Rights of the Child*, New York, UNICEF, 2002, at 39.

17   Bellon, Christina M., "The Promise of Rights for Children: Best Interests and Evolving Capacities," in Alaimo, Kathleen, and Brian Klug, eds, *Children as Equals: Exploring the Rights of the Child*, Lanham (Maryland), University Press of America, 2002.

18   Minow, Martha, *Making All the Difference: Inclusion, Exclusion, and American Law*, Ithaca, Cornell University Press, 1990.

19   Cantwell, Nigel, "The impact of the CRC on the concept of 'best interests of the child,'" in Bruning, Mariëlle, and Geeske Ruitenberg, eds, *Rechten van het kind in (inter)nationaal perspectief*, Amsterdam, Amsterdam Centrum voor Kinderstudies, 2005, at 66–67.

20   Van Bueren, Geraldine, "Child-Oriented Justice – An International Challenge for Europe," 6 *International Journal of Law and the Family* 381, 1992, at 381–382.

21   Zermatten, Jean, *The Swiss Federal Statute on Juvenile Criminal Law*, presented at the Conference of the European Society of Criminology, Amsterdam, 25–28 August, 2004.

- Penal offenses must be defined in law by the time of alleged crimes (Art. 40(2)(a)).
- The law should stipulate an age below which children are presumed incapable of committing offenses (Art. 40(3)(a)).
- Children are presumed innocent until proven guilty (Art. 40(2)(b)(i)).
- Right to be notified promptly of charges (Art. 40(2)(b)(ii)).
- Right to legal assistance (Art. 40(2)(b)(ii-iii)).
- Right to the presence of parents or guardians except where not in child's best interest (Art. 40(2)(b)(iii)).
- Determination without delay by a competent, independent and impartial authority or judicial body in a fair hearing (Art. 40(2)(b)(iii)).
- Right to remain silent and to confront and cross-examine witnesses (Art. 40(2)(b)(iv)).
- Right to judicial review of decisions (Art. 40(2)(b)(v)).
- Right to a free language interpreter (Art. 40(2)(b)(vi)).
- Right to full respect for privacy at all stages (Art. 40(2)(b)(vii)).

These protections are required for all children alleged as, accused of, or recognized as having infringed the penal law, who have already reached the MACR. The far-reaching procedural guarantees, however, do not by any means suggest free range for the justice approach. For example, in the words of the 1985 United Nations Standard Minimum Rules for the Administration of Juvenile Justice (the Beijing Rules), "the well-being of the juvenile should also be emphasized in legal systems that follow the criminal court [i.e. justice] model, thus contributing to the avoidance of merely punitive sanctions."[22] International juvenile justice standards reserve space for both best interests and procedural guarantees, yet other principles provide even greater context.

Respect for the Views of the Child and Effective Participation at Trial

Children's rights to respect for their views and to effective participation at trial are critical in international juvenile justice standards' mediation along the welfare–justice continuum. CRC Article 12 on respect for views of the child—deemed one of the four CRC "general principles" by the Committee on the Rights of the Child, and applying to all children in all contexts—is a useful starting point as such:[23]

> 1. States Parties shall assure to the child who is capable of forming his or her own views the right to express those views freely in all matters affecting the child, the views of the child being given due weight in accordance with the age and maturity of the child.

---

22 Commentary to Rule 5.
23 Committee on the Rights of the Child, *supra* note 6.

2. For this purpose, the child shall in particular be provided the opportunity to be heard in any judicial and administrative proceedings affecting the child, either directly, or through a representative or an appropriate body, in a manner consistent with the procedural rules of national law.

The balance between CRC Articles 3 and 12, for example, is immediately clear. As seen above, Article 3 on the best interests of the child, in and of itself, does not stipulate an active role for children in the actions concerning them. Adults must effectively determine and protect children's best interests on their behalf. Article 12, however, guarantees children's right to be heard in all matters affecting them; here children automatically have a seat at the table and an opportunity to express themselves. The process at hand is thus entirely different, even if adults still hold final authority and responsibility for decisions: "[t]he outcome will be decided by adults but informed and influenced by the views of the child."[24] In this sense, Article 12 imposes obligations on how adults interpret and implement the best interests of the child under Article 3.

Beyond children's right to express their views, the right to a fair trial in juvenile justice—for children upon MACRs and alleged as, accused of, or recognized as having infringed the penal law—requires that children be able to participate effectively in relevant proceedings. The Committee on the Rights of the Child has noted that "Alleging that the child is criminally responsible implies that he/she should be competent and able to effectively participate in the decisions regarding the most appropriate response to allegations of his/her infringement of the penal law."[25] Thus, effective participation requires competencies far beyond Article 12's basic standard of forming one's own views:

> A fair trial requires that the child alleged as or accused of having infringed the penal law be able to effectively participate in the trial, and therefore needs to comprehend the charges, and possible consequences and penalties, in order to direct the legal representative, to challenge witnesses, to provide an account of events, and to make appropriate decisions about evidence, testimony and the measure(s) to be imposed. Article 14 of the Beijing Rules provides that the proceedings should be conducted in an atmosphere of understanding to allow the child to participate and to express himself/herself freely. Taking into account the child's age and maturity may also require modified courtroom procedures and practices.[26]

The requirements for children's effective participation have profound implications for juvenile justice processes. If an individual child is not capable of participating

---

24 Lansdown, Gerison, *The Evolving Capacities of the Child*, Florence, UNICEF Innocenti Research Centre, 2005, at 4.
25 Committee on the Rights of the Child, *supra* note 4, par. 45.
26 *Ibid.*, par. 46.

effectively in decisions about his or her alleged infringement of the penal law, it may be necessary to significantly modify procedures and practices, including substantial direct assistance to the child. If the child is ultimately unable to participate effectively, the logical consequence is that the child must not be submitted to any process alleging, accusing, or recognizing the child as having infringed the penal law. In effect, any actions taken must avoid any connotation whatsoever of criminal responsibility, penalty, and punishment. No longer a question of juvenile justice per se, the matter becomes a question of welfare-oriented responses to children for whom criminal responsibility is excluded. In effect, the child's case follows the rights, guarantees, and guidance delineated above for children who have not reached MACRs. Therein, an array of effective responses to the child's behavior are available, while still fully respecting all relevant children's rights. This fundamental emphasis of children's rights upon participation is a striking contrast to the mere acceptance of participation in most welfare and justice approaches.

The European Court of Human Rights has maintained a similar view regarding the fair trial provisions of the Convention for the Protection of Human Rights and Fundamental Freedoms: "Article 6 ..., read as a whole, guarantees the right of an accused to participate effectively in a criminal trial. In general this includes, inter alia, not only his right to be present, but also to hear and follow the proceedings. Such rights are implicit in the very notion of an adversarial procedure... ."[27] In child-specific cases, it explored the components of children's right to effective participation:

> "effective participation" in this context presupposes that the accused has a broad understanding of the nature of the trial process and of what is at stake for him or her, including the significance of any penalty which may be imposed. It means that he or she, if necessary with the assistance of, for example, an interpreter, lawyer, social worker or friend, should be able to understand the general thrust of what is said in court. The defendant should be able to follow what is said by the prosecution witnesses and, if represented, to explain to his own lawyers his version of events, point out any statements with which he disagrees and make them aware of any facts which should be put forward in his defence... .[28]

These criteria closely resemble the standards for effective participation cited by the Committee on the Rights of the Child. Moreover, even where children met the United Kingdom's standard of "fitness to plead," or the minimum competence required to proceed to trial, the European Court of Human Rights has found that

---

27 European Court of Human Rights, *Case of Stanford v. the United Kingdom: Judgment*, 1994, par. 26.

28 *Id.*, *Case of S.C. v. the United Kingdom: Judgment*, Strasbourg, 2004, par. 29. See also *Id.*, *Case of T. v. the United Kingdom: Judgment*, Strasbourg, 1999; *Id.*, *Case of V. v. the United Kingdom: Judgment*, Strasbourg, 1999.

they were not necessarily capable of participating effectively in their defenses.[29] Consequently, it found that such proceedings violated children's right to effective participation and to fair trials.[30]

Articles 10 and 11 of the Universal Declaration of Human Rights are the predecessors to the fair trial guarantees of both the CRC and the Convention for the Protection of Human Rights and Fundamental Freedoms, as well to broadly similar guarantees in other international and regional instruments.[31] The international law basis for children's right to effective participation is thus particularly strong. Chapter 6 further examines these questions from the perspective of research on the ages at which children typically acquire relevant competencies, and by considering the implications for MACR age levels and policies.

The Evolving Capacities of the Child

The CRC introduces for the first time in international human rights treaties the concept of the evolving capacities of the child.[32] Article 5, particularly in its second half, poses the most complete expression of the concept:

> States Parties shall respect the responsibilities, rights and duties of parents or, where applicable, the members of the extended family or community as provided for by local custom, legal guardians or other persons legally responsible for the child, to provide, in a manner consistent with the evolving capacities of the child, appropriate direction and guidance in the exercise by the child of the rights recognized in the present Convention.

Similarly, Article 14(2) stipulates in the context of freedom of thought, conscience, and religion that "States Parties shall respect the rights and duties of the parents and, when applicable, legal guardians, to provide direction to the child in the exercise of his or her right in a manner consistent with the evolving capacities of the child."

Both articles relate to the role of parents and caregivers in children's guidance and upbringing, but their emphasis on the relationship of individual children to their rights is fundamental, and their principles hold true for children of all ages in all contexts. Lansdown identifies three conceptual frameworks for the evolving capacities of the child: as a developmental concept, as a participatory or

---

29   See, e.g., *ibid.*, par. 36.

30   *Ibid.*; *Id.*, *supra* note 28 (*Case of T. v. the United Kingdom*, and *Case of V. v. the United Kingdom*).

31   See, e.g., International Covenant on Civil and Political Rights, Art. 14; American Convention on Human Rights, Art. 8; and African Charter on the Rights and Welfare of the Child, Art. 17.

32   Lansdown, *supra* note 24.

emancipatory concept, and as a protective concept.[33] These three angles explain how evolving capacities are pivotal to children's rights in mediating welfare–justice tensions.

First, as a developmental concept, it is incumbent upon adults to respect and foster children's abilities and capacities, just as CRC Article 6(2) holds that "States Parties shall ensure to the maximum extent possible the ... development of the child." Development in this sense includes all children's skills, knowledge, abilities, and competencies that grow over time. In general, the fullest possible development of children proves to be a core concern for children's rights, the CRC, and international juvenile justice standards.[34]

The heart of the second conceptual framework for evolving capacities—as a participatory or emancipatory concept—lies in the transition wherein children increasingly exercise their rights on their own behalf. Whereas Article 3 states children's right to have their best interests be a primary consideration (by adults) in all actions concerning them, and Article 12 guarantees children's right to express their views in all matters affecting them (with those views given due weight by adults), Articles 5 and 14 instead shift to children exercising their own rights. In citing "the child in the exercise of his or her rights," and "in the exercise by the child of the rights recognized in the present Convention," these articles imply "a transfer of responsibility for decision-making from responsible adults to children, as the child acquires the competence, and of course, willingness to do so."[35] The concept is linked directly to the transition wherein children become full moral agents with the capacity to exercise competency-based liberty rights on their own behalf, as described in Chapter 1.[36] State action based on the best interests of the child is further tempered, as protectionist interventions must take into account the child's evolving capacities or the guidance of responsible adults.[37]

As discussed in Chapter 1, individual children's skills and capacities do not develop uniformly per se, as they may quickly become competent in some contexts while needing further encouragement and growth in others, such that they begin to exercise distinct rights for themselves at different points in time.[38] Nonetheless, in general, children may justifiably expect to gain various liberties and responsibilities with some degree of consistency, and to see protection rights decrease in importance. As their capacities grow over time, and as they participate more actively, both liberty rights and responsibilities should generally follow. It is logically inconsistent, as well as inconsistent with children's rights, to push these

---

33   *Ibid.*
34   For example, CRC Preamble and Arts. 23(3), 27(1), and 29(1)(a); and Beijing Rules 1.2 and 17 Commentary.
35   Lansdown, *supra* note 24, at 4.
36   Bellon, *supra* note 17.
37   Ronen, Ya'ir, "Protection for Whom and from What? Protection Proceedings and the Voice of the Child at Risk," in Douglas, Gillian, and Leslie Sebba, eds, *Children's Rights and Traditional Values*, Aldershot (England), Ashgate/Dartmouth, 1998.
38   Lansdown, *supra* note 24.

rights and responsibilities in opposite directions. Instead, children's own capacities should act as the ballast for carrying both ahead on course.

Here, the concept of evolving capacities means not only encouraging children on their way towards greater participation and autonomy, but also fostering their sense of control over and responsibility for their own lives, and for their roles in society. These aspects are recurring themes in relevant international instruments, including in juvenile justice standards.[39] Thus, as children develop their capacities overall, they are encouraged to assume greater autonomy and responsibility as individuals and as fully participating members of their communities.

Finally, Lansdown's third and final lens on evolving capacities—as a protective concept—insists that the very level of children's evolving capacities guide the progression towards responsibilities and independence. Children should not be forced to accept responsibilities that they are not equipped to handle with appropriate support. Responsibilities must accrue only in alignment with the relevant prerequisites of knowledge, experience, and other competencies. For example, a child's inability to participate meaningfully in a given context indicates his or her need for further assistance and growth before assuming the responsibility of making relevant decisions.

Children are also due protection from responsibilities that may expose them, or the continuing development of their capacities, to harm. To be sure, there are strong moral arguments that children are "entitled to have both their present autonomy recognized and their capacity for future autonomy safeguarded. And this is to recognize that children, particularly younger children, need nurture, care and protection."[40] Maintaining these delicate balances according to the demands of children's evolving capacities is no simple task:

> One of the most fundamental challenges posed by the Convention on the Rights of the Child is the need to balance children's rights to adequate and appropriate protection with their right to participate in and take responsibility for the exercise of those decisions and actions they are competent to take for themselves.[41]

Part of the difficulty lies in the nature of the balance; it is not a dichotomy but a continuum between protection and liberty rights, where both are necessary, just as in the tensions along the welfare–justice continuum.[42] Likewise, the national

---

39 See, e.g., the CRC Preamble and Art. 29(1)(d); the 1966 International Covenant on Civil and Political Rights, Preamble; the 1990 UN Guidelines for the Prevention of Juvenile Delinquency, Guidelines 18 and 23; and the 1990 UN Rules for the Protection of Juveniles Deprived of their Liberty, Rule 12.

40 Freeman, Michael, *The Moral Status of Children: Essays on the Rights of the Child*, The Hague, Kluwer Law International, 1997, at 37.

41 Lansdown, *supra* note 24, at 32.

42 Freeman, M.D.A., *The Rights and Wrongs of Children*, London, Frances Pinter Publishers, 1983.

minimum age limits for various liberty rights, mentioned in Chapter 1, refer in a sense to points along this continuum. The Committee on the Rights of the Child reviews these limits and related measures to ensure "that children are not forced to participate in activities that expose them to responsibilities, risks or experiences that are inappropriate or harmful in view of their youth," that is, in view of their still evolving capacities in different contexts and at different ages.[43]

Evolving Capacities, Responsibility, and Criminal Responsibility

Children's evolving capacities have particularly important implications for the welfare–justice continuum in juvenile justice. As they participate and mature in decision-making, children must learn that responsibility entails accountability for their decisions, both good and bad. In juvenile justice, "children are regarded not only as vulnerable and developing individuals, but also—and equally—as individuals who are developing the capacity for rational choice, more independent decision making, and, hence, a growing moral and legal responsibility."[44] As their capacity for responsibility grows, children should be encouraged towards accountability for their decisions in a supportive and learning environment that respects all their rights, including in juvenile courts.[45] International juvenile justice standards broadly support this developmental perspective, reaffirming children's right to effective participation in juvenile justice matters, and to enjoy proceedings and treatment that take into account their age.[46] This implicitly requires that juvenile justice mechanisms be adapted to fit the needs of children at different ages and of different capacities.

The concept of criminal responsibility lies clearly embedded in this framework, as seen most specifically in Beijing Rule 4.1, its related Commentary, and CRC Article 40(3)(a). Beijing Rule 4.1 states that MACRs "… shall not be fixed at too low an age level, bearing in mind the facts of emotional, mental and intellectual maturity." The rule appeals to the protective aspect of evolving capacities. In consideration of children's growing emotional, mental, and intellectual maturity, children at young ages may not have the necessary competency to sustain individual responsibility for their choices and actions—particularly in the sense of criminal responsibility and the gravity of its implications. Therefore, MACRs should be set high enough to protect children from a type of responsibility, and

---

43 Lansdown, *supra* note 24, at 7.
44 Doek, Jaap E., "Modern Juvenile Justice in Europe," in Rosenheim, Margaret K., Franklin E. Zimring, David S. Tanenhaus, and Bernardine Dohrn, eds, *A Century of Juvenile Justice*, Chicago, University of Chicago Press, 2002, at 522.
45 *Id.*, "The Future of the Juvenile Court," in Junger-Tas, Josine, et al., eds, *The Future of the Juvenile Justice System/L'avenir du système pénal des mineurs*, Leuven, Acco, 1991.
46 For example, CRC Arts. 12 and 40(1); Beijing Rule 14.2; and the 1966 International Covenant on Civil and Political Rights, Art. 14(4).

from experiences that may potentially follow, for which they are not prepared and that may cause them undue harm.

Rule 4.1's Commentary reinforces these points, describing the modern trend:

> to consider whether a child can live up to the moral and psychological components of criminal responsibility; that is, whether a child, by virtue of her or his individual discernment and understanding, can be held responsible for essentially antisocial behaviour. If the age of criminal responsibility is fixed too low or if there is no lower age limit at all, the notion of responsibility would become meaningless. In general, there is a close relationship between the notion of responsibility of delinquent or criminal behaviour and other social rights and responsibilities (such as marital status, civil majority, etc.).

By directing attention to moral and psychological development, discernment, and understanding, the Commentary stresses certain competencies—among children's overall evolving capacities—with particular relevance to criminal responsibility. The mentioned "close relationship" alludes to the principle that as children acquire greater competency, they accrue more liberty rights (in contrast to protection rights), autonomy, and the responsibility that follows from them. It is unreasonable to expect that young children are competent enough to bear criminal responsibility, just as they would not be granted independence and liberty rights in other contexts. As children mature over time in the prerequisite competencies for criminal responsibility—in line with their broader evolving capacities—it is fitting that they increasingly and independently exercise their own rights and bear responsibility. Upon the appropriate legal age, this can also include bearing criminal responsibility.

CRC Article 40(3)(a) states similarly "States Parties shall seek to promote ... the establishment of a minimum age below which children shall be presumed not to have the capacity to infringe the penal law." This language continues the same discourse as the Beijing Rules. It instructs States Parties to establish a minimum age, linked directly to children's evolving capacities, which is explicitly protective. It is protective in the sense that all minimum ages protect children from liberty rights and responsibilities for which they may not yet be prepared, and in the sense that the CRC's language addresses immature capacities of children beneath the minimum age.

The content and intent of Article 40(3)(a), however, cannot be interpreted exclusively as a protective measure. In spinning upon the axis of children's evolving capacities, it must also be seen from a developmental and emancipatory angle.[47] The article's developmental content, for example, is inherent in its very language: it is fundamentally posed as a matter of children's capacity. Children's capacity at younger ages will generally be insufficient; it can be expected over time to grow with support and encouragement; and at older ages it will generally be sufficient. Children deserve support, encouragement, and developmentally appropriate

---

47 Lansdown, *supra* note 24.

opportunities to learn as part of this process. This is true even though the specific context is the evolving capacities necessary for criminal responsibility.

In an emancipatory light, Article 40(3)(a) also has relevance for older children. At a certain age, they will be presumed to have the legal capacity to infringe the penal law; they will reach the MACR, the formal starting point to juvenile justice. Once they reach that threshold, and if they are alleged as, accused of, or recognized as having infringed the penal law, they may claim for themselves the wide range of rights and guarantees spelled out in the rest of Article 40 and related articles. Younger children—and children not alleged as, accused of, or recognized as having broken the law—are not guaranteed these context-specific rights.

The very inclusion of the notion of children's criminal responsibility within international juvenile justice standards—and directly in the context of children's evolving capacities—underscores that it can have an appropriate role in rights-based juvenile justice. Children's criminal responsibility is indeed an integral and necessary part of children's rights—a logical extension of the concept of children's evolving capacities insofar as it is an appropriate step in respecting children's progression from lesser to greater competence, which gradually prepares them for adult rights and responsibilities in society.

Therefore, from the theoretical viewpoint of children's rights, it is untenable to argue that children should never be held criminally responsible, or that MACRs should be increased to the age of 18 years. There are many scenarios in which criminal responsibility is not an appropriate step as such, and here it must be rejected: for example, in exposing children to undue risks or harm to their future development, or by launching them directly into the adult criminal justice system. In this sense, a rights framework assumes that the onset of children's criminal responsibility occurs against the backdrop of rigorous application of all other juvenile justice standards. There can be no connotation that criminal responsibility somehow legitimizes deprivation of liberty, excessive punishments, sheerly retributive penalties, and so on, as all of these are prohibited or very strictly limited and regulated under international standards.

Furthermore, the possibility of criminal responsibility does not necessarily mean that a penal approach should or will be taken in response to children in conflict with the law. The international standards do envision both penal and non-penal responses to delinquency, yet sustain a decided preference for diversion and non-penal approaches. In addition, whenever children are found guilty of committing delinquent acts, their evolving capacities continue to be a guiding principle in consideration of possible responses. CRC Article 40(4) identifies the appropriate purpose therein: to "ensure that children are dealt with in a manner appropriate to their well-being and proportionate both to their circumstances and the offence." For a response to be proportionate to children's circumstances, "Not only the committed crime is important, but also the degree of culpability of a child with a growing capacity to be held responsible."[48]

---

48 Doek, *supra* note 45, at 206.

In other words, all children adjudicated responsible for offenses should see some appropriate response, calibrated for both their developmental maturity and the actual offense. The concept of evolving capacities demands no less: children must experience some consequence to the offenses that they commit—some meaningful response that encourages them to understand and take personal responsibility for their choices, and which demonstrates the expectation that they be increasingly accountable for their actions as they mature. A non-response to children's delinquency does not foster their capacities for autonomous life in society. Instead, international juvenile justice standards direct states to create and employ a range appropriate responses that will serve this developmental purpose.[49]

Children's evolving capacities uphold the same underlying principles for younger children, even when criminal responsibility is barred due to their age. Their evolving capacities still need to be developed, respected, and fulfilled. Insofar as they are competent in relevant ways, children should have both the opportunity to exercise their autonomy and the opportunity to learn from the results of such practice. All children should be granted developmentally appropriate independence, with encouragement and support as they become willing to accept that independence, as well as developmentally appropriate responsibility.

Therefore, *all children* who commit unlawful acts should experience some response to their actions—an individualized and developmentally appropriate response that respects their competence, helps develop it further, and yet protects them from excessive responsibilities and harm. As noted below, this does not necessarily signify formal or government intervention. Younger children, including those younger than MACRs, can certainly commit delinquent acts, and these children also deserve the learning experience of an appropriate response to their acts:

> Though the message of the Convention on the Rights of the Child is that criminalisation of children should be avoided, this does not mean that young offenders should be treated as if they have no *responsibility*. On the contrary, it is important that young offenders are held responsible for their actions and, for instance, take part in repairing the damage that they have caused.[50]

This is not a discourse about punishment per se, which as explained in Chapter 6 is decidedly counterproductive for at least the youngest offenders. Penal charges, treatment, procedures, and punishments are ruled out for children younger than respective MACRs, and responses must generally be non-coercive, respecting all relevant children's rights.[51] At levels where children can engage and communicate, appropriate responses should focus on the teachable moment at hand—a dialogue

---

49   For example, CRC Art. 40(4).

50   Hammarberg, Thomas, *The Human Rights Dimension of Juvenile Justice*, presented at the Conference of the Prosecutors General of Europe, Moscow, 5–6 July 2006.

51   The 1990 UN Guidelines for the Prevention of Juvenile Delinquency provide relevant context. See Guidelines 2–4, 5(a), 5(d), 6, 7, 10, 20, and 52.

aimed at fostering moral awareness of the significance of the harm caused.[52] A talk with a respected elder, the experience of offering an apology, mediation, and restorative justice may provide effective channels not only to express disapproval to children, but also to give them the counsel, support, and inclusion that they need.[53] Formal justice institutions may actually block meaningful communication of this sort.

Reintegration into Society

The final principle within international juvenile justice standards that helps mediate welfare–justice tensions is the goal of reintegration. CRC Article 40(1) includes children's reintegration into society as one of the core aims of juvenile justice: "the right of every child ... to be treated in a manner consistent with the promotion of the child's sense of dignity and worth, ... which takes into account ... the desirability of promoting the child's reintegration and the child's assuming a constructive role in society." At the same time, the principle generally applies to children older and younger than MACRs, particularly in all cases involving the deprivation of liberty.

Beginning with the CRC, reintegration has become increasingly prominent within international juvenile justice standards.[54] It rejects the assumption that individual children are the source of problems that emerge, and instead looks at structural influences and the role and responsibilities of society at large. For example, there is an emphasis on societies' active *integration* of children into community life in general, before delinquency is even an issue, and on ensuring all children's welfare as a starting point.[55] Children deprived of their liberty or in conflict with the law should enjoy contact with their families, continuing links to their communities, vocational skill training, early release arrangements, and guidance and other services so as to lay the foundation for successful reintegration back into their communities.[56] The standards emphasize the role of communities in ensuring the full reintegration of children, as successful reintegration requires that societies be willing to accept and welcome children back into community life.[57]

---

52 Weijers, Ido, "The Moral Dialogue: A Pedagogical Perspective on Juvenile Justice," in Weijers, Ido, and Antony Duff, eds, *Punishing Juveniles: Principle and Critique*, Oxford, Hart, 2002.

53 Walgrave, Lode, "Not Punishing Children, but Committing Them to Restore," in Weijers, Ido, and Antony Duff, eds, *Punishing Juveniles: Principle and Critique*, Oxford, Hart, 2002.

54 Van Bueren, *supra* note 20.

55 For example, Beijing Rule 1 Commentary; and 1990 UN Guidelines for the Prevention of Juvenile Delinquency, Guidelines 2 and 21.

56 For example, Beijing Rules 26.1 and 29 and Commentary; and 1990 UN Rules for the Protection of Juveniles Deprived of their Liberty, Rules 3, 8, 38, 59, and 79–81.

57 See 1990 UN Rules for the Protection of Juveniles Deprived of their Liberty, Rules 8 and 80.

The principle of reintegration acts to restrain the excesses of both the welfare and justice approaches—including their common weakness of approaching delinquency as a question of individual children, in isolation from the obligations and consequences of broader society and systemic-structural factors. In a children's rights approach to juvenile justice, the obligations of society-at-large are directly addressed. In addition, as a primary goal of juvenile justice, all of the various aspects of reintegration must be weighed and duly pursued with respect to all children in conflict with the law. Any treatment, procedure, or penal sanction that tends to demonize children, use children as moral or political scapegoats, remove them from society and effectively isolate them, and so on, must be considered in violation of the principle of reintegration, among other children's rights. International juvenile justice standards' emphasis on reintegration thus holds a light up to every juvenile justice function and asks, at a minimum, "Is this consistent with children's full reintegration into society?"

Conclusion

This chapter surveys the main children's rights principles that help mediate tensions along the welfare–justice continuum, and that consequently give meaning to the MACR in a full children's rights context. International children's rights insist upon a richer conceptualization of children than either the traditional welfare or justice approach, and provide a more comprehensive account of the relationship among state, family, and child. By staking out a broader set of central principles, they also seek to avoid the systemic flaws in the welfare and justice approaches. At their core, children's rights demand greater respect for individual dignity, such as where CRC Article 40(1) emphasizes the fundamental principle of juvenile justice that children "be treated in a manner consistent with the promotion of the child's sense of dignity and worth."

International juvenile justice standards apply such principles through a progression of rights across welfare and justice. First, children younger than MACRs who may have committed delinquent acts enjoy special considerations in any response to their behavior. The best interests of the child are central, and any welfare, care, protection, education, or other proceeding or action must focus on appropriate assistance to families and schools in addressing children's behavior. The deprivation of liberty of such children is almost never permissible, and CRC States Parties must report details of all such incidences to the Committee on the Rights of the Child.

An even broader range of guarantees is provided to children who have attained the MACR and are alleged as, accused of, or recognized as having infringed the penal law. In this sense, it is true that children younger than MACRs enjoy fewer specific protections than children at or above MACRs who are involved in juvenile justice. For older children, the best interests of the child continue to be a primary consideration, yet a detailed range of juvenile justice rights and guarantees further ensures for them a fair trial and other protections. These differences are part of why the MACR is such an important marker in juvenile justice and for children's rights generally. For example, higher MACRs exclude a larger cohort of children from juvenile justice, but signify a relatively narrower range of context-specific rights for those same children.

Other principles further restrain the excesses of welfare and justice approaches. Respect for the views of the child, and children's right to effective participation at trial, assert a truly central role for participation that goes far beyond welfare and justice approaches. If children are unable to express themselves freely and participate effectively at trial, they are due greater assistance and modifications to procedures and settings. If such measures are insufficient, cases must generally be removed from the juvenile justice context and referred to relevant welfare-oriented actions used to address the behavior of children free from criminal responsibility, as mentioned above.

Similarly, the international standards' emphasis on reintegration addresses a criticism of both the welfare and justice approaches: both view individual children in isolation, either as objects needing aid to fix their problems, or as subjects who simply decide to commit crimes and deserve punishment. In contrast, the international standards explicitly advocate a structural-institutional understanding of juvenile delinquency, as well as a principled approach to the individual child, that stresses the outcome of children assuming constructive roles in society.

The concept of children's evolving capacities is also critical, refusing any assumption that children are incompetent. All children have competencies that must be respected and nurtured. It is generally expected that as those competencies grow, protection rights become less prominent, and both liberty rights and responsibilities accrue. Children's criminal responsibility is embedded in this developmental approach, which supports children's progression towards a larger role in decision-making, in exercising their rights on their own behalf, and in maturing responsibility for their own actions. As such, children's rights principles do not support an across-the-board rejection of children's criminal responsibility, such as the setting of MACRs at 18 years of age. Children's evolving capacities mean that all children of all ages should see appropriate responses to their problematic behaviors or actions—including before the MACR in the context of assistance to families and schools, as well as beginning at the MACR, which can mean responses in the context of juvenile justice.

Such principles illustrate that international children's rights are not neutral in the ongoing construction of childhood's meaning. Beyond the welfare and justice approaches, they communicate their own distinct conception of children, their rights, and responsibility. This vision brings important advantages, including greater transparency, international legitimacy, a coherent moral framework and basis, and a corresponding set of principles that guide societies' understanding of children. In this sense, international children's rights demand new interpretations of childhood and children. This features an integrated (rather than fragmented) account of protection rights and liberty rights, including their respective prerequisites, their balance and interaction, the conditions for their implementation, and the roles of adults and society overall. This children's rights narrative also opens space for a richer and more principled account of children's morality. It transcends justice approach morality myths and blaming, and addresses both individual justice and social justice.

Yet around the principles of international children's rights, there also remains space for cultural differences, varying conceptions of childhood, and debate. There are in fact many ambiguities and points of friction, but this is only a natural consequence of what is fundamentally a dynamic and evolving project.[58] Much of the vitality of children's rights lies in the universal relevance of its principles, and this point underscores the need for vigilance in constantly revisiting and remaining faithful to them. Indeed, the continued value of children's rights as a way of framing issues about children depends to some extent on how these principles are applied in practice over time, and on how successfully they can be adapted with integrity to address the new challenges that will continue to arise.

---

58 See, for example, Nelken, David, "Afterword: Choosing Rights for Children," in Douglas, Gillian, and Leslie Sebba, eds, *Children's Rights and Traditional Values*, Aldershot (England), Ashgate/Dartmouth, 1998.

Chapter 3
MACRs and States' Obligations under Regional and International Law Instruments

A wide array of regional and international legal instruments gives specific consideration to the minimum age of criminal responsibility (MACR), and at times creates legal obligations for relevant countries. This chapter chronologically surveys the main instruments, paying particular attention to the evolution and drafting history behind relevant provisions, as well as their subsequent interpretation by monitoring bodies and other judicial bodies.[1] A number of points remain open to debate or beg further clarification, but the available guidance is both detailed and extensive, thanks principally to the work of the Committee on the Rights of the Child. The Committee's recommendations, largely affirmed over time by other instruments and bodies, suggest a general convergence in international standards for countries' MACRs and their implementation. This chapter departs from Chapter 2's analysis of the broader juvenile justice framework to document this very specific practical guidance on MACRs.

International Covenant on Civil and Political Rights

Like the Convention on the Rights of the Child (CRC), the 1966 International Covenant on Civil and Political Rights (ICCPR) is one of the core international human rights treaties.[2] ICCPR States Parties include the only two countries in the world that have not ratified the CRC, Somalia and the United States of America. While the ICCPR applies to both adults and children, it is the first international human rights treaty to explicitly mandate States Parties to provide special treatment and procedures for children in criminal matters. Even though the treaty does not define "juvenile persons," Article 14(4) clearly uses the term to refer to the span of years between the MACR and the minimum age of penal majority.[3] This presupposes that there is a precise lower age limit for "juvenile persons,"

---

1 Information included in this chapter is believed to be complete through at least June 2008.
2 Adopted by the UN General Assembly, Resolution 2200A (XXI), 16 Dec 1966.
3 ICCPR Art. 14(4): "In the case of juvenile persons, the procedure shall be such as will take account of their age and the desirability of promoting their rehabilitation."

and scholars have noted that the ICCPR's provisions occasion the following conclusions:

- Each State Party is obligated to establish a respective MACR.
- Each State Party may choose its respective age level, provided that it falls within the general limits of internationally recognized norms.
- Each State Party must apply its same respective MACR to boys and girls alike.[4]

The Human Rights Committee—the ICCPR's monitoring body—has long interpreted the Covenant accordingly.[5] In its General Comment on the implementation of Article 14, the Human Rights Committee noted that few States Parties' reports provided sufficient information on MACRs and on how these took account of the desirability of promoting juveniles' rehabilitation, as stipulated by Article 14(4).[6] The Committee has also examined and critiqued the MACR provisions of specific States Parties. In summary terms, the Committee has held MACRs of 7, 8, and 10 years to be unacceptably low and incompatible with international standards—particularly ICCPR Articles 10(2)(b), 14(4), and 24(1)—and has recommended respective increases.[7]

The Committee has appraised MACR-related provisions besides age levels, including the *doli incapax* doctrine, which exists in scores of countries and is examined closely at various points in this study. In brief, *doli incapax* is a legal presumption that children between the MACR and a higher age limit are not capable of bearing criminal responsibility. Theoretically, the presumption may be rebutted by evidence before the court of an individual child's maturity or understanding. If the presumption is rebutted as such, the possibility for criminal responsibility

---

4   Muhammad, Haji N.A. Noor, "Due Process of Law for Persons Accused of Crime," in Henkin, Louis, ed., *The International Bill of Rights: The Covenant on Civil and Political Rights*, New York, Columbia University Press, 1981; and Nowak, Manfred, *U.N. Covenant on Civil and Political Rights: CCPR Commentary*, Kehl (Germany), N.P. Engel, 1993.

5   In general, see Cipriani, Don, *The Minimum Age of What? Criminal Responsibility, Juvenile Justice, and Children's Rights*, unpublished draft, Florence, UNICEF Innocenti Research Centre, 2002.

6   "General Comment 13 (Twenty-first session, 1984)," in *Compilation of General Comments and General Recommendations adopted by Human Rights Treaty Bodies*, HRI/GEN/1, 1992, par. 16.

7   See, inter alia, the following: *Concluding observations*: *Cyprus*, CCPR/C/79/Add.39, 21 Sept 1994; *Kenya*, CCPR/CO/83/KEN, 29 Apr 2005, par. 24; *Sri Lanka*, CCPR/C/79/Add.56, 27 Jul 1995; and *Suriname*, CCPR/C/80/SUR, 4 May 2004, par. 17. ICCPR Art. 10(2)(b): "Accused juvenile persons shall be separated from adults and brought as speedily as possible for adjudication."; Art. 14(4): *supra* note 3; and Art. 24(1): "Every child shall have, without any discrimination as to race, colour, sex, language, religion, national or social origin, property or birth, the right to such measures of protection as are required by his status as a minor, on the part of his family, society and the State."

opens, and the trial proceeds. If it is not rebutted, the child is not legally capable of criminal responsibility, and penal proceedings are in theory excluded. The Human Rights Committee, in consideration of Sri Lanka's statutes, noted the *doli incapax* system as a matter of profound concern—apparently for judges' wide discretion on children's potential criminal responsibility.[8]

International Covenant on Economic, Social and Cultural Rights

The 1966 International Covenant on Economic, Social and Cultural Rights does not explicitly address juvenile justice concerns, but its monitoring body—the Committee on Economic, Social and Cultural Rights—views Article 10 as having important MACR implications.[9] It noted concern for MACRs of 7 and 9 years as being too low, and explicitly encouraged and called upon respective States Parties to increase them in accord with the obligations of Article 10.[10]

American Convention on Human Rights

Two bodies are responsible for overseeing compliance with provisions of the 1969 American Convention on Human Rights: the Inter-American Commission on Human Rights and the Inter-American Court of Human Rights.[11] In 2001, the former requested before the latter an Advisory Opinion on the Juridical Condition and Human Rights of the Child.[12] Although the request was much broader than MACRs, it was driven by a concern for law and practice regarding officials' discretion to find children as lacking full discernment. As noted in Chapter 1, such decisions have historically led to measures that in practice curtail children's rights, legal protections, and guarantees, particularly in criminal law, despite justification as the best interests of the child.

In its wide-ranging discussion on these matters, the majority opinion of the Inter-American Court of Human Rights briefly discusses the notion of minimum capacity for criminal responsibility, which it terms "chargeability":

---

8   *Ibid.* (*Sri Lanka*). Cipriani, *supra* note 5.

9   Adopted by the UN General Assembly, Resolution 2200A (XXI), 16 Dec 1966. Somalia is a State Party to the treaty. Among other issues, Article 10 addresses protection and assistance to families, especially in children's care and education, and special measures of protection and assistance to children.

10   See the following: *Concluding observations: Malta*, E/C.12/1/Add.101, 14 Dec 2004, pars. 21 and 38; and *(Hong Kong):China*, E/C.12/1/Add.58, 21 May 2001, pars. 24 and 43.

11   Adopted 22 Nov 1969 by the Inter-American Specialized Conference on Human Rights, Organization of American States, Treaty Series, No. 36.

12   Inter-American Court of Human Rights, *Juridical Condition and Human Rights of the Child*, Advisory Opinion OC-17/2002 of August 28, 2002.

From a criminal perspective—associated with conduct that is defined and punishable as a crime, and with the consequent sanctions—chargeability refers to a person's capacity for culpability. If the person does not have this capacity, it is not possible to file charges in a lawsuit as in the case of a person who is chargeable. Chargeability is not an option when the person is unable to understand the nature of his or her action or omission and/or to behave in accordance with that understanding. It is generally accepted that children under a certain age lack that capacity. This is a generic legal assessment, one that does not examine the specific conditions of the minors on a case by case basis, but rather excludes them completely from the sphere of criminal justice.[13]

The opinion subsequently refers to relevant provisions of the CRC and the United Nations Standard Minimum Rules for the Administration of Juvenile Justice, as discussed below, and refutes application of the criminal law under the *situación irregular* doctrine.[14] As seen in this excerpt, the majority opinion reaffirms the notion that MACRs must be established by law, and apparently rejects the notion of individual assessments for the capacity for criminal responsibility, as in the case of *doli incapax* tests. One concurring opinion does raise doubts about the establishment of a standard MACR without appraising individuals' capacity for criminal responsibility.[15]

Protocol I Additional to the Geneva Conventions of 12 August 1949

In the case of the 1977 Additional Protocol I to the 1949 Geneva Conventions (relating to the Protection of Victims of International Armed Conflicts), the implications for states' MACR obligations emerge not from the protocol text—as it includes no references to MACRs—but from the extensive MACR debates that transpired in its drafting. Through the decades after World War II, international support grew to further develop humanitarian law, and in particular to update the 1949 Geneva Conventions.[16] The International Committee of the Red Cross (ICRC) composed an initial text of two draft Protocols to the 1949 Geneva Conventions, which were distributed to all governments in 1973. The Swiss Government then convened a Diplomatic Conference in sessions from 1974–77, inviting all States Parties to the Geneva Conventions and all United Nations Members.

---

13 *Ibid.*, par. 105.
14 *Ibid.*, par. 106 *et seq.*
15 Judge Sergio García Ramírez, Concurring Opinion, ibid., pars. 10–12.
16 See Pictet, Jean, "General introduction: The task of the development of humanitarian law," in Sandoz, Yves, et al., eds, *Commentary on the Additional Protocols of 8 June 1977 to the Geneva Conventions of 12 August 1949*, Geneva, International Committee of the Red Cross, 1987.

Of particular interest in the ICRC's draft Additional Protocol I, Article 68(3) prohibited the pronouncement of the death penalty against persons under 18 at the time of their offenses related to certain international armed conflicts.[17] This scope is relatively limited, arguably excluding ordinary criminal offenses in general, as is the case for the version adopted as Article 77(5) in the final text.[18] In consideration of draft Article 68(3), the Brazilian delegation proposed the addition of the following sentence, still referring to offenses related to certain international conflicts: "Penal proceedings shall not be taken against, and sentence shall not be pronounced on, persons who were under sixteen years of age at the time the offence was committed."[19]

Of the three main plenary committees of the Diplomatic Conference, Committee III took up consideration of draft Article 68 and the amendments proposed to it. In the committee's first meeting on the article, the representative of Brazil formally introduced his delegation's proposal and made explicit reference to Brazilian criminal law's age of penal majority of 18. At the time, 18 was also technically Brazil's MACR, as no penal proceedings, sentences, or punishments were foreseen for people younger than 18 at the time of alleged criminal offenses. The representative explained that his delegation's amendment proposed an age limit of 16 to penal proceedings and sentences, rather than 18, "in the hope that it would prove generally acceptable."[20] Even if 16 was not acceptable, he still considered it desirable to specify some fixed age limit. Interestingly, Committee III's debate specifically on the Brazilian proposal, examined here in detail, looked to and commented primarily upon domestic criminal law provisions.

---

17 International Committee of the Red Cross, "Article 68 – Protection of children," *Draft Additional Protocols to the Geneva Conventions of August 12, 1949*, Geneva, 1973, reprinted in "Volume I," *Official Records of the Diplomatic Conference on the Reaffirmation and Development of International Humanitarian Law applicable in Armed Conflicts, Geneva, 1974–1977*, Bern, Federal Political Department, 1978.

18 "The death penalty for an offence related to the armed conflict shall not be executed on persons who had not attained the age of eighteen years at the time the offence was committed." See Pilloud, Claude, and Jean Pictet, "Protocol I: Article 77 – Protection of children," par. 3205, in Sandoz, Yves, et al., eds, *Commentary on the Additional Protocols of 8 June 1977 to the Geneva Conventions of 12 August 1949*, Geneva, International Committee of the Red Cross, 1987, at 904.

19 *Amendments to Draft Additional Protocol I and Annex: Article 68, Protection of Children [Art. 77 of the Final Act]: Brazil*, CDDH/III/325, 30 Apr 1976, reprinted in "Volume III," *Official Records of the Diplomatic Conference on the Reaffirmation and Development of International Humanitarian Law applicable in Armed Conflicts, Geneva, 1974–1977*, Bern, Federal Political Department, 1978, at 301.

20 *Summary Record of the Forty-Fifth Meeting held on Wednesday, 5 May 1976, at 10.20 a.m.: Article 6—Protection of children*, CDDH/III/SR.45, par. 12, reprinted in "Volume XV," *Official Records of the Diplomatic Conference on the Reaffirmation and Development of International Humanitarian Law applicable in Armed Conflicts, Geneva, 1974–1977*, Bern, Federal Political Department, 1978, at 66.

In the first direct comment on the Brazilian proposal, the representative of Japan observed that many countries' criminal laws set the age of 14 years as the minimum age limit for penal proceedings; Japan's MACR at the time was ostensibly 14 years. As such, he suggested that the Brazilian proposal would have to be lowered to 14 to make it acceptable.[21] Apparently, the committee's strong preference for decision-making by consensus implicitly favored a lowest-common-denominator approach that would accommodate existing domestic criminal laws.

Canada's representative, instead, declined to support Brazil's amendment and noted the following:

> The fixing of the age of criminal responsibility was a national responsibility which each State would exercise having regard to its own peculiar culture, state of development and requirements. To attempt to formulate a provision in the Protocol impinging on the exercise of that sovereign right would be unacceptable to many States as an unwarranted interference.[22]

Canada's relatively low MACR—which remained 7 years of age until 1984—may have influenced the representative's argument on the principle of sovereign rights, thus avoiding the practical issue of accommodating diverse national laws.

Various governments' representatives commented on the proposal and raised broadly similar points, including the Uruguayan representative's rejection of the amendment on the basis that "it would be difficult to arrive at a provision that would be universally applicable."[23] Finally, it was suggested that the committee's Working Group carefully consider the precise age limit to be included. Committee III agreed to refer the entire draft Article 68 to the Working Group for further debate.[24]

The Working Group discussed the draft article for one week, and reported back the following with regard to the Brazilian proposal:

> One representative wished to have it noted in the report that he would have preferred to add a new paragraph 6 prohibiting any penal prosecution and punishment of a child who was not old enough at the time the offence was committed to understand the implications of his acts. The Working Group, however, decided that the definition of such standards was better left to national law.[25]

---

21   *Ibid.*, par. 20 at 67.
22   *Ibid.*, par. 24 at 68.
23   *Ibid.*, par. 28 at 69. See also *Ibid.*, par. 25 at 68, par. 31 at 69, par. 34 at 70, and par. 36 at 71.
24   *Ibid.*, pars. 37 and 40 at 71.
25   *Report to Committee III on the work of the Working Group, submitted by the Rapporteur*, CDDH/III/391, reprinted in "Volume XV," *Official Records of the Diplomatic Conference on the Reaffirmation and Development of International Humanitarian Law applicable in Armed Conflicts, Geneva, 1974–1977*, Bern, Federal Political Department, 1978, at 522.

It returned the draft article without the Brazilian amendment, despite the suggestion of a new paragraph that would have cemented into international law a central principle underlying MACRs. The article was largely ready for adoption by consensus.

In seeking to complete its business overall, Committee III closed discussion on draft articles, but allowed delegations to explain their votes on articles after the fact.[26] Following adoption of draft Article 68, the Italian representative offered a statement:

> Mr. BARILE (Italy) said there was an ommission [sic] in Article 68 of draft Protocol I and Article 32 of draft Protocol II. No mention was made in those articles of the universally recognized principle that a child, whatever its age, could not be sentenced if, at the time of the offence, it was incapable of cognizance. Should it be impossible to set a specific age for cognizance, a general principle should at least be included both in a separate paragraph of Article 68 of Protocol I, and as a general rule in Protocol II. That paragraph might be worded as follows: "No sentence in respect of an offence related to armed conflict shall be pronounced on children who, by reason of their age, did not have the capacity of discernment at the time of the offence". His delegation felt that it had been deemed unnecessary to spell out that rule, which occurred in every legal system, but that it must nevertheless be applied. Both that interpretation and the general principle should therefore be mentioned specifically in the final report.[27]

No such provisions were inserted into either Protocol I or Protocol II, but when Committee III later debated the section of its final work report dedicated to draft Article 68, an Italian representative interjected to pursue the same point:

> he took it as understood that no one in the Working Group had ever questioned the existence of a general principle to the effect that any person who, at the time when an offence was committed, was incapable of understanding the meaning of his own acts could not be regarded as guilty of the offence. He believed that it would be desirable to refer to that principle in paragraph 65, and proposed that the last sentence should be replaced by the following text:
>
> "The Committee recognized that it was a principle of general international law that no person could be convicted of a criminal offence if, at the time the offence was committed, he was unable to understand the consequences of his

---

26 *Summary Record of the Fifty-Ninth Meeting held on Tuesday, 10 May 1977, at 3.15 p.m.: Proposals submitted by the Working Group for further study*, pars. 1 and 17–18, CDDH/III/SR.59, reprinted in "Volume XV," *Official Records of the Diplomatic Conference on the Reaffirmation and Development of International Humanitarian Law applicable in Armed Conflicts, Geneva, 1974–1977*, Bern, Federal Political Department, 1978, at 209 and 212.

27 *Ibid.*, par. 62 at 219.

act. The Committee nevertheless decided that the application of this principle should be left to national legislation."[28]

Immediately thereafter, the Working Group's Rapporteur confirmed "that the proposed text seemed to him an accurate and clear reflection of the Committee's intentions."[29] As such, Committee III's official report on its work—albeit without any trace in the adopted text of Additional Protocol I—notes the following:

> One representative wished to have it noted in the report that he would have preferred to add a new paragraph 6 prohibiting any penal prosecution and punishment of a child who was not old enough at the time the offence was committed to understand the implications of his acts. The Committee recognized that it was a principle of general international law that no person could be convicted of a criminal offence if, at the time the offence was committed, he was unable to understand the consequences of his act. The Committee, nevertheless, decided that the application of this principle should be left to national legislation.[30]

Additional Protocol I was adopted on June 8, 1977, but in the end it does not stipulate any age limits to criminal prosecution. However, Committee III's final report records the first formal claim that a general principle of international law exists in this domain. The participants agreed upon, and indeed never even questioned, the existence of the principle that no person could be convicted of a criminal offense if, at the time the offense was committed, he or she was unable to understand the consequences of his or her act. In the end, this arguably includes a number of relevant contexts: it was understood with specific regard to children, and as related to children's understanding at different ages; it bars criminal prosecution, conviction, and punishment; it holds true without regard to the nature of the offense; and its validity is independent of the presence or absence of conflict situations. Apparently due to the difficulty in agreeing upon one common age limit, it was held that national legislation should regulate the application of the principle. Recent scholarship has tentatively supported the conclusion of Committee III that a general principle of law existed, while noting that as presented the rule

---

28 *Summary Record of the Sixtieth (Closing) Meeting held on Friday, 13 May 1977, at 10.20 a.m., [Fourth Session], Adoption of the Draft Report of Committee III*, CDDH/III/SR.60, par. 4, reprinted in "Volume XV," *Official Records of the Diplomatic Conference on the Reaffirmation and Development of International Humanitarian Law applicable in Armed Conflicts, Geneva, 1974–1977*, Bern, Federal Political Department, 1978, at 221–222.

29 *Ibid.*, par. 5 at 222.

30 *Report of Committee III*, CDDH/407/Rev. 1, par. 65, reprinted in "Volume XV, Annex II," *Official Records of the Diplomatic Conference on the Reaffirmation and Development of International Humanitarian Law applicable in Armed Conflicts, Geneva, 1974–1977*, Bern, Federal Political Department, 1978, at 466.

would seemingly permit either a fixed age limit or a case-by-case examination of individual children's potential criminal responsibility.[31] These points are explored further in Chapter 5, upon presentation of current MACRs worldwide.

Convention against Torture

The 1984 Convention against Torture and Other Cruel, Inhuman or Degrading Treatment or Punishment (CAT) is one of the core international human rights treaties, and the Committee Against Torture monitors its implementation by States Parties, which include Somalia and the United States of America.[32] The CAT applies equally to children and adults, and the Committee Against Torture regularly dedicates particular attention to children in CAT implementation. In terms of the MACR, it expressed concern for MACRs of 7, 8, and 10 years as being too low, and has recommended relevant MACR increases, at times "as a matter of urgency."[33] It also encouraged Burundi to complete its proposed MACR increase from 13 to 15 years.[34]

In the case of Argentina, the Committee focused on the inherent links between MACRs and certain grievous children's rights violations. At the time, Argentina's MACR of 16 years overlapped with its minimum age for responsibility in adult criminal court, with *situación irregular* provisions applying to younger children, as discussed in Chapter 1. With regard to these younger children, the Committee expressed:

> concern at ... reports of arrests and detention of children below the age of criminal responsibility, most of them "street children" and beggars, in police stations, where they are held together with adults, as well as on the alleged torture and ill-treatment suffered by such children, leading to death in some cases ... .[35]

---

31 Happold, Matthew, *Child Soldiers in International Law*, Manchester, Manchester University Press, 2005, at 144.

32 Adopted by the UN General Assembly, Resolution 39/46, 10 Dec 1984.

33 See the following: *Concluding observations: Yemen*, CAT/C/CR/31/4, 5 Feb 2004, pars. 6(i) and 7(l); *Indonesia*, CAT/C/IDN/CO/2, 16 May 2008, Advance Unedited Vers., par. 17 ("urgency"); *Zambia*, CAT/C/ZMB/CO/2, 26 May 2008, par. 18; *New Zealand*, CAT/C/CR/32/4, 11 Jun 2004, par. 5(e).

34 *Concluding observations: Burundi*, CAT/C/BDI/CO/1, 15 Feb 2007, par. 13. Burundi's MACR and age of penal majority coincide at 13 years. In this and similar cases, it is not clear if the Committee was specifically motivated by concern for MACRs and/or adult criminal court responsibility at low ages.

35 *Concluding observations: Argentina*, CAT/C/CR/33/1, 10 Dec 2004, par. 6(f).

United Nations Standard Minimum Rules for the Administration of Juvenile Justice

4. Age of Criminal Responsibility
4.1 In those legal systems recognizing the concept of the age of criminal responsibility for juveniles, the beginning of that age shall not be fixed at too low an age level, bearing in mind the facts of emotional, mental and intellectual maturity.

Commentary
The minimum age of criminal responsibility differs widely owing to history and culture. The modern approach would be to consider whether a child can live up to the moral and psychological components of criminal responsibility; that is, whether a child, by virtue of her or his individual discernment and understanding, can be held responsible for essentially antisocial behaviour. If the age of criminal responsibility is fixed too low or if there is no lower age limit at all, the notion of responsibility would become meaningless. In general, there is a close relationship between the notion of responsibility of delinquent or criminal behaviour and other social rights and responsibilities (such as marital status, civil majority, etc.).

Efforts should therefore be made to agree on a reasonable lowest age limit that is applicable internationally.

Among international human rights instruments, the 1985 United Nations Standard Minimum Rules for the Administration of Juvenile Justice (commonly known as the Beijing Rules) provide the first and most detailed treatment of both juvenile justice and the MACR.[36] Rule 4 and its Commentary, intended to be read as an integral part of the Rule, offer the only direct note in international instruments on appropriate considerations for selecting an MACR, and the only direct caution that the MACR should not be too low. Even though they are not binding, the Committee on the Rights of the Child has recommended that the Beijing Rules be applied to all children. Furthermore, as discussed below, the Beijing Rules were the direct source for the CRC's MACR provisions and their subsequent interpretations. A closer examination of the Beijing Rules' history provides even greater insights for understanding the MACR.[37]

In 1980, the Sixth United Nations Congress on the Prevention of Crime and the Treatment of Offenders created the mandate for the Beijing Rules. In its proceedings, the Congress approved the report of its Committee that had considered "Juvenile justice: before and after the onset of delinquency." That report noted the following:

---

36 Adopted by the UN General Assembly, Resolution 40/33, 29 Nov 1985.
37 In general, see Cipriani, *supra* note 5.

Many countries discussed their respective ages of criminal or social responsibility, and it was discernible from the various discussions that such ages, by and large, represented the point(s) when the youth was regarded as socially responsible in the sense of legal liability for the consequences of his actions, although there were intermediate age-shades between absolute non-responsibility and responsibility. Some problems were noted on this issue, prominent among which was that of the criteria for the age(s) of responsibility: should such age be chronological or mental? Again, having regard to the now generally accepted welfare aims of juvenile justice, ought society to continue to base juvenile justice on age of responsibility or on stages and types of welfare programmes? The legalistic demarcation, with its attendant attraction of constitutional rights, in particular due process, is known to result in a blockage of the applicability of the much needed welfare programmes beneficial to the youth involved.[38]

This commentary demonstrates an ironic perspective on the evolution of juvenile justice and the MACR. Although the welfare approach continues to enjoy adherents worldwide, three key United States Supreme Court decisions from 1966 to 1970—discussed in Chapter 1—clearly pushed the justice approach into ever-greater prominence. It appears skewed to refer in 1980 to "the now generally accepted welfare aims of juvenile justice." Essentially advocating the welfare approach, the Committee suggests that the MACR blocks the provision of needed and beneficial welfare programs to children, to the point of implying that it is a disposable anachronism. In contrast, the drafters of Additional Protocol I to the Geneva Conventions believed that a general principle of law existed by 1977 for the establishment of specific national MACRs. Revealingly, the Committee recognizes yet downplays the attachment of constitutional and due process rights to the MACR. The necessary corollary, unstated yet preferred, is that rights do not necessarily attach to welfare actions imposed by adults upon children. Such a position is incompatible with a children's rights approach.

More generally, the Congress's final resolutions called for the development of model rules on juvenile justice administration, the future Beijing Rules. Following the Congress, the Crime Prevention and Criminal Justice Branch of the United Nations Centre for Social Development and Humanitarian Affairs held primary responsibility for the proposed rules, and it requested Professor Horst Schüler-Springorum to independently compose an initial working draft.[39] As seen in the following excerpt, Professor Schüler-Springorum's original summer 1983 version—which he submitted to the United Nations—is very similar to the final Beijing Rules text: "The beginning of criminal responsibility should not be fixed

---

38 "Report of Committee II," par. 150, in UN Department of International Economic and Social Affairs, *Sixth UN Congress on the Prevention of Crime and the Treatment of Offenders: Caracas, Venezuela, 25 August–5 September 1980: Report prepared by the Secretariat*, A/CONF.87/14/Rev.1, New York, United Nations, 1981, at 65.
39 In general, see Cipriani, *supra* note 5.

at too low an age level. An age between 12 and 14 years being internationally widespread, an even lower age seems hardly compatible with the legal and social implications of criminal responsibility."[40]

With regard to the existing ICCPR provisions on age, and their implicit requirement for MACRs, the 1966 Covenant had no influence on Professor Schüler-Springorum at the time of his draft.[41] The ICCPR did not have any direct bearing on the subsequent elaboration and ratification of the Beijing Rules either. Apparently, the ICCPR only served as an early forerunner to the Beijing Rules and the CRC in its general consideration of age. Explicit MACR interpretations were not fully matured or recognized by the time of the Beijing Rules. The same can be said for the findings in drafting Additional Protocol I to the Geneva Conventions.

The essence of Professor Schüler-Springorum's 1983 draft—that the MACR should "not be fixed at too low an age level"—was reproduced verbatim in the Beijing Rules, while international negotiations and debate led to secondary revisions.[42] However, this process did not reflect any deeper understanding about the MACR or its implications for children's rights.[43] Arguments on the basis of history, culture, and legal tradition were central in drafting revisions. Through a series of regional conferences around the world, and at the conclusive Beijing conference, it became evident that a broader consensus on the MACR was impossible. Official MACRs, where they existed around the world at the time, spanned from 0 years to 18 years. Among other national and regional concerns, countries with Islamic *shari'a* law played a forceful role.[44] As a result, Schüler-Springorum's suggestion that 12–14 years would be an appropriate lowest MACR level was discarded, and the hopes for designating a worldwide baseline MACR became a recommendation for the future.

In the adopted text, the Beijing Rules' guidance for United Nations Member States on the MACR conveys a strong concern for establishing MACRs that are not too low.[45] This is true both at the state level and in the hopes of agreeing upon a reasonable lowest MACR applicable internationally. However, this advice should be seen in the context of the incomplete understanding of the MACR's implications from which it emerged. Although there is no formal record of the final negotiators and drafters' intentions, there may have been a continuing preference for higher MACRs in order to preserve discretion in welfare interventions. To some extent, the push for higher MACRs is linked in the text to the "modern approach" of responsibility, in consideration of "the facts" of maturity and development.

---

40   Schüler-Springorum, Horst, *Report on the standard minimum rules for the administration of juvenile justice and the handling of juvenile offenders*, unpublished draft, Summer 1983, e-mail correspondence with author, May 2002.
41   In general, see Cipriani, *supra* note 5.
42   *Ibid.*
43   Schüler-Springorum, Horst, e-mail correspondence with author, May 2002.
44   See Chapter 4 on the history of political shifts in the uses of Islamic law.
45   In general, see Cipriani, *supra* note 5.

However, it assumes a prejudiced view of children as insufficiently mature and developed until older ages, even implying that criminal responsibility should be delayed until approximately the age of civil majority or for consent to marriage. At the same time, there seems to have been a desire to spare younger children the legal and social implications of responsibility. From there, it appears plausible that the conceptual bases may be inferred as the following: (1) countries should establish definitive lower boundaries for juvenile justice delinquency jurisdiction; and (2) it is preferable to keep young children outside the purview of juvenile justice systems, and consequently it is preferable to not hold young children criminally responsible.

Beyond this foundation, the MACR provisions in the Beijing Rules reflect certain political consequences of the drafting process and other contradictions. For example, there is the concession of Rule 4.1, virtually outdated as it was written, that some countries may not even recognize the very concept of the MACR. The Rule then endorses the onset of criminal responsibility based upon criteria related to emotional, mental, and intellectual maturity, and moral and psychological development. While these are indeed relevant factors in considering MACR levels, the Rule vaguely suggests that *individual* children may be assessed for criminal responsibility based on their *individual* development in such areas.[46] This implies recourse to *doli incapax* provisions, whose compatibility with key international human rights guarantees has subsequently been rejected.

Despite these shortcomings, the Beijing Rules serve as a cornerstone in international law for MACRs.[47] They recognize the importance of MACRs in juvenile justice, support the establishment of national MACRs, suggest in basic terms the relationship between children's evolving capacities and their increasing rights and responsibilities over time, and acknowledge the variations among national MACRs for historical and cultural reasons. Only four years later, with the MACR stage set by the Beijing Rules, the United Nations General Assembly adopted the CRC.

Convention on the Rights of the Child

During 1979 deliberations on the initial draft of what would become the 1989 CRC, delegates already identified the MACR as one of a number of key issues for consideration.[48] Nonetheless, neither the drafting process through 1988 nor the

---

46 *Ibid.*
47 *Ibid.*
48 "Report of the Working Group," E/CN.4/L.1468, 12 Mar 1979, par. 6, reprinted in Office of the UN High Commissioner for Human Rights, *Legislative History of the Convention on the Rights of the Child*, vol. 1, New York, 2007. Records refer to "the age of criminal responsibility of children," and it is possible that the Working Group was actually referring to the age of penal majority. See Annex 1 for the full CRC text.

preliminary text adopted at first reading that year led to any further reference to the MACR. In the subsequent technical review, the Social Development Division of the United Nations Centre for Social Development and Humanitarian Affairs noted the absence of the MACR as its very first critique of the draft article on juvenile justice:

> *Paragraph 1* does not make any reference to the fact that children, in principle, should neither be considered criminally responsible, nor be incarcerated. In this respect, your attention is drawn to "Beijing Rule" 4. Accordingly, and with due respect to national laws, it should be clearly stated that there should be no criminal responsibility of children until they reach a certain age.[49]

Later in 1988, based on such comments, UNICEF requested that the Crime Prevention and Criminal Justice Branch of the same United Nations Centre for Social Development and Humanitarian Affairs formulate a new draft article on juvenile justice. This branch, which had not contributed directly to the elaboration of the convention up to that point, was the same office that led the drafting of the Beijing Rules. It drew directly and extensively from the Beijing Rules in providing two options for a new juvenile justice article. The first option, which was ultimately discarded, sought to minimize changes to the draft text already adopted. The second option based the draft article comprehensively around the Beijing Rules, and included the following:

> States Parties recognize the right of children who are accused or recognized as being in conflict with the penal law not to be considered criminally responsible before reaching a specific age, according to national law, and not to be incarcerated. The age of criminal responsibility shall not be fixed at too low an age level, bearing in mind the facts and circumstances of emotional, mental and intellectual maturity and stage of growth.[50]

This draft—the first specific MACR proposal during the CRC drafting process—pulls language directly from Beijing Rule 4. It abandons the Rule's notation that some legal systems may not recognize the concept of the MACR, and proposes the higher standard that all States Parties set MACRs. It also omits the Beijing Rules' discussion of different approaches to MACRs, and their support for efforts towards

---

49 "Comment by the Social Development Division, Centre for Social Development and Humanitarian Affairs," E/CN.4/1989/WG.1/CRP.1, reprinted in Office of the UN High Commissioner for Human Rights, *Legislative History of the Convention on the Rights of the Child*, vol. 2, New York, 2007.

50 "Background note submitted by the Crime Prevention and Criminal Justice Branch, Centre for Social Development and Humanitarian Affairs," E/CN.4/1989/WG.1/CRP.1/Add.2, reprinted in Office of the UN High Commissioner for Human Rights, *Legislative History of the Convention on the Rights of the Child*, vol. 2, New York, 2007.

a common lowest-acceptable age. These omissions are likely a consequence of the fruitless efforts to set a common lowest MACR age limit during the Beijing Rules' drafting. They also probably spared CRC drafters the contentious debates seen in finalizing both the Beijing Rules and Additional Protocol I to the Geneva Conventions. The draft proposal maintains the focus on MACRs not being set too low, however, and specifies that incarceration is ruled out below MACRs. In a surprisingly loose construction, it also hinges its stipulations on children not being "considered" criminally responsible. This phrasing allows formal accusations and recognition of children being in conflict with the law, at the same time that they are not "considered" criminally responsible.

Subsequently, a drafting group took into consideration the proposed juvenile justice article and related motions, and forged a new text that eventually became CRC Article 40. This new text's exact MACR language, in fact, became Article 40(3)(a) in the final adopted convention:[51]

> 3. States Parties shall seek to promote the establishment of laws, procedures, authorities and institutions specifically applicable to children alleged as, accused of, or recognized as having infringed the penal law, and, in particular:
> (a.) the establishment of a minimum age below which children shall be presumed not to have the capacity to infringe the penal law

It is not clear why the drafting group pared down the earlier proposed MACR text, omitting its consideration for "emotional, mental and intellectual maturity and stage of growth," its prohibition of incarceration for children under the MACR, and its language on children being "considered" responsible.[52] Even though many different aspects of Article 40 were debated before final adoption, there is no record of any MACR-specific debate at any point in the *Travaux Préparatoires*.[53] The result is treaty language with a rather simple thrust: for countries to set definitive lower boundaries, via formal MACRs, to juvenile justice delinquency jurisdiction.

The CRC text's innovation is that it frames the establishment of MACRs as an explicit treaty obligation for the first time ever. However, several problems immediately follow, including its very definition of the MACR as the age "below which children shall be presumed not to have the capacity to infringe the penal law."[54] This formulation is ambiguous and may carry little weight in legal traditions not familiar with such phraseology, which is closely linked to English common law.

---

51   "Discussion and adoption at second reading," E/CN.4/1989/48, reprinted in Office of the UN High Commissioner for Human Rights, *Legislative History of the Convention on the Rights of the Child*, vol. 2, New York, 2007.

52   In general, see Cipriani, *supra* note 5.

53   See Detrick, Sharon, ed., *The United Nations Convention on the Rights of the Child: A Guide to the "Travaux Préparatoires,"* Dordrecht, Martinus Nijhoff, 1992.

54   In general, see Cipriani, *supra* note 5.

Thus, the provision allows wide conceptual interpretation without any substantive guidance. Moreover, the depiction of the MACR as a presumption, and not a rule, leaves the CRC silent on some of the most difficult questions at hand. It implies recourse to *doli incapax* tests, albeit not to the extent of the Beijing Rules. There is no indication of the contextual understanding of criminal responsibility or its consequences, such as the respective implications for children above and below the age limit. In contrast, the original draft MACR language, submitted by the United Nations Centre for Social Development and Humanitarian Affairs, defined the MACR clearly as a right of children, not as a presumption in their favor. It also prohibited, explicitly and as a matter of right, incarceration beneath the MACR age limit. On the same points where the CRC remains unclear, countless countries have manipulated or disregarded the MACR, as documented in Chapter 6. Indeed, the CRC's definition of the MACR is not sufficiently descriptive or practical, in the absence of further interpretation, to serve as a conceptual foundation or meaningful legal provision for children's rights.

Guidance and Interpretations of the Committee on the Rights of the Child

The Committee on the Rights of the Child, the international body that monitors CRC implementation, has been the most frequent commentator on the MACR, and bears the challenging responsibility of interpreting the CRC's MACR provisions.[55] From its first consideration of States Parties reports in 1993 through and including its 48th Session in May–June 2008, the Committee on the Rights of the Child has commented on MACR-related provisions in almost 160 different Concluding Observations. These Concluding Observations convey the Committee's formal appraisal and suggestions to 117 of 193 CRC States Parties.

Drawing from such experience, the Committee issued in 2007 a General Comment on "Children's rights in juvenile justice," which expounds the Committee's interpretations as such.[56] The General Comment devotes extensive coverage to the MACR, and represents its most authoritative statement to-date on the topic. In it, the Committee defines the CRC's provisions:

> as an obligation for States parties to set a minimum age of criminal responsibility (MACR). This minimum age means the following:
> – Children who commit an offence at an age below that minimum cannot be held responsible in a penal law procedure ... .
> – Children at or above the MACR at the time of the commission of an offence (or: infringement of the penal law) but younger than 18 years ... can be formally charged and subject to penal law procedures ... .[57]

---

55 *Ibid.*
56 Committee on the Rights of the Child, *General Comment No. 10: Children's rights in juvenile justice*, CRC/C/GC/10, 25 Apr 2007, pars. 30–39.
57 *Ibid.*, par. 31.

While the CRC itself proffers unassertively that "States Parties shall seek to promote the establishment ... in particular" of MACRs, the Committee stresses that States Parties are obligated under the CRC to establish MACRs, and that children younger than MACRs at the time of alleged crimes cannot be charged or held criminally responsible. Indeed, on numerous occasions, the Committee has recommended to individual States Parties without MACRs or with insufficiently clear MACRs that they establish them, and has specifically emphasized that relevant laws be enforced and implemented.[58]

The Committee on the Rights of the Child also intervenes in the CRC's difficult definition of the MACR as "a minimum age below which children shall be presumed not to have the capacity to infringe the penal law." After referring to this provision, yet seeming to downplay its awkward phraseology, the Committee notes that:

> Even (very) young children do have the capacity to infringe the penal law but if they commit an offence when below MACR the irrefutable assumption is that they cannot be formally charged and held responsible in a penal law procedure. For these children special protective measures can be taken if necessary in their best interests ... .[59]

The Committee accepts that children, and even very young children, are capable of committing acts that are against the law. Rather than capacity, the Committee stresses in this context the tangible function of MACRs, to demarcate at what age children may potentially face criminal responsibility for such acts. Regardless of the act that a child below that age may have committed, no formal charges may follow, and criminal law's processes are excluded. Such children may be held accountable for their otherwise illegal actions through special protective measures—if necessary in their best interests. These measures and what they may entail are discussed in detail in the following section. The Committee's explanations also clarify ambiguities discussed above regarding the MACR as a presumption or rule.

The General Comment notes that the pertinent moment in time for considering a child's age is at the moment of the alleged offense—not at the time of arrest, trial, sentencing, or execution of sanctions—which affirms its previous recommendations.[60] Likewise, it underscores children's right to birth registration, and where there is no proof of age, children's entitlement to reliable medical or

---

58 See respective *Concluding observations*, inter alia: *Marshall Islands*, CRC/C/MHL/CO/2, 2 Feb 2007, pars. 70–71, and *United Republic of Tanzania*, CRC/C/TZA/CO/2, 2 Jun 2006, par. 71; and *Lebanon*, CRC/C/15/Add.169, 1 Feb 2002, par. 22, and *Bangladesh*, CRC/C/15/Add.221, 3 Oct 2003, par. 27.

59 Committee on the Rights of the Child, *supra* note 56, par. 31.

60 *Ibid.*, par. 75. *Concluding observations: India*, CRC/C/15/Add.228, 26 Feb 2004, pars. 78–80.

social investigations. In cases where "it cannot be established that the child is at or above the MACR, the child shall not be held criminally responsible."[61] Chapter 6 discusses related issues in detail.

The General Comment also addresses the appropriate age levels for MACRs, recommending that States Parties increase their MACRs to at least 12 years of age, and that they continue increasing them to even higher ages:

> Rule 4 of the Beijing Rules recommends that the beginning of MACR shall not be fixed at too low an age level, bearing in mind the facts of emotional, mental and intellectual maturity. In line with this rule the Committee has recommended States parties not to set a MACR at a too low level and to increase an existing low MACR to an internationally acceptable level. From these recommendations, it can be concluded that a minimum age of criminal responsibility below the age of 12 years is considered by the Committee not to be internationally acceptable. States parties are encouraged to increase their lower MACR to the age of 12 years as the absolute minimum age and to continue to increase it to a higher age level.[62]

Indeed, the Committee notes the "commendable high level of age 14 or 16" of some countries' MACRs, apparently for their support of diversion away from formal judicial proceedings.[63] It also explicitly urges countries not to lower their MACRs to the age of 12 where they are already at higher levels.

This guidance on age levels is largely confirmed in the Committee's recommendations to individual States Parties through June 2008. On nearly 110 different occasions, it observed or expressed concern for low MACRs, or recommended that MACRs be increased, with regard to MACRs generally below 12.[64] Otherwise, the Committee specifically welcomed or recommended MACRs, or proposals for MACR increases, from 12 through 16 years of age.[65] MACR increases to only 10 years of age, both proposed and enacted, have been deemed insufficient.[66] The Committee has disapproved of MACR decreases, including

---

61   Par. 35. See also pars. 39 and 72.

62   Par. 32.

63   Pars. 30. See also par. 33.

64   For unclear reasons, the Committee recommended that two countries respectively increase MACRs of 12 and 14 years. See respective *Concluding observations*: *Jamaica*, CRC/C/15/Add.210, 4 Jul 2003, pars. 21–22; and *Slovenia*, CRC/C/15/Add.65, 30 Oct 1996, pars. 19 and 27.

65   See, inter alia, the following: *Concluding observations*: *Ghana*, CRC/C/GHA/CO/2, 27 Jan 2006, pars. 4 and 73; and *Mexico*, CRC/C/MEX/CO/3, 2 Jun 2006, par. 71. The welcoming of a proposed increase to 18 years was most likely a semantic mix-up; the Committee apparently saw the proposal as creating juvenile court jurisdiction from 7 to 18. See, e.g., *Nigeria*, CRC/C/15/Add.61, 30 Oct 1996, par. 39; and *Summary record of the 323rd meeting*, CRC/C/SR.323, 1 Oct 1996, par. 66.

66   See, inter alia, *Concluding observations: Australia*, CRC/C/15/Add.79, 10 Oct 1997, par. 29.

both proposals and actual decreases, even when the lowered age limit was 12 or 14 years—and on one occasion strongly urged that the pre-existing MACR be reinstated "as a matter of urgency."[67] It has never expressed disapproval of an MACR for it being set too high per se.

In light of the foregoing calculations, although the Committee does not suggest a recommended or optimal age level for MACRs, it would appear to be most comfortable with MACRs of 16 years. There remains some uncertainty as to the desirability of setting MACRs at 17 or 18 years of age. On the one hand, the Committee's counsel to "continue to increase [MACRs] to a higher age level" seems to suggest the view that the higher the MACR, the better, although this is not the only logical conclusion. On the other hand, as explored in Chapter 2, it would be difficult to argue from children's rights principles that children should never be held criminally responsible, or that MACRs should be increased to the age of 18 years. It appears likely that such ambiguity is a reflection of the underlying interrelated debates on liberty and protection rights, and the justice-welfare continuum in juvenile justice.

The General Comment critiques provisions setting multiple age limits for responsibility. In particular, it notes problems with age ranges for rebuttable presumptions of non-responsibility (e.g., *doli incapax* tests), and for different age limits applicable to ostensibly more serious and less serious offenses. The Committee observes that *doli incapax* frequently substitutes for age limits by offense, wherein the *doli incapax* presumption is rebutted in cases of more serious crimes. This type of system is "often not only confusing, but leaves much to the discretion of the court/judge and may result in discriminatory practices."[68] Consequently, the Committee "strongly recommends that States parties set a MACR that does not allow, by way of exception, the use of a lower age."[69] The General Comment thus resolves the Committee's wide-ranging recommendations in the past regarding *doli incapax*,[70] and reaffirms its positions on multiple age limits by type or seriousness of offense.[71]

Anti-terrorism and other emergency laws, where they set different ages of criminal responsibility or otherwise circumvent existing MACRs, should be interpreted in the same light. In the General Comment, the Committee recommends

---

67 *Concluding observations: Georgia*, CRC/C/GEO/CO/3, 6 Jun 2008, Advance Unedited Vers., par. 73. See also, inter alia, *Concluding observations: Japan*, CRC/C/15/Add.231, 26 Feb 2004, par. 53.

68 Committee on the Rights of the Child, *supra* note 56, par. 30.

69 *Ibid.*, par. 34. The present study defines the MACR as the lowest possible age for responsibility. Thus, where the Committee refers to an MACR with an exceptional lower age limit for serious offences, this study deems the same provisions as an MACR for specified serious offences plus a higher general limit.

70 See, inter alia, the following *Concluding observations*: *United Kingdom of Great Britain and Northern Ireland – Isle of Man*, CRC/C/15/Add.134, 16 Oct 2000, pars. 18–19; and *Seychelles*, CRC/C/15/Add.189, 9 Oct 2002, par. 54.

71 For example, *Concluding observations: New Zealand*, CRC/C/15/Add.71, 24 Jan 1997, pars. 10 and 23.

that criminal law provisions to prevent and combat terrorism "do not result in retroactive or unintended punishment of children."[72] More explicitly, the Committee has stated its concern over reports on Nepal's "Terrorist and Disruptive Activities (Control and Punishment) Ordinance (TADO) which has no set minimum age."[73]

In the past, the Committee has raised two other issues related to multiple ages of criminal responsibility. First, it expressed grave concern that Nigeria featured wide disparities among state MACRs, and it urged the country to ensure that one MACR was applicable in all its states.[74] Similarly, it noted concern for discrepancies among the statutory MACR and age limits in other legislation and jurisprudence, recommending that different standards not be imposed upon different children in conflict with the law.[75] It would seem, generalizing from these recommendations, that each State Party is expected to establish a single MACR that applies to all children throughout its territory.

These points allude to the principle of non-discrimination, which the General Comment characterizes as one of the "leading principles of a comprehensive policy for juvenile justice."[76] The Committee has stressed this theme in relation to the MACRs of several States Parties. It was concerned for the determination of minimum ages by arbitrary criteria, including puberty, which allowed for discrimination between girls and boys in Sudan, and recommended that legislation be reviewed for gender neutrality.[77] Gender neutrality of MACRs has been a recurring concern.[78] Discrimination based on socio-economic status has also arisen in the context of MACRs, particularly under former *situación irregular* legislation in Latin America. The doctrine "paves the way for the stigmatization and frequent institutionalization and deprivation of liberty of children on the basis of their economic and socially disadvantaged situation."[79]

Committee's Guidance on Responding to Children Younger than MACRs

The Committee's General Comment offers important guidance on one of the most complex issues at hand—how countries may respond to children younger than MACRs who come into conflict with the law. In brief, it notes that children

---

72 Par. 41.

73 *Concluding observations: Nepal*, CRC/C/15/Add.260, 3 Jun 2005, par. 98.

74 *Concluding observations: Nigeria*, CRC/C/15/Add.257, 28 Jan 2005, pars. 12, 78, and 81.

75 *Concluding observations: Malaysia*, CRC/C/MYS/CO/1, 2 Feb 2007, pars. 102–103.

76 Committee on the Rights of the Child, *supra* note 56, par. 5. See also par. 6. Non-discrimination is also one of the four "general principles" of the CRC.

77 *Concluding observations: Sudan*, CRC/C/15/Add.190, 9 Oct 2002, pars. 24–25.

78 See the following: *Concluding observations: Jordan*, CRC/C/15/Add.125, 2 Jun 2000, par. 28; *Lebanon,* CRC/C/15/Add.169, 1 Feb 2002, par. 22(b); and *Iran (Islamic Republic of)*, CRC/C/15/Add.123, 28 Jun 2000, pars. 19–20.

79 *Concluding observations: Uruguay,* CRC/C/15/Add.62, 30 Oct 1996, par. 14. See also *Concluding observations: Bolivia*, CRC/C/15/Add.1, 18 Feb 1993, par. 11.

younger than MACRs "cannot be formally charged and held responsible in a penal law procedure," but that "special protective measures can be taken if necessary in their best interests."[80] Although these basic notions seem straightforward, their application is complicated by unclear distinctions among protective measures, especially when such measures may deprive children of their liberty.

The Committee's recommendations to individual States Parties help round out this core meaning. For example, children younger than MACRs should not be subject to criminal proceedings; have penal responses applied against them; be treated in a criminalized manner; or be held in police custody, detained, or imprisoned.[81] Criminal responsibility is always ruled out, even if assigned through juvenile court procedures, and low MACRs may be problematic even if criminal penalties are not applicable.[82]

Clearly, child protection procedures are more appropriate than the criminal justice system for handling children younger than MACRs.[83] However, responses generally deemed special protective measures are not necessarily acceptable. For example, the Committee recommended that Liberia apply only "protective and educative measures" to children younger than its MACR, while it noted that Poland should not sentence such children to either "correctional or educational measures."[84] The differences between *educative* measures and *educational* measures, and among protective measures generally, depend on the particular contexts at hand. Accordingly, the Committee declines to take a prescriptive approach to States Parties' policies:

> States parties should inform the Committee in their reports in specific detail how children below the MACR set in their laws are treated when they are recognized as having infringed the penal law, or are alleged as or accused of having done so, and what kinds of legal safeguards are in place to ensure that their treatment is as fair and just as that of children at or above MACR.[85]

This further suggests the Committee's general expectations for policies regarding children younger than MACRs. The description of such children facing recognition,

---

80   Par. 31.

81   See, e.g., the following *Concluding observations*: *Jordan*, CRC/C/15/Add.21, 25 Apr 1994, par. 16; *Chile*, CRC/C/CHL/CO/3, 2 Feb 2007, par. 71; *Russian Federation*, CRC/C/15/Add.274, 30 Sept 2005, par. 86; *Burundi*, CRC/C/15/Add.133, 16 Oct 2000, pars. 73–74; *Seychelles*, CRC/C/15/Add.189, 9 Oct 2002, par. 56; and *Ukraine*, CRC/C/15/Add.191, 9 Oct 2002, par. 70.

82   *Concluding observations: Liberia*, CRC/C/15/Add.236, 1 Jul 2004, par. 66. *Concluding observations: Cameroon*, CRC/C/15/Add.164, 6 Nov 2001, pars. 66 and 68.

83   *Concluding observations: Syrian Arab Republic*, CRC/C/15/Add.212, 10 Jul 2003, par. 53.

84   *Concluding observations: Liberia*, CRC/C/15/Add.236, 1 Jul 2004, par. 68. *Concluding observations: Poland*, CRC/C/15/Add.194, 30 Oct 2002, par. 26.

85   Committee on the Rights of the Child, *supra* note 56, par. 33.

allegation, or accusation of penal law infringement—which is not technically possible beneath MACRs—broadly indicates young children in conflict with the law who may face protection procedures. Therein, children are entitled to fair and just treatment, although the legal safeguards applicable in protection procedures are not as extensive as fair trial requirements for children at and above MACRs, as detailed in Chapter 2.

In consideration of special protective measures, the Committee does not exclude the possibility of the deprivation of liberty of children younger than MACRs. Although not specifically citing the MACR, the Committee repeats in its General Comment one of the most pertinent rules:

> Note that the rights of a child deprived of his/her liberty, as recognized in CRC, apply with respect to children in conflict with the law, and to children placed in institutions for the purposes of care, protection or treatment, including mental health, educational, drug treatment, child protection or immigration institutions.[86]

Tacitly, this concedes that children may be legally and appropriately deprived of their liberty—in highly restricted circumstances detailed in Chapter 2—for purposes of care, protection, or treatment, including in educational and child protection institutions.

The Committee has implied the same point with respect to various States Parties. For example, it emphasized to Nigeria that "legal safeguards ... must be provided to all children, whether the deprivation of their liberty results from the application of a welfare or a criminal procedure."[87] The Committee recommended the Republic of Korea ensure that "all juveniles involved in protection dispositions that may result in deprivation of liberty have access to legal counsel at an early stage."[88] Likewise, it recommended to Madagascar to "[m]ake sure that children below the age of 13 years are not brought before a criminal court and that educational measures permit deprivation of liberty only as a measure of last resort."[89] The Committee does not prohibit the deprivation of liberty in any of the foregoing examples. Instead, it emphasizes some of the many restrictions on its application: legal safeguards and assistance are required, and its use must be only as a measure of last resort.

At other times—including when such restrictions are violated—the Committee has criticized protective responses depriving the liberty of children, and has cited them as evidence of MACRs that are unclear or meaningless. For example, it

---

86 *Ibid.*, footnote 1.
87 *Concluding observations: Nigeria*, CRC/C/15/Add.61, 30 Oct 1996, par. 39.
88 *Concluding observations: Republic of Korea*, CRC/C/15/Add.197, 18 Mar 2003, par. 57(b).
89 *Concluding observations: Madagascar*, CRC/C/15/Add.218, 3 Oct 2003, par. 69(b). See also *Concluding observations: Kyrgyzstan*, CRC/C/15/Add.244, 1 Oct 2004, par. 66.

suggested that the Czech Republic's protective custody provisions for young children were inconsistent with the meaning of the MACR, and cited Bahrain's provisions for the detention of young children in social welfare centers—for up to 10 years—as evidence of no MACR.[90] With similarities, the Committee found no effective MACR in France or Senegal, despite their respective citations of purported MACR provisions.[91] Former *situación irregular* provisions, respectively abrogated by 2007, followed this same pattern in most Latin American countries. On multiple occasions the Committee deemed that there was no effective MACR in force.[92]

These various scenarios lying along the distinction between protection measures and penal measures are both difficult and controversial. With many conditions, the Committee does support the possibility of special protective measures for children younger than MACRs who come into conflict with the law. Such measures are in effect welfare responses triggered by the apparent commission of delinquent acts. At the same time, the Committee has repeatedly stressed the need to differentiate child protection from juvenile delinquency policies.[93] *Situación irregular* provisions repeatedly brought this paradox to light.[94] The distinction is thus desirable, yet its balance remains along the fault line between welfare-oriented and justice-oriented approaches—a challenging balance as discussed in Chapter 1.

There are further ambiguities about the suitable remedy when procedures or measures constitute de facto punishment beneath the MACR. For example, the Committee has occasionally suggested that full juvenile justice due process rights be extended to children younger than MACRs, in order to ensure fairness of treatment, particularly in cases involving the deprivation of liberty.[95] However, this approach may bring unintended consequences. When children face punitive procedures masqueraded as welfare or protection hearings, the introduction of due process guarantees to assist them may accommodate rather than challenge what are fundamentally illegitimate state actions. The distinction between welfare and delinquency cases also erodes further. In contrast, it may be preferable to demand that very distinction and the full realization of children's rights, respectively, in welfare proceedings, in cases of deprivation of liberty, and in juvenile justice

---

90 See respective *Concluding observations: Czech Republic*, CRC/C/15/Add.201, 18 Mar 2003, par. 66(b); and *Bahrain*, CRC/C/15/Add.175, 7 Feb 2002, par. 47. See also, inter alia, *Poland*, CRC/C/15/Add.194, 30 Oct 2002, par. 25.

91 *Concluding observations: France*, CRC/C/15/Add.240, 4 Jun 2004, pars. 16–17. *Concluding observations: Senegal*, CRC/C/15/Add.44, 27 Nov 1995, pars. 11 and 25.

92 See respective *Concluding observations: Chile*, CRC/C/15/Add.173, 1 Feb 2002; *Panama*, CRC/C/15/Add.68, 24 Jan 1997; and *Guatemala*, CRC/C/15/Add.58, 7 Jun 1996.

93 *Concluding observations: Portugal*, CRC/C/15/Add.162, 6 Nov 2001, par. 3. *Concluding observations:* Chile, CRC/C/CHL/CO/3, 23 Apr 2007, par. 8.

94 *Concluding observations: Chile*, CRC/C/15/Add.173, 1 Feb 2002, par. 53. *Concluding observations: Guatemala*, CRC/C/15/Add.154, 9 Jul 2001, par. 11.

95 For example, *Concluding observations: Denmark*, CRC/C/15/Add.273, 30 Sept 2005, par. 58(c).

proceedings, as delineated in Chapter 2. In this scenario, the remedy would be to dispute the legitimacy of punitive-oriented procedures and measures beneath MACRs, and to insist upon immediate transfer to appropriate welfare-based procedures, measures, and rights. There are no easy answers in such cases, but the MACR's role is prominent for drawing crucial lines among societies' responses to children.

In summary, the Committee on the Rights of the Child has developed detailed guidance for States Parties on the CRC's MACR provisions, covering a wide range of concerns. Taken collectively, as seen most authoritatively in the General Comment on juvenile justice and in Concluding Observations to respective States Parties, the following represents a synopsis of its key points:

- Each State Party must establish and enforce one clear MACR, applicable throughout its territory, at the level of 12 years of age at a minimum. States Parties should continue to increase their MACRs to higher age levels, and should not decrease them.
- Secondary and multiple ages of criminal responsibility are not compatible with CRC provisions. These include *doli incapax* and similar age ranges for rebuttable presumptions; multiple age limits according to type or supposed seriousness of offense; and age limits in anti-terrorism and other emergency laws. (The minimum age of penal majority, which must be set at 18 years or higher, is unrelated.)
- MACRs must fully respect in law and practice the principle of non-discrimination (e.g., in the contexts of gender, socio-economic status, and vulnerable groups).
- If there is no proof of age for children in conflict with the law, they are entitled to reliable medical or social investigations. If evidence is inconclusive on whether children are younger than MACRs or not, children shall not be held criminally responsible.
- Children younger than MACRs at the time of alleged offenses cannot be formally charged, or be held responsible in or be subject to penal law procedures or responses, via either juvenile or adult criminal court. Furthermore, they cannot be treated in a criminalized manner, including, inter alia, by detention in police custody or other forms of detention.
- Special protective measures can be taken if necessary in the best interests of children who are younger than MACRs at the time of alleged offenses, through non-penal judicial proceedings or without resorting to judicial proceedings. In all such cases, legal safeguards must be in place to ensure that treatment is fair and just. In cases involving the deprivation of liberty via special protective measures, all rights of children deprived of their liberty additionally apply.

African Charter on the Rights and Welfare of the Child

The 1990 African Charter on the Rights and Welfare of the Child effectively restates the obligation found in the CRC that States Parties establish an MACR.[96] The treaty's monitoring body, the African Committee of Experts on the Rights and Welfare of the Child, has not yet begun to review States Parties' reports on their implementation efforts.

European Social Charter

The 1996 revised European Social Charter, which replaces the original 1961 Charter over time, is the major European treaty for children's rights.[97] Member States report annually to the European Committee of Social Rights, the body responsible for monitoring compliance, which consistently remarks upon MACR provisions.

The Committee has found MACRs under 12 to be incompatible with Article 17 of the Charter, even citing MACRs of 11 years as "manifestly too low."[98] Where MACRs remain higher than 12 years of age, any decrease may still be problematic. In the case of Slovakia, the Committee expressed concern over and asked the reasons for a proposal to decrease the MACR from 15 years to 14 years—a possibly "retrograde step."[99] In contrast, it often notes without objection MACRs of 12 and higher.[100]

More importantly, the European Committee of Social Rights has scrutinized MACR provisions reported by States Parties, with particular attention to the treatment in law and in practice given to children younger than MACRs. In the case of Turkey, which had reported an MACR of 12 years, the Committee found that the Juvenile Courts Law established an effective MACR of 11 years. It noted that even children younger than 11 were subject to various measures of

---

96 Adopted 11 Jul 1990 by the Organisation of African Unity Assembly of Heads of State and Government, OAU Doc. CAB/LEG/24.9/49. Article 17(4): "There shall be a minimum age below which children shall be presumed not to have the capacity to infringe the penal law."

97 Council of Europe Secretariat of the European Social Charter, *Children's Rights Under the European Social Charter*, Strasbourg, 2005. European Treaty Series, No. 35, 18 Oct 1961. Council of Europe Treaty Series, No. 163, 3 May 1996.

98 Article 17 concerns the right of children to broad social, legal, and economic protections, but does not specifically address juvenile justice. *Conclusions XVII–2 (Turkey)*, 2005, at 30. See also *Second Addendum to Conclusions XV–2 (Ireland)*, 2001; *Conclusions XVII–2 (Malta)*, 2005; and *Conclusions XVII–2 (United Kingdom)*, 2005.

99 *Conclusions XVI-2 (Slovakia)*, 2003, at 103.

100 Member States with MACRs of 12 and higher included Croatia, Finland, Germany, Greece, Hungary, Iceland, Italy, Latvia, Lithuania, Netherlands, Norway, Romania, Spain, and Sweden.

deprivation of liberty, and requested detailed information on the placement system and procedures, relevant age limits, and the number of children younger than 11 deprived of their liberty.[101]

European Convention on Human Rights

The 1950 European Convention on Human Rights, or the Convention for the Protection of Human Rights and Fundamental Freedoms, is interpreted and applied by the European Court of Human Rights.[102] In 1999, the Court heard jointly and delivered decisions on two critical cases involving the MACR.[103]

The context for the decisions was the infamous Bulger case, which is described in detail in Chapter 5.[104] In brief, the original 1993 case involved two 10-year-old boys, in Liverpool, England, who kidnapped and beat to death a 2-year-old toddler, James Bulger. The boys then left the toddler's body on railroad tracks where it was later severed by a passing train. Their three-week trial saw unprecedented public outrage and media sensationalism, with angry protests upon the arrival of the boys to court, including attempts to attack the vehicle transporting them. The adult courtroom and trial proceedings, despite some adaptations on the boys' behalf, were generally formal. At the time, England's MACR was 10 years of age, with a rebuttable presumption of non-responsibility between the ages of 10 and 14 years based on a child's discernment of right from wrong. This presumption was rebutted, the trial jury found both children guilty, and the presiding judge sentenced them to detention "during Her Majesty's pleasure" as required under law. Both children subsequently complained before the European Court of Human Rights that this trial and sentencing had violated a number of their fundamental rights.

The Court considered whether the effects of England's MACR, in and of itself, constituted a violation of Article 3—the right not to be subjected to torture or to inhuman or degrading treatment or punishment. In doing so, the Court took account of the MACR provisions among Council of Europe Member States, as well as relevant international texts and instruments. While noting England's low MACR, the Court did not find a commonly accepted lowest age for MACRs in Europe, nor did it see England's MACR so low as to differ disproportionately from prevailing standards. It did not find a clear tendency, either, for a lowest acceptable age limit, in the Beijing Rules or the CRC.[105] As such, the Court held

---

101 *Conclusions XVII–2 (Turkey)*, 2005, at 29.
102 European Treaty Series, No. 5, 4 Nov 1950.
103 European Court of Human Rights, *Case of T. v. the United Kingdom: Judgment*, Strasbourg, 1999; *Id.*, *Case of V. v. the United Kingdom: Judgment*, Strasbourg, 1999.
104 In general, see Cipriani, *supra* note 5.
105 Among other developments, the General Comment on juvenile justice by the Committee on the Rights of the Child, clarifying relevant international standards, was completed after the Court's hearing.

that the attribution of criminal responsibility to the boys did not constitute by itself a violation of Article 3.

One of the partly dissenting opinions to the Court's decisions, signed by nearly one-third of its judges, opposed this interpretation.[106] In particular, these judges maintained that the low MACR, prosecution in adult court, and subjection to an indeterminate sentence (i.e., detention during Her Majesty's pleasure) collectively created a level of mental and physical suffering for the boys that constituted inhuman and degrading treatment in violation of Article 3. They also argued that the majority erred in considering the MACR in isolation from the trial process, and in failing to find a clear tendency in MACRs among European states and international instruments. The partly dissenting opinion noted that only four of 41 Member States then had an MACR as low as or lower than England's MACR, and argued that this disparity constituted a disproportionate difference. The judges observed that despite the absence of a specific recommendation in the Beijing Rules, the concepts of maturity and criminal responsibility were undoubtedly linked, and nearly all Member States held that children younger than 13 or 14 years of age lacked the appropriate maturity.

Despite this vigorous dissent, the Court's judgment declined to link England's low MACR to a rights violation, and the Court maintained this position in a subsequent case.[107] As discussed elsewhere in this study, however, these cases are critical in the jurisprudence on children's right to effective participation at trial. Moreover, given subsequent clarification by the Committee on the Rights of the Child as to international standards for MACR age levels, it seems nearly certain that the European Court of Human Rights will be asked to revisit its reasoning on the MACR in coming years.

Conclusion

Over the course of several decades, an array of international law instruments has scrutinized MACRs and their implications—in regional and international settings; in human rights and humanitarian instruments; in instruments' drafting histories and final language; via regional and international jurisprudence; and in binding and advisory contexts. The corresponding legal obligations for MACRs that have arisen depend, from country to country, on such variables and leave several points for future debate. These include the possibility that there exists a general principle

---

106 European Court of Human Rights, "Joint Partly Dissenting Opinion of Judges Pastor Ridruejo, Ress, Makarczyk, Tulkens, and Butkevych," *Case of T. v. the United Kingdom: Judgment*, Strasbourg, 1999; and *Id.*, "Joint Partly Dissenting Opinion of Judges Pastor Ridruejo, Ress, Makarczyk, Tulkens, and Butkevych," *Case of V. v. the United Kingdom: Judgment*, Strasbourg, 1999.

107 European Court of Human Rights, *Case of S.C. v. the United Kingdom: Judgment*, Strasbourg, 2004.

of international law regarding MACRs, as first raised during deliberations on Additional Protocol I to the Geneva Conventions, and as discussed in further detail in Chapter 5. Nonetheless, in a more general sense, it does seem possible to infer a basic convergence on MACRs, their establishment, and their implementation, drawing most visibly from the work of the Committee on the Rights of the Child.[108] Indeed, the Committee has examined the MACR in the greatest detail, and it brings added authority as the monitoring body for the most widely legally binding instrument, which is also specific to children. Moreover, the other instruments and related monitoring bodies surveyed in this chapter have largely reaffirmed several of the key points emphasized by the Committee. Arguably, this international convergence includes the following points:

- Each State Party must establish and enforce one clear MACR, applicable throughout its territory, at the level of 12 years of age at a minimum. States Parties should continue to increase their MACRs to higher age levels, and should not decrease them.
- Secondary and multiple ages of criminal responsibility are not compatible with CRC provisions. These include *doli incapax* and similar age ranges for rebuttable presumptions; multiple age limits according to type or supposed seriousness of offense; and age limits in anti-terrorism and other emergency laws. (The minimum age of penal majority, which must be set at 18 years or higher, is unrelated.)
- MACRs must fully respect in law and practice the principle of non-discrimination (e.g., in the contexts of gender, socio-economic status, and vulnerable groups).
- If there is no proof of age for children in conflict with the law, they are entitled to reliable medical or social investigations. If evidence is inconclusive on whether children are younger than MACRs or not, children shall not be held criminally responsible.
- Children younger than MACRs at the time of alleged offenses cannot be formally charged, or be held responsible in or be subject to penal law procedures or responses, via either juvenile or adult criminal court. Furthermore, they cannot be treated in a criminalized manner, including, inter alia, by detention in police custody or other forms of detention.
- Special protective measures can be taken if necessary in the best interests of children who are younger than MACRs at the time of alleged offenses, through non-penal judicial proceedings or without resorting to judicial proceedings. In all such cases, legal safeguards must be in place to ensure that treatment is fair and just. In cases involving the deprivation of liberty via special protective measures, all rights of children deprived of their liberty additionally apply.

---

108   In general, see Cipriani, *supra* note 5.

Among other implications, the progressive consolidation of these standards would seem to favor further judicial review of national MACRs, particularly in national and regional tribunals. The European Court of Human Rights, which has closely examined the MACR in influential decisions, appears to be a likely forum as such.

Behind this convergence, however, the antecedents, drafting histories, instrument texts, and formal interpretations periodically demonstrate inconsistencies in their ideas about the significance and purpose of MACRs. To a large extent, these are further reflections of the historic debates and tensions described in Chapter 1. They are also related to the growth in conceptual sophistication over time, as children's rights scholarship has progressed and its principles have been applied in practice. The early history behind the Beijing Rules' specific consideration of the MACR, for example, suggests a notable welfare bias and loss of conceptual clarity; children's rights thinking no longer doubts the need for due process rights for children. Isolated consideration of the MACR can also create, ironically, distractions from an appropriate sense of perspective vis-à-vis the broader children's rights framework. As noted in Chapter 2, this framework contains its own ambiguities and points of contention, yet its principles generally provide sufficient clarity for a grounded perspective. They demand much broader context than, for example, just the protective rationale that underlies many calls for very high MACRs. Although these calls are typically motivated to protect children from the harmful practices that abound in many juvenile justice systems, they do not sufficiently explain their own implicit characterization of children as incompetent, nor do they generally give a convincing account of how to respond appropriately to the larger group of children younger than MACRs as these are increased.

The question of appropriate responses to children younger than MACRs is already one of the most complicated issues, even without raising the MACR to very high levels. International standards do envisage state responses to children younger than MACRs in conflict with the law, and there are specific restrictions and guidance on such responses. Chapter 2 additionally argues that children's rights principles support developmentally appropriate responses to all such children. Nevertheless, these standards do not simply rule out deprivation of liberty in all cases for children younger than MACRs, which might seem to be the easy answer. Although all pertinent international rules apply, protection measures may at times include the deprivation of liberty, even if its use should be seen as exceptionally rare. Moreover, in looking at other responses which seem to suggest non-custodial approaches—such as many protection, education, welfare, treatment, and other measures—these may amount to de facto punishment and criminal responsibility. Thus, even though international guidance gives some direction, it is not always clear how states may or should respond to children younger than MACRs, nor which responses are a sign of criminal responsibility and thus inadmissible for such children.

This is perhaps the area where further interpretive guidance by both monitoring and judicial bodies would be most useful in clarifying international standards—

teasing out in practical terms how relevant principles apply to children younger than MACRs. It would seem particularly helpful as such to promote greater transparency and disclosure on national provisions and practices for children younger than MACRs, including among respective governments and national and international non-governmental organizations, and to foster dialogue and exercise closer scrutiny. Ideally, these steps would progressively reaffirm in greater detail what is desirable for children younger than MACRs in conflict with the law, and what state responses are prohibited.

Chapter 4
Historical Influences on MACRs

Chapter 1 of this study surveys the direct roots of modern juvenile justice reaching back into feudal England, while the present chapter offers a complementary overview of the major historical trends behind minimum ages of criminal responsibility (MACRs) themselves. To a significant extent, these histories are part of the same narrative, thus the present chapter touches again upon the foundations of juvenile justice history. However, the legal history of MACRs merits distinct consideration as it offers an important explanatory perspective on relevant provisions across the world today, and brings to light the common threads behind a number of recurring problems and challenges. In fact, ancient Roman law, European colonial law, Islamic criminal law, and Soviet law explain most countries' current MACR provisions, which are documented in Chapter 5. Beneath the surface of national law, various customary, traditional, and religious law systems regulate children's criminal responsibility for large segments of many countries' populations.

Roman Law, European Law, and European Colonial Law

Among other ancient bodies of law, Babylonian law, Hebrew law, and Greek law all referred to the severity of punishments for various crimes as contingent upon the degree of conscious wrongdoing.[1] The Romans' earliest written legal code, the Law of the Twelve Tables (c. 450 B.C.), applied such notions more directly to children. The Twelve Tables mention pre-pubescent children in two dispositions in penal-related law, and distinguish between voluntary and involuntary crimes as a basis for mitigating punishments. Thus, as pre-pubescence constituted a presumed lack of discernment, it led to an attenuation of punishment for most crimes, although not a total exemption as such from criminal responsibility.[2]

The growing influence of Greek philosophy upon Roman law led to greater consideration of moral criteria in general and with respect to children in

---

1 Perrin, Bernard, "La minorité pénale en droit romain et dans les législations européennes antérieures au XIX⁰ siècle," in Donnedieu de Vabres, Henri, and Marc Ancel, eds, *Le problème de l'enfance délinquante: l'enfant devant la loi et la justice pénales*, Paris, Librairie du Recueil Sirey, 1947; and Thomas, J.A.C., "Delictal and Criminal Liability of the Young in Roman Law," in Société Jean Bodin pour l'histoire comparative des institutions (ed.) *L'enfant, Recueils de la Société Jean Bodin pour l'histoire comparative des institutions*, vol. 38, Bruxelles, Éditions de la Librairie encyclopédique, 1977.

2 Perrin, *ibid.*

particular.[3] By the time of the *Lex Cornelia* (c. 81 B.C.), pre-pubescent children's criminal acts were excused, beyond simple mitigation of their punishment, on the basis that they lacked the capacity to intend harm.[4] Upon reaching puberty, children were liable to all punishments.[5]

Over time, children beneath the limit of puberty for criminal responsibility were further divided into three distinct groups, reflecting the continuing focus on the development of children's comprehension; upon reaching puberty children still faced criminal liability. The first group, that of *infantia* or infancy, referred to children who were considered incapable of *dolus*, or guilty intention, and who could thus never be held criminally responsible.[6] Initially, this group apparently included children (*infantes*) from birth until they literally gained the ability of *fari*, that is, "to use words according to grammatical and lexical rules of speech."[7] By the 300s A.D., this physical test was replaced in law by a standard age limit of 7 years denoting the end of *infantia*.[8]

The subsequent two periods were *infantiae proximus*, near infancy, and *pubertati proximus*, near puberty. It seems that ancient Roman law did not establish an age-based division between these groups, distinguishing between them instead upon individuals' physical appearances. Similarly, potential criminal responsibility was determined within both groups on an individual basis, according to whether children were deemed *doli capax*—capable of forming guilty intentions.[9] Children among *infantiae proximus* generally faced the presumption that they were *doli incapax* (incapable of guilty intentions), while those among *pubertati proximus* were presumed *doli capax*. In both cases, the presumptions were rebuttable, based on the presentation of clear and certain evidence showing a child's intentions.[10] Those ultimately held *doli capax* and found criminally responsible were treated as adults with mitigation of their punishments.[11] Commentary from the 100s A.D. notes that the majority of jurists agreed with such an approach.

---

3   *Ibid.*

4   Platt, Anthony, and Bernard L. Diamond, "The Origins of the 'Right And Wrong' Test of Criminal Responsibility and its Subsequent Development in the United States: An Historical Survey," 54 *California Law Review* 1227, 1966.

5   Crofts, Thomas, *The Criminal Responsibility of Children and Young Persons: A Comparison of English and German Law*, Aldershot (England), Ashgate, 2002.

6   Perrin, *supra* note 1; and Robinson, Olivia F., *The Criminal Law of Ancient Rome*, London, Duckworth, 1995.

7   Voigt, Moritz, *Die XII Tafeln*, vol. 1, 1883, reprinted Aalen, Scientia, 1966, at 314, paraphrased by Crofts, *supra* note 5, footnote 3 at 93.

8   Perrin, *supra* note 1.

9   Crofts, *supra* note 5.

10   *Ibid.*; and Platt et al., *supra* note 4.

11   Stettler, Martin, *L'évolution de la condition pénale des jeunes délinquants examinée au travers du droit suisse et de quelques legislations étrangères: Les seuils de minorité pénale absolue ou relative confrontés aux données de la criminologie juvénile et aux impératifs de la prévention*, Geneva, Librairie de l'université, 1980.

These divisions among pre-pubescent children were at times clouded by the notion of *malitia supplet aetatem*—malice or wickedness supplies age—meaning that the demonstrated vice of a child could justify criminal responsibility despite his or her youthfulness. The joint emperors Maximian and Diocletian had invoked this principle in related circumstances around 300 A.D., yet there is evidence of its use even at the beginning of the Roman Empire.[12] In later centuries of the Empire, with heavier state penal repression and public order measures, recourse to *malitia supplet aetatem* led to the increasing assimilation of *pubertati proximus* directly into adulthood.[13] At the same time, *infantiae proximus* were progressively incorporated into the group of *infantia* with no criminal responsibility.[14] Consistently, however, the beginning of puberty triggered criminal responsibility. Whereas examination for physical signs of puberty was the earlier practice, by the 500s A.D. explicit age limits were established as the accepted onset of puberty: 14 years for boys, and 12 years for girls.[15] Thus, by that point in Roman law, children younger than 7 were *doli incapax*; girls 7–11 years old and boys 7–13 years old were only presumed *doli incapax*; and girls 12 and older and boys 14 and older were *doli capax*.

The resurgence in the study of ancient Roman law began by roughly the 1000s, and scholars began reestablishing the Roman age periods regarding children's criminal responsibility, drawing extensively from the Justinian Code of the 500s A.D.[16] With the influence of its instruction at universities, most of Europe eventually adapted Roman law and gradually applied it by the 1500s. Different peoples and nations often had their own penal rules and practices regarding children, which had evolved over the intervening centuries. However, these were influenced across the board by the reception of Roman law, which eventually became the common rule among almost all legal traditions of Europe.

Nonetheless, the meaning and age boundaries of children's criminal responsibility were determined in practice by independent appraisal of judges. Despite a common legal framework, case law shows that legal practice was logically incoherent and contradictory, and the supposed rules were often violated. It seems most likely that children's status in the criminal law typically led to mitigation of sentences and not exclusion of responsibility. In particular, the principle of *malitia supplet aetatem* saw a great revival in the Middle Ages, and frayed away the special considerations attached to the respective age groups. Scholars, who widely commented upon the principle, found in it the justification to hold even very young children criminally responsible— as seen in numerous cases where it was invoked to punish children.[17]

---

12   Laingui, André, *La responsabilité pénale dans l'ancien droit (XVIe – XVIIIe siècle)*, Paris, Librairie générale de droit et de jurisprudence, 1970; and Perrin, *supra* note 1.

13   Perrin, *ibid.*

14   Stettler, *supra* note 11.

15   Crofts, *supra* note 5; and Platt et al., *supra* note 4.

16   Perrin, *supra* note 1.

17   Laingui, *supra* note 12; and Perrin, *ibid.*

In fact, all the governments of monarchical Europe used *malitia supplet aetatem* as a cornerstone in criminal law practice for children.[18]

Despite its watering-down in practice, Roman law often remained legally in force until national codification efforts began in the 1700s. Just prior to the French Revolution, most European states still applied a system of mitigation for children, with criminal liability withheld only for some of the youngest children.[19] By this time, age limits certainly varied among countries and even regions, and judges continued to exercise great discretion in considering the individual circumstances of children's cases and applying unwritten laws. Importantly, the French Penal Codes of 1791 and 1810 eliminated the stages of penal minority and set a simplified age of penal majority of 16 years. For children under the age of 16, it was determined in court whether they had acted with discernment or not. If they had not exercised discernment, criminal responsibility was technically excluded and no penal sanctions were permitted. If children before 16 years had acted with discernment, without any lower age limit, criminal responsibility and mitigated penalties ensued. The drafters for these codes drew inspiration directly from Roman law *doli capax* provisions.[20] Nonetheless, with their elimination of the minimum age limit for criminal responsibility, French penal law did not feature any MACR between 1791 and 1912, when an MACR of 13 years was codified. In conjunction with the original Roman law formulation, the 1791 and 1810 French Penal Codes were influential models through the 1800s in Europe and the Americas.[21] After the first half of the 1800s, many countries that had adopted the French model began adding MACRs to their respective codes, and the inclusion of MACRs became common practice.[22]

England was the principal exception to the European trend of receiving Roman law, yet England's own history on children's criminal liability is nonetheless a mixed evolution of Anglo-Saxon and Roman law. Ancient Anglo-Saxon law, as early as 688 A.D. and through the 900s, showed special concern for young offenders, generally exempting youth from the severe punishments given to adults.[23] Through this period, age limits for such clemency ranged from roughly 10 to 15 years of age in various circumstances. Over time, this general notion of leniency for children developed in law and jurisprudence into two distinct age limits: the first, an age below which punishment was never possible; and the second, a higher age limit

---

18 Perrin, *ibid.*
19 Stettler, *supra* note 11.
20 Laingui, André, *Histoire du droit pénal*, Paris, Presses Universitaires de France, 1985.
21 Cieślak, Marian, "De la répression a la protection des mineurs: Histoire de la délinquance juvénile: Rapport de synthese," in Société Jean Bodin pour l'histoire comparative des institutions (ed.), *supra* note 1.
22 *Ibid.*; and Nillus, Renée, "La minorité pénale dans la législation et la doctrine du XIXe siècle," in Donnedieu de Vabres, Henri, and Marc Ancel, eds, *Le problème de l'enfance délinquante: l'enfant devant la loi et la justice pénales*, Paris, Librairie du Recueil Sirey, 1947.
23 Crofts, *supra* note 5.

beneath which children could be punished in certain circumstances. Regarding the former, from roughly the late 1200s to the early 1600s there is evidence of evolution, albeit neither linear nor consistent, towards a concrete minimum age below which no punishment could be given. Such evidence suggests that judges held significant discretion in deciding if individual children were old enough to face punishment or not, while guideline age limits of 7 and 8 years were occasionally cited. These limits, especially that of 7 years, are probably related to the influence of the Catholic Church, whose Canon Law drew directly from ancient Roman law in its provisions on children's criminal responsibility. Indeed, over time, 7 years became the consensus lower age limit below which no punishment could be given, understood as the age where children first began to understand the difference between good and evil. As such, it marked the beginning of the possibility for punishment depending upon individual children's development and understanding.

By the early 1300s, a conditional range for children's criminal responsibility became common, in which responsibility depended in broad terms on individual children's knowledge or understanding of the difference between good and evil.[24] In general, as commonly cited by judges and legal scholars, children beginning at the minimum age limit of 7 years were presumed to lack the minimum mental capacity to commit crimes and to understand the moral implications of their acts. The prosecution had to submit evidence of children's actions, demonstrating their understanding, in order to rebut this presumption and open the possibility for criminal responsibility.[25] The upper boundary to this conditional range evolved over time, hovering around 12 and 14 years, and became fixed by consensus at 14 years probably by the end of the 1600s.[26] Before the introduction of systematic birth registration systems in the early 1600s, it fell upon judges to decide individual children's maturity as a question of fact based on physical appearances.[27]

In summary, by the early 1700s English common law held that children beneath the age of 7 years could not be punished for any crime, and that children between the ages of 7 and 14 years were (rebuttably) presumed incapable of understanding the gravity of their acts, while children from 14 were subject to criminal responsibility. These rules, notwithstanding variations in practice, remained unchanged until England raised the MACR from 7 to 8 years by statute in 1932, and again so from 8 years to 10 years in 1963. As discussed later in this study, the United Kingdom abolished the *doli incapax* presumption for children between 10 and 14 years in 1998.

In addition to the influence of the French Penal Code as a model for national legal codification efforts in the 1700s–1800s, both French law and English common law are particularly important for propagating MACRs worldwide through respective

---

24   Crofts, *ibid.*; and Platt et al., *supra* note 4.
25   Crofts, *ibid.*
26   *Ibid.*; and Platt et al., *supra* note 4.
27   Kean, A.W.G., "The History of the Criminal Liability of Children," 53 *Law Quarterly Review* 364, 1937; and Platt et al., *ibid.*

colonies and protectorates. France, for example, pursued a strategy from 1921–1928 to introduce across its colonies the measures of the *Loi du 22 juillet 1912 sur les tribunaux pour enfants et adolescents et sur la liberté surveillée*.[28] This is the law that established an MACR of 13 years, but that also maintained the stipulation that children between 13 and 18 years must have acted with discernment in order to face imprisonment.[29] The French Ministry of Colonies elaborated a text based on that law, which subsequently went into force in numerous French colonies. As discussed below in this chapter, there were widespread challenges in taking account of indigenous customs in implementing the law, and not all colonies adopted the measure. Where the text went into force, it established an MACR of 13 years, while other colonies and protectorates maintained laws based on earlier French statutes and strict discernment tests without age limits.[30] In later decades, new countries typically retained the colonial law that stood in force directly prior to independence. Consequently, among 26 countries that were French colonies or protectorates in the 1900s, 15 have an MACR of 13 years, while six maintain some form of test for children's discernment before criminal responsibility may ensue. In other countries in this group, overlapping influences of Soviet law, Islamic law, and English law have often held greater sway.

Indeed, the impact of English common law on MACRs around the world is even more notable.[31] As Great Britain settled colonies, it carried and adapted provisions for children's criminal responsibility under colonial law. Typically, common law countries received common law as it stood in effect in England on a specified date, while in many cases penal codes were established in diverse forms and drew from complex sources. Statutory changes were often made over time, mirroring amendments undertaken in Great Britain or otherwise modifying the language of provisions. All the same, former British colonies generally share "underlying unity" in the realm of English criminal law.[32] By extension, the strongest indications are that most former British colonies and protectorates derived their MACRs from English common law or later amending statutes. Indeed, out of some 75 countries that were once British colonies or protectorates, or that otherwise received common law, 51 set a related age limit at 7, 8, or 10 years. Furthermore, out of the 55 countries that do have *doli incapax* or similar provisions, approximately 40 have been directly influenced by English common law.[33]

---

28 Bouvenet, Gaston Jean, *La minorité pénale dans les colonies françaises*, doctoral dissertation, Université de Nancy, Faculté de droit, 1936.

29 Griffe, Clément, *Les tribunaux pour enfants: Étude d'organisation judiciaire et sociale*, Paris, Fontemoing, 1914.

30 In general, see Cipriani, Don, *The Minimum Age of What? Criminal Responsibility, Juvenile Justice, and Children's Rights*, unpublished draft, Florence, UNICEF Innocenti Research Centre, 2002.

31 *Ibid.*

32 Read, James S., "Criminal Law in the Africa of Today and Tomorrow," 7 *Journal of African Law* 5, 1963, at 5.

33 See Chapters 5 and 6 for further considerations.

Other European countries with colonies and protectorates tended to transplant their MACR provisions overseas as well. As discussed above, most continental European countries shared the legacy of Roman law, if not the influence of the first French Penal Codes, and these were the basic models carried forth despite numerous variations. Due to the breadth of their colonial reach, however, France and England bear disproportionate and more direct influence on MACR provisions worldwide.

Islamic Law

At first glance, Islamic law may seem to hold far less influence on MACR provisions across the 192 countries of the world. Among the 64 nations that are part of the Islamic world, only 10 clearly base their MACR provisions to some extent upon Islamic law.[34] The majority of the others can trace their MACR provisions through the history of English, French, or Soviet influences. However, respect in practice for these provisions may depend upon their legitimacy under Islamic law, and Islamic law has played a primary role in various debates on MACR reform.[35] This section highlights classic Islamic criminal law doctrine on children's responsibility, discusses problematic issues in that doctrine and in its transcription to modern statutory law and practice, and illustrates how Islamic jurists have applied classic law to further harmonize MACR provisions with international standards.

There are eight major schools of thought within Islamic law, and they hold diverse viewpoints even on some questions of children's age and responsibility. Among these eight, the four Sunni schools (i.e., Hanafites, Malikites, Shafi'ites, and Hanbalites) and two Shi'a schools are of critical importance, as virtually all Muslims are either Sunni or Shi'a, respectively 85–90 per cent and 10–15 per cent. Already in the 700s, Islamic philosophers and jurists—including founders of some of the legal schools—held vigorous debates on the implications of childhood and responsibility for child protection, such that by the 900s classic Islamic law on children had fully evolved.[36]

---

34 The estimate of 64 countries is based upon a composite list of the Member States of the Organization of the Islamic Conference and the countries profiled by the Islamic Family Law program at Emory University School of Law (www.law.emory.edu/ifl/index2.html) that are also United Nations Member States.

35 See An-Na'im, Abdullahi Ahmed, "Human Rights in the Muslim World: Socio-Political Conditions and Scriptural Imperatives: A Preliminary Inquiry," 3 *Harvard Human Rights Journal* 13, 1990.

36 Fahd, Toufy, and Muhammad Hammoudi, "L'enfant dans le droit islamique," in Société Jean Bodin pour l'histoire comparative des institutions (ed.) *L'enfant*, *Recueils de la Société Jean Bodin pour l'histoire comparative des institutions*, vol. 35, Bruxelles, Éditions de la Librairie encyclopédique, 1975; and Sait, M. Siraj, "Islamic Perspectives on the Rights of the Child," in Fottrell, Deidre, ed., *Revisiting Children's Rights: 10 Years of the United Nations Convention on the Rights of the Child*, London, Kluwer Law International, 2000.

In all cases, Islamic law predicates criminal responsibility, for adults and children alike, upon certain individual characteristics, among which the capacity for intelligent reason (*akl*) and the existence of free choice are central.[37] *Akl* bears special, broader importance as a prerequisite to understanding and appreciating the significance of divine morality and judgment. As such, it is tied to the capacity for comprehension and to the faculty of discerning between good and evil. Indeed, in Islamic criminal law, only those who can understand a legal norm, and act according to that understanding, are liable to criminal responsibility for violating that norm. In turn, penal sanctions depend upon the nature of the offender's intentions, reflecting an underlying conception of criminal responsibility based on the existence and degree of fault. *Akl*, however, is a capacity that develops over time, but not in immediately or objectively visible ways. The *Qur'an* does not provide explicit age guidelines regarding the development of *akl*, thus Islamic legal and religious scholars interpret relevant ages as objective criteria to denote its growth.[38] In particular, they designate ages by which children are presumed to have acquired *akl*; where it is lacking, criminal responsibility is not possible.

With this basic conceptual foundation, Islamic law recognizes three age groups with respect to children and criminal responsibility:

1. From birth to age 7: The general view among classical scholars is that children up to the age of 7 years are considered non-discriminating, without the capacity of *akl*, and are not held criminally responsible for any reason.[39]
2. From age 7 to the onset of puberty: During this "age of discretion," children's reasoning is still incomplete in its development, and therefore precludes any criminal responsibility.[40] Even where individual children demonstrate discernment, they are not held criminally responsible.[41] However, as described further below, beginning with at least this age group various schools apparently contemplate *ta'dīb* punishments for certain offenses committed by such children.

    The temporal end of this period, the onset of puberty, is calculated differently by the various schools. Most establish an age range—from a minimum age before which puberty can never be established, to a maximum age upon which puberty is assumed—within which puberty must be ascertained according to an individual child's physical development.[42]

---

[37] El Accad, Mohamed, *La responsabilité pénale en droit musulman*, doctoral dissertation, Université de Droit, d'Économie et de Sciences Sociales de Paris, 1984.

[38] Pearl, David, "A Note on Children's Rights in Islamic Law," in Douglas, Gillian, and Leslie Sebba, eds, *Children's Rights and Traditional Values*, Aldershot (England), Ashgate/Dartmouth, 1998.

[39] Bahnassi, Ahmad Fathi, "Criminal Responsibility in Islamic Law," in Bassiouni, M. Cherif, ed., *The Islamic Criminal Justice System*, London, Oceana Publications, 1982.

[40] *Ibid.*

[41] Fahd et al., *supra* note 36.

[42] *Ibid.*

Table 4.1 Selected Islamic school age ranges (in years) for individual determinations of puberty

School(s)	Hanafites	Malikites	Shafi'ites	Hanbalites	Shiites
Boys	12–15	9–18	9–15	10–15	none – 15
Girls	9–15	9–18	9–15	9–15	none – 9

Source: Adapted from Peters, Rudolph, *Crime and Punishment in Islamic Law: Theory and Practice from the Sixteenth to the Twenty-First Century*, Cambridge, Cambridge University Press, 2006, Tables 2.1–2.2, at 21.

Peters compiles the authoritative opinions of most Islamic schools' age ranges for the consideration of puberty, which sometimes vary for boys and girls under the same school, as seen in Table 4.1.

In consideration of children within their respective age ranges, Islamic schools also hold divergent views on the admissible physical evidence of puberty.[43] In all cases, puberty remains a proxy for the intellectual capacity of individual children, with puberty of course varying both by gender and among individuals.[44] In terms of physical signs, boys are commonly accepted as having attained puberty when they are capable of producing sperm, and girls upon their first menstruation.[45] Further proof in Shi'a Islam includes the growth of pubic hair, and in other schools pregnancy and the deepening of the voice.[46]

3. From the onset of puberty and beyond: Even after the onset of puberty, children are not automatically held criminally responsible for their illicit acts. For such responsibility to follow, children must have reached puberty and be of sound mind.[47] If these conditions are met, complete maturity and full criminal responsibility are accepted, with penal sanctions for such children's delinquent acts.[48]

ta'dīb: Punishing Children Before Criminal Responsibility?

Within this tiered system of criminal responsibility, one clarification is necessary regarding children younger than the age of puberty. In brief, for one category of offenses (*ta'zīr*) that are punishable at judges' discretion, some children may face punishment or disciplining (*ta'dīb*) despite the general Islamic criminal law

---

43 Bahnassi, *supra* note 39. Nobahar, Rahim, Mofid University, Iran, e-mail correspondence with author, July 2001.
44 El Accad, *supra* note 37.
45 *Ibid.*
46 Nobahar, *supra* note 43.
47 Bahnassi, *supra* note 39.
48 Fahd et al., *supra* note 36.

age divisions.[49] It appears that *ta'dīb* may be imposed conditionally in certain contexts against children of all ages, and by judges against any child committing a *ta'zīr* offense and deemed to possess *akl*.[50] However, it does seem that there are varying interpretations of *ta'zīr* offenses regarding the possibility of *ta'dīb* for children younger than 7, and that at least the Sunni Shafi'ites and Hanafites do not allow such punishments until the age of 7.[51] Regardless, even though *ta'dīb* in theory "serves more as a lesson or warning than as a punishment," the disciplining generally consists of explicit corporal punishment in the form of flogging.[52]

In larger terms, this issue derives from classical Islamic government theory, wherein the head of state may delegate authority to courts staffed by individual judges (*qādīs*), who then decide cases based on Islamic legal doctrine.[53] Although trials before *qādīs* are generally regulated by formal adversarial procedures, these procedures are greatly relaxed and judges are granted wide-ranging discretion when alleged offenses regard *ta'zīr*. *Ta'zīr* itself is a broad category, and is in practice the most important base for punishment.[54] Under it, *qādīs* may order measures from a nearly unlimited range of punishments, including reprimand, public scorn, flogging, banishment or imprisonment until repentance, and the death penalty. There are few limits on *qādīs'* authority as such, and these generally relate to the maximum number of lashes that may be ordered in flogging.

At the same time, such punishments are justified as rehabilitation for the offender, and accordingly they are individualized based upon the circumstances—as well as social and economic status—of each offender.[55] The primary goal of *ta'zīr* punishments is to prevent repeat offending, either by punishing past offenses or by coercing the fulfillment of religious duties. Within this scheme, *ta'dīb* in particular seeks to correct prohibited conduct.[56] Indeed, the root of *ta'dīb* is *'adab*,

---

49 Peters, Rudolph, *Crime and Punishment in Islamic Law: Theory and Practice from the Sixteenth to the Twenty-First Century*, Cambridge, Cambridge University Press, 2006.

50 Fahd et al., *supra* note 36; and Peters, *ibid*.

51 See Bahnassi, *supra* note 39; and Khan Nyazee, Imran Ahsan, *General Principles of Criminal Law (Islamic and Western)*, Islamabad, Advanced Legal Studies Institute, 1998.

52 Serrano, Delfina, "Legal Practice in an Andalusi-Maghrib Source from the Twelfth Century CE: The *Madhāhib al-ḥukkām fī nawāzil al-aḥkām*," 7 *Islamic Law and Society* 199, 2000, at footnote 63. See also Fahd et al., *supra* note 36.

53 Peters, *supra* note 49.

54 *Ta'zīr* concerns discretionary punishment for all the following: forbidden or sinful behavior, including punishment for acts similar to but not meeting the strict legal definition of crimes in Islamic criminal law; the refusal to perform religious duties; and acts that could not otherwise be convicted for procedural reasons. Al Awabdeh, Mohamed, *History and prospect of Islamic Criminal Law with respect to the Human Rights*, dissertation, Berlin, Humboldt-Universität, 2005; and Peters, *ibid*.

55 Peters, *ibid*.

56 See Serrano, *supra* note 52; and Tuşalp, Emine Ekin, *Treating Outlaws and Registering Miscreants in Early Modern Ottoman Society: A Study on the Legal Diagnosis of Deviance in Şeyhülislam Fatwas*, thesis, Istanbul, Sabancı University, 2005.

broadly meaning manners or culture, which gives context to *ta'dīb*'s meaning as "education conceived as moral discipline, our means to the refinement of character."[57] The concept is used widely in the fields of Islamic education and child rearing, and has variously been described in more succinct terms as "education, discipline, refinement," "corrective punishment," "admonition," "formation of character," and "teaching a lesson."[58] As such, at least some legal schools strictly consider *ta'dīb* to be non-criminal and non-penal in nature.[59]

The complex nature of *ta'dīb* for children actually parallels several aspects of juvenile justice systems that employ substantially punitive measures as welfare responses. Both systems draw upon elaborate historical and theoretical foundations; they grant almost unfettered discretion to judges in meting out punishments; they justify punishments on the basis of children's own best interests or rehabilitation; they are sometimes defended as non-penal approaches despite fundamentally punitive responses; and there is limited legal and statistical information available, if any, on relevant procedures and practices. Additionally, as discussed more generally in Chapter 5, *ta'zīr*'s primary goal of preventing recidivism would automatically characterize *ta'dīb* as a punishment indicative of criminal responsibility.

However, further research is needed on the doctrine and practice of applying *ta'dīb* to children younger than 7 and/or the age of puberty, both in countries where the statutory MACR already reflects Islamic law and where *ta'dīb* may be handed down independently of such provisions. As one example of the intricate legal standards at hand, Pakistan allowed whipping as *ta'dīb* for *ta'zīr* offenses committed by children 7 and older with sufficient mental maturity—irrespective of puberty—until the practice was prohibited in 1996.[60] At the same time, other laws still apparently sanction *ta'zīr* punishments for any child, regardless of puberty or age, including fines and/or imprisonment up to five years for certain offenses.[61] Beyond corporal punishment as a children's rights violation, such norms require analysis on a case-by-case basis to determine how they interact with and potentially undermine MACRs.

57 Goodman, Lenn E., *Jewish and Islamic Philosophy*, Edinburgh, Edinburgh University Press, 1999, at 131; and *Id.*, "Humanism and Islamic Ethics," in Carr, Brian, ed., *Morals and Society in Asian Philosophy*, Richmond (England), Curzon Press, 1996.

58 Respectively, *Ibid.* ("Humanism ... "), at 4; Peters, *supra* note 49, at 196; Wansbrough, John, and Andrew Rippin, *Quranic Studies: Sources and Methods of Scriptural Interpretation*, Amherst (New York), Prometheus Books, 2004, at 231; Haddad, Fuad Said, "An Early Arab Theory of Instruction," 5 *International Journal of Middle East Studies* 240, 1974, at 243; and Peters, Rudolph, "For His Correction and as a Deterrent Example for Others – Mehmed Ali's First Criminal Legislation (1829–1830)," 6 *Islamic Law and Society* 169, 1999, at footnote 23.

59 See Fahd et al., *supra* note 36; and Khan Nyazee, *supra* note 51.

60 Khan Nyazee, *ibid.*

61 For example, Offence of *Zina* (Enforcement of *Hudood*) Ordinance, 1979, Arts. 7 and 10; and the Prohibition (Enforcement of *Hadd*) Ordinance, 1979, Arts. 2 and 11.

MACRs under Islamic Law: Divergences and Reharmonizations

To be sure, Islamic countries' modern legislation does not necessarily correspond to classical Islamic criminal law doctrine, which was essentially consolidated by the 900s. Western powers began to influence and colonize parts of the Islamic world by the late 1700s, and new Western-style penal codes most often replaced Islamic criminal law in Asia and Africa through the 1800s.[62] Under the surface, scholars across the Islamic world have continuously studied and taught traditional doctrine, and informal Islamic law has often enjoyed greater legitimacy and importance than official state laws. In modern times, this popular appeal—as well as discontent over Western influences and secularization—has fed into a major political-religious resurgence. Beginning in the 1970s, Islamist movements sought to establish Muslim states, and to consolidate and expand their legitimacy where already in power. The reestablishment of Islamic law was the most visible objective, and the enforcement of criminal law was generally the first step. Although Saudi Arabia, Qatar, and Yemen never interrupted their systems, Iran, Libya, Malaysia, Nigeria, Pakistan, Sudan, and the United Arab Emirates all passed legislation to reintroduce Islamic criminal law.

In the context of MACRs in particular, current research confirms that Afghanistan, Comoros, Iran, Malaysia, Maldives, Nigeria, Pakistan, Saudi Arabia, Somalia, and Sudan all derive their provisions to some extent from Islamic criminal law principles.[63] These provisions are not necessarily part of broader Islamic criminal law frameworks. In other countries, there may be limited information available on MACR provisions or their basis in Islamic law.[64]

In almost all cases, MACR provisions under Islamic law breach international standards against gender discrimination; they explicitly assign criminal responsibility on the basis of puberty. At times, the application and enforcement of legal norms exacerbate such inherent discrimination against girls. For example, Pakistan's 1979 Offence of *Zina* (Enforcement of *Hudood*) Ordinance specifically regulates adultery, premarital sex, rape, and other related crimes.[65] In basic terms, girls—due to the earlier onset of puberty—potentially bear criminal responsibility

---

62 This discussion is drawn primarily from the summary and analysis in Peters, *supra* note 49.

63 See Table 5.1.

64 Libya, Qatar, United Arab Emirates, and Yemen. For example, Libya has broadly described its MACR-related provisions with the logic of classic Islamic doctrine, but without making any direct reference to Islamic law. See Committee on the Rights of the Child, *Summary record of the 432nd meeting: Libyan Arab Jamahiriya*, CRC/C/SR.432, 12 Jan 1998, pars. 68–74. This study concludes that the MACRs of Libya, Qatar, United Arab Emirates, and Yemen are all 7 years of age; historic British legal influences in all of these countries may also be relevant.

65 In general, see Cipriani, *supra* note 30.

several years before their male cohorts for this class of crimes.[66] In addition, procedural and evidentiary requirements for puberty tend to delay and even avoid the conferral of responsibility upon boys. Instead, for girls, menstruation and/or pregnancy are clear and irrefutable signs. In practice, this is equally true for consensual sex and for cases where girls have ostensibly been raped. In the absence of direct proof of rape, the fact that a girl is pregnant proves that she has committed adultery or has had premarital sex. Since promulgation of the *Zina* Ordinance, the percentage of girls in prison accused of *zina* has become extremely disproportionate to the percentage of girls accused of other crimes; UNICEF has cited cases where even 12- and 13-year old girls were punished for adultery because rape could not be proven.[67]

In general, MACRs derived from Islamic law not only deviate from international norms against discrimination, but also from core principles of classical Islamic doctrine. For example, in contradiction to the elaborate consideration of age, reasoning, and puberty in classical Islamic criminal law, MACRs in Pakistan, Somalia, and Sudan hold all children criminally responsible for various categories of crimes, without any clear minimum age limit. Nigeria and Comoros show other discrepancies between classical Islamic law and modern provisions, by setting MACRs that undercut scholars' consensus on the lowest possible age range for puberty, and by allowing marriage to trigger responsibility.

However, MACRs derived from Islamic law are reconcilable with both international children's rights standards and classical Islamic criminal law, due to Islamic law's intrinsic flexibility as a scholars' body of law. Where legal questions are not already resolved by the definitive sources of law, a number of juridical tools may be available to develop the jurisprudence and supplement its content.[68] Modern scholarly debate has applied these tools to adapt Islamic legal principles to human rights norms, including arguments that support an underlying harmony between Islamic texts and children's rights. In particular, "modern Muslim scholars would mostly agree that many of the legal principles in this area of child law are developments of *Ijma* or consensus of the scholars (in particular using the notion of *ijtihad* or independent search)," which allows for further jurisprudential elaboration that is not possible in other areas of law.[69] The use of such techniques may lend greater legitimacy and credibility to children's rights claims vis-à-vis

---

66 See Di Martino, Kirsten, *Analysis of the Juvenile Justice System in Pakistan for the UN Juvenile Justice Project*, draft, Geneva, UN Centre for Human Rights, 1996.

67 Amnesty International, *Pakistan: Denial of basic rights for child prisoners*, London, 2003; Committee on the Rights of the Child, *Summary record of the 134th meeting: Pakistan*, CRC/C/SR.134, 11 Apr 1994, par. 6; and Tufail, Pervaiz, et al., *Street Children and Juvenile Justice in Pakistan*, London, AMAL Human Development Network and the Consortium for Street Children, 2004.

68 For example, analogy, juristic preference or equitable solution, common good or public interest, and necessity. Sait, *supra* note 36.

69 Pearl, *supra* note 38, at 90.

Islamic law, which is fundamental in light of the moral, political, social, and cultural authority of Islamic law.[70]

Oftentimes, the purported disconnect between Islamic law and children's rights discourses is not a question of religion, but of political dynamics and political will.[71] Indeed, in the case of the MACR, one may even argue that classic Islamic criminal law doctrine lies closer to international standards than to some countries' contradictory provisions. Several countries have considered that religious scholarship supports such a conclusion. In Iran, Oman, and Maldives, scholars and officials have taken initial steps towards better aligning MACR provisions with children's rights standards.[72]

Afghanistan probably offers the best example in the world of juvenile justice legislation that integrates traditional Islamic principles with international children's rights standards for the MACR. The Hanafi school is the most influential in Afghanistan, yet Article 72 of the 1976 Penal Code formerly set the MACR at 7 years, beneath the Hanafi age range for puberty consideration. A high-level working group, including United Nations agencies, international donor countries, and government officials from various ministries and courts, convened for over a year to draft a new Juvenile Code to replace such provisions. In essence, they modeled the legislation after classic Islamic criminal law doctrine, defining as "non-discerning" children younger than 7, as "discerning" those between 7 and 12, and as juveniles those between 12 and 18; only juveniles bear criminal responsibility.[73] In effect, the law pegs criminal responsibility within the classic Hanafi age ranges for boys and girls, but sets it at the same level for both without further consideration of puberty. As enacted, these provisions meet international children's rights standards for MACRs in all respects, and importantly are gender-neutral, yet are based upon and are considered compatible with Islamic criminal law.

Soviet Law

Soviet law has left an unmistakable legacy for the MACR provisions of almost 35 countries, primarily in Asia and Central and Eastern Europe.[74] Although certainly a more recent historical phenomenon than Islamic law or European colonial law,

---

70   An-Na'im, *supra* note 35.
71   Sait, *supra* note 36.
72   In general, see Cipriani, *supra* note 30.
73   Arts. 4–5. The law also makes available a range of non-punitive measures of accountability for children younger than the MACR. For children older than the MACR, *akl* and related factors are included wherein judges are duty bound to consider the degree of psychological development, character and aptitude, and behaviour of each child during and after offenses. The age of penal majority is set at 18 years.
74   In general, see Cipriani, *supra* note 30.

a brief overview of relevant Soviet provisions helps explain the context for such trends. In pre-revolutionary Russia, the Law of 2 June 1897 and the Penal Code of 1903 established an MACR of 10 years, while courts appraised individual children's capacity for discernment between the ages of 10 and 17 in order to determine their potential criminal responsibility.[75] Indeed, Russian criminal law in this period was a part of progressive continental European legal trends, and these provisions parallel the French model.[76]

After transitory legal frameworks in the early revolutionary period, the Union of Soviet Socialist Republics adopted its first Constitution in 1924.[77] This Constitution left penal law codification to the union republics, although their respective codes had to reflect the Fundamental Principles of Criminal Legislation, which were handed down by the all-union authority.[78] The first Fundamental Principles were also enacted in 1924, but MACR provisions underwent a long series of modifications, with the MACR varying at least from 11 years to 16 years, until 1958.[79]

That year saw the enactment of new Fundamental Principles of Criminal Legislation, in itself the culmination of a series of legal reforms undertaken following Stalin's death in 1953 that sought to liberalize and rationalize Soviet penal law.[80] The 1958 Fundamental Principles led to the enactment of new criminal codes in all 15 republics between 1959 and 1961. Across the board, these apparently set MACRs of 14 years for specific "serious crimes," and higher limits of 16 years for responsibility for other crimes. For example, Article 10 in both the 1960 Russian Soviet Federated Socialist Republic Criminal Code and the 1958 Fundamental Principles lists the "serious crimes" as the following:

---

75 Griffe, *supra* note 29; and Cieślak, Marian, "Organisation de la lutte contre la délinquance juvénile dans les pays socialistes européens," in Société Jean Bodin pour l'histoire comparative des institutions (ed.), *supra* note 1.

76 Naumov, Anatolii V., *Rossiiskoe Ugolovnoe Pravo, Obshchaia chast'* (Russian Criminal Law. The General Part), Moscow, Beck, 1996, cited in Pomorski, Stanislaw, "Review Essay: Reflections on the First Criminal Code of Post-Communist Russia: On the Occasion of Anatolii V. Naumov's *Rossiiskoe Ugolovnoe Pravo, Obshchaia chast'* (Russian Criminal Law. The General Part). Moscoe: Beck, 1996. P. 550.," 46 *American Journal of Comparative Law* 375, 1998.

77 Butler, W.E., *Soviet Law*, 2nd ed., London, Butterworths, 1988; and Hooker, M.B., *Legal Pluralism: An Introduction to Colonial and Neo-colonial Laws*, Oxford, Oxford University Press, 1975. In general, see Cipriani, *supra* note 30.

78 Berman, Harold J., *Soviet Criminal Law and Procedure: The RSFSR Codes*, Cambridge (Massachusetts), Harvard University Press, 1966; and Savitsky, Valery M., and Victor M. Kogan, "The Union of Soviet Socialist Republics," in Cole, George F., et al., eds, *Major criminal justice systems: a comparative survey*, 2nd ed., Newbury Park, Sage, 1987.

79 Cieślak, *supra* note 75.

80 In general, see Cipriani, *supra* note 30.

homicide, intentionally inflicting bodily injuries causing an impairment of health, rape, assault with intent to rob, theft, robbery, malicious hooliganism, intentionally destroying or damaging state or social property or the personal property of citizens, with grave consequences, or intentionally committing actions that can cause a train wreck.[81]

Embedded within this structure, Soviet criminal law conceptualized a much narrower idea of culpability than common and civil law systems, based upon the now broadly rejected "psychological theory" of culpability.[82] Nonetheless, criminal responsibility rested upon an account of intentionality in committing crimes, and recognized the need for sufficient maturity.[83]

The 1958 Fundamental Principles remained in force until the dissolution of the Soviet Union in 1991, although relatively minor changes in MACR provisions were undertaken over time among respective criminal codes of Union Republics.[84] The codes were then received directly as the criminal codes for the respective newly independent countries. As these have been modified or replaced since 1991, essentially the same MACR provisions have generally been maintained. For example, Article 20 of the 1996 Criminal Code of the Russian Federation repeats the pre-existing MACR age structure and further expands the list of "serious crimes."[85] Of the 15 former Soviet republics, 13 still reserve an MACR for "serious crimes" and a higher limit for other crimes. With the exception of Uzbekistan and Georgia, these countries maintain the historical 14 years/16 years division.

Beyond the former republics themselves, numerous countries with strong Soviet legal influences have followed these basic patterns.[86] The respective Penal Codes of Albania, Bulgaria, China, Mongolia, Poland, Romania, and Viet Nam, presumably originating from historic Soviet influence, all establish lower age limits for more serious offenses and higher age limits for other offenses, and the majority of these follow the predominant 14 years/16 years division. Although further research is necessary to confirm the respective legal histories of exact

---

81 "The Criminal Code of the RSFSR: October 27, 1960, as amended to July 3, 1965," in Berman, *supra* note 78. Compare to Cieślak, *ibid.*, at 294.

82 Pomorski, Stanislaw, "Review Essay: Reflections on the First Criminal Code of Post-Communist Russia: On the Occasion of Anatolii V. Naumov's *Rossiiskoe Ugolovnoe Pravo, Obshchaia chast'* (Russian Criminal Law. The General Part). Moscoe: Beck, 1996. P. 550.," 46 *American Journal of Comparative Law* 375, 1998.

83 Savitsky et al., *supra* note 78.

84 *Ibid.* In general, see Cipriani, *supra* note 30.

85 Butler, W.E., *Russian Law*, Oxford, Oxford University Press, 1999; Osheev, Oleg, "The Age of Criminal Responsibility in Accordance with the Criminal Code of the Russian Federation (1996)," 11 *Chronicle (International Association of Youth and Family Judges and Magistrates)* 13, July 2002; and UNICEF Innocenti Research Centre, "Young People in Changing Societies: The MONEE Project CEE/CIS/Baltics," *Regional Monitoring Report* 7, 2000.

86 In general, see Cipriani, *supra* note 30.

provisions, it also seems likely that such influences contributed to related age limits in Bosnia and Herzegovina, Cuba, Croatia, Czech Republic, Democratic People's Republic of Korea, Hungary, Lao People's Democratic Republic, the former Yugoslav Republic of Macedonia, Montenegro, Serbia, Slovakia, and Slovenia. Three-quarters of these countries have MACRs of 14.

A final influence of Soviet law seems to be the problematic institutional response to children in conflict with the law who are younger than formal MACRs, as discussed in detail in Chapter 6. Due to the scarcity of information available on their legal bases, it is difficult to establish a clear historic link to Soviet law, yet there is a discernible pattern among former Soviet republics and countries historically influenced by Soviet law.[87] Some cases show a direct link, such as the introduction of "re-education through labor" in China by the Soviet Union, where it had been a measure for juvenile punishment.[88] In broad terms, most of these countries rely upon streamlined administrative procedures to consider young children suspected of having committed illegal acts. Relevant authorities—sometimes deemed Commissions on Minors or on Minors' Affairs—regularly order the deprivation of liberty of such children, in places such as special correction schools and re-education institutions. This trend among former Soviet republics and related countries is salient in the problems worldwide of inappropriate responses to children younger than MACRs.

Customary, Traditional, and Religious Law Systems

While European colonial law, Soviet law, and Islamic law explain the trends behind most official MACR provisions around the world, traditional, customary, religious, and other informal law systems are often primary for determining children's criminal responsibility.[89] Colonial-era legislation, for example, has never played a decisive role in the lives of most people; 80–90 per cent of the population is unaffected by it in some countries. This is largely because Western colonialization processes never fully displaced pre-existing law systems. The main powers took various approaches in establishing colonial legal structures, and usually acquiesced to customary law's local jurisdiction as long as it did not

---

87 Azerbaijan, Bulgaria, China, Cuba, Kazakhstan, Kyrgyzstan, Lao People's Democratic Republic, the Russian Federation, Slovenia, Tajikistan, Ukraine, Uzbekistan, and Viet Nam. Estonia, Poland, and Romania also show recent signs of comparable responses to young children, as well as similar Penal Code provisions, yet the results of the present study set these countries slightly apart. See Annex 2 for details.

88 Shengshan, Pan, "Chinese Re-education through Labor System in Relation to Religious Freedom: Hua'en Research Report Issued September 2006," 2 *Chinese Law & Religion Monitor* 5, 2006.

89 In general, see Cipriani, *supra* note 30.

negatively affect European authority, sovereignty, or settlers.[90] They selectively supported and intervened in customary systems to help ensure stability and administrative ease, without necessarily attempting modernization or alignment with Western-style laws. In Africa, for example, customary law continued to exist as one of several layers of jurisprudence, and "the overwhelming majority of Africans continued to follow the traditional customary laws."[91]

As noted previously, British and French colonization was especially important in setting MACR trends across continents.[92] In basic terms, the British typically favored colonial administration by a simple protectorate system and indirect rule, which allowed greater deference to existing indigenous institutions and laws.[93] British colonial rulers even recognized customary law on an ad hoc basis and consistently used indigenous institutions, including clan/lineage structures and customary courts, to facilitate their rule. However, criminal responsibility was historically a point of conflict with customary law. In both Asia and Africa, a significant problem for judges was "the fixing of the age necessary to support capacity for criminal responsibility."[94] Even if the underlying assumption derived from English common law, concessions were made arbitrarily according to local realities, including use of puberty and adulthood norms.

Although the French viewed colonialism as a process of complete assimilation, requiring full harmonization of native customs with French legal-institutional models, administrative and financial limitations meant that customary law continued to thrive.[95] As a result, most of French law "remained inapplicable to the bulk of the population."[96]

After achieving independence, former colonies generally retained the statutory law that had been in force, while customary laws remained complex mixtures of pre-colonial customary law and colonial influences.[97] Over time, many countries sought to update their codified legislation, frequently inspired by contemporary European models, while sometimes recognizing, codifying, or integrating customary law. Yet in the end, customary law was and often remains far more important. In the post-independence period, for instance, African traditional courts in many countries heard roughly 90 per cent of all criminal trials.[98] For

---

90 Mommsen, W.J., and J.A. De Moor, eds, *European Expansion and Law: The Encounter of European and Indigenous Law in 19th- and 20th-Century Africa and Asia*, Oxford, Berg Publishers, 1992.

91 Menski, Werner F., *Comparative law in a global context: The legal systems of Asia and Africa*, London, Platinium Publishing Limited, 2000, at 405.

92 In general, see Cipriani, *supra* note 30.

93 Hooker, *supra* note 77.

94 *Ibid.*, at 177.

95 Hooker, *supra* note 77.

96 *Ibid.*, at 220.

97 Mann, Kristin, and Richard Roberts, eds, *Law in Colonial Africa*, Portsmouth, Heinemann, 1991. In general, see Cipriani, *supra* note 30.

98 Read, *supra* note 32.

most Africans, "the laws cloned from the colonial countries have been irrelevant to what the people do and the factors that determine their life style."[99] Strong anthropological evidence suggests that villagers resist hybrid customary law in state courts by using "massive avoidance tactics."[100]

Customary law is considered especially important in children's lives in rural areas, as children may not have access to formal legal channels.[101] For example, there are more than 40 different ethnic communities in Kenya which define children and childhood differently, based upon rites of passage, periodic and seasonal circumcision ceremonies, physical feats, retreats and socialization rites, etc.[102] These definitions continue to be used in many communities, and regardless of chronological age they confer adult status, duties, and responsibilities.

There are, in fact, many examples of traditional and religious law systems that respond to children in conflict with the law in place of formal juvenile justice systems, such as in South Africa, Lesotho, Samoa, Ethiopia, and Yemen. More specifically, there are numerous examples where such systems address MACRs or the assignment of criminal responsibility to children. Throughout Somalia, both customary/traditional and Islamic law play a crucial role, due in part to historically weak state institutions.[103] Since there has never been a functioning juvenile justice system in the country, families resort first to community elders to address relevant cases, where customary/traditional law in effect supports an MACR of 15 years. In Nepal, the majority of cases of children in conflict with the law are apparently handled locally without any government involvement of any sort. Indeed, there is a multitude of traditional, village-based systems that operate on principles of religion and religious law. Where these derive from Hindu law and philosophy, fundamental Hindu precepts strongly support the notion of the innocence of children, and tend to lend support to higher MACRs.[104]

Further examples suggest countless variations and complexities in attributing criminal responsibility to children. Customary law predominates over statutory law in 70–90 per cent of Sierra Leone, with non-formal courts at the village level, but it varies by the beliefs and practices of roughly 14 different ethnic groups.[105]

---

99 Okupa, Effa, *International bibliography of African customary law*, Hamburg, LIT and International African Institute, 1998, at ix, quoted in Menski, *supra* note 91, at 438.

100 Menski, *supra* note 91, at 425.

101 Menski, *supra* note 91.

102 Committee on the Rights of the Child, *Initial reports of States parties due in 1992: Kenya*, CRC/C/3/Add.62, 16 Feb 2001, pars. 97–99.

103 UNICEF Somalia, "Juvenile Justice in Post-Conflict Situations: Somalia," unpublished draft presented at the conference *Juvenile Justice in Post-Conflict Situations*, UNICEF Innocenti Research Centre, Florence, May 2001.

104 Sangroula, Yubaraj, "The Roles Opportunities and Challenges of the Juvenile Justice System in Nepal: Need of a Diversion from the Criminal Justice System," *Kathmandu School of Law Journal*, 2004.

105 Man, Nathalie, "Juvenile Justice in Sierra Leone," unpublished draft presented at the conference *Juvenile Justice in Post-Conflict Situations*, UNICEF Innocenti Research

Adults generally take full responsibility for children's actions, while the passage from childhood to adult responsibilities may be variously indicated by factors such as physical ability/maturity, familial role, initiation ceremonies, marriage, and school attendance. In Afghanistan, statutory, *shari'a*, and customary law overlap in diverse forms throughout the country, yet in practice, courts typically apply Islamic and customary law rather than national laws.[106] Islamic law generally governs criminal law matters, and almost all courts, including the Supreme Court, rely directly upon it. At the same time, roughly 80 per cent of the population lives by any one of various highly localized forms of tribal or customary law, particularly in rural areas.[107] Among other provisions, the traditional law MACR is apparently 12 in Kabul, and 15 in Masar, as children beneath these ages are held accountable by their families. Upon reaching these ages, children's cases are referred to the local *shura*, a type of traditional dispute resolution council.[108]

Conclusion

To a large extent, this chapter's historical sketch flows into the earlier discussion of welfare and justice approaches in juvenile justice, whose contrasting emphases involve almost all juvenile justice systems in the world. Of course, such prevailing trends over time often led to reforms in overall design as well as in MACRs. Customary, traditional, and religious law systems add another dimension because of their predominance in determining children's criminal responsibility in many countries. All the same, the historical role and explanatory power of Roman law, continental European law and common law, colonial law, Islamic law, and Soviet law remain strong. The majority of MACRs across countries today can still be traced back to these broad historical trends. Historic influences also contribute to modern recurring problems, such as the low MACRs of English common law, gender discrimination in assigning criminal responsibility in Islamic criminal law, and highly problematic welfare responses to children younger than MACRs in Soviet-influenced legal systems.

Centre, Florence, May 2001. Likewise, almost 90 per cent of Malawi's population lives in areas where customary law applies, and communities estimate children's ages under customary law or by different ethnic groups' rites of passage.

106 Lau, Martin, *Afghanistan's Legal System and its Compatibility with International Human Rights Standards*, Geneva, International Commission of Jurists, 2002.

107 Cappelaere, Geert, *"Crime has no future. You have!": Juvenile Justice Mission to Afghanistan: 6–20 February 2002: Trip Report*, draft, UNICEF, 2002; and Winter, Renate, *Children's Rights: A Comparative Study of the Convention on the Rights of the Child and the Legislation of Afghanistan*, Kabul, UNICEF Afghanistan, 2004.

108 Kabul University Faculty of Law and Political Science, *Customary Law Survey and Children Rights: Report on Customary Law Survey Results*, draft, UNICEF Afghanistan, December 2003.

Despite varying elements, formulations, and problems, these central legal sources share a number of common attributes. Importantly, they all recognize some concept of maturity or moral agency before criminal responsibility may follow. This tenet was expressed as a minimum age limit beneath which no criminal responsibility or punishment could theoretically be applied, with the exception of obsolete French Penal Codes that omitted MACRs. In Roman law, former English common law, and classic Islamic law, this minimum age limit was held at 7 years, with a secondary stage of children's development typically extending from 7 years until mid-adolescence. Soviet law, instead, first opened the possibility for criminal responsibility at 14 years. In both early Roman law and Islamic law, the secondary stage concluded upon the onset of puberty. The Roman formulation, in addition, led directly to English common law's *doli incapax* and the French test of discernment. Chapters 5 and 6 examine dozens of countries that still apply these tests in various forms.

While the respective traditions are compatible in general terms, they carry forth their own dynamic constructions of childhood, their own accounts of children's development and its consequences, and their own statements about society's responsibility towards children. Upon these layers, the children's rights perspective adds a further understanding of childhood, which has been endorsed almost universally in the form of the United Nations Convention on the Rights of the Child (CRC). Given the historic parallels, there would seem to be space for convergence among the various legal traditions and children's rights. Modern Islamic law scholarship in several countries demonstrates the possibilities for such harmonization. Arguably, part of the commitment to children's rights under the CRC is in fact to reassess historical bases for MACRs, and the notions of childhood imbedded within them, against children's rights principles. Where dissonance remains, modern MACR provisions should be realigned with contemporary conceptions of children, the CRC, and international MACR standards. Indeed, Chapter 5 further illustrates the impact of historical influences on modern national MACR provisions, as well as the overwhelming trend in recent years to reconcile those provisions with standards set out largely under the CRC.

Chapter 5
Current MACRs Worldwide and Modern Trends

This chapter presents the first worldwide compilation of minimum ages of criminal responsibility (MACRs), including all key provisions by country with statutory citations and excerpts in most cases. Modern trends in MACR reform are analyzed in extensive detail, focusing on the major influence of the reporting process of the Convention on the Rights of the Child (CRC) on MACR increases. Volatile dynamics surrounding MACR decreases are also scrutinized. The chapter concludes by detailing the comprehensive evidence for a general principle of international law, which obligates all countries to establish respective MACRs.

Making Sense of MACRs and Punishment: Methodological Considerations

A series of caveats must be taken into account for this chapter's data and discussions, which form the basis for much of the current study. In the attempt to provide the most detailed examination to-date of MACRs around the world, research methodology has necessarily relied upon countless primary and secondary sources.[1] These included governments' own accounts and third-party accounts about national MACR provisions, which regularly provided unclear, contradictory, and even self-contradictory information. In large part, such conflicts are due to widespread conceptual misunderstanding of the MACR; confusion with the minimum age of penal majority (i.e., responsibility in adult criminal court), which contrary to international law coincides with MACRs in many countries; confusion with and limited information on relevant civil welfare and protection measures; and certain attempts to downplay practices that would undermine formal claims about MACR provisions and policy. To cite one among many examples, Lebanon has simultaneously claimed that no one younger than 18 is considered criminally responsible, that no criminal charges may be brought against a child younger than 15, but that children as young as 7 may be sued and penalized when they commit crimes.[2]

---

1 In general, see Cipriani, Don, *The Minimum Age of What? Criminal Responsibility, Juvenile Justice, and Children's Rights*, unpublished draft, Florence, UNICEF Innocenti Research Centre, 2002.

2 Committee on the Rights of the Child, *Initial reports of States parties due in 1993: Lebanon*, CRC/C/8/Add.23, 3 Feb 1995.

The frequency of such accounts makes it highly unreliable to accept governments' own characterizations of their MACRs, or even third-party descriptions about them, in the absence of further substantiation. As explored in Chapter 3, the Committee on the Rights of the Child has appraised MACR claims piecemeal against international children's rights standards. On numerous occasions—where it found that treatment of children younger than nominal MACRs amounted to punishment or implied criminal responsibility—the Committee has directly refuted countries' characterizations of supposed MACRs, and has recommended the establishment of clear MACRs. Thus, the MACR is certainly not just a question of what governments interpret as their minimum age limits for criminal responsibility, but also a matter of the age limit beneath which no treatment or penalty indicative of criminal responsibility can be applied by law.

However, the Committee has typically emphasized the relevant principles that apply in juvenile justice, without necessarily finding the need to exposit or dictate a precise common standard—and thus there remain some grey areas on what treatment is reconcilable with MACRs. At the same time, there are occasions when the Committee did not have the benefit of full clarifying information, or simply lacked the time to analyze and make sense of inaccurate claims, and consequently misinterpreted the meaning of different age limits or treatments.

As a result, there is still some need for objective criteria against which any provision or treatment could be judged, both as an analytical tool for better understanding respective national provisions, and as a roughshod mechanism to compare vastly different systems. Indeed, just as understandings of punishment are dynamic and culture- and time-specific, questions of how to interpret and compare the treatment of children arise throughout this study, including in the context of the classic welfare approach, *situación irregular* doctrine and practice, classical Islamic criminal law, and patterns of provisions across countries influenced by Soviet law.[3] Oftentimes, across such different contextual backdrops, it is very difficult to ascertain effective age limits. This is particularly true when provisions and practices for children younger than the presumed MACR seem to contradict the very meaning of the MACR.

Classic criminal law scholarship is helpful in delineating a more robust practical definition of punishment and criminal punishment. One seminal work in this respect is Packer's *The Limits of the Criminal Sanction*.[4] In basic terms, Packer holds that the first fundamental component of punishment in general is something "done to a person that he would not wish to have done to him," or intentional "pain or other consequences normally considered unpleasant."[5] The severity or degree of unpleasantness of the measure is not relevant.

---

3 See Garland, David, *Punishment and modern society: A study in social theory*, Oxford, Clarendon Press, 1994.

4 Packer, Herbert L., *The Limits of the Criminal Sanction*, Stanford, Stanford University Press, 1968.

5 *Ibid.*, at 23.

The second defining component of punishment is the predominant justifying purpose for its imposition: the prevention of and/or retribution for offending conduct. Any sanction that is triggered by some offending conduct and that primarily seeks to protect people (i.e., by preventing future offenses) is a form of punishment. The same is true for any sanction driven by the determination that a person has committed a wrongful act. This generally includes "whatever happens to people in the criminal process."[6] More specifically, criminal punishments—a subset of punishments—include all dispositions available for those judged guilty of crimes through criminal law processes. The hallmark of criminal punishment is a formal judgment of guilt, which as discussed in Chapter 2 signifies the community's moral condemnation of the act.[7]

Of particular interest, criminal punishment is frequently justified in juvenile justice on the basis of rehabilitation—in the sense of rehabilitative or reformatory sanctions that seek to promote changes in the offender's behavior and/or personality, such that s/he will avoid future conflicts with the law. In such cases, the underlying purpose remains crime prevention, albeit with intended benefits for the offender, and this is a social justification not driven by the child's interests. Euphemisms that avoid calling such measures punishment are misleading:

> However benevolent the purpose of reform, however better off we expect its object to be, there is no blinking the fact that what we do to the offender in the name of reform is being done to him by compulsion and for *our* sake, not for his. Rehabilitation may be the most humane goal of punishment, but it is a goal of *punishment* so long as its invocation depends upon finding that an offense has been committed, and so long as its object is to prevent the commission of offenses.[8]

In contrast to punishment, Packer defines treatment as a type of sanction wherein the primary justifying purpose is to benefit or help the person being treated, with the expectation that treatment will be ameliorative. Offending conduct may bring attention to the need for treatment, but such conduct is not necessary or formally confirmed, and is in fact generally disregarded. The focus remains steadfastly on helping the person, thus crime control and protecting other people play no role.

Although presented here in simplified terms, these distinctions among punishment, criminal punishment, criminal punishment justified as rehabilitation, and treatment are broadly useful in deciphering the validity of claims about

---

6   *Ibid.*, at 27.
7   For further discussion on this aspect of punishment, see, inter alia, Greenawalt, Kent, "Punishment," 74 *Journal of Criminal Law & Criminology* 343, 1983; Hart, Jr., Henry M., "The Aims of the Criminal Law," 23 *Law and Contemporary Problems* 401, 1958; Packer, *ibid.*; and Von Hirsch, Andrew, *Past or Future Crimes: Deservedness and Dangerousness in the Sentencing of Criminals*, Manchester, Manchester University Press, 1986.
8   Packer, *ibid.*, at 53–54.

national MACRs. This is especially true since such claims are scattered across divergent adult criminal justice, juvenile justice, and child protection and welfare systems. Packer's definitions are an important step towards objective standards against which sanctions may generally be compared, regardless of what system or institution hands them down.

The majority of MACRs clearly overlap with criminal processes and punishments in the sense that they are stipulated, as seen in this chapter, in respective penal codes, criminal codes, and juvenile delinquency laws. Here there is little doubt about the MACR; it is the limit for unpleasant sanctions in response to offending conduct, either as retribution for that conduct or prevention for such future conduct.

Where criminal punishment is further justified as rehabilitation, Packer's definitions clarify which measures are indicative of criminal responsibility. Therapeutic, rehabilitative, and reformatory sanctions that are contingent upon the determination of a past offense, and that primarily seek to prevent future offenses, remain criminal punishments. Many juvenile justice sanctions fall into this category of mitigated punishments that intend to assist children, and are therefore instances of criminal punishments.

However, measures that claim to meet Packer's definition of treatment—primarily seeking to help the recipient, with limited or no consideration of offending conduct, and not concerning public safety—often need closer scrutiny. The justification for treatment in this sense is a central tenet of the classic welfare approach to juvenile justice, and of many child protection systems, as discussed in Chapter 2. The welfare approach is one model along a continuum, and it is difficult for related systems to permanently fend off competing political and public policy pressures, such as crime control and the drive for retribution. As these pressures seep in, they undermine claims to treatment and begin to spread into the realm of punishment. This chapter surveys several historically welfare-based juvenile justice systems in which this has transpired. In such systems, legal categories may avoid denominating measures as punishments, even once they have become substantially punitive, and the component of condemnation in the punishment becomes implicit. Relevant institutions and the public understand that children are getting what they deserve, not that they are getting above all else the help they need. For example, this was arguably the case in Belgium in the past, where in practice "educative measures" were "pronounced with a retributive undertone" and effectively punished children younger than the nominal MACR of 16 years.[9] In many cases, supposed child protection measures also follow such patterns. Get-tough crime control rhetoric surrounds their application, discrediting higher nominal MACRs. This is perhaps the margin where MACRs require the closest scrutiny, and where they often merit rejection as effective bars to punishment of children.

---

9   Walgrave, Lode, "Restorative Juvenile Justice: A Way to Restore Justice in Western European Systems?," in Asquith, Stewart, ed., *Children and Young People in Conflict with the Law*, London, Jessica Kingsley Publishers, 1996, at 181.

In the present study, in cases of unclear or contradictory accounts of MACR provisions, additional research pursued the most reliable, complete, and current data available to the furthest practical extent possible. Particular attention has been given to the provisions and practices regarding the treatment of children vis-à-vis the distinctions described here. However, Packer's criteria are not used as a hard and fast rule, mainly in light of the contextual nuances that are beyond the scope of this study, and the inherent risks of holding all legal systems up against the concepts of predominantly one legal tradition. Reference to his work is partly an invitation to further research and debate towards the elaboration of definitive standards with international validity and applicability. This study applies a fairly restrained methodology for the time being, and classifies MACRs with significant deference to governments' own characterizations. Nonetheless, alternative age limits that contradict governments' characterizations are presented as MACRs where they are confirmed by an extensive preponderance of evidence—in light of the broad standards suggested by Packer and the Committee on the Rights of the Child. In such cases, governments' own claims about their MACRs are sometimes but not always noted; statutory language often provides such abundant evidence that contrary government claims do not offer additional insight. Dozens of cases fall in between; footnotes point out strong evidence that places nominal MACRs in doubt, but that is not sufficiently complete to label alternative age limits as MACRs.

Indeed, the collation of varied sources could not confirm with certainty all information, and information is often scarcest on countries where dubious signs are most abundant. In this sense, there is a hidden bias against countries with the most highly documented juvenile justice systems. For such reasons, the MACR listings are in part a subjective and interpretive exercise, in which it is unfortunately assumed that unknown errors remain. Nonetheless, the listings seek to present the most authoritative evidence found about the ages before which countries do not submit their children to penal or substantially punitive procedures or measures. It is hoped that this world overview provides a useful starting point for future research that may more properly assess national law, policy, institutions, and procedures—across the spheres of criminal justice, juvenile justice, and child protection and welfare—in detailed national contexts.

Current MACRs Worldwide

Table 5.1 (presented over the following pages) summarizes the basic MACR provisions of all 192 United Nations Member States. Where known to exist, the table includes secondary ages of criminal responsibility for defined categories of offenses (ACR specific crimes), and age ranges for *doli incapax* or similar assessments of individual children's potential responsibility (*doli incapax* test).[10]

---

10 In general, see Cipriani, *supra* note 1.

Table 5.1 Summary of worldwide MACR provisions by country

Country	MACR	ACR specific crimes	*Doli incapax* test
Afghanistan	12	–	–
Albania	14	16	–
Algeria	13[1]	–	–
Andorra	12	–	–
Angola	12	–	–
Antigua and Barbuda	8	–	–
Argentina	16[2]	18	–
Armenia	14	16	–
Australia	10	–	10–14
Austria	14	16	–
Azerbaijan	14[3]	16	–
Bahamas	7	–	7–12
Bahrain	0[4]	–	–
Bangladesh	9	–	9–12
Barbados	11	–	–
Belarus	14	16	–
Belgium	12	–	–
Belize	9	–	9–12
Benin	13	–	–
Bhutan	10	–	–
Bolivia	12	–	–
Bosnia and Herzegovina	14	–	–
Botswana	8	12	8–14
Brazil	12	–	–
Brunei Darussalam	7	–	7–12
Bulgaria	14[5]	–	14–18

1. While the Criminal Code stipulates that "Only protective or re-education measures may be applied to a minor aged under 13," such measures apparently include placement in any of roughly 30 specialized re-education centers administered by the Ministry of Justice. Nearly 2000 children in conflict with the law between the ages of 8 and 13 were deprived of their liberty in these centers in 2005. See Committee on the Rights of the Child, *Second periodic reports of States parties due in 2000: Algeria*, CRC/C/93/Add.7, 3 Mar 2005, par. 332; and *Id.*, *Compte rendu analytique de la 1057e séance*, CRC/C/SR.1057, 20 Sept 2005, par. 91.
2. The 2005 *Ley de protección integral de los derechos de las niñas, niños y adolescentes* explicitly abrogates the 1919 Agote law, which was the basis for Argentina's *situación irregular* policy of, in effect, discretionary deprivation of liberty of children of any age. The 2005 law would also seem to annul provisions in this spirit in the 1980 *Ley 22.278, Régimen Penal de la Minoridad*. However, final analysis may hinge upon pending legislation on juvenile criminal responsibility.
3. Under the 2002 Law on "Commission on minors and the protection of the rights of the children," administrative commissions may consider the cases of all children younger than 14 years of age suspected of having committed crimes, and they may impose disciplinary measures on such children including confinement in "special correction schools." See Azerbaijan NGO Alliance for Children's Rights, *Juvenile Justice in Azerbaijan: NGO Alternative Report on Situation of Juvenile Justice System in Azerbaijan within the period of 1998–2005*, Baku, 2005; and Committee on the Rights of the Child, *Second periodic reports of States parties due in 1999: Azerbaijan*, CRC/C/83/Add.13, 7 Apr 2005, pars. 436–444.
4. Bahrain has held that its 1976 Penal Code, Article 32, establishes an MACR of 15 years, and that Juveniles Act No. 17 of 1976 provides non-criminal reform and protection responses to younger children. In reality, 15 years is the age of penal majority, and there is no lower age limit to what are clearly punitive responses, "such as detention in social welfare centres for up to 10 years for felonies (e.g., article 12 of the 1976 Juvenile Law)." The Committee on the Rights of the Child observed that there is no MACR. See *Concluding observations: Bahrain*, CRC/C/15/Add.175, 7 Feb 2002, par. 47; and *Initial reports of States parties due in 1994: Bahrain*, CRC/C/11/Add. 24, 23 Jul 2001.
5. Art. 32(2) of the Penal Code allows corrective measures, as defined under the Juvenile Delinquency Law, to be applied against children under 14 who have committed socially dangerous acts.

Table 5.1   Continued

Country	MACR	ACR specific crimes	*Doli incapax* test
Burkina Faso	13[6]	–	13–18
Burundi	13	–	–
Cambodia	0	–	–
Cameroon	10	–	–
Canada	12	–	–
Cape Verde	16	–	–
Central African Republic	13	–	–
Chad	13	–	–
Chile	14	16	–
China	14[7]	16	–
	Hong Kong: 10	–	10–14
	Macao: 12	–	–
Colombia	14	–	–
Comoros	13; or 14–15 or physical maturity (boys) or marriage (girls)[8]	–	–
Congo (Republic of the)	13[9]	–	–
Costa Rica	12	–	–
Côte d'Ivoire	10	–	–

Commissions for Prevention of Juvenile Delinquency may administratively order such measures, including deprivation of liberty in Social-pedagogic boarding schools for children as young as 7, and in Correctional boarding schools for children as young as 8. See, e.g., Bulgarian Helsinki Committee, *Memorandum of the Bulgarian Helsinki Committee*, Sofia, 17 Oct 2005; and National Statistical Institute of the Republic of Bulgaria, *Anti-Social Acts of Minor and Juvenile Persons in 2005*, 31 Mar 2006, www.nsi.bg/index_e.htm.

6   Although children younger than 13 are technically not criminally responsible, Act No. 19/61 of 9 May 1961 on juvenile offenders and children at risk does not prevent their deprivation of liberty by law enforcement officials: "Act No. 19/61 does not regulate the police phase of the deprivation of liberty.... Consequently, minors under the age of 13 who are presumed not to be responsible for their actions may be held in police custody...." Committee on the Rights of the Child, *Initial reports of States parties due in 1997: Burkina Faso*, CRC/C/65/Add.18, 13 Feb 2002, par. 440.

7   The *laodong jiaoyang* system is one of the administrative detention systems used to punish most minor offences without official charge, trial, or judicial review. A patchwork regulatory framework apparently restricts its use to children 13 and older, although in the past children as young as 11 were detained. Deprivation of liberty is currently possible for up to four years total, based in large part upon the discretion of public security officials. Re-education is formally justified as a child protection measure of assistance for reintegration into society, yet the UN Special Rapporteur on Torture has considered the system a form of inhuman and degrading treatment or punishment. See, inter alia, Committee of Experts on the Application of Conventions and Recommendations, *Individual Observation concerning Worst Forms of Child Labour Convention, 1999 (No. 182): China*, 2007; Trevaskes, Susan, "Severe and Swift Justice in China," 47 *British Journal of Criminology* 23, 2007; and UN Commission on Human Rights, *Report of the Special Rapporteur on torture and other cruel, inhuman or degrading treatment or punishment, Manfred Nowak: Mission to China*, E/CN.4/2006/6/Add.6, 10 Mar 2006.

8   Comoros has indicated that, as stipulated in the Criminal Code, its MACR is 13 years. However, the Criminal Code and Islamic law are both legally recognized sources, and there are no fixed age limits under Muslim law. Physical maturity or the age of 14–15 years confers criminal responsibility on boys, while marriage at any age confers criminal responsibility upon girls. Committee on the Rights of the Child, *Initial reports of States parties due in 1995: Comoros (Additional Info from State Party)*, CRC/C/28/Add.13, 7 Oct 1998, pars. 52, 79, and 141–142.

9   Although apparently classified as protection, assistance, and education measures, children younger than 13 may be declared guilty, held in remand institutions, and placed in "a suitable educational or professional training establishment, or any public or private institution providing care for children, or in an appropriate boarding school for offenders of school age." See *Id.*, *Initial reports of States parties due in 1999: Congo*, CRC/C/COG/1, 20 Feb 2006, pars. 428–430.

Table 5.1   Continued

Country	MACR	ACR specific crimes	Doli incapax test
Croatia	14	–	–
Cuba	0[10]	–	–
Cyprus	10	12	10–12
Czech Republic	15	–	–
Democratic People's Republic of Korea	14	–	–
Democratic Republic of the Congo	0	–	–
Denmark	15[11]	–	–
Djibouti	13	–	–
Dominica	12	–	–
Dominican Republic	13	–	–
Ecuador	12	–	–
Egypt	7	–	–
El Salvador	12	–	–
Equatorial Guinea	16	–	–
Eritrea	12	–	–
Estonia	7	–	–
Ethiopia	9	–	–
Fiji	10	12	10–12
Finland	15	–	–
France	0[12]	–	0–18
Gabon	13	–	–
Gambia	12	–	–
Georgia	12	14	–
Germany	14	–	14–18
Ghana	12	–	–

10   Cuba claims its MACR is 16, but this limit is actually the age of penal majority as stipulated in Penal Code Art. 16(2). The main juvenile justice legislation, *Decreto-Ley No. 64 del Sistema para la Atención a Menores con Trastornos de Conducta del 30 de diciembre de 1982*, does not contain any minimum age for its application. Under this system, relevant children are seen as offenders in conflict with the law, and administrative "prevention and social welfare commissions" may order their deprivation of liberty indefinitely in specialized re-education centers. See, inter alia, Committee on the Rights of the Child, *Initial reports of States parties due in 1993: Cuba*, CRC/C/8/Add.30, 15 Feb 1996; Romero, Lidia, and Luis Gómez, *La Política Cubana de Juventud Entre 1995 y 1999: Principales Características (La Experiencia del Pradjal en Cuba)*, La Habana, Centro de Estudios Sobre la Juventud, 2000; and Zaragoza Ramírez, Alina, and Bárbara Mirabent Garay, "Administración de justicia de menores: un desafío a la contemporaneidad," *Cubalex: Revista Electrónica de Estudios Jurídicos*, no. 9, July–September 1999.

11   The Administration of Justice Act (as of 2004), part 75b, grants police the authority to detain suspects as young as 12 years of age in waiting rooms, holding cells, etc. Detention may be extended for up to 24 hours, and solitary confinement is permitted for up to six hours. Police may also conduct wiretaps, surveillance, searches, and seizures against such children. See Committee on the Rights of the Child, *Written Replies by the Government of Denmark Concerning the List of Issues (CRC/C/Q/DNK/3)*, CRC/C/RESP/91, 19 Aug 2005; and National Council for Children, *Report to the UN Committee on the Rights of the Child: Supplementary report to Denmark's 3rd periodic report*, Copenhagen, 2005.

12   All children deemed capable of discernment and found to have committed illegal acts are considered criminally responsible. The measures that such children may face vary according to their ages, as stipulated in the *Ordonnance relative à l'enfance délinquante* (as of March 2007). Adjudicated children of all ages are subject to "mesures de protection, d'assistance, de surveillance et d'éducation" (see, inter alia, Arts. 1–2). "Sanctions éducatives," which in certain cases deprive children of their liberty, are applicable to children ages 10 and older (Art. 15–1). "Peines," which also in certain cases deprive children of their liberty, are applicable to children 13 and older (Arts. 20–2 to 20–9).

Table 5.1   Continued

Country	MACR	ACR specific crimes	*Doli incapax* test
Greece	13[13]	–	–
Grenada	7	–	7–12
Guatemala	13	–	–
Guinea	13	–	–
Guinea–Bissau	16	–	–
Guyana	10	–	–
Haiti	13	–	–
Honduras	12	–	–
Hungary	14	–	–
Iceland	15	–	–
India	7	–	7–12
Indonesia	8	–	–
Iran (Islamic Republic of)	9/15[14]	–	–
Iraq	9	–	–
Ireland	10	12	–
Israel	12	–	–
	Occupied Palestinian Territory: 9	–	–
Italy	14	–	14–18
Jamaica	12	–	–
Japan	11[15]	–	–
Jordan	7	–	–
Kazakhstan	14[16]	16	–
Kenya	8	12	8–12

13 The Penal Code formally assigns criminal responsibility at age 13. However, juvenile courts have jurisdiction over children ages 8 and older in conflict with the law (Penal Code, Arts. 121 and 126), and may order rehabilitation and therapeutic measures (Arts. 122–123, respectively) for children that may deprive them of their liberty. See, inter alia, World Organisation Against Torture et al., *State Violence in Greece: An Alternative Report to the UN Committee Against Torture 33rd Session*, Athens, 2004.

14 The MACR is 9 lunar years (8 years and 9 months) for girls and 15 lunar years (14 years and 7 months) for boys.

15 May 2007 amendments to the Juvenile Law allow Family Courts to order their most severe disposition against children as young as 11 in conflict with the law—commitment to Juvenile Training Schools, which are supervised by the Ministry of Justice Correction Bureau. Previously, the minimum age for such placements was generally 14 years. Under the amendments, such children may also be subject to police questioning, searches, and seizures. The age limit of 14 years is also frequently cited because it is the lowest possible age for waiver to adult criminal court for certain serious crimes (Penal Code Art. 41). See, inter alia, Ito, Masami, "Diet lowers incarceration age to 'about 12'," *The Japan Times*, 26 May 2007; Jin, Guang-Xu, "Japan: The Criminal Responsibility of Minors in the Japanese Legal System," 75 *International Review of Penal Law* (*Revue internationale de droit pénal*) 409, 2004; and "Juvenile crime wave prompts Justice Ministry crackdown," *The Japan Times*, 25 Aug 2004.

16 Criminal Code Art. 15 (Commentary) notes courts' authority, under certain conditions, to apply coercive measures of correctional education to children 11 and older. This signifies placement for up to three years in special educational institutions, which are reorganized correctional colonies (i.e., juvenile prisons). Also, Centers of temporary isolation, adaptation and rehabilitation may admit children younger than the MACR who have committed acts harmful to the public. See, e.g., Children's Fund of Kazakhstan et al., *Alternative Report of Non-Governmental Organizations of Kazakhstan with Commentaries to the Initial Report of the Government of Kazakhstan*, Almaty, 2002; Committee on the Rights of the Child, *Second and third periodic reports of States parties due in 2006: Kazakhstan*, CRC/C/KAZ/3, 23 Aug 2006, pars. 28 and 458–466; and Kazakhstan NGOs' Working Group "On Protection of Children's Rights," *Alternative Report of Non-Governmental Organizations with the Comments to the Second and Third Reports of the Government of the Republic of Kazakhstan*, Almaty, 2006.

Table 5.1   Continued

Country	MACR	ACR specific crimes	Doli incapax test
Kiribati	10	12	10–14
Kuwait	7	–	–
Kyrgyzstan	14[17]	16	–
Lao People's Democratic Republic	15[18]	–	–
Latvia	14	–	–
Lebanon	7	–	–
Lesotho	7	–	7–14
Liberia	7	–	–
Libyan Arab Jamahiriya	7[19]	–	–
Liechtenstein	14	–	–
Lithuania	14	16	–
Luxembourg	0[20]	–	–
Madagascar	13	–	13–18
Malawi	7	12	7–12
Malaysia	0[21]	puberty/10/13	10–12
Maldives	puberty[22]	10/15	–
Mali	13	–	13–18
Malta	9	–	9–14
Marshall Islands	0[23]	–	–

17 Administrative bodies (Commissions on Minors' Affairs) have jurisdiction over children younger than 14 who are in conflict with the law. They may place children from the age of 11 in "special correctional schools" for one to five years, in effect depriving them of their liberty. See Meuwese, Stan, ed., *KIDS BEHIND BARS: A study on children in conflict with the law*, Amsterdam, Defence for Children International The Netherlands, 2003; and Youth Human Rights Group, *Alternative NGO Report to the UN Committee on the Rights of the Child*, Bishkek, 2004.

18 Special measures are applied under the Penal Code against children at least as young as 12, including deprivation of liberty in custodial re-education institutions. See Committee on the Rights of the Child, *Initial reports of States parties due in 1993: Lao People's Democratic Republic*, CRC/C/8/Add.32, 24 Jan 1996, pars. 161 and 166; and UNICEF East Asia and Pacific Regional Office, *Overview of Juvenile Justice in East Asia and the Pacific Region*, Bangkok, 2001.

19 Although Libya generally maintains that its MACR is 14 years, relevant Penal Code articles provide that children between 7 and 14 who are proven culpable of acts classified as misdemeanours or felonies may be the subject of preventive measures, which include commitment for a period of less than one year to a juvenile education and guidance centre. See, inter alia, Committee on the Rights of the Child, *Second periodic reports of States parties due in 2000: Libyan Arab Jamahiriya*, CRC/C/93/Add.1, 19 Sept 2002, pars. 29–30 and 76.

20 In essence, Luxembourg holds that 16 years is its MACR and minimum age for penal majority (*Loi relative à la protection de la Jeunesse*, Art. 32), and that only protection measures of care, therapy, and education are available for younger children. However, several juvenile court measures indicate a penal-correctional response to children's actions without any lower age limit. These may deprive children of their liberty, and in some cases, solitary confinement may be ordered for up to 10 consecutive days as a disciplinary sanction. See, e.g., *Id.*, *Concluding observations of the Committee on the Rights of the Child: Luxembourg*, CRC/C/15/Add.250, 31 Mar 2005.

21 Among explanations on various provisions regarding children and responsibility, Malaysia has suggested that Penal Code Section 82 establishes an MACR of 10 years. Other provisions clearly set a lower age threshold. *Id.*, *Initial report of States parties due in 1997: Malaysia*, CRC/C/MYS/1, 22 Dec 2006, par. 131(f).

22 Maldives has described its MACR as 10 years under Art. 4(a) of the Regulation on Conducting Trials, Investigations and Sentencing Fairly for Offences Committed by Minors. However, this same Regulation attributes criminal responsibility upon puberty, without consideration for age, for certain offences. *Id.*, *Second and third periodic reports of States parties due in 1998 and 2003: Maldives*, CRC/C/MDV/3, 10 Apr 2006.

23 Marshall Islands describes its MACR as 10 years according to Criminal Code Section 107. However, juvenile delinquency statutes establish procedures to adjudicate children as delinquent, without any lower age limit, and to order their deprivation of liberty as a consequence. The Committee on

Table 5.1   Continued

Country	MACR	ACR specific crimes	*Doli incapax* test
Mauritania	7	–	–
Mauritius	0[24]	–	–
Mexico	12	–	–
Micronesia	0[25]	–	–
Moldova	14	16	–
Monaco	13	–	–
Mongolia	14	16	–
Montenegro	14	–	–
Morocco	12	–	–
Mozambique	0[26]	–	–
Myanmar	7	–	7–12
Namibia	7	–	7–14
Nauru	0[27]	–	–
Nepal	0[28]	10	–
Netherlands	12[29]	–	–

the Rights of the Child observed that there is no MACR. *Id.*, *Concluding observations: Marshall Islands*, CRC/C/MHL/CO/2, 2 Feb 2007; and *Id.*, *Initial reports of States parties due in 1995: Marshall Islands*, CRC/C/28/Add.12, 18 Nov 1998.

24 Children younger than 14 that the court deems not capable of discernment, apparently without any lower age limit at all, may be sent under certain circumstances to a correctional institution until their 18th birthdays. The court may place children deemed capable of discernment, again without any lower age limit, in a correctional institution. See *Id.*, *Second periodic reports of States parties due in 1997: Mauritius*, CRC/C/65/ADD.35, 19 Jul 2005, pars. 125 and 477–478.

25 Micronesia has suggested that 16 is the MACR and the minimum age for penal majority under the Laws of the Federated States of Micronesia (Title 12 §1101, and in parallel provisions of respective state codes). However, juvenile delinquency statutes establish procedures to adjudicate children as delinquent, without any lower age limit, and to order their deprivation of liberty as a consequence. The Committee on the Rights of the Child observed that there is no clearly defined MACR. *Id.*, *Concluding observations: Micronesia (Federated States of)*, CRC/C/15/Add.86, 4 Feb 1998; and *Id.*, *Initial reports of States parties due in 1995: Micronesia (Federated States of)*, CRC/C/28/Add.5, 17 Jun 1996.

26 Mozambique has alternatively suggested that its MACR is 10 years (Penal Code Art. 43) or 16 years (Penal Code Art. 42), stating in particular that children younger than 16 may only face punishment vis-à-vis protection, assistance, or educational measures, without deprivation of liberty. Instead, 16 years appears to be the age of penal majority, while younger children fall under the jurisdiction of the Juvenile Court as stipulated in the Statute of Legal Aid to Minors. Art. 16 of this Statute allows corrective measures, including measures of deprivation of liberty, to be ordered for children who have committed acts deemed crimes or misdemeanours in the penal law. See *Id.*, *Initial reports of States parties due in 1996: Mozambique*, CRC/C/41/Add.11, 14 May 2001.

27 Children ages 14 and older are held criminally responsible in adult court, although the court also has the discretion to try younger children accused of murder. In general, children under the age of 14 are considered minors and their criminal responsibility is decided on a case-by-case basis without any lower age limit. Russell Kun, Principal Legal Adviser, Department of Justice, telephone interview with author, 19 Sept 2002.

28 Nepal has noted its MACR as 10 years according to Children's Act Art. 11, but the Terrorist and Disruptive Activities (Control and Punishment) Ordinance applies to children of all ages for certain offences. Committee on the Rights of the Child, *Second periodic report of States parties due in 1997: Nepal*, CRC/C/65/Add.30, 3 Dec 2004. UNICEF Regional Office for South Asia, *Juvenile Justice in South Asia: Improving Protection for Children in Conflict with the Law*, Kathmandu, 2006.

29 Police officers may arrest children younger than 12 and interrogate them at police stations for up to six hours. Some authors have described these and related measures as effective criminal responsibility at age 10. Detrick, Sharon, et al., *Violence against Children in Conflict with the Law: A Study on Indicators and Data Collection in Belgium, England and Wales, France and the Netherlands*, Amsterdam, Defence for Children International – The Netherlands, 2008. Uit Beijerse, Jolande, and Rene van Swaaningen, "The Netherlands: Penal Welfarism and Risk Management," in Muncie, John, and Barry Goldson, eds, *Comparative Youth Justice*, London, Sage, 2006.

Table 5.1   Continued

Country	MACR	ACR specific crimes	*Doli incapax* test
New Zealand	10	14	10–14
Nicaragua	13	–	–
Niger	13	–	13–18
Nigeria	Northern States: 7	–	7–12
	Southern States: 7	12	7–12
	various States: puberty[30]	7	–
Norway	15	–	–
Oman	9	–	–
Pakistan	0[31]	7	7–12
Palau	10	–	10–14
Panama	14	–	–
Papua New Guinea	7[32]	14	7–14
Paraguay	14	–	–
Peru	14	–	–
Philippines	15[33]	–	15–18
Poland	0[34]	–	–
Portugal	12	–	–
Qatar	7	–	7–18
Republic of Korea	14[35]	–	–
Romania	14	–	14–16
Russian Federation	14[36]	16	–

30   Among many conflicting statements, Nigeria has cited various ages as the MACRs under state laws. However, 12 states' *shari'a* criminal laws assign criminal responsibility upon puberty, without regard to age per se, for adultery or fornication; rape; sodomy; incest; lesbianism; bestiality; acts of gross indecency; and false accusation of adultery or fornication. For other crimes, children are potentially responsible at 7 years of age. See, e.g., *Id., Initial reports of States parties due in 1993: Nigeria*, CRC/C/8/Add.26, 21 Aug 1995; and Nigerian Federal Ministry of Women Affairs, *Convention on the Rights of the Child: Second Country Periodic Report*, CRC/C/70/Add.24/Rev.2, Abuja, 2004.

31   Pakistan cites its MACR as 7 years according to Penal Code Sect. 82. However, various other legal provisions set no minimum age for responsibility for certain offences. Committee on the Rights of the Child, *Second periodic reports of States parties due in 1997: Pakistan*, CRC/C/65/Add.21, 11 Apr 2003.

32   Besides the Criminal Code's MACR provisions, the 1961 Child Welfare Act (as of 1990) allows the Children's Court to deprive the liberty of child offenders of any age (see, inter alia, Arts. 32(2)(a)(ii) and 41(1)(b)(iii)).

33   The MACR is technically 15 years and one day. See Bayoran, Gilbert, "56 minors to be cleared of criminal liability soon," *The Visayan Daily Star*, Bacolod City (Philippines), 23 May 2006, www.visayandailystar.com/2006/May/23.

34   In response to evidence of any child's "demoralization," which includes his or her commission of an offense, courts may order educative, protective, and therapeutic measures. In some cases, these measures signify the deprivation of liberty for indeterminate periods of time. See, inter alia, Committee on the Rights of the Child, *Periodic reports of States parties due in 1998: Poland*, CRC/C/70/Add.12, 6 Feb 2002, par. 360; and Stando-Kawecka, Barbara, *The Juvenile Justice System in Poland*, presented at the Conference of the European Society of Criminology, Amsterdam, 25–28 August, 2004.

35   Children 12 and older accused of committing criminal offences, or deemed likely to do so and also beyond parental control, are handled as juvenile protection cases. Such children are not subject to sentences in juvenile prisons, as children 14 and older are, but they may face protection dispositions that include placement in child welfare institutions, juvenile protection institutions, and juvenile training schools or reformatories. See, inter alia, Republic of Korea, *The Juvenile Protection Education Institution*, www.jschool.go.kr/HP/JSC80/jsc_01/jsc_1020.jsp.

36   The 1999 law on "The Bases of the System of Preventing/Combating Homelessness and Juvenile Offenses" allows for the placement of children younger than the MACR in centers for the

Table 5.1   Continued

Country	MACR	ACR specific crimes	Doli incapax test
Rwanda	14	–	–
Saint Kitts and Nevis	8	–	–
Saint Lucia	12	–	–
St. Vincent and the Grenadines	8	–	–
Samoa	8	–	8–14
San Marino	12	–	12–18
Sao Tome and Principe	16[37]	–	–
Saudi Arabia	puberty[38]	7 or 12[39]	–
Senegal	13	–	–
Serbia	14	–	–
Seychelles	7	12	7–12
Sierra Leone	14	–	–
Singapore	7	–	7–12
Slovakia	14	–	14–15
Slovenia	14[40]	–	–
Solomon Islands	0[41]	–	–
Somalia	0[42]	–	–

temporary confinement of juvenile delinquents, via a judicial sentence or judge's order in response to "socially dangerous acts." Although placement is limited to 30 days, there were 54,800 such placements in 1999, 30,000 in 2000, and 24,400 in 2001. See Committee on the Rights of the Child, *Third periodic reports of States parties due in 2001, Russian Federation*, CRC/C/125/Add.5, 15 Nov 2004, par. 323; and Stoecker, Sally W., "Homelessness and criminal exploitation of Russian minors: Realities, resources, and legal remedies," *Demokratizatsiya*, Spring 2001.

37 Under the Statute on judicial assistance for minors, children younger than 16 who have committed acts deemed offences or crimes are only subject to protection, assistance, or education measures ordered by juvenile courts. Such measures may involve the deprivation of liberty, as in the case of placement in educational institutions and private educational establishments, although these do not appear to be used in practice. See, inter alia, *Id.*, *Initial reports of States parties due in 1993: Sao Tome and Principe*, CRC/C/8/Add.49, 1 Dec 2003, pars. 103, 107, and 109.

38 Children who have reached puberty may face the death penalty for crimes including adultery, apostasy, "corruption on earth," drug trafficking, sabotage, (political) rebellion, murder during armed robbery, murder, and manslaughter, as well as for actions within the broad category allowing courts' discretionary punishment (*ta'zīr*). In addition, judges may consider physical characteristics of puberty at the time of trial or upon sentencing, rather than considering children's ages at the time of alleged offenses, and may exercise significant discretion over which physical characteristics to assess. Human Rights Watch, *Adults Before Their Time: Children in Saudi Arabia's Criminal Justice System*, New York, 2008.

39 At least until recent years, the age of criminal responsibility for crimes besides capital offenses was 7 years. Government statements/policies regarding an intended or approved increase to 12 years are largely inconsistent, and in either case may only apply to boys. *Ibid.* Committee on the Rights of the Child, *Initial reports of States parties due in 1998: Saudi Arabia*, CRC/C/61/Add.2, 29 Mar 2000, par. 55.

40 Despite the nominal MACR of 14, welfare agencies called "Social Work Centers" have the authority to commit younger children to juvenile institutions, which are substantially equivalent to educational institution placements for older children in criminal cases. See Filipcic, Katja, "Slovenia: Dealing with Juvenile Delinquents in Slovenia," 75 *International Review of Penal Law* (*Revue internationale de droit pénal*) 493, 2004.

41 Solomon Islands has indicated that Penal Code Section 14 sets the MACR at 8 years. However, the Juvenile Offenders Act does not set any lower age limit for holding children guilty of offences and depriving them of their liberty as a consequence. Committee on the Rights of the Child, *Initial reports of States parties due in 1997: Solomon Islands*, CRC/C/51/Add.6, 12 Jul 2002.

42 Although overlapping customary/traditional law, Islamic law, and codified criminal law all contain relevant standards, there is no effective MACR. In customary/traditional law, the MACR is understood to be 15 years. Islamic law grants judges the authority to decide on the dangerous

Table 5.1 Continued

Country	MACR	ACR specific crimes	Doli incapax test
South Africa	7	–	7–14
Spain	14	–	–
Sri Lanka	8	–	8–12
Sudan	0[43]	7/15/18/puberty	–
Suriname	10	–	–
Swaziland	7	–	7–14
Sweden	15	–	–
Switzerland	10	–	–
Syrian Arab Republic	10	–	–
Tajikistan	14[44]	16	–
Thailand	7	–	–
The former Yugoslav Republic of Macedonia	14	–	–
Timor–Leste	12	–	–
Togo	13	–	–
Tonga	7	–	7–12
Trinidad and Tobago	7	–	10–14
Tunisia	13	–	13–15
Turkey	12[45]	–	12–15
Turkmenistan	14	16	–
Tuvalu	10	12	10–14
Uganda	12	–	–

character of juvenile delinquents under the age of 15, and to order them to periods of up to three months in reformatory facilities. Under the Penal Code, Article 59 nominally sets an MACR of 14 years, yet Article 177 details circumstances under which judges may commit younger children who have committed offences to reformatories for two years or more. UNICEF Somalia, "Juvenile Justice in Post-Conflict Situations: Somalia," unpublished draft presented at the conference *Juvenile Justice in Post-Conflict Situations*, UNICEF Innocenti Research Centre, Florence, May 2001.

43 Regardless of Sudan's various claims, Criminal Code Articles 3 and 9 only nominally limit criminal responsibility to children 15 or older who have attained puberty, and to adults 18 or older. Article 47 allows courts to order children 7 and older who have committed offenses to correctional institutions for two to five years, and there is no minimum age limit at all for offences including alcohol or drug handling or consumption, and sexual relations outside of marriage. Moreover, under certain circumstances, Article 27(2) allows capital punishment for children ages 7 to 18 who commit murder, *hadd* offences, or offences subject to *qasas*. Committee on the Rights of the Child, *Initial reports of States parties due in 1992: Sudan*, CRC/C/3/Add.3, 16 Dec 1992, par. 33. *Id*., *Periodic reports of States parties due in 1997: Sudan*, CRC/C/65/Add.17, 6 Dec 2001, pars. 40–41, 52, and 347.

44 Under Order no. 178 of the President of the Republic of Tajikistan, of 23 Feb 1995 (Regulations on the Commission on Minors), administrative Commissions consider the cases of children younger than 14 suspected of having committed criminal acts. There is no minimum age limit to Commissions' mandate in this respect, and they may apply punishments including the deprivation of liberty for children apparently as young as 7. There are indications that even younger children, contrary to Regulations, have been deprived of their liberty. See, e.g., World Organisation Against Torture, *Human Rights Violations in Tajikistan: Alternative Report to the UN Committee Against Torture 37th Session*, Geneva, 2006.

45 Under the Criminal Code, children younger than 12—as well as children between 12 and 15 deemed unable to perceive the legal meaning and consequences of their offences or as lacking the ability to control their actions—may face security measures/precautions. Furthermore, under the 2005 Juvenile Protection Law, any child in conflict with the law and deemed not criminally responsible may face "protective and supportive measures" that include deprivation of liberty in educational, governmental, and private care institutions. There is no lower age limit to the application of such measures, they may be imposed through a child's 18th birthday, and judges are not required to hold hearings before ordering them. See, inter alia, Arts. 3(1)(a)(2), 5(1)(b–c), 7(6), 11(1) and 13(1).

Table 5.1   Continued

Country	MACR	ACR specific crimes	*Doli incapax* test
Ukraine	14[46]	16	–
United Arab Emirates	7	–	7–n/a
United Kingdom of Great Britain and Northern Ireland	England and Wales: 10	–	–
	Northern Ireland: 10	–	–
	Scotland: 8	–	–
	Others: vary 8–10	varies	varies
United Republic of Tanzania	10	–	10–12
	Zanzibar: 12	–	12–14
United States of America[47]	CA,	–	CA[50]: 0–14
	NJ,[48]	–	–
	PA,	PA: 10	–
	VT, and others: 0[49]	VT: 10	–
	NC: 6	–	–
	MD, MA, NY: 7	–	–
	AZ, WA: 8	–	WA: 8–12
	AR, CO, KS, LA, MN, MS, SD, TX, WI: 10	–	–

46 Criminal Code Chapter XV on "Specific Features of Criminal Liability and Punishment of Minors" casts doubt upon the effective MACR. Article 97(2) states that "A court shall also apply compulsory reformation measures … to a person, who committed a socially dangerous act … before he/she attained the age of criminal liability." Such measures include "placing a minor in a special educational and correctional institution for children and teenagers until the minor's complete correction but for a term not exceeding three years" (Art. 105(2)). Translation by the Organization for Security and Co-operation in Europe, Office for Democratic Institutions and Human Rights, www.legislationline.org.

47 Juvenile justice is principally regulated and administered under respective state law. The states, plus the District of Columbia, and their respective abbreviations are the following: Alabama–AL, Alaska–AK, Arizona–AZ, Arkansas–AR, California–CA, Colorado–CO, Connecticut–CT, Delaware–DE, District of Columbia–DC, Florida–FL, Georgia–GA, Hawaii–HI, Idaho–ID, Illinois–IL, Indiana–IN, Iowa–IA, Kansas–KS, Kentucky–KY, Louisiana–LA, Maine–ME, Maryland–MD, Massachusetts–MA, Michigan–MI, Minnesota–MN, Mississippi–MS, Missouri–MO, Montana–MT, Nebraska–NE, Nevada–NV, New Hampshire–NH, New Jersey–NJ, New Mexico–NM, New York–NY, North Carolina–NC, North Dakota–ND, Ohio–OH, Oklahoma–OK, Oregon–OR, Pennsylvania–PA, Rhode Island–RI, South Carolina–SC, South Dakota–SD, Tennessee–TN, Texas–TX, Utah–UT, Vermont–VT, Virginia–VA, Washington–WA, West Virginia–WV, Wisconsin–WI, and Wyoming–WY.

48 New Jersey jurisprudence, exemplified in two juvenile sex offender cases, arguably upholds the availability of the common law *doli incapax* presumption in juvenile court delinquency proceedings (see State of New Jersey in the Interest of J.P.F., 845 A.2d 173 (2004); In the Matter of Registrant J.G., 777 A.2d 891 (2001); and Carter, Andrew M., "Age Matters: The Case for a Constitutionalized Infancy Defense," 54 *Kansas Law Review* 687, 2006). However, neither decision attempts to reconcile such availability with the provision, referring to the Code of Criminal Justice chapter on sex offenses, that "No actor shall be presumed to be incapable of committing a crime under this chapter because of age…." (New Jersey Statutes §2C:14–5(b)). One lower court in another juvenile sex offender case interpreted this provision as a "clear statutory disavowal of the old common law three-tiered rule." (State of New Jersey in the Interest of C.P. & R.D., 514 A.2d 850, 854 (1986)).

49 In statutory and/or case law, these states either have no minimum age for adjudicating children delinquent in juvenile court proceedings, or have no minimum age for original adult criminal court jurisdiction. In addition, the federal government has no minimum age limit to adjudicating children delinquent; federal law enforcement officials arrest approximately 400 children per year, but cases may be transferred under certain conditions to state courts. "Others" include AL, AK, CT, DC, DE, FL, GA, HI, ID, IL, IN, IA, KY, ME, MI, MO, MT, NE, NV, NH, NM, ND, OH, OK, OR, RI, SC, TN, UT, VA, WV, and WY. See, inter alia, King, Melanie, and Linda Szymanski, "National Overviews," *State Juvenile Justice Profiles*, Pittsburgh, National Center for Juvenile Justice, 2006,

Table 5.1   Continued

Country	MACR	ACR specific crimes	Doli incapax test
Uruguay	13	–	–
Uzbekistan	13[51]	14/16	–
Vanuatu	10	–	10–14
Venezuela	12	–	–
Viet Nam	14[52]	16	–
Yemen	7	–	–
Zambia	8	12	8–12
Zimbabwe	7	12	7–14

www.ncjj.org/stateprofiles; and Snyder, Howard N., and Melissa Sickmund, *Juvenile Offenders and Victims: 2006 National Report*, Washington, United States Department of Justice, Office of Juvenile Justice and Delinquency Prevention, 2006.

50 This table notes the two states—California and Washington—where some type of *doli incapax* test is currently available in juvenile delinquency proceedings (see also note 48 regarding New Jersey). Case law in roughly 20 other states upholds the common law *doli incapax* provisions only in adult criminal courts, without necessarily barring delinquency proceedings in juvenile courts. Although such provisions are theoretically applicable to all relevant children in adult courts, *doli incapax* has generally fallen into disuse, and respective case law is typically dated. See Carter, *supra* note 48; Thomas, Tim A., *Annotation: Defense of Infancy in Juvenile Delinquency Proceedings*, 83 ALR4th 1135, 1991 and August 2002 Supplement; and King et al., *ibid*.

51 Regional and municipal Commissions on Minors' Affairs have primary responsibility, subject to public prosecutor supervision, for responding to children younger than 13 in conflict with the law. Commissions may return such children to parental supervision or send them to children's institutions for at least three years. See Danish Centre for Human Rights and UNICEF, *Juvenile Justice in Uzbekistan: Assessment 2000*, Copenhagen, 2001; and World Organisation Against Torture, *Rights of the Child in Uzbekistan*, Geneva, 2006.

52 Under the administrative procedures of Government Decree No. 33/CP of 1997, Art. 1, and the Ordinance on Sanctions against Administrative Violations, 2002, Art. 5(1)(a), children from age 12 who commit Penal Code violations are subject to placement in reform schools for six months to two years. See Human Rights Watch, *"Children of the Dust": Abuse of Hanoi Street Children in Detention*, New York, 2006; and Committee on the Rights of the Child, *Periodic reports of States parties due in 1997: Viet Nam*, CRC/C/65/Add.20, 5 Jul 2002, pars. 114(b) and 232(a).

Annex 2 to this study additionally excerpts and/or cites the most explicit sources of these provisions, which are often repeated in various law articles and/or laws, for most countries of the world. It also includes clarification on the reasoning for MACRs listed, and information on other complex and/or overlapping age limits.

Figure 5.1 depicts the distribution of MACR age levels worldwide and provides a platform for interpreting some of the main characteristics of MACR provisions detailed in Table 5.1. As seen in Figure 5.1, the current range of MACRs across countries is from 0 to 16 years. The median MACR—that is, the age level with as many MACRs at and below it as there are MACRs at and above it—is 12 years. In comparison, the average MACR of roughly 10 years is not as useful a measure because, among other reasons, the mean is skewed by the 23 countries classified as having MACRs of 0 in Figure 5.1.[11] This does not necessarily signify that such

---

11 Bahrain, Cambodia, Comoros, Cuba, Democratic Republic of the Congo, France, Luxembourg, Malaysia, Maldives, Marshall Islands, Mauritius, Micronesia, Mozambique,

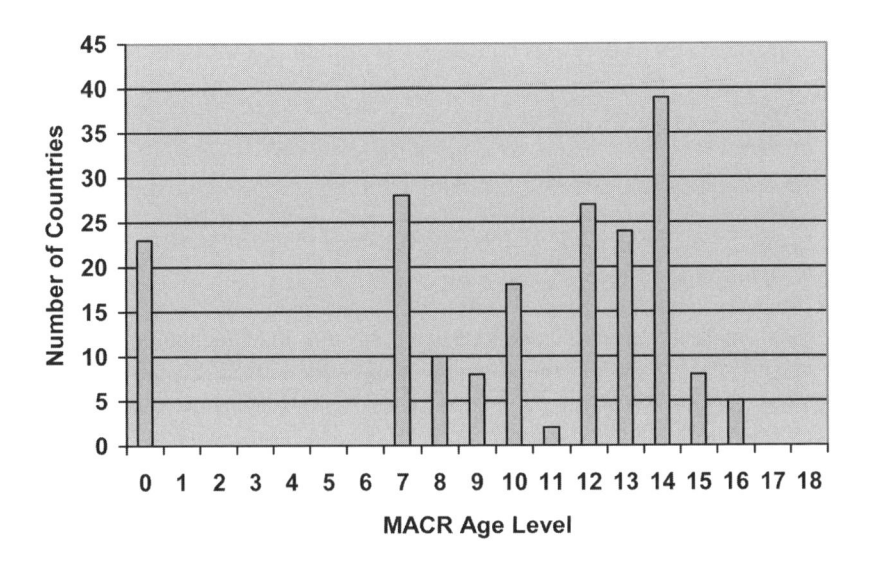

Figure 5.1   Current MACR distribution worldwide

countries hold infants and toddlers criminally responsible for their acts; instead, they have no clear lower age limit below which criminal responsibility and/or sanctions are ruled out in all cases, as per the criteria outlined above in this chapter.

In moving along the columns of Figure 5.1 from left to right, and recalling the historical overviews of Chapter 4, it appears likely that most of the MACRs set at 7, 8, and 10 years are linked to the influences of English common law.[12] Many of the MACRs of 12 years are in African, Latin American, and other countries that have amended their MACRs since the adoption of the CRC. The high number of countries with MACRs of 13 is due largely to historic influences of French law; those at 14 years are often related to Soviet law influences; and those at 15 are mostly in Scandinavian countries.

Several provisions and features are found in the details of Table 5.1 but are not reflected in Figure 5.1. First, within China, Israel, Nigeria, Tanzania, the United Kingdom, and the United States, respective political/administrative subdivisions have different MACR age levels. In terms of multiple national ages of criminal responsibility according to the type and/or category of offense, at least 42 different countries have both MACRs and one or more higher age limits. Of these, 17 are former Soviet republics or other countries heavily influenced by Soviet law.[13] The

---

Nauru, Nepal, Nigeria, Pakistan, Poland, Saudi Arabia, Solomon Islands, Somalia, Sudan, and the United States of America.

12   In general, see Cipriani, *supra* note 1.

13   Albania, Armenia, Azerbaijan, Belarus, China, Georgia, Kazakhstan, Kyrgyzstan, Lithuania, Moldova, Mongolia, Russia, Tajikistan, Turkmenistan, Ukraine, Uzbekistan, and

group also includes 14 countries with secondary criminal responsibility age limits only for boys for offenses such as rape and sexual offenses, provisions which are apparently a remnant of English common law.[14] Also related to English common law in many cases, there are at least 55 countries with *doli incapax* or substantially similar age ranges for considering potential criminal responsibility on a case-by-case basis.[15]

At this summary level alone, the broad characteristics of MACRs worldwide show significant differences from the consensus international standards for MACRs as discussed in Chapter 3. One of the few points of convergence is the age of 12 years: the international standard holds that MACRs should be at least 12 years of age, just as the international median of MACRs is 12 years. However, this also means that 89 countries have MACRs of 11 years or lower, including the 23 countries with MACRs tied to puberty or cited as 0 in this study. All of these countries' provisions fall outside the boundaries of the international standards. The same is true for six countries' multiple MACRs by political subdivision, 42 countries' dual or multiple age limits by type of offense, and 55 countries' *doli incapax* or similar tests.

Even though these characteristics sometimes overlap within respective countries' laws, it is clear that the majority of countries in the world have one or more traits that are incompatible with the consensus international standards. In fact, fewer than 75 countries meet the basic standards at this level of analysis. This designation, however, still says almost nothing about respect for children's rights. Chapter 6 surveys practical challenges in national implementation, and one or more of these challenges probably affects every country in the world. Ironically, some become more menacing particularly as MACRs grow higher and ostensibly more compatible with the standards. Although not a part of the international consensus on MACRs per se, another point of difference with state practice is the apparent preference of the Committee on the Rights of the Child for MACRs of 16 years. Only five countries set their MACRs this high, and none set them higher.

Viet Nam. Others include Argentina, Austria, Chile, Ireland, Malaysia, Maldives, Nepal, New Zealand, Nigeria (various states), Pakistan, Saudi Arabia, Sudan, and the United States (Pennsylvania and Vermont).

14 Botswana, Cyprus, Fiji, Kenya, Kiribati, Malawi, Malaysia, Nigeria, Papua New Guinea, Seychelles, Tuvalu, the United Kingdom (British Virgin Islands), Zambia, and Zimbabwe. In Papua New Guinea, the provision is formulated as a rebuttable presumption for boys between the MACR of 7 years and 14 years. Although they have been cited as a protection for boys against unjust prosecutions, such provisions discriminatorily assign criminal responsibility to girls for sex-related crimes.

15 Several other countries have limits on boys' responsibility for sex offenses or *doli incapax* tests, but it appears that these only apply in adult criminal courts while MACRs and criminal responsibility independently apply at lower ages in juvenile courts.

Scrutiny under the CRC and Rising MACRs

Driven largely by CRC-related attention, countries have overwhelmingly raised and sought to raise their MACRs over the past two decades. This section offers an overview of this pattern and related considerations.[16]

Table 5.2 portrays the basic trends in MACRs worldwide. Moving top to bottom, the table lists by year from the CRC's adoption (1989) through 2008 the 40 countries that have established or increased their MACRs, and the seven countries that have lowered their MACRs. Beneath 2008 are the countries that have formally stated their intentions to amend MACRs, or are currently considering or have recently considered specific proposals as such: 23 to create or increase MACRs, and two to decrease them.[17] Where the Committee on the Rights of the Child raised relevant concerns prior to proposed or enacted increases, countries names are in bold.

Above all else, the sweeping number of countries that have increased or proposed to increase their MACRs—nearly 65 since the United Nations General Assembly's adoption of the CRC in 1989—is a visible testament to the CRC's impact overall and to the CRC country reporting process in particular. In contrast, although historical research becomes progressively less reliable, the matching 19-year span including 1970 through 1988 brings just 10 known MACR changes: seven increases and three decreases. The nearly constant attention of the Committee on the Rights of the Child to the MACR, as detailed in Chapter 3, appears to be the driving force behind the number of modern changes. The Committee's frequent recommendations to increase MACRs also explain the lopsided international trend—a 7:1 ratio of increases and proposed increases to decreases and proposed decreases. The pace of post-CRC MACR increases even appears to be quickening. For example, in the 10 years including 1989 through 1998, there were 11 MACR increases, while the nine years including 1999 through 2007 have brought 28 increases, with 23 more proposed increases in the waiting. Twenty-one of these 23 proposals are in countries with which the Committee on the Rights of the Child has raised the issue of the MACR in its Concluding Observations.

Of course, these MACR patterns are an indicator of the CRC's larger impact for children's rights in juvenile justice systems. Table 5.2 includes many countries

---

16 In general, see Cipriani, *supra* note 1.

17 MACR proposals, for both increases and decreases, only include legislatively oriented proposals that appear to be pending or that are recurring. They omit those that have been considered and subsequently abandoned, as well as calls for MACR reform from academics, non-governmental organizations (NGOs), and advocacy groups. Table 5.2 does not include changes or proposed changes strictly to *doli incapax* provisions or to secondary age limits. It also excludes several presumed MACR changes where the resultant age limit is not considered the effective MACR in this study, or where the nature of former provisions remains unclear. The establishment of effective MACRs where there appears to have been no meaningful age limit previously (e.g., following abrogation of *situación irregular*) is tallied as the creation of new MACRs.

112   *Children's Rights and the Minimum Age of Criminal Responsibility*

Table 5.2   MACR trends since adoption of the CRC (1989)

	Year	MACR Decreases (7 Enacted)		MACR Increases (41 Enacted)	
	1989				
	1990		Brazil		
	1991				
	1992		Nepal / Peru		
	1993				
	1994		**El Salvador**		
	1995		Australia*		
	1996		Costa Rica / Honduras	Uganda	
	1997		Indonesia		
	1998		Barbados / **Ghana**	Nicaragua / Venezuela	
	1999	Andorra	**Belize** / **Bolivia**	Cyprus / Panama	Portugal
	2000		Spain / Timor-Leste	United Kingdom**	
	2001		Paraguay		
	2002	France			
	2003		**China (Hong Kong)** / Dominican Republic	Ecuador / **Guatemala**	Switzerland / Syria
	2004	Nepal	**Bangladesh** / **Bhutan**	Uruguay	
	2005	Mauritania / Slovakia	Afghanistan / **Argentina**	Gambia / Mexico	
	2006		Chile / Ireland	Philippines	
	2007	Georgia / Japan	Colombia / Peru	Sierra Leone	
	2008				

---- *Recently Proposed* ----

MACR Decreases (2 Proposed)		MACR Increases (23 Proposed)	
Czech Republic	**Bahrain**	Kenya	South Africa
Philippines	Belize	Lebanon	Suriname
	Bhutan	Lesotho	Swaziland
	Burundi	Malawi	Tanzania
	Cambodia	Maldives	Thailand
	France	Namibia	Timor-Leste
	Indonesia	**Oman**	U.K. (Bermuda)
	Jordan	Samoa	

Countries that amended their MACRs through mid-2008 are listed alphabetically by year.
Names in bold = concerns raised by the Committee on the Rights of the Child prior to proposed or enacted increases.
* Commonwealth; others vary
** The Overseas Territories of Anguilla and Cayman Islands increased their MACRs from 8 years to 10 years between 2000 and 2007, with both maintaining *doli incapax* tests between 10 and 14 years.

where MACR amendments are just one limited aspect of broader reform. For example, the CRC pushed a fundamental rethinking and redefining of children's place in law and society across Latin America, and it spurred the intensive advocacy efforts that uprooted the *situación irregular* doctrine. Thus, the 18 relevant countries listed in Table 5.2 as having created or increased their MACRs have, more importantly, legally defined children as holders of clear rights and guarantees, in both juvenile justice and child protection realms. In Mexico, for instance, respective states had independently regulated and administered their juvenile justice systems, in the spirit of *situación irregular*, with formal MACRs that ranged from 0 through 14 years.[18] Constitutional amendments passed in 2005 require states to create rights-based juvenile justice systems, MACRs of 12 years, minimum ages of penal majority of 18 years, strict limits on the deprivation of liberty, and only protection-oriented measures for children younger than the MACR in conflict with the law.[19]

All the same, juvenile justice debates around the world regularly focus on the MACR as a central challenging issue. In many cases, this has spurred constructive engagement, such as in Syria's civil society and government discussions that resulted in MACR reform.[20] Hong Kong examined its MACR in exceptional detail, soliciting public and academic comment, which eventually led to legal reform in 2003.[21] Similarly, upon ministerial request the Scottish Law Commission produced a thorough discussion paper on the topic, convened a debate forum, and published a formal report, which collectively prompted wide comment although ultimately no MACR change.[22]

Even if geared towards age limit increases, such MACR debates are not necessarily constructive. For example, prior to the Philippines' increase from 9 years to 15 years in 2006, a UNICEF-supported study of out-of-school children was conducted in support of advocacy efforts.[23] Its manipulation of language and imagery, however, is extremely problematic from a children's rights perspective. The report claims that "[a]t 18 years of age, the out-of-school children and youth tested in this study were at a level of discernment comparable to that of the average 7-year-old," and that "[c]learly, most child offenders have a low level of moral development and an equally dismal level of discernment." Ironically, the

---

18   García, Dilcya Samantha, UNICEF Mexico, correspondence with author, October 2005.

19   *Constitución Política de los Estados Unidos Mexicanos*, as of 2006, Art. 18.

20   Uddin Siddiqui, Kamal, "The Age of Criminal Responsibility and Other Aspects of the Children Act, 1974," presented at the workshop *Raising the Age of Criminal Responsibility and Other Aspects of the Children Act, 1974*, Dhaka, 16 Jan 2004.

21   See, inter alia, Law Reform Commission of Hong Kong, *Consultation Paper on the Age of Criminal Responsibility in Hong Kong*, Wanchai, 1999.

22   See, inter alia, Scottish Law Commission, *Report on Age of Criminal Responsibility*, Edinburgh, 2002.

23   Ortiz, Will P., *Arrested Development: The Level of Discernment of Out-of-School Children and Youth*, Manila, Philippine Action for Youth Offenders, 2000.

report has been cited as a good practice for arguing that only older children have sufficient discernment to bear criminal responsibility. Not surprisingly, legislators submitted a bill just two years later to lower the age limit back down to 10, arguing that immature children were apt to commit dangerous offences.

In considering MACR increases, other countries have focused more on the appropriateness of welfare responses to young children. Germany saw growing pressure through the 1970s to raise its MACR from 14 to 16, yet this dissipated in the 1980s because of concerns about how children younger than 16 might subsequently be treated.[24] There were fears that welfare approach responses could erode procedural guarantees and increase the indeterminate deprivation of liberty of children. In Canada, a general consensus by the early 1980s held that it was more appropriate for young children to access services through child welfare and mental health frameworks, rather than the criminal law, and the MACR was increased from 7 to 12 in 1984.[25] However, as discussed in the following section, both Germany and Canada subsequently faced pressures to decrease their MACRs.

Downward Pressures: Isolated Crimes and Widespread Hype

All MACR amendments mark critical points in societies' changing definitions of childhood. Debates on MACRs access a wide and often contradictory range of images and assumptions about children, about what children are capable of doing, and about what is fitting as a response to children's actions. Consequently, they regularly involve some of the most heated public dialogues on child-related issues. Even though movements to reduce MACRs are in the minority, this section shows that related dynamics are particularly unwieldy. Case studies suggest that media and political grandstanding and other factors prey upon isolated cases of juvenile crime. This explosive mix often threatens to upend MACR-related provisions, to redefine understandings of childhood, and even to trigger major setbacks for overall national children's rights implementation. Such patterns have a number of implications for juvenile justice and MACR reform efforts.

The United Kingdom and James Bulger

The single most important and influential example is the United Kingdom and the Bulger case, even though its main repercussions affected *doli incapax* and

---

24   Dünkel, Frieder, "Juvenile Justice Systems in Europe – Legal Aspects and Actual Developments," in UN Asia and Far East Institute for the Prevention of Crime and the Treatment of Offenders, 52 *Resource Material Series* 275, Tokyo, 1998.

25   Augimeri, Leena K., et al., "Appendix B: Children Under Age 12 Years Who Commit Offenses: Canadian Legal and Treatment Approaches," in Loeber, Rolf, and David P. Farrington, eds, *Child Delinquents: Development, Intervention, and Service Needs*, Thousand Oaks, Sage Publications, 2001.

not the MACR itself.[26] The backdrop to the case was a period of plunging public opinion about the general state of affairs in the United Kingdom.[27] By the 1980s, crime policy began to take a prominent and dramatic role in the national discourse, including in legislative and policy arenas.[28] A number of violent youth crimes, broadly and visibly reported, added to the volatile mix that lacked only a final spark.[29] Then, in Liverpool in 1993, while being filmed by a mall security camera, two 10-year-old boys lured 2-year-old James Bulger away from his mother in a shopping center.[30] The boys took the toddler to a secluded area, used an iron bar and bricks to torture and brutally murder the child, and left his body on railroad tracks to be sliced in half. At the time, England's MACR was 10 years of age, and the *doli incapax* presumption of non-responsibility between 10 and 14 was rebutted based on the boys' discernment of right from wrong. A trial jury found both children guilty, and the presiding judge sentenced them to detention for an indeterminate period, which the Home Secretary held discretion to specify.

The case prompted unprecedented public hysteria. During the trial, hostile crowds awaited the defendants' arrival to the courthouse, and protesters attempted to attack the vehicle carrying the boys. The boys themselves continued in a state of psychological and emotional shock, yet were denied therapeutic treatment until after the trial (i.e., for approximately eight months) for fear of altering potential evidence.[31] Despite some modifications of the formal adult court setting and procedures, the boys were unable to effectively participate or even follow the trial. Following their conviction, the judge allowed only the names of the boys to be published, but the next day tabloids throughout the country nonetheless published their names, photographs, and other details about their lives. The Bulger family started a public campaign seeking sentences of life imprisonment for the two boys, and submitted a petition with over 275,000 signatures to that effect. Even beyond the tabloid press, the mass media demonized the boys and leveled "a kind of moral condemnation that is usually reserved for the enemy in times of war."[32] In the end, the boys were recommended to serve at least eight years in a secure juvenile jail, and have since been released with new identities.

Extensive commentary has focused on the dynamics of the media in particular and the broad "moral panic" surrounding and following the Bulger case. This

---

26 In general, see Cipriani, *supra* note 1.

27 Freeman, Michael, *The Moral Status of Children: Essays on the Rights of the Child*, The Hague, Kluwer Law International, 1997.

28 Sparks, Richard, et al., "Children talking about justice and punishment," 8 *International Journal of Children's Rights* 191, 2000.

29 Freeman, *supra* note 79.

30 European Court of Human Rights, *Case of T. v. the United Kingdom: Judgment*, Strasbourg, 1999.

31 Freeman, *supra* note 79.

32 King, Michael, "The James Bulger Murder Trial: Moral Dilemmas, and Social Solutions," 3 *International Journal of Children's Rights* 167, 1995, at 172.

is in line with commentary since the late 1970s on the disconnect between successive moral panics over youth crime and actual levels of youth crime.[33] Both the mass media and the justice system fueled the panic by paring down the case to simplified elements, and by presenting a dramatic and seemingly complete account with "straightforward moral messages" ready for mass consumption.[34] The two boys convicted in the Bulger case became the incarnation of evil and brutal children—to which other stereotypes of good and innocent children were the foil. This narrative carried forward the larger public fears about the country's path and what was seen as the crumbling of public safety.[35] At the same time, it excluded any serious discussion about the causes of crime, possible effects of social and economic inequality and injustice, or societies' responsibility for providing appropriate children's services.[36] Instead, once the MACR allowed the case to be branded as a criminal matter, these larger perspectives faded away and the blame and scapegoating carried forth.[37] As such, the case illustrates many of the inherent weaknesses of the justice approach as explored in Chapter 1.

Politicians picked up on these images and narratives, and strategically exploited them in policy and political debates.[38] In large part due to the Bulger case, youth crime and punishment became a salient battleground between the Conservative and Labour parties through the 1990s, with each side escalating its rhetoric and policy proposals.[39] There was a showdown over which party could win the public's confidence that it could reinstate order in the midst of chaos, and be tougher on dangerous children.[40] The shadow Home Secretary at the time, Tony Blair, thus developed his justice agenda by the time Labour assumed power in 1997.[41] In

---

[33] Ruddick, Susan, "Abnormal, the 'New Normal,' and Destabilizing Discourses of Rights," 18 *Public Culture* 53, 2006.

[34] Hay, Colin, "Mobilization Through Interpretation: James Bulger, Juvenile Crime and the Construction of a Moral Panic," 4 *Social and Legal Studies* 197, 1995; and King, *supra* note 84, at 178.

[35] Davis, Howard, and Marc Bourhill, "'Crisis': The Demonization of Children and Young People," in Scraton, Phil, ed., *'Childhood' in 'Crisis'?*, London, University College London Press, 1997.

[36] Respectively, Freeman, *supra* note 79; Asquith, Stewart, "When Children Kill Children: The Search for Justice," 3 *Childhood* 99, Feb 1996; and Davis and Bourhill, *supra* note 87.

[37] Fionda, Julia, "Youth and Justice," in Fionda, Julia, ed., *Legal Concepts of Childhood*, Oxford, Hart Publishing, 2001.

[38] Franklin, Bob, "Children's rights and media wrongs: Changing representations of children and the developing rights agenda," in Franklin, Bob, ed., *The New Handbook of Children's Rights: Comparative Policy and Practice*, London, Routledge, 2002; and King, Michael, "The James Bulger Murder Trial: Moral Dilemmas, and Social Solutions," 3 *International Journal of Children's Rights* 167, 1995.

[39] Sparks et al., *supra* note 80.

[40] Freeman, *supra* note 79.

[41] Sparks et al., *supra* note 80.

1998, the Crime and Disorder Act passed, and as the Labour government sought, it eliminated outright the *doli incapax* presumption. The fallout continues and is difficult to understate, even 15 years after James Bulger's murder, as captured in Prime Minister Gordon Brown's citation of juvenile delinquency as a key priority for his government.[42]

More generally, the Bulger case demonstrates how a single incident can provoke truly dramatic shifts in the ways societies are willing to think about children and respond to them. Almost 700 years after the inception of *doli incapax* in England, but not even five years after the Bulger case, the doctrine was discarded.

The case even sparked shock and debate around the world, particularly in Europe and common law countries. At the time, popular support surged in several European countries to lower national MACRs. Both Uganda and Ghana, respectively in 1996 and 1998, increased their MACRs and abrogated their *doli incapax* provisions, in part to avoid the problems that arose in England. The Bulger case and domestic youth crime also led to related proposals in Australia, which continue to resurface on the public agenda.[43] Even in 2008, the case continues to resonate strongly; the press focused almost exclusively on the Bulger case and the MACR in covering parliamentary debate on South Africa's Child Justice Bill.

The United States of America

Although there are some similarities to the United Kingdom, the scenario in the United States brings other paradoxes and insights for the MACR, including a debate that has remained curiously and uniquely abandoned in the past.[44] Both historically and today, the United States is widely influential in juvenile justice and youth crime policy, and it is arguably the single most widely-studied national context. Regardless, in contrast to every other country in the world with substantive juvenile justice debates, international children's rights remain new concepts, and there is no national discussion whatsoever about the MACR. Ironically, such reasons make the United States an especially important case study for understanding how the MACR can come to be sidelined with extreme implications for children.

In the United States, the respective states and the District of Columbia legislate and operate their own juvenile justice systems. As seen in Table 5.1, only 15 states have established MACRs, which range from 6 to 10 years and thus fall uniformly short of the emerging international standard of a minimum of 12 years. In the remaining states,

---

42 Hinsliff, Gaby, "Children's tsar seeks to ban sonic weapon used on hoodies," *Observer*, 10 Feb 2008.

43 Crofts, Thomas, "Doli Incapax: Why Children Deserve its Protection," 10 *Murdoch University Electronic Journal of Law*, no. 3, 2003. "NSW Opposition wants criminal responsibility lowered to 10," *ABC News Online*, 2 Mar 2007. Urbas, Gregor, "The Age of Criminal Responsibility," *Trends & Issues in Crime and Criminal Justice* 181, Australian Institute of Criminology, November 2000.

44 In general, see Cipriani, *supra* note 1.

and under the very limited federal juvenile justice jurisdiction, there is no minimum age for adjudicating child delinquents. It appears that this situation is a historical remnant of the original justifications and stated purposes of early juvenile justice systems. As described in Chapter 1, since the intention of the welfare approach was treatment instead of punishment, it would have been unreasonable to impose a lower age cut-off for presumed assistance to children. Indeed, this logic has generally led states to abrogate, either legislatively or by judicial decision, the availability of the common law *doli incapax* presumption of non-responsibility in juvenile courts.[45] The growth in the range of clearly punitive and retributive sanctions over time—and historic Supreme Court decisions on children's procedural rights—has failed to trigger any reconsideration of the role for MACRs.

Realistically, in the contemporary United States discourse there may simply be very little space for the MACR. The debate on age and children has typically been dominated by delinquency sensationalism and fear, and by political maneuvering on the age upon which children may enter the adult criminal justice system. After essentially constant levels through most of the 1980s, arrest rates for violent youth crimes made unparalleled increases from 1989 through 1993, and then followed a long decline from 1994 through at least 2003 to levels lower than the 1980s.[46] Regardless, the brief years of violent crime increases were sufficient to trigger an unprecedented public obsession through the 1990s, consistently fueled by the mass media.[47] Sensationalist publicity increased exponentially on school violence and shootings, so-called "superpredator" youth, and brutal acts committed by the very young.

This level of imagery and vitriol sabotaged discussions on juvenile justice. For example, a 1994 study on the coverage of children in national news media, in news broadcasts and selected national newspapers, showed that almost half of all television news coverage and roughly 40 per cent of newspaper articles on children were about violence and crime.[48] Child poverty and welfare were covered

---

45 See Carter, Andrew M., "Age Matters: The Case for a Constitutionalized Infancy Defense," 54 *Kansas Law Review* 687, 2006; and Thomas, Tim A., *Annotation: Defense of Infancy in Juvenile Delinquency Proceedings*, 83 ALR4th 1135, 1991 and August 2002 Supplement. Criminal proceedings were considered a wholly separate matter, however, and common law rules on children's criminal responsibility (i.e., an MACR of 7 years and *doli incapax* presumption between 7 and 14 years) generally continued to apply in adult criminal courts both before and after the emergence of distinct juvenile justice systems. In fact, jurisprudence in approximately 20 states still holds the *doli incapax* presumption available in adult criminal courts, although case law is dated and largely ignored.

46 Snyder, Howard N., and Melissa Sickmund, *Juvenile Offenders and Victims: 2006 National Report*, Washington, United States Department of Justice, Office of Juvenile Justice and Delinquency Prevention, 2006.

47 Dorfman, Lori, and Vincent Schiraldi, *Off Balance: Youth, Race & Crime In The News*, Washington, Justice Policy Institute, 2001.

48 Shepherd, Jr., Robert E., "Film at Eleven: The News Media and Juvenile Crime," 18 *Quinnipiac Law Review* 687, 1999.

in approximately 4 per cent of television and newspaper reports on children, with limited discussion of policy options and strategies on youth issues. The public's knowledge base was clearly affected, especially since most people have little or no personal knowledge or experience of juvenile crime, and form their opinions based solely on media coverage.[49] Despite ten years of continuously falling violent youth crime rates, and the lowest juvenile crime rate in over 25 years, a national opinion poll showed that more than 90 per cent of the public still believed that the percentage of teenagers who commit violent crimes had increased or stayed the same over the previous ten years.[50]

With such an outlook on juvenile justice, every state but Nebraska amended its laws between 1992 and 1999 to make it easier to prosecute children as adults, prompting steep increases in the number of children prosecuted as adults.[51] Already by 1996, approximately 20–25 per cent of all youth offenders—between 210,000 and 260,000 children—were prosecuted in adult criminal courts annually.[52] Only very recently have states begun to reconsider these policies, in light of the overwhelming evidence of negative and criminogenic effects of adult trials and sentencing of children.[53]

In addition, the resultant overlaps between MACRs and adult court trials are extensive. In 18 states where there is no MACR applicable in juvenile courts, there is no minimum age limit for responsibility in adult courts either.[54] Under various stipulations, children in these states are subject to prosecution as adults at any age. Moreover, five of these 18 states actually mandate adult prosecution for children of all ages charged with certain offenses.[55]

These radical legal developments reflect an intensive episode in redefining the meaning and boundaries of childhood. They are also a major rethinking of the institutions built around childhood, and a notable distraction from the underlying

---

49 Dorfman and Schiraldi, *supra* note 99.

50 Guzman, Lina, et al., "How Children Are Doing: The Mismatch between Public Perception and Statistical Reality," *Child Trends Research Brief*, Washington, Child Trends, July 2003.

51 Griffin, Patrick, "National Overviews," *State Juvenile Justice Profiles*, Pittsburgh, National Center for Juvenile Justice, 2000; Shook, Jeffrey J., "Contesting Childhood in the US Justice System: The transfer of juveniles to adult criminal court," 12 *Childhood* 461, 2005.

52 Bishop, Donna M., "Juvenile Offenders in the Adult Criminal Justice System," 27 *Crime and Justice* 81, 2000.

53 Campaign for Youth Justice, *The Consequences Aren't Minor: The Impact of Trying Youth As Adults and Strategies for Reform*, Washington, 2007.

54 Alaska, Delaware, District of Columbia, Florida, Georgia, Hawaii, Idaho, Indiana, Maine, Nebraska, Nevada, Oklahoma, Oregon, Pennsylvania, Rhode Island, South Carolina, Tennessee, and West Virginia. See Table 5.1 and Griffin, Patrick, "Transfer Provisions," *State Juvenile Justice Profiles*, Pittsburgh, National Center for Juvenile Justice, 2006.

55 Delaware, Florida, Indiana, Nevada, and Pennsylvania. See Table 5.1 and Griffin, *supra* note 106.

social and economic policies that affect youth.[56] Schools—part of the so-called school to prison pipeline—now host within their walls degrading treatment, abusive disciplinary measures, police intervention in disciplinary measures, and even arrest and excessive police use of force.[57] Targeted children are intentionally counseled to leave, suspended, transferred, or expelled out of school. Targeting also includes the family; it is now quite common for states to hold parents criminally liable for their children's illegal acts.[58] This vast expansion of the reach of criminal law transgresses common law standards, and has been explicitly discouraged for other countries by the Committee on the Rights of the Child.[59]

Patterns Repeated Around the Globe

Many aspects of the dynamics in the United Kingdom and the United States have played a direct role in MACR debates worldwide. In some, disproportionate fear over youth crime has blocked debate on MACRs and scaled back the age limit increases that were originally envisioned. Switzerland's MACR increase, from the former 7 years to possibly as high as 12, 14, or 16 years, was stopped at 10 years over concerns about serious crime by young children and how to respond to it.[60] Reform efforts have been opposed or scaled back due to similar resistance in countries such as New Zealand, Bangladesh, and Uruguay. In other countries, public opinion has created pressure for lowering the MACR. Fears about violent juvenile crime led to calls in Finland to reduce the MACR, as well as significant discussions to this effect, and the Netherlands and Saint Lucia have seen similar tensions.[61] In some Latin American countries, since the establishment of respective

---

56   Shook, Jeffrey J., "Contesting Childhood in the US Justice System: The transfer of juveniles to adult criminal court," 12 *Childhood* 461, 2005.

57   See, inter alia, Christle, Christine A., et al., "Breaking the School to Prison Pipeline: Identifying School Risk and Protective Factors for Youth Delinquency," 13 *Exceptionality* 69, 2005; and Sullivan, Elizabeth, *Deprived of Dignity: Degrading Treatment and Abusive Discipline in New York City & Los Angeles Public Schools*, New York, National Economic and Social Rights Initiative, 2007.

58   Brank, Eve M., et al., "Parental Responsibility Statutes: An Organization and Policy Implications," 7 *Journal of Law & Family Studies* 1, 2005.

59   See Brank et al., *ibid.*; Committee on the Rights of the Child, *General Comment No. 10: Children's rights in juvenile justice*, CRC/C/GC/10, 25 Apr 2007, pars. 8 and 23g; Nicholas, Deborah A., "Parental Liability for Youth Violence: The Contrast Between Moral Responsibilities and Legal Obligations," 53 *Rutgers Law Review* 215, 2000.

60   Zermatten, Jean, *The Swiss Federal Statute on Juvenile Criminal Law*, presented at the Conference of the European Society of Criminology, Amsterdam, August 25–28, 2004.

61   Marttunen, Matti, "Finland: The Basis of Finnish Juvenile Criminal Justice," 75 *International Review of Penal Law (Revue internationale de droit pénal)* 315, 2004. Meuwese, Stan, ed., *KIDS BEHIND BARS: A study on children in conflict with the law*, Amsterdam, Defence for Children International The Netherlands, 2003. Committee on the Rights of the Child, *Compte rendu analytique de la 1026e séance*, CRC/C/SR.1026, 24 May 2005.

post-*situación irregular* juvenile justice systems and MACRs, public hostility has been common and has led to proposals for MACR decreases.[62]

Public pressures also threatened MACR decreases in Germany and Canada, which had seen movements to increase MACRs, as discussed above in this chapter. In Germany, by the 1990s, rising youth crime rates led to some politicians' calls to lower the MACR from 14 to 12.[63] More recently, after a Greek teenager and a young Turkish adult brutally attacked a German senior citizen in the Munich subway, one state governor began to vigorously campaign for state parliamentary elections around tough-on-crime themes. In particular, he proposed a lower MACR of 12 years strictly applicable to immigrant children, one of several discriminatory campaign proposals that were generally supported by Chancellor Angela Merkel.[64]

Canada saw a major shift of thinking during the decade after its 1984 MACR increase from 7 to 12.[65] General misconceptions and public anger about the causes, rates, and supposedly lenient responses to youth crime—fueled by the media— were linked to some 75 per cent of the public supporting a subsequent decrease in the MACR.[66] The Department of Justice lobbied to decrease the MACR from 12 to 10 years in a 2002 juvenile justice act, based largely on the belief that there was no effective way to address crime by young children, but this proposal ultimately failed.

Among countries that have decreased their MACRs, Japan follows the United Kingdom and the United States most closely with May 2007 reforms that effectively lowered the MACR of 14 to 11. To restore their image after negative coverage of 1990s police scandals, law enforcement officials increasingly reported relatively minor offenses.[67] Official crime rates soared, which in turn prompted broad malaise over the supposed crumbling of public safety. Surveys in 1998 and 2004 showed a doubling of the proportion of the public that thought crime was worsening, even though Japan has continued to have a low violent crime rate, and is consistently

---

62 For example, Brazil, Honduras, and Nicaragua.

63 Kerner, Hans-Juergen, "Crime Prevention, Prospects and Problems: The Case of Effective Institutional Versus Community-Based Treatment Programmes for Prevention of Recidivism Among Youthful Offenders," in UN Asia and Far East Institute for the Prevention of Crime and the Treatment of Offenders, 68 *Resource Material Series* 35, Tokyo, 2006.

64 "German coalition shaky over juvenile crime row," *EuroNews*, 15 Jan 2008. Kulish, Nicholas, "Attack Jolts Germany Into Fray on Immigrant Crime," *New York Times*, 14 Jan 2008.

65 See, inter alia, Covell, Katherine, and R. Brian Howe, "Public attitudes and juvenile justice in Canada," 4 *International Journal of Children's Rights* 345, 1996.

66 Roberts, Julian V., "Public Opinion and Juvenile Justice," in Tonry, Michael, and Anthony N. Doob, eds, *Youth Crime and Youth Justice: Comparative and Cross-National Perspectives*, Chicago, University of Chicago Press, 2004.

67 Hamaia, Koichi, and Thomas Ellis, "Crime and criminal justice in modern Japan: From re-integrative shaming to popular punitivism," 34 *International Journal of the Sociology of Law* 157, 2006.

one of the most crime-free industrialized countries. With this backdrop, the media seized upon a statistically isolated series of extremely violent crimes by children in the early 2000s, resorting to sensationalist coverage, shocking headlines, and partial and inaccurate reporting.[68] This upended the public's view of children and distorted the reality of youth crime. In a country of approximately 127 million people, children younger than the former MACR of 14 years committed roughly two murders per year through the 1990s, 10 murders in 2001, and between three and six per year since 2001.[69]

The sensationalism–fear chain reaction continued with the Japanese public's increasing support for punitive control measures and sanctions.[70] Crime and public safety became more central politically than they had been in decades, and political pressure translated into legal and policy reform.[71] Japan first lowered its age of penal majority—the lowest age for adult criminal court trial—from 16 to 14 in 2001. In seeking further reform, one Justice Minister specifically identified juvenile crime and international terrorism, in the same breath, as great concerns under the Prime Minister's get-tough security agenda.[72] In pushing this agenda ahead, the government's initial draft legislation set an effective MACR of 0.[73] In the end, enacted reforms set an effective MACR of 11 years by allowing commitment of children from that age to Juvenile Training Schools, supervised by the Ministry of Justice Correction Bureau.

France has witnessed similar pressures challenging the welfare precepts of its juvenile justice system, beginning with a 1990s context of conservative politics, racial tensions, and apprehensions about immigrant youths.[74] Increasing child crime rates helped cement the view that juvenile crime was more dangerous than ever before. Pressure for harsher juvenile justice led to amendments, enacted in a 1996 emergency measure, that encouraged faster and more explicit punishment. Further reform in 2002 continued this trend, by describing all children with discernment as penally responsible—thus returning to standards in force from 1791 through 1912—and by creating a new class of tougher educative sanctions.[75]

---

68 Arudou, Debito, "Upping the fear factor," *The Japan Times*, 20 Feb 2007.

69 Kinoshita, Tsukasa, "Juvenile Law change raises questions; Reform or punishment – how young is too young to send kids to reformatories?," *The Daily Yomiuri*, 21 Apr 2007.

70 Hamaia and Ellis, *supra* note 119. See also Foljanty-Jost, Gesine, ed., *Juvenile Delinquency in Japan: Reconsidering the "Crisis,"* Leiden, Brill, 2003.

71 Arudou, *supra* note 120; and Hamaia and Ellis, *supra* note 119.

72 Ito, Masami, "Justice chief's mandate: make Japan safe, refugee-friendly," *The Japan Times*, 2 Oct 2004.

73 "Lawmakers eye lowering age for sending juveniles to reformatory to 12," *Kyodo News Service*, 17 Apr 2007.

74 Peeler, Calvin, "Always a Victim and Never a Criminal: Juvenile Delinquency in France," 22 *North Carolina Journal of International Law and Commercial Regulation* 875, 1997.

75 Bongert, Yvonne, "Délinquance juvénile et responsabilité pénale du mineur au XVIIIe siècle," in Abbiateci, André, et al., *Crimes et criminalité en France sous l'Ancien*

Subsequently, as one of his main policy objectives, then-Interior Minister Nicolas Sarkozy wielded shocking statistics to push through more punitive measures still.[76] Upon assuming office, President Sarkozy acted quickly on one of his key campaign promises and lobbied for an "anti-crime" bill with adult criminal sentences for some children.[77]

Georgia, another country that has reduced its MACR, has struggled to address continuing social transitions; with youth crime, this includes much fear, angst, and clearly retributive reactions. Until 1999, the MACR of 14 years only applied in cases of certain relatively serious offenses, while criminal responsibility began at 16 years for all other offenses. In 1999, as a get-tough measure, the age limit of 14 years began to apply in all cases, and convictions of 14- and 15-year-olds have steadily increased since then.[78] Meanwhile, inflammatory media reports about the murders of several teenagers prompted wide popular unease about youth crime, and led to growing support for an MACR decrease from 14 to 12 years.[79] Juvenile justice policy increasingly became one of zero-tolerance and over-reliance on the deprivation of liberty. In schools, reminiscent of the United States, the Ministry of Education was rolling out metal detectors, security video cameras, and police authority to enter and conduct student searches. In terms of the proposal to decrease the MACR, perhaps the most commonly-cited justification was that 12- and 13-year-olds "were acting as 'Kingpins' and were involved in significant amounts of crime and boasting of their impunity," yet this was supported only by anecdotal evidence and not born out by crime statistics.[80] In its explanatory note to the new

---

Régime: 17e-18e siècles, Paris, Librairie Armand Colin, 1971. Pradel, Jean, "Quelques observations sur le statut pénal du mineur en France depuis la loi No 2002–1138 du 9 septembre 2002," 56 *Revue internationale de droit comparé* 187, 2004.

76 *Loi 2007–297 du 5 Mar 07 relative a la prévention de la délinquance*. Associated Press, "French Interior Minister says youth delinquency has soared 80 percent in 10 years," *International Herald Tribune*, 13 Sept 2006.

77 Associated Press, "Tougher punishments for repeat offenders, including children," *International Herald Tribune*, 9 Jul 2007.

78 Hamilton, Carolyn, *Analysis of the Juvenile Justice System in Georgia*, Tbilisi, UNICEF Georgia, 2007. World Organisation Against Torture, *Violence Against Children in Georgia: An Alternative Report to the UN Committee on the Rights of the Child on the implementation of the Convention on the Rights of the Child: 47th session, January 2008*, Geneva and Tbilisi, 2007.

79 Rimple, Paul, "Georgia Grapples with Rising Teenage Crime," www.eurasianet.org, 19 Jun 2007.

80 Hamilton, *supra* note 130, at 47. Georgia has claimed that incomplete facilities arrangements will prevent the amendments from entering into force for the foreseeable future, and that its Ministry of Justice supports discussions in Parliament to nullify the amendments completely. Committee on the Rights of the Child, *Written Replies by the Government of Georgia to the List of Issues Prepared by the Committee on the Rights of the Child in Connection with the Consideration of the Third Periodic Report of Georgia*, CRC/C/GEO/Q/3/Add.1, 20 May 2008, par. 48. Georgia, *Additional Information on the*

law, which was intended to enter into force in 2008 and lower the MACR to 12 for specified serious offenses, the government described the change as a tool to make children more accountable for their actions and to make them "fear punishment."[81] Slovakia recently lowered its MACR from 15 to 14 through a similar series of pressures and responses, while the Czech Republic seems poised to do the same with the additional element of strong racist and discriminatory overtones.[82]

Treading Carefully in Amending MACRs

The foregoing survey of national debates is aimed at exploring the major contemporary influences in redefining childhood under the MACR. Clearly, this is one particularly contentious point in the larger, constant redefining of childhood's boundaries, and of societies' regulation, protection, and blaming of children. In recent years, the most powerful influence internationally is undoubtedly the CRC reporting process, which is related to nearly 65 MACR increases or proposed increases. Yet behind this more visible MACR trend lies the explosive mix in many countries of isolated violent crimes by young children, sensationalist media coverage, public misperceptions about youth crime, and populist maneuvering that seizes upon fears for political gain. The point of this review is not to downplay juvenile crime, in the consequences of individual acts or at the societal level, nor to condemn the media and politicians. On the contrary, public safety is undeniably important, as acknowledged by international juvenile justice standards.[83] Public opinion, mass media information and images, and political compromises are all generally legitimate pressures and dynamics in national contexts.[84]

The long-term viability of children's rights in juvenile justice depends upon coming to terms with public opinion; actual and perceived youth crime; the media; and political realities. In the absence of common ground, threats emerge for distorted debates, retributive tendencies, and the curtailing of children's procedural and substantive rights in the guise of safety and justice. Such policies go far beyond MACR amendments, and are indeed problematic in causing tangible harm to the broader children's rights agenda.[85]

Implementation of the Convention on the Rights of the Child in Respect of the Third Periodic Report of Georgia, circa May 2008.

81 Human Rights Watch, *Georgia: Lowering the Age of Criminal Responsibility Flouts International Standards*, New York, 11 Jun 2007.

82 ČTK, "Extremist National Guard to watch Karlovy Vary school," *Prague Daily Monitor*, 24 Jun 2008. O'Nions, Helen, "A litmus test for civil society," *Guardian Unlimited*, 31 July 2002.

83 For example, Beijing Rules, Rule 17 and Commentary.

84 See, e.g., CRC Art. 17, and UN Standard Minimum Rules for Non-Custodial Measures, Rule 18.3.

85 Hamilton, Carolyn, and Rachel Harvey, "The Role of Public Opinion in the Implementation of International Juvenile Justice Standards," 11 *International Journal of Children's Rights* 369, 2004.

The role of responsible and ethical journalism in presenting images of children is one of the clear implications of this review.[86] Likewise, there is a role for the state to develop law and policy in good faith, which includes the state's ultimate responsibility for ensuring implementation of children's rights. Political exploitation of youth crime is not reconcilable with this responsibility, despite its practice at the highest levels of government in countries such as France, Japan, and the United Kingdom. Children's rights implementation is also facilitated through an increasingly informed and engaged populace, including through human rights and children's rights education, as well as through stable democratic institutions and decision-making. Governments have leading roles in all of these areas, with clear mandates for civil society, children's rights organizations, and other sectors.[87]

Other implications include lessons for MACR reform efforts in coming to terms with such dynamics. As explored in Chapter 2, the children's rights framework offers a richer understanding of children than welfare–justice and victim–perpetrator bifurcations. Where advocates base their strategy on children-as-victim and/or children-as-innocent discourses in MACR reform, there is a failure to faithfully imagine and convey the meaning of rights-based justice. Such strategy also overlooks the trap into which it unintentionally leads. National experiences repeatedly suggest that it is easy to depict MACR increases as going lightly on children, sometimes accurately in terms of supporters' intentions. A single violent youth crime is sufficient to smash victim–perpetrator divisions, and children-as-victims narratives then capitulate quickly to children-as-perpetrator panics. These bring real consequences for individual children, and the backlash undercuts larger fronts in the children's rights agenda. That broader agenda includes fostering an enduring social value on treating all children fairly and with dignity, and creating institutions that consistently do so. Some narrow MACR reforms may skew the debate and distract attention and pressure away from necessary system reforms.

Advocates obviously need to be savvy about media influence, public opinion, and political decision-making pressure points, yet these are means to an end—effective implementation of rights for all children—and the means must be consistent with the ends. This principle does not envisage, for example, further manipulation of imagery about children supposedly for their own benefit, such as in the Philippines' discernment study mentioned above. One alternative, pursuant to arguments laid out in Chapter 2, is to pair reform with comprehensive policies for responding to younger children that provide some appropriate form of accountability.[88] An effective range of measures preempts claims that children are somehow unaccountable, helps defuse the threat of children-as-perpetrator panics, and fully respects international standards.

---

86 Tobin, John, "Partners worth courting: The relationship between the media and the Convention on the Rights of the Child," 12 *International Journal of Children's Rights* 139, 2004.

87 See also Hamilton and Harvey, *supra* note 137.

88 See also Chapter 6 on responses to children younger than MACRs.

The MACR as a General Principle of International Law

As sought in Japan and achieved in France, some campaigns to toughen juvenile justice attempt not only to decrease MACRs, but to eliminate them altogether. In the United States, roughly two-thirds of the states do not have MACRs due in part to the overwhelming dynamics of retributive juvenile justice. These examples challenge the various moral and legal mandates for creating MACRs described in previous chapters, especially those of regional and international law instruments described in Chapter 3. Moreover, they raise the question whether or not countries face any additional requirements—in particular beyond treaty law obligations—to establish respective MACRs.

Chapter 3 also documents the first claim that a general principle of international law exists around the MACR, which arose during the drafting of Additional Protocol I to the Geneva Conventions. General principles of international law are a binding source of international law—that is, giving rise to international legal obligations that are independent from treaty law.[89] The recognition or confirmation of such a principle regarding MACRs would thus be no minor matter. At the time of Additional Protocol I drafting, participants agreed on the existence of a general principle that no person could be convicted of a criminal offense if, at the time of the offense, he or she was unable to understand the consequences of his or her act. Due to disagreements on the lowest age for potential criminal responsibility, application of the principle was deferred to respective national law, and the matter has largely been forgotten ever since.

The worldwide MACR information presented in this study permits a fresh appraisal of the existence of a relevant general principle of international law. General principles or rules of international law are, above all else, "expressions of national legal systems" that can be derived from the general principles common to the world's major legal systems.[90] Roughly speaking, they are deemed to have been accepted by countries as rules of international law because they are derived directly from legal systems around the world.[91] In fact, the best way to determine whether a certain fundamental principle of justice meets the threshold of a general principle of international law is by its existence in the national laws of United Nations Member States.[92] The inductive method of research is used to identify "the existence of a legal principle," and the more a given principle is reiterated, the more deference it deserves.[93] The focus is on the sameness of the legal principle or precept that underlies norms across countries.

---

89 Bassiouni, M. Cherif, "A Functional Approach to 'General Principles of International Law'," 11 *Michigan Journal of International Law* 768, Spring 1990; and "General principle of law," *Black's Law Dictionary*, 7th ed., 1999.

90 Bassiouni, *ibid.*, at 768.

91 Kennel, John R., "International Law," 48 *Corpus Juris Secundum* §2, June 2007.

92 Bassiouni, *supra* note 141.

93 *Ibid.*, at 809.

As seen most comprehensively in Annex 2, and as discussed above in this chapter, nearly every country in the world has established an MACR. Many shades of meaning are discernible behind these ages, including the certainty of law, jurisdictional concerns, children's capacity to bear criminal responsibility, and youth policy. However, all of these interests lead to one broad legal reason for establishing MACRs in the law: children below some specified, fixed age limit should never be held criminally responsible for their actions. Chapter 4 illustrates how this common principle stems from respective historical developments in all of the major legal families, and how the sole exception of puberty in Islamic law is reconcilable with it. Furthermore, as explained in this chapter and identified country-by-country, the principle includes the notion that children younger than the stipulated age limit shall not face punishments or sanctions implying criminal responsibility or procedures. The nearly universal acceptance of this general criminal law principle would seem to raise it to the status of a general principle of international law.

There are, in fact, only eight countries that either do not claim to have an MACR in law or that effectively acknowledge not having one.[94] The other 15 countries whose MACRs are classified as 0 or as puberty in this study still cite or describe related statutory age limits as their MACRs.[95] In other words, they formally support the underlying legal principle and refer to relevant norms, but empirical research either rebuts these norms as effective MACRs or identifies further provisions that assign criminal responsibility for certain offenses from puberty or without age restrictions. In this sense, the present study is concerned with children's criminal responsibility both in law and in practice. General principles, in contrast, are based upon the empirical evidence of subscription to the principle at hand—vis-à-vis the presence of relevant norms—leaving aside arguments over its application or the extent to which it is actually protected in practice.[96] The fact that countries still publicly and formally claim to have MACRs in law, and that they cite statutes and age limits to that effect, is evidence of their subscription to the principle despite inconsistencies or questionable practices.

Although the CRC has greatly influenced MACR trends, it is not the case that current MACRs only reflect state efforts to comply with CRC provisions.[97]

---

94 Cambodia (currently in the process of establishing an MACR), Democratic Republic of the Congo, France, Mauritius, Nauru, Poland, Somalia, and the United States of America. See Annex 2 as well as respective documents related to consideration by the Committee on the Rights of the Child.

95 See respective footnotes in Table 5.1 for Bahrain, Comoros, Cuba, Luxembourg, Malaysia, Maldives, Marshall Islands, Micronesia, Mozambique, Nepal, Nigeria, Pakistan, Saudi Arabia, Solomon Islands, and Sudan.

96 See Bassiouni, M. Cherif, "Human Rights in the Context of Criminal Justice: Identifying International Procedural Protections and Equivalent Protections in National Constitutions," 3 *Duke Journal of Comparative & International Law* 235, 1993; and Bassiouni, *supra* note 141.

97 See related discussions in Happold, Matthew, *Child Soldiers in International Law*, Manchester, Manchester University Press, 2005.

As noted above, this study counts 40 countries that have established or increased MACRs since the CRC's adoption in 1989, again from the perspective of both law and practice; 19 of these were MACR increases. Eighteen were Latin American countries that abandoned the *situación irregular* doctrine and codified substantive MACR provisions. Similarly, Portugal is counted as a country with a welfare juvenile justice approach that in the past appears not to have had any effective lower age limit for punitive sanctions, and that created a clear juvenile justice delinquency jurisdiction and MACR in 1999. In the past, this set of countries consistently claimed to have had MACRs in their national laws—which were actually minimum ages of penal majority in respective penal codes. Their claims to subscribe to the principle of the MACR were continuous while their enforcement faltered. Since the CRC's adoption, only Bhutan and Indonesia appear to have supported the precept behind the MACR for the first time and codified their first MACRs. In effect, a general principle of international law behind MACRs seems to predate the CRC.

However, the variations, range, and distribution of MACR provisions worldwide generally prevent further conclusions about such a general principle of international law. It does not seem possible to make any claims as such in terms of a mandatory age level, secondary age limits for other offenses, or *doli incapax* and related individual assessments of children's potential responsibility. At most, it may correctly be argued—as broadly reflected across rationales for MACRs worldwide—that countries must not set their MACRs at levels where children cannot normatively be expected to understand the consequences of their actions.[98] As discussed in this study, however, this is a highly ambiguous standard that is malleable across divergent constructions of childhood. As suggested in Chapters 2 and 6, future research and legal developments around children's right to effective participation at trial could conceivably lead to a more objective basis.

In the end, the current analysis maintains that there exists a binding general rule of international law that all countries must establish by law an age limit before which children, at the time of their acts, can never be held criminally responsible or face punitive sanctions. This rule brings legal obligations for all countries regardless of treaty law commitments. Depending on the legal system, it may be argued directly in domestic, regional, and/or international courts. It is especially relevant for the 23 countries noted in this study as having no MACR or no effective MACR. In particular, the jurisprudence of the European Court of Human Rights suggests that it is a likely forum for consideration of this apparent general principle.

Conclusion

This chapter documents the wide variety and characteristics of MACRs around the world. Among the limitations and interpretive pitfalls that this presentation

---

98   *Ibid.*

necessarily entails, the practical meaning of criminal responsibility is particularly troublesome. As detailed in Chapter 3, the Committee on the Rights of the Child has set out a range of criteria that are useful as a basic standard in gauging what may be considered indicative of criminal responsibility. Where ambiguities remain, this chapter takes further cues from the work of Herbert Packer in seeking to assess, with as universal and objective a standard as possible, the different laws and practices under consideration.[99] Where sanctions and measures meet his definition of criminal punishment, they arguably signal the presence of effective criminal responsibility for children. Although many welfare-oriented juvenile justice systems and child protection systems claim to deliver only treatment in Packer's terms, both legal provisions and actual practices in numerous countries belie such claims. In classifying MACR provisions in this study, close attention is paid to such considerations, although at the same time significant deference is paid to respective governments' claims about their MACR provisions and practices.

Even though these criteria suggest that 23 countries do not have clear or effective MACRs, virtually all countries in the world either have an MACR or consistently claim to have one anyway.[100] The median age limit worldwide is 12 years, which coincides with the international standard that MACRs be set at 12 years or higher. However, in looking at major characteristics of MACRs across countries, it is clear that the strong majority fall short of international consensus standards. At the same time, there is a very strong and increasing trend since the 1989 adoption of the CRC to establish, increase, and to seek to increase respective MACRs—involving 63 countries, almost one-third of all United Nations Member States. This predominant contemporary trend in MACRs is due above all else to the CRC reporting process, including the constant attention of the Committee on the Rights of the Child.

A less conspicuous but critical trend lies in the dynamics of debates surrounding MACR reform. Media and political sensationalism have steamrolled the debates in numerous countries, thus blocking MACR reforms or lowering age limits to explicitly punish more children. Perhaps the greatest implications are for efforts to reform national MACRs on a children's rights basis. The volatility surrounding MACR amendments, with potentially extensive harm to children's rights in general, suggests serious drawbacks to stand-alone MACR reform efforts. Quick-fix age amendments, without deeper changes towards a culture of children's rights, seem especially vulnerable to equally quick unraveling in the face of crime and fear juggernauts.

The interdependent nature of human rights is a central concern, as the prospects for successful and sustainable MACR reform need to be weighed carefully in the overall balance of juvenile justice and children's rights implementation. In view of the leitmotif of public safety and retribution in many MACR debates, particular

---

99 Packer, *supra* note 4.

100 See Chapter 6 for further discussion on nominal MACRs that do not effectively bar criminal penalties.

attention needs to be paid to procedures and measures for children both younger and older than MACRs. These issues are doubly important because the mere impression that there is no system of responses to children in conflict with the law can create intense pressure to make juvenile justice more retributive and to lower MACRs.

Great care should be taken in advocacy strategies to avoid playing into simplistic binary notions of children as innocent or evil, or as victim or perpetrator. In carving out boundaries where children should largely be excused, other children will be forced inevitably and more decidedly into areas where they shall largely be punished. It also seems unrealistic to expect that contemporary societies will both extend the area of innocence until adulthood and at the same time treat all the children beneath it in truly appropriate ways. This does not appear to be a battle that can be won with age lines, or by forestalling a necessary coming to terms with juvenile crime. The children's rights perspective encourages a much richer appreciation of children and their development anyway—one that focuses on dignity, participation, reintegration, and full respect for all children. Reliance upon tactics and imagery contrary to this conception will carry societies further away from the values it fundamentally seeks to advance.

The rancor that is often generated around youth crime has even led to calls to annul MACRs entirely. However, beyond the various moral and legal obligations for MACRs described in this study, there exists compelling evidence of a general principle of international law that countries must establish respective MACRs. Regardless of treaty obligations, this rule would seem to mandate national MACRs in law, although disparity among ages across countries prevents any conclusions about the appropriate age level.

Chapter 6
Practical Implications and Challenges of MACR Implementation

Throughout the present study, different perspectives shed light on challenges related to minimum ages of criminal responsibility (MACRs), such as in the context of theoretical foundations, modern international interpretations, and historical influences. Some challenges, notably gender and socio-economic discrimination, are visibly recurrent. Others are similar to widespread problems in juvenile justice systems for children older than MACRs, but lie beyond the scope of this study where there is no direct relation to MACRs. This chapter, in particular, offers a closer examination of some of the major difficulties and implications of practical MACR implementation.

Beginning with the seemingly straightforward question of determining children's ages so as to apply MACRs, each of these difficulties proves to be surprisingly complex. Responses to children younger than MACRs who come into conflict with the law—for which there are effective, rights-compliant, and economical options—are generally not provided or are problematic. Low MACRs themselves may consistently threaten children's right to effective participation at trial. Other challenges include problems related to *doli incapax* and similar tests for criminal responsibility; the instrumental use of children younger than MACRs for criminal activities; and the limited applicability and implementation of MACR provisions. All told, one or more of the challenges highlighted in this chapter probably affects every country in the world.

No Proof of Age or Reliable Age Estimates

Any age limit becomes problematic when a child has no birth certificate or other proof of age, and this scenario materializes regularly in juvenile justice systems worldwide with respect to the MACR. This section offers an overview of the frequency and extent of such difficulties, the checkered legal and procedural solutions that countries have pursued, the broad limitations of scientific age estimates, and the extent of children's rights guidance in mediating the confusion.

Overall, it is fairly common for children not to have proof of their ages. In 2003, for example, some 36 per cent of births went unregistered around the world.[1]

---

1 UNICEF, *The "Rights" Start to Life: A Statistical Analysis of Birth Registration*, New York, 2005, at 3.

Percentages of unregistered births vary widely by region and country, for example reaching 63 per cent in South Asia, and almost 94 per cent in countries such as Tanzania. However, migration patterns make the issue relevant in every country. Furthermore, percentages of unregistered births in the past—regarding children near MACRs today, for example—were often higher.[2]

Juvenile justice systems face greater difficulties wherever more children in conflict with the law are missing proof of age, which often multiplies underlying socio-economic disadvantages. They approach age estimates in many different ways.[3] The most common scenario, apparently, is for judges to exercise full discretion in ascertaining children's ages, without any clear guidelines at all. Many countries provide limited procedural guidance and protections. For example, a 2006 law in the Philippines instructs courts to decide in children's favor when there is doubt over their ages, yet allows any person to contest the ages of children in conflict with the law.[4] Based more upon children's rights principles, recent juvenile justice reform across Latin America has also led to close regulation of age estimates and guarantees for procedural fairness.[5] Finally, some countries add confusion over the point in time at which a child's age should be considered: at the time of the alleged offense, arrest, trial, sentencing, or actual sentence.[6] The Committee on the Rights of the Child holds that age should be counted at the time of the alleged offense, as does standard criminal law practice worldwide.[7]

The practical outcomes for children without proof of age are often deplorable.[8] Most often, as in Bangladesh, judges simply guess children's ages by appearance—a fast route to discrimination in judicial processes.[9] Almost as

---

2 Compare to UNICEF Innocenti Research Centre, 'Birth Registration: Right from the Start', *Innocenti Digest* 9, Florence, 2002.

3 See, inter alia, Campos, Niza, "El 55% menores infractores carece de actas nacimiento," *Listín Diario*, digital edition, Santo Domingo, 24 April 2002. In general, see Cipriani, Don, *The Minimum Age of What? Criminal Responsibility, Juvenile Justice, and Children's Rights*, unpublished draft, Florence, UNICEF Innocenti Research Centre, 2002.

4 Juvenile Justice and Welfare Act of 2006, Sect. 7.

5 For example, Paraguay, *Código de la Niñez y la Adolescencia*, 2001, Art. 2.

6 See, e.g., Committee on the Rights of the Child, *Second periodic reports of States parties due in 2000: India*, CRC/C/93/Add.5, 16 Jul 2003, par. 1005; Warren, H.D., and C.P. Jhong, "Annotation: Age of Child at Time of Alleged Offense or Delinquency, or at Time of Legal Proceedings, as Criterion of Jurisdiction of Juvenile Court," 89 ALR2d 506, 2004; and Human Rights Watch, *Adults Before Their Time: Children in Saudi Arabia's Criminal Justice System*, New York, 2008.

7 See, e.g., Afghanistan, Juvenile Code, 2005, Art. 6(4); Belarus, Criminal Code, as of 1 May 1994, Art. 10; Cameroon, *Code Pénal*, Art. 80(5); Cuba, *Código Penal*, as of 2004, Art. 16(2); and Germany, *Jugendgerichtsgesetz* (Youth Court Act), 1953, §3.

8 In general, see Cipriani, *supra* note 3.

9 See, e.g., Uddin Siddiqui, Kamal, "The Age of Criminal Responsibility and Other Aspects of the Children Act, 1974," presented at the workshop *Raising the Age of Criminal Responsibility and Other Aspects of the Children Act, 1974*, Dhaka, 16 Jan 2004.

frequently—as in Oman, Ethiopia, and Sri Lanka—courts request age estimates by medical professionals, who are not readily available, and children languish in pre-trial detention. In Nigeria, further complications arise when parents submit false evidence on the ages of their children; this is facilitated by the low cost of, and easy access to, counterfeit certificates issued directly from government hospitals.[10] On the contrary, prosecutors and police officers in many countries regularly overstate children's ages—even registering children younger than MACRs as adults—for retribution against young alleged offenders and to boost arrest and prosecution rates.[11] They may target street children and poor children in particular, who are often less likely to have proof of age, and judges readily accept inflated age claims.

In response to challenges regarding proof of age, both in the context of immigration and juvenile justice, officials are increasingly turning to forensic medical examinations to estimate children's ages. Among proponents, the most widely recommended method is to collate the independent results of a psychosocial assessment, a general physical examination, a dental examination looking in particular at the mineralization of third molars, and an X-ray of the wrist that is compared to reference atlases of standard images by age and sex.[12] Each exam is meant to be completed by an expert with forensic experience in the respective test.

Although relevant scientific knowledge is growing, practitioners themselves point out a number of limitations to this approach, beginning with reference data and validation.[13] Socio-economic status and ethnicity correlate to five to six year differences in some age estimates, yet their influence is not fully understood, and little or no baseline data may be available.[14] As such, the risk of misinterpreting individual examinations can be very high. Even when examinations are conducted

---

10   Owasanoye, Bolaji, and Marie Wernham, *Street Children and the Juvenile Justice System in Lagos State: Nigerian Report*, Lagos, Human Development Initiatives and the Consortium for Street Children, 2004.

11   See, inter alia, Amnesty International, *Children in South Asia: Securing their Rights*, London, 1998; Society for the Protection of the Rights of the Child, *The State of Pakistan's Children 2003*, Islamabad, 2004; and Child Rights Coalition Sierra Leone, *A Complementary Report by Non-Governmental Organizations to the State Party Report of Sierra Leone (2005) on the Implementation of the Convention on the Rights of the Child*, Freetown, 2007.

12   International Organization for Migration and the Austrian Federal Ministry of the Interior, *Resource Book for Law Enforcement Officers on Good Practices in Combating Child Trafficking*, Vienna, 2006; Olze, A., et al., "Age estimation of unaccompanied minors: Part II. Dental aspects," 159 *Forensic Science International* S65, May 2006 Supplement; and Schmeling, A., et al., "Age estimation of unaccompanied minors: Part I. General considerations," 159 *Forensic Science International* S61, May 2006 Supplement.

13   Schmeling, A., et al., "Age estimation," 165 *Forensic Science International* 178, 2007. Schmeling, A., et al., "Forensic age diagnostics of living individuals in criminal proceedings," 54 *Homo* 162, 2003.

14   Olze et al., *supra* note 12.

and interpreted correctly, none of the recommended components can establish an exact age of a child.[15] When combining the various examinations, there is currently no scientifically valid method to determine the overall margin of error.[16] One validation study—based on a sample of 43 court case files where age was judged to be verified beyond doubt—found that scientific age estimates carried a deviation of plus or minus 12 months.

Critics lodge an even broader range of complaints. One study cites medical experts' opinions that X-rays and dental exams are inaccurate methods to determine age, and that discrepancies among different estimation methods vary by up to five years.[17] Others describe a growing consensus that such exams are ethically questionable, especially in ordering against a child's will invasive X-ray examinations that are not medically necessary, and in the difficulties of ensuring respect for the principle that physicians review all results and pursue medical interventions as necessary, even based on incidental findings.[18] For such reasons, Austrian courts grew increasingly unconvinced of forensic experts' ability to estimate accurately children's ages. The Vienna Juvenile Court dismissed one forensic expert over the limitations of the wrist X-ray method, and the procedure is no longer used at all in Austria due to radiation exposure and its wide margin of error.[19]

Costs per child are an important practical consideration; wrist X-rays may cost roughly 60 to 85 euros in Europe, while the dental examination may cost approximately 90 euros. Between the need for highly trained professionals and these immediate costs, such examinations would not seem to be financially practicable for most countries.

Although there are no easy answers for estimating children's ages, some guidance is available in terms of relevant principles, developed largely in the context of immigration and juvenile justice. As noted in Chapter 3, the Committee on the Rights of the Child has emphasized that "If there is no proof of age and it cannot be established that the child is at or above the MACR, the child shall not be held criminally responsible."[20] The Committee further stressed that "If there is no proof of age, the child is entitled to a reliable medical or social investigation that

---

15 International Organization for Migration et al., *supra* note 12.

16 Schmeling et al., *supra* note 12.

17 Physicians for Human Rights and The Bellevue/NYU Program for Survivors of Torture, *From Persecution to Prison: The Health Consequences of Detention for Asylum Seekers*, Boston, 2003. Royal College of Paediatrics and Child Health, *The Health of Refugee Children - Guidelines for Paediatricians*, London, 1999.

18 Physicians for Human Rights et al., *supra* note 17. Schmeling et al. ("Age ... "), *supra* note 12.

19 Höpfel, Frank, "Austria: Criminal Responsibility of Minors," 75 *International Review of Penal Law* (*Revue internationale de droit pénal*) 121, 2004; and International Organization for Migration et al., *supra* note 12.

20 *General Comment No. 10: Children's rights in juvenile justice*, CRC/C/GC/10, 25 Apr 2007, par. 35.

Practical Implications and Challenges of MACR Implementation 135

may establish his/her age and, in the case of conflict or inconclusive evidence, the child shall have the right to the rule of the benefit of the doubt."[21] It has also cited the need for official systems of age verification, focusing on objective evidence such as birth and school records.[22]

In even greater detail, the Committee addressed the question in its General Comment on unaccompanied children:

> identification measures include age assessment and should not only take into account the physical appearance of the individual, but also his or her psychological maturity. Moreover, the assessment must be conducted in a scientific, safe, child and gender-sensitive and fair manner, avoiding any risk of violation of the physical integrity of the child; giving due respect to human dignity ... .[23]

The Committee's guidance complements related Guidelines issued earlier by the UN High Commissioner for Refugees:

> b) When scientific procedures are used in order to determine the age of the child, margins of error should be allowed ... .
> c) The child should be given the benefit of the doubt if the exact age is uncertain.
> Where possible, the legal consequences or significance of the age criteria should be reduced or downplayed. It is not desirable that too many legal advantages and disadvantages are known to flow from the criteria because this may be an incentive for misrepresentation. The guiding principle is whether an individual demonstrates an "immaturity" and vulnerability that may require more sensitive treatment.[24]

Finally, one study on unaccompanied minors offers useful suggestions on how such principles might be best translated into practice:

> Age assessment should be based on the totality of available evidence, taking account of: claims made by the child; physical and psychological maturity; documentation held (such as passports or identity cards); evaluation by healthcare professionals; information from family members; and any x-ray or

---

21 *Ibid.*, par. 39.

22 *Concluding observations: Nepal*, CRC/C/15/Add.260, 3 Jun 2005, par. 97. *Concluding observations: Bangladesh*, CRC/C/OPAC/BGD/CO/1, 17 Mar 2006, par. 16(a).

23 *General Comment No. 6: Treatment of Unaccompanied and Separated Children Outside their Country of Origin*, CRC/GC/2005/6, 1 Sept 2005, par. 31(i).

24 Office of the UN High Commissioner for Refugees, *Guidelines on Policies and Procedures in dealing with Unaccompanied Children Seeking Asylum*, Geneva, 1997, par. 5.11.

other examinations. Where the outcome of age determination affects decisions about detention, independent experts should make the final determination.[25]

Thus, there is a fairly stable base of authoritative principles to guide countries in their age estimation practices. Nonetheless, the survey of national practices above suggests that these principles are currently neither widely known nor widely practiced.

In summary, the challenge of reliably ascertaining children's ages is exceedingly widespread, complex, and difficult to resolve. The bottom line is that the MACR loses both legitimacy and practical value as a basis for children's rights in juvenile justice, leading to an array of problems and indeed violations of those rights.

Problematic State Responses to Children Younger than MACRs

In dozens of countries, state responses to children younger than MACRs who come into conflict with the law are effectively criminal procedures and punishments, forming one of the most widespread MACR-related dilemmas worldwide.[26] Such treatment is typically categorized under domestic laws as welfare, care, protection, or education measures—despite clear resort to retribution-oriented deprivation of liberty—and it sometimes amounts to cruel or inhuman treatment.[27]

Comparative assessments of states' responses are difficult, beginning with a scarcity of authoritative information. Civil law and administrative protection procedures, rather than criminal law procedures, are typically the route to such interventions, and result in less publicly available information. The nature of interventions is rarely clear in practice, and the line between acceptable versus inappropriate measures under the MACR is also elusive.

For such reasons, Chapter 3 examines international monitoring bodies' classification of certain practices as punitive or implying criminal responsibility— and thus unacceptable beneath MACRs. Despite countries' prerogative to respond appropriately to children younger than MACRs in conflict with the law, and in the rarest of circumstances to contemplate their deprivation of liberty, many national measures undoubtedly conflict with the international bodies' standards. For guidance beyond international opinion, Chapter 5 introduces Packer's definition

---

25 Crock, Mary, *Seeking Asylum Alone: A Study of Australian Law, Policy and Practice Regarding Unaccompanied and Separated Children*, Sydney, Themis Press, 2006, at 230.

26 In general, see Cipriani, *supra* note 3.

27 For example, UN General Assembly, *Human rights questions: implementation of human rights instruments: Question of torture and other cruel, inhuman or degrading treatment or punishment: Interim report of the Special Rapporteur of the Commission on Human Rights on the question of torture and other cruel, inhuman or degrading treatment or punishment*, A/55/290, 11 Aug 2000, pars. 11–12.

of criminal punishment as an additional standard against which national provisions and practices may be compared.[28] Ideally, national level research would evaluate the full legal context, relevant institutions, and MACR implementation against international guidance and such definitions. Even within the limited scope of the present study, and compared to these benchmarks, many countries' approaches constitute serious problems.[29]

Table 5.1 and Annex 2 to this study document such patterns, particularly in their respective footnotes on relevant countries. For instance, at one point in 2005, Algeria was depriving the liberty of nearly 2000 children between 8 and the nominal MACR of 13 in specialized re-education centers—ostensibly as protective or re-education measures.[30] Such MACRs are often so problematic—in terms of implicit justifications, procedures, and outcomes—that they cannot reasonably be accepted as effective limits to responsibility. For example, Bahrain cites its MACR in the Penal Code clause that "a person under 15 years of age cannot be held responsible for the commission of an act constituting an offence," while the Juveniles Act applies to younger children.[31] However, this Act's measures for protection, education, reform, and rehabilitation include detention in social welfare centres for up to 10 years, leading the Committee on the Rights of the Child to find there was no effective MACR.[32] In France, following amendments in recent years, the Penal Code holds that all children deemed capable of discernment who have committed illegal acts are criminally responsible.[33] Again, the Committee on the Rights of the Child found no effective MACR.[34] Other related examples include, inter alia, Burkina Faso, Greece, Luxembourg, Libya, Kenya, Papua New Guinea, Republic of the Congo, the Republic of Korea, Turkey, and Sao Tome and Principe.

Former Soviet republics and countries historically influenced by Soviet law form a central trend in this respect, including nearly half of such countries. Typically, local administrative bodies—often termed Commissions on Minors' Affairs—exercise wide authority over children in conflict with the law who are younger than nominal MACRs, and may order their deprivation of liberty in special correction schools and re-education institutions.[35] For example, China's "re-education through labor" system—introduced by the former Soviet Union—

---

28 Packer, Herbert L., *The Limits of the Criminal Sanction*, Stanford, Stanford University Press, 1968.

29 See Chapter 5 for further methodological considerations.

30 See Committee on the Rights of the Child, *Second periodic reports of States parties due in 2000: Algeria*, CRC/C/93/Add.7, 3 Mar 2005, par. 332; and *Id.*, *Compte rendu analytique de la 1057e séance*, CRC/C/SR.1057, 20 Sept 2005, par. 91.

31 Committee on the Rights of the Child, *Initial reports of States parties due in 1994: Bahrain*, CRC/C/11/Add.24, 23 Jul 2001, pars. 115 and 315–316.

32 *Concluding observations: Bahrain*, CRC/C/15/Add.175, 7 Feb 2002, par. 47.

33 See Art. 122–8. Only the applicable measures vary according to children's ages.

34 *Concluding observations: France*, CRC/C/15/Add.240, 4 Jun 2004, par. 16.

35 See also Moestue, Helen, *Lost in the Justice System – Children in conflict with the law in Eastern Europe and Central Asia*, UNICEF, 2008.

deprives children of their liberty for minor offenses on an administrative basis, and the UN Special Rapporteur on Torture has considered the system a form of inhuman and degrading treatment or punishment.[36] In Cuba—which incorrectly cites its age of penal majority of 16 years as the MACR—"prevention and social welfare commissions" may order children's deprivation of liberty indefinitely in specialized re-education centers, without any lower age limit at all. Likewise, Polish courts may impose educative, protective, and therapeutic measures against children in conflict with the law of any age, amounting in some cases to indefinite deprivation of liberty—leading the Committee on the Rights of the Child to find no clear MACR.[37] In Russia, despite the formal MACR of 14 years, a 1999 law allows for the placement of younger children in centers for the temporary confinement of juvenile delinquents, with over 24,000 such placements occurring in 2001.[38] Azerbaijan, Bulgaria, Kazakhstan, Kyrgyzstan, Laos, Slovenia, Tajikistan, Ukraine, Uzbekistan, and Viet Nam provide examples of similar systems and problems.

Effective arrest, deprivation of liberty, and other punitive-oriented responses to young children around the world not only are serious rights violations, but also increase juvenile delinquency over time. For example, studies consistently show that when arrest has any impact, it is most likely to add to future delinquent behavior.[39] Deterrence programs used in some countries for young children, such as "scared straight" approaches and boot camps, are ineffective or harmful.[40] Children who are arrested and incarcerated are substantially more likely to be imprisoned as adults, and there are "no studies showing that incarceration of serious child delinquents results in a substantial reduction in recidivism or the prevention of later serious and violent offending."[41] In general, interventions that aggregate high-risk youth—such as institutional placements described in this

---

36   See, inter alia, UN Commission on Human Rights, *Report of the Special Rapporteur on torture and other cruel, inhuman or degrading treatment or punishment, Manfred Nowak: Mission to China*, E/CN.4/2006/6/Add.6, 10 Mar 2006.

37   See, inter alia, Committee on the Rights of the Child, *Periodic reports of States parties due in 1998: Poland*, CRC/C/70/Add.12, 6 Feb 2002, par. 160; and *Id., Concluding observations: Poland*, CRC/C/15/Add.194, 30 Oct 2002, par. 25.

38   See *Id., Third periodic reports of States parties due in 2001, Russian Federation*, CRC/C/125/Add.5, 15 Nov 2004, par. 323; and Stoecker, Sally W., "Homelessness and criminal exploitation of Russian minors: Realities, resources, and legal remedies," *Demokratizatsiya*, Spring 2001.

39   Thornberry, Terence P., et al., "The Causes and Correlates Studies: Findings and Policy Implications," 9 *Juvenile Justice* 3, 2004.

40   Farrington, David P., "Early Identification and Preventive Intervention: How Effective is this Strategy?," 4 *Criminology & Public Policy* 237, 2005; and US Government Accountability Office, *Residential Treatment Programs: Concerns Regarding Abuse and Death in Certain Programs for Troubled Youth*, Washington, 2007.

41   See Loeber, Rolf, et al., "Child Delinquency: Early Intervention and Prevention," *Child Delinquency Bulletin Series*, Washington, US Department of Justice, Office of Juvenile Justice and Delinquency Prevention, May 2003; and Thornberry et al., *supra* note 39.

section—may lead to increases in problem behavior.[42] When young children are placed with older adolescent offenders, they may face both negative influences and victimization, with both phenomena tending to lead to further delinquent behavior.[43] Such options are also notoriously more expensive per child than the effective non-custodial programs discussed in the following section.

No Effective Response to Children Younger than MACRs

If it is not problematic responses to children younger than MACRs, then the most common outcome worldwide for young children in conflict with the law seems to be no systematic response at all. Many countries essentially treat the MACR as an absolute cut-off; there are no substantial provisions for what to do with children below its limit, and so there is no effective state response to their actions. The lack of any visible or effective response can even add pressure to lower MACRs, in the belief that criminal law responses are needed to fill the void. This was the case in the United Kingdom following reports that children who had committed almost 3000 crimes in one year were not prosecuted, due to ages below the MACR, placing doubt upon earlier calls to increase the MACR.[44] In light of such challenges, this section discusses why younger children's delinquent acts are systematically ignored, how this non-response allows them to develop into more serious offenders, and alternatively, which programs for young children are effective, economical, and rights-compatible.

Ignoring Problem Behaviors until Bad and Getting Worse

Many countries have identified or attempted to address their lack of effective responses to children younger than MACRs. For example, countries of Southern and Eastern Africa convened in 2004 to discuss juvenile justice reform, and identified the issue as a core regional challenge.[45] In Switzerland's recent debate on MACR reform, the "lack of appropriate structures to deal with" crime among younger

---

42 Dishion, Thomas J., "Features of Ineffective and/or Unsafe Interventions," in conference report *Preventing Violence and Related Health-Risking Social Behaviors in Adolescents: An NIH State-of-the-Science Conference, October 13–15, 2004*, Bethesda (Maryland), National Institutes of Health, 2004.

43 See Loeber, Rolf, and David P. Farrington, eds, *Child Delinquents: Development, Intervention, and Service Needs*, Thousand Oaks, Sage Publications, 2001; and Loeber et al., *supra* note 41.

44 "Criminal age 'should rise to 18'," *BBC News*, 17 May 2007; "Lock up your sons and daughters," *Economist*, 6 Sept 2007; and "Thousands of crimes by under-10s," *BBC News*, 2 Sept 2007.

45 Gallinetti, Jacqueline, "Child Justice Advocacy Initiatives in South Africa, Southern and Eastern Africa," in *Kids Behind Bars: A Child Rights Perspective: Conference Report*, Defence for Children International Palestine Section, Bethlehem, 2005.

children emerged as a central concern and stumbling block.[46] Canada successively increased its MACR to prioritize welfare responses to young children, and then faced pressures to roll it back when intervention systems for young children didn't develop widely.[47]

In particular, United States scholars have analyzed why states do not systematically respond to young children in conflict with the law, even though juvenile courts' jurisdiction there is generally not restricted by age. First, children 12 and younger who commit delinquent acts make up a small proportion of overall offenses.[48] Even when they are repeat offenders, such children rarely accumulate long records or commit very serious or violent offenses; for example, they compose an infinitesimal portion of juvenile arrests for murder.[49] Consequently, most juvenile justice, child welfare, and school resources are aimed at older children and children with persistent problem behaviors.[50] Parents of the youngest delinquent boys are roughly half as likely to receive help from any service-providing agency as parents of the oldest delinquent boys.[51] Juvenile courts, historically and as a general expectation, "do not adjudicate very young, first-time offenders," and step in only when other relevant institutions have failed.[52] Unclear or overlapping roles of relevant systems mean that young offenders are more likely to slip through the cracks, and may not even be identified or referred to courts.[53]

The irony is that the most difficult juvenile offender cases involve children who are very likely to have exhibited problem behavior or committed offenses when they were younger. Before considering such evidence, however, it must be emphasized that the majority of young children with disruptive behavior will not become child offenders, and it is not realistically possible to predict which

---

46 Zermatten, Jean, *The Swiss Federal Statute on Juvenile Criminal Law*, presented at the Conference of the European Society of Criminology, Amsterdam, 25–28 August 2004.

47 See Augimeri, Leena K., et al., "Appendix B: Children Under Age 12 Years Who Commit Offenses: Canadian Legal and Treatment Approaches," in Loeber, Rolf, and David P. Farrington, eds, *Child Delinquents: Development, Intervention, and Service Needs*, Thousand Oaks, Sage Publications, 2001; and Burns, Barbara J., et al., *Treatment, Services, and Intervention Programs for Child Delinquents*, Washington, US Department of Justice, Office of Juvenile Justice and Delinquency Prevention, 2003.

48 Snyder, Howard N., et al., *Prevalence and Development of Child Delinquency*, Washington, US Department of Justice, Office of Juvenile Justice and Delinquency Prevention, 2003.

49 McGarrell, Edmund F., "Restorative Justice Conferences as an Early Response to Young Offenders," *Juvenile Justice Bulletin*, Washington, US Department of Justice, Office of Juvenile Justice and Delinquency Prevention, August 2001; and Snyder et al., *ibid*.

50 See Burns et al., *supra* note 47; and Loeber et al., *supra* note 41, at 11.

51 Thornberry et al., *supra* note 39.

52 Loeber et al., *supra* note 41, at 11.

53 US Department of Justice, Office of Juvenile Justice and Delinquency Prevention, "Serious and Violent Juvenile Offenders," *Juvenile Justice Bulletin*, Washington, May 1998.

children will commit offenses.[54] So many children exhibit problem behaviors at some point, and then discontinue on their own, that it is practically impossible to select out the comparatively few that will not eventually do so.[55] Specifically, there is no accurate method to predict which young boys with disruptive behavior will worsen or improve their behavior over time, or which children with serious behavior problems will move on to delinquency.[56] Furthermore, attempts at such predictions must weigh far-ranging ethical considerations, including potential uses and implications for discrimination and coercive intervention.[57]

Within this carefully qualified context, delinquency research shows that "the foundations for both prosocial and disruptive behaviors are laid in the first 5 years of life."[58] Certain preschool problem behaviors are correlated to later conduct disorder and child delinquency, while early antisocial behavior may be the most highly correlated factor to later delinquency. In particular, early aggression appears to be the social behavior characteristic that is most significantly tied to delinquent behavior before age 13.[59] Moreover, "[s]ix longitudinal studies conducted in five countries (Canada, England, New Zealand, Sweden, and the United States) ... confirmed that childhood antisocial behavior tends to be the best predictor of early-onset delinquency for boys."[60]

For children who become serious and violent offenders, compared to other offenders, correlations are stronger to both minor behavior problems at very young ages and early-onset delinquency.[61] In fact, children who begin to commit delinquent acts between the ages of 7 and 12 are two to three times as likely to become serious, violent, and chronic offenders versus children who begin to offend at older ages.[62] Results from the most comprehensive investigation ever of the causes and correlates of delinquency attest to such conclusions.[63] In all of the major "pathways" observed in the study that children followed to delinquency, "an early age of onset of problem behavior or delinquency was associated with escalation to more serious behaviors."[64] The study also confirmed that boys exhibited relevant disruptive behaviors an average of seven and a half years before

---

54   *Ibid.*
55   Szmukler, G., "Violence risk prediction in practice," 178 *British Journal of Psychiatry* 84, 2001.
56   See Loeber et al., *supra* note 41; and Thornberry et al., *supra* note 39.
57   Grisso, Thomas, and Paul S. Appelbaum, "Is It Unethical to Offer Predictions of Future Violence?," 16 *Law and Human Behavior* 621, 1992.
58   Loeber et al., *supra* note 41, at 8.
59   Wasserman, Gail A., et al., "Risk and Protective Factors of Child Delinquency," *Bulletin Series*, Washington, US Department of Justice, Office of Juvenile Justice and Delinquency Prevention, April 2003.
60   Loeber et al., *supra* note 41, at 6.
61   *Ibid.*; and US Department of Justice, *supra* note 53.
62   *Ibid.* (Loeber et al.).
63   Thornberry et al., *supra* note 39.
64   *Ibid.*, at 6.

they first came into contact with the juvenile court for certain serious offences. Research findings have consistently shown as much.[65]

In other words, children and youth policies systematically miscalculate in a sort of continuous loop. They focus extensively on adolescent offenders and largely overlook early problem behavior and young and first-time offenders, who without positive interventions are more likely to continue offending or to have persistent behavior problems as adolescents, and to become serious and violent offenders. From there, the cycle begins again.

Cheap, Effective, and Rights-compliant Options for Young Children

In contrast to this dead-end loop, the most effective, economical, and rights-based approach is early prevention and intervention based upon proven programs. Systematic universal prevention efforts, plus early intervention for disruptive behavior and offenses, refuse to ignore young children and are central in international juvenile justice standards. Certain early prevention programs address factors linked to delinquency, and reduce persistent disruptive behavior and early delinquency:

> Of all known interventions to reduce juvenile delinquency, preventive interventions that focus on child delinquency will probably take the largest "bite" out of crime. Specifically, these efforts should be directed first at the prevention of persistent disruptive behavior in children in general; second, at the prevention of child delinquency, particularly among disruptive children; and third, at the prevention of serious and violent juvenile offending, particularly among child delinquents. "The earlier the better" is a key theme in establishing interventions to prevent child delinquency ... .[66]

Universal prevention programs should therefore begin from at least the beginning of elementary school onward, when they are more likely to be effective as compared to interventions at later stages towards delinquency.[67]

The type of prevention or early intervention is absolutely critical, and extensive research documents both the key characteristics for effective programs as well as specific proven models.[68] For example, effective interventions "must account for the wide range of individual, family, peer, school, and community" factors, since

---

65 Loeber et al., *supra* note 41. See also Sagel-Grande, Irene, "Juvenile Delinquency and Age," in Junger-Tas, Josine, et al., eds, *The Future of the Juvenile Justice System/ L'avenir du système pénal des mineurs*, Leuven, Acco, 1991.

66 Loeber et al., *supra* note 41, at 9.

67 See Burns et al., *supra* note 47; Loeber et al., *ibid.*; and Thornberry et al., *supra* note 39.

68 See, inter alia, the Blueprints Model Programs, Center for the Study and Prevention of Violence, www.colorado.edu/cspv/blueprints/model/overview.html.

these present dynamic influences counteracting or contributing to the development of disruptive behavior and delinquency.[69] Programs that focus on parents and other family members, and that are based in the home or school, have proven to be most effective for younger children.[70] In schools, for example, certain social competence promotion programs consistently reduce young children's aggressive and antisocial behaviors.[71] One showed effects on antisocial behavior during the actual program intervention, immediately after its completion, as well as 6 years later when participants turned 18 years old. In general, however, these various model programs must be replicated faithfully, which requires extensive training and program oversight, in order to maintain such positive and lasting results.

To be sure, these basic characteristics hold true for both universal prevention programs (i.e., implemented with all children) and for individual responses to specific disruptive behaviors and offenses by young children. For children 12 and younger, "the best intervention and service programs provide a treatment-oriented, nonpunitive framework that emphasizes early identification and intervention."[72] The early intervention programs that are most successful in preventing serious and violent offending "involve simultaneous interventions in the home and in the school," and are delivered through mental health and child welfare systems.[73] These research findings generally hold true for older children—13 years and older—as well.[74]

Toronto, Canada, hosts the best example of providing effective early interventions for young children's aggressive, disruptive, and/or delinquent behavior. For over 20 years—one success spurred by Canada's 1984 MACR increase from 7 to 12 in favor of such approaches—the SNAP Under 12 Outreach Project has taken a multisystemic approach to children younger than the MACR through simultaneous interventions for children, parents, schools, and communities.[75] The Project mobilized city police and fire departments, children's aid societies, school boards, and other children's service agencies to establish a centralized, single-entry access point for services. The same citywide mechanism thus receives all referrals and responds to children engaging in antisocial behaviors or delinquent

---

69   Wasserman et al., *supra* note 59, at 10.

70   Burns et al., *supra* note 47. Farrington, *supra* note 40.

71   See also US Department of Health and Human Services, Centers for Disease Control and Prevention, "The Effectiveness of Universal School-Based Programs for the Prevention of Violent and Aggressive Behavior: A Report on Recommendations of the Task Force on Community Preventive Services," 56/RR-7 *Morbidity and Mortality Weekly Report* 1, 2007.

72   Burns et al., *supra* note 47, at 12.

73   Loeber et al., *supra* note 41. US Department of Justice, *supra* note 53, at 3.

74   See, inter alia, Greenwood, Peter, *Changing Lives: Delinquency Prevention as Crime Control Policy*, Chicago, University of Chicago Press, 2005.

75   Augimeri, Leena K., et al., *A Comprehensive Strategy: Children Under 12 in Conflict With the Law: "The Forgotten Group,"* Toronto, Center for Children Committing Offenses, Child Development Institute, 2006.

acts. After initial screening, all participating children learn cognitive behavior skills in structured groups, while their parents learn effective family and child management strategies. Depending on individual needs, children may also receive mentoring partners, counseling, in-home academic tutoring, school advocacy, teacher consultations, and other services. Extensive research, including controlled experiments, consistently demonstrates positive effects in treating children, and the program has been widely replicated.[76]

In conclusion, the absence of systematic responses to young child offenders—and to children younger than MACRs—opens a complex set of issues. As argued in Chapter 2, the lack of appropriate responses poses various problems for children's rights. Empirically, it also allows worse delinquency problems to develop over time, which are in turn much more difficult and costly to resolve. In contrast, the most effective and cost-effective approach—and one that fits neatly in the context of overall children's rights implementation—is comprehensive delinquency prevention that begins with universal programs at young ages, and that provides early and appropriate interventions as needed based on model programs.

MACRs that Threaten Children's Right to Effective Participation at Trial

Chapter 2 highlights children's right to effective participation in their own defense at trial, which rules out criminal responsibility, procedures, and punishments when their effective participation is not ultimately possible. Indeed, it is fundamentally unjust to order punishments based upon procedures in which children are not capable of assisting in their own defense, or that they cannot sufficiently understand.[77] This section considers how low MACRs may systematically threaten this right by enabling penal proceedings against children who cannot normatively be expected to participate effectively in them. In particular, it addresses research on the ages at which children acquire specific abilities necessary for effective participation at trial, and discusses critical implications for MACRs.

Legal standards for trial competency vary substantially by country, but as discussed in Chapter 2, the Committee on the Rights of the Child has outlined basic minimum criteria that reflect regional and international human rights standards:

> A fair trial requires that the child alleged as or accused of having infringed the penal law be able to effectively participate in the trial, and therefore needs to comprehend the charges, and possible consequences and penalties, in order to direct the legal representative, to challenge witnesses, to provide an account

---

76 See, inter alia, Augimeri, Leena K., et al., "The SNAP Under 12 Outreach Project: Effects of a Community Based Program for Children with Conduct Problems," *Journal of Child and Family Studies*, published online 10 Jan 2007.

77 Archard, David, *Children: Rights and childhood*, 2nd ed., London, Routledge, 2004.

of events, and to make appropriate decisions about evidence, testimony and the measure(s) to be imposed. Article 14 of the Beijing Rules provides that the proceedings should be conducted in an atmosphere of understanding to allow the child to participate and to express himself/herself freely. Taking into account the child's age and maturity may also require modified courtroom procedures and practices.[78]

Although these international children's rights standards set an even higher threshold, they broadly resemble the main groups of abilities required for "adjudicative competency" under United States case law: "Understanding of Charges and Potential Consequence," "Understanding of the Trial Process," "Capacity to Participate with Attorney in a Defense," and "Potential for Courtroom Participation."[79] These requirements, in turn, are the subject of the most extensive research available on children's relevant abilities at different ages.

Much of this research suggests that the age range of 11–13 years is critical for developing the abilities necessary for trial participation. For example, the largest and most comprehensive effort to date studied roughly 1400 youth ages 11–24, drawn from the justice system and the general community at four different US locations.[80] Nearly one-third of children 11–13 years old were generally incompetent to stand trial, showing the same level of trial-related understanding and reasoning as adults whom courts have found incompetent. These children performed significantly worse than all older children, and were nearly three times more likely than the oldest children to fall short of typical levels for trial competence.

Prior investigations on a more limited scale offer consistent results, such as one study of 247 incarcerated children's competency to stand trial.[81] Those 12 and younger performed significantly worse than older children in all the fundamental areas of adjudicative competence. In another investigation of 136 case files of children clinically assessed for competency, the percentages of children held clearly competent to stand trial declined precipitously as children's ages decreased: 68 per cent at age 14; 56 per cent at age 13; 27 per cent at age 12; 18 per cent at age

---

78 *General Comment No. 10: Children's rights in juvenile justice*, CRC/C/GC/10, 25 Apr 2007, par. 46.

79 Dohrn, Bernardine, "'I'll Try Anything Once': Using the Conceptual Framework of Children's Human Rights Norms in the United States," 41 *University of Michigan Journal of Law Reform* 29, 2007. Grisso, Thomas, "What We Know about Youths' Capacities as Trial Defendants," in Grisso, Thomas, and Robert G. Schwartz, eds, *Youth on Trial: A Developmental Perspective on Juvenile Justice*, Chicago, University of Chicago Press, 2000, at 142.

80 Grisso, Thomas, et al., "Juveniles' Competence to Stand Trial: A Comparison of Adolescents' and Adults' Capacities as Trial Defendants," 27 *Law and Human Behavior* 333, 2003.

81 LaVelle Ficke, Susan, et al., "The Performance of Incarcerated Juveniles on the MacArthur Competence Assessment Tool-Criminal Adjudication (MacCAT-CA)," 34 *Journal of the American Academy of Psychiatry and the Law* 360, 2006.

11; and 0 per cent at ages 10 and 9.[82] Similarly, statistical analysis in another case review found that children 12 and younger were significantly more likely than older children to have been declared incompetent to stand trial.[83]

Other research goes beyond formal US standards for trial competence, and examines broader influences on children's practical ability to participate in justice processes. For example, emotional maturity in legal decision-making contexts is generally lower among children 11–13 years old as compared to older children— in crucial areas such as considering long-term consequences, perceiving risks, resisting peer influences, and complying with authority figures.[84]

Such research carries both limitations and advantages. It focuses on just one country's constitutional standards, with state-level variations within that country. These US requirements are broadly related to international children's rights standards for effective participation, but are not a proxy for them. Moreover, investigations to date do not provide definitive answers on precise age levels for children's adjudicative competency, even within the US context, let alone for other countries and legal standards. They indicate important age-competency links, but cannot be extrapolated to a global scale. At the same time, these studies do suggest promising avenues for future research on the specific competencies required for children's effective participation as defined under international standards. Functional thresholds may be more objective and easily measured, and less prone to value judgments overall, than the contested boundaries of moral agency, moral responsibility, and criminal responsibility, as discussed in Chapter 1. Related knowledge could play an important role among considerations for appropriate MACR age levels, as discussed below, whereas research on children's moral development has generally failed to impact relevant debates.

This research raises other important implications, such as the role of courts in assessing children's ability to participate before proceeding to trial. Across countries, there is little evidence of widespread attempts to assess or ensure children's abilities, or for defense attorneys to raise relevant claims. If children and their representatives were to raise claims in all legitimate cases of doubt, courts might not be prepared for the human and financial burden of handling a flood of competence assessments.[85] Application of the *doli incapax* doctrine in

---

82   Cowden, Vance, and Geoffrey McKee, "Competency to Stand Trial in Juvenile Delinquency Proceedings: Cognitive Maturity and the Attorney-Client Relationship," 33 *Louisville Journal of Family Law* 629, 1995.

83   Baerger, Dana Royce, et al., "Competency to Stand Trial in Preadjudicated and Petitioned Juvenile Defendants," 31 *Journal of the American Academy of Psychiatry and the Law* 314, 2003.

84   See, e.g., Grisso et al., *supra* note 80; and Abramovitch, Rona, et al., "Young people's understanding and assertion of their rights to silence and legal counsel," 37 *Canadian Journal of Criminology* 1, 1995.

85   See Scott, Elizabeth S., and Thomas Grisso, "Developmental Incompetence, Due Process, and Juvenile Justice Policy," 83 *North Carolina Law Review* 793, 2005.

courts around the world, discussed below in this chapter, suggests that competence assessments would not be given due consideration anyway.

Even where children are identified as unable to participate effectively at trial, it may not be possible to provide adequate assistance to facilitate their participation. In the relatively few cases of adults held incompetent by courts, United States procedures are usually effective in providing sufficient instruction, assistance, and treatment so that trials may proceed.[86] In the case of children, however, trial incompetence is correlated with age, and the nature of their incompetencies suggests that the only way to overcome them is to grow older and mature. For example, when researchers provided instruction on core legal concepts to children 13 and younger, they were less likely than older children to improve in their legal understanding.[87] Informal efforts to modify court settings and procedures, and to provide instruction and assistance, appear to be the most common actions taken by countries—yet they may not have any impact on children's ability to participate effectively.

In cases where children's effective participation is not possible, courts may refer children to the types of welfare-oriented proceedings and measures described in Chapter 2. Therein, children's right to participation is largely guided by Article 12 of the Convention on the Rights of the Child: the right of children to express their views freely, and for their views to be given due weight in accordance with their age and maturity. If courts instead proceed with criminal responsibility, procedures, or punishments—in the absence of children's effective participation—they directly violate a central right of children under international standards.

In light of the foregoing considerations, low MACRs create a number of difficulties. They systematically place at risk of criminal trials children who are unable to participate effectively in them. Although not all defendants as young as MACRs should or will face penal proceedings, most countries neither identify children unable to participate effectively, nor are they able to provide children with sufficient assistance to enable participation. Preliminary research on US children and standards suggests that the range of 11–13 years is critical for developing the abilities necessary for trial participation, and that it may be improbable for children 12 and younger to have these abilities. Although not directly comparable, these results at least cast doubt upon the MACRs lower than 12 in nearly 90 countries, and the likelihood that children participate effectively in their trials in such countries.

The most practicable and just approach may be to establish MACRs that limit potential criminal responsibility to children who, more likely than not, are capable of effective participation. Children incapable of effective participation would be the exception, and officials could more easily identify and assist them, and if

---

86   Ibid.
87   Viljoen, Jodi L., et al., "Teaching Adolescents and Adults about Adjudicative Proceedings: A Comparison of Pre- and Post-Teaching Scores on the MacCAT-CA," 31 *Law and Human Behavior* 419, 2007.

necessary, refer them to welfare-based programs and proceedings. However, this does not signify that MACRs should be raised continuously higher strictly for the sake of ensuring children's effective participation in penal procedures. In addition to other considerations raised throughout this study, significantly higher MACRs also have the effect of truncating the opportunity of children to respond to the accusations and allegations made against them, when they may be fully capable of doing so. Under welfare proceedings—no longer subject to fair trial requirements of criminal law—children have right to an important but narrower construction of participation. For older children capable of effective participation, such a policy conflicts with the right to have all of their capacities recognized, respected, and fostered. In addition, if a sizeable group of children were excluded from criminal responsibility on the basis of participation—like the effect of setting high MACRs on this basis—it would not be broadly acceptable in society, institutional crises would likely ensue, and systems may fail to handle children appropriately.[88] Future research on children's abilities for effective participation—as defined under international children's rights standards and applied at national levels—could play an important and potentially decisive role in MACR debates. However, the balance of considerations is still a delicate one, and these debates must weigh the broader range of rights and policy considerations.

Undermining of *Doli Incapax* and Similar Presumptions

Chapter 4 sketches the Roman law origins of the *doli incapax* doctrine—the rebuttable presumption of children's non-responsibility between the MACR and a higher age limit—and describes English common law's influence in carrying it around the world.[89] Across respective countries, the doctrine underwent innumerable modifications as it was disseminated, codified, amended, and judicially interpreted over time. Further variations arise in similar tests, such as historic French law's discernment test. *Doli incapax* has prompted vigorous national and international contemporary debates—variously supported and opposed, both on the basis of children's rights and of harsher justice.[90] However, as noted in Chapter 3, human rights bodies have recently reached the consensus that these systems are irreconcilable with children's rights, which is the departure point for this section. The following pages overview *doli incapax* and parallel tests across legal systems, finding that their protective intent is regularly undermined as the presumption is ignored; it is subverted into a presumption of responsibility;

---

88 Scott and Grisso, *supra* note 85.
89 In general, see Cipriani, *supra* note 3.
90 See, inter alia, Crofts, Thomas, "Doli Incapax: Why Children Deserve its Protection," 10 *Murdoch University Electronic Journal of Law*, no. 3, 2003; and Bradley, Lisa, "The Age of Criminal Responsibility Revisited," 8 *Deakin Law Review* 71, 2003.

application is inconsistent; the evidence used is problematic; and the ascription of responsibility becomes more than anything a form of discrimination.

England's *doli incapax* provisions were the cause for energetic debate over many decades before they were ultimately revoked in 1998.[91] Even by 1883, one commentator criticized that the test was "practically inoperative" and applied "capriciously."[92] In 1960, a prominent law review committee recommended that the presumption be abrogated, citing evidence that it still "was not consistently applied and that courts differed in the degree of proof which they required of guilty intention."[93] Evidentiary requirements for rebuttal remained unclear in the final period before England abolished *doli incapax*.[94] The preferred evidence, children's statements upon being questioned by police, was fraught with difficulties related to children's understanding of their legal rights, the lack of legal assistance, police intimidation and threats, and so on. In either case, as Parliament debated whether to abolish the *doli incapax* presumption, government officials admitted that there was no broad empirical data available anyway on the operation of the test.

Similar problems are evident in Australia—where the *doli incapax* presumption applies in theory to all children between the MACR of 10 years and the age of 14—and relevant law "has been consistently criticised for over a century."[95] Moreover, the presumption is usually ignored, and children are assumed capable of responsibility. In some rural and other areas, many practitioners are apparently not even familiar with the concept or application of *doli incapax*. When it is pleaded, courts admit a wide range of evidence that seems to undermine procedural fairness for children—including confessions to police officers in the absence of legal counsel—and commentators have stated that the presumption is rebutted upon very little evidence anyway.

In common law countries of Asia and Africa, *doli incapax* has often become a presumption of responsibility or a means of socio-economic discrimination. In Bangladeshi and Kenyan courtrooms, for example, children with sufficient maturity may simply mean street children, child prostitutes, and poor children, as criminal responsibility is often ascribed to such groups without any true assessment of maturity.[96] When assessments do occur, they tend to be informal judgments about

---

91 Crofts, Thomas, *The Criminal Responsibility of Children and Young Persons: A Comparison of English and German Law*, Aldershot (England), Ashgate, 2002.

92 Paraphrased by Crofts, *supra* note 90, pars. 39 and 10, respectively.

93 Crofts, *supra* note 91, at 24.

94 See in general Crofts, *supra* notes 90 and 91.

95 Mathews, Benjamin Peter, *Australian Laws Ascribing Criminal Responsibility to Children*, PhD thesis, Queensland University of Technology, 2001, at 132. See in general Bradley, *supra* note 90; and Crofts, *supra* note 90.

96 CRADLE et al., *Street Children and Juvenile Justice in Kenya*, London, 2004. Uddin Siddiqui, *supra* note 9. See also past Ugandan practices, in Nsereko, D.D.N., "Uganda," 1995, in Fijnaut, Cyrillus, and Frankk Verbruggen, eds, "Criminal Law," in Blanpain, Roger, ed., *International Encyclopaedia of Laws*, The Hague, Kluwer Law International, 2004.

children's backgrounds and their alleged offenses. In Myanmar, Pakistan, and Sri Lanka, judicial practices reverse the *doli incapax* burden of rebuttal. Instead of prosecutors' evidence to prove the maturity of children in relevant age ranges, children are presumed responsible unless proven insufficiently mature.[97]

South Africa and Namibia, two countries in the limited Roman–Dutch legal tradition, have encountered similar difficulties with their common law *doli incapax* presumptions. Research indicates that Namibia's presumption of non-responsibility for children between 7 and 14 is usually ignored or simply transformed into a presumption of responsibility, and findings of non-responsibility are the exception.[98] In South Africa, contemporary *doli incapax* case law is elaborate, yet in practice lower courts usually accept incomplete, invalid, and/or simplified inquiries that fail to consider all of the required questions for rebuttal.[99]

In the civil law tradition, German courts individually assess children between 14 and 18 years for potential criminal responsibility based upon related criteria.[100] Jurisprudence is highly refined on the exact requirements, but "in practice there seems to be a tendency to circumvent the requirements."[101] Critics argue that the test no longer has any meaningful role, and empirical evidence suggests that it is often ignored as criminal responsibility becomes the rule. One study showed that where case judgments did include maturity assessments, children's criminal responsibility was justified summarily in almost every case.[102]

Finally, in historic French civil law tradition, children's criminal responsibility within relevant age ranges depends upon evidence of their individual capacity of discernment. As in other countries, socio-economic discrimination is a common result. In Niger, for example, only court experts can determine if children 13 and older have acted with discernment at the time of alleged offenses.[103] Families are required to pay the experts' fees, but since most families cannot afford these costs, assessments are rarely conducted. In practice, most children become criminally responsible at 13 years, while wealthy children can pay experts' fees and avoid responsibility until 18 years.

---

97 Committee on the Rights of the Child, *Summary record of the 872nd Meeting: Sri Lanka*, CRC/C/SR.872, 1 Jul 2003. Amnesty International, *Pakistan: Denial of basic rights for child prisoners*, London, 2003; and Jillani, Anees, *Cries Unheard: Juvenile Justice in Pakistan*, Islamabad, Society for the Protection of the Rights of the Child, 1999. UNICEF East Asia and Pacific Regional Office, correspondence with author, July 2001.

98 Schulz, Stefan, and Marthinus Hamutenya, "Juvenile Justice in Namibia: Law Reform towards Reconciliation and Restorative Justice?," *Restorative Justice Online*, June 2004.

99 Sloth-Nielsen, Julia, *The Influence of International Law upon Juvenile Justice Reform in South Africa*, LLD thesis, University of the Western Cape, 2001.

100 Crofts, *supra* note 91.

101 *Ibid.*, at 177.

102 *Ibid.*

103 UNICEF Niger, correspondence with author, July 2001. In general, see Cipriani, *supra* note 3.

Instrumental Use of Young Children by Adults for Crimes

Experts believe that adults instrumentally use children for criminal activities in every country of the world.[104] For example, organized crime, drug-trafficking and child prostitution rackets, and other criminal gangs exploit disadvantaged and young children in Europe generally, and in Italy, Russia, and Australia.[105] Although the instrumental use of children is certainly not limited to children younger than MACRs, it may present a larger threat to them. In addition to greater vulnerability at younger ages, there is oftentimes no significant response to such children involved in criminal activities. This probability, compared to the threat of arrest and prosecution for both older children and adults, makes them particularly useful in the eyes of adult criminals. It also means young children are less likely to be tracked in official records, allowing adults to manipulate them less conspicuously than older children.[106] Limited efforts to prosecute adults enables further instrumentalization, while child protection efforts are complicated and often ineffective. Different countries, and levels and branches of governments, alternatively address the issue as a question of international criminal organizations, child labor, child trafficking, child welfare and protection, and/or juvenile justice.[107] Further examples illustrate some of these challenging dynamics.

Criminal instrumentalization is a significant problem in Pakistan.[108] Adult drug-traffickers pay children to carry wrapped packages, without necessarily telling

---

104 David, Pedro, "The Instrumental Use of Juveniles in Criminal Activities," in UN Centre for Human Rights et al., *Children in Trouble: UN Expert Group Meeting*, report of the "UN Expert Group Meeting: Children and Juveniles in Detention: Application of Human Rights Standards, Vienna, 30 October to 4 November 1994," Vienna, Austrian Federal Ministry for Youth and Family, 1995.

105 Committee on the Rights of the Child, *Concluding observations: Italy*, CRC/C/15/Add.41, 27 Nov 1995, par. 11. *Id.*, *Compte rendu analytique de la 1077e séance*, CRC/C/SR.1077, 18 Oct 2005, par 18. International Organization for Migration et al., *supra* note 12. Bell, Duane, and Bruce Heathcote, "Gangs and Kinship: Gang Organisation Amongst Contemporary Indigenous Culture in Western Australia," presented at *Children and Crime: Victims and Offenders Conference*, Brisbane, Australian Institute of Criminology, 17–18 June 1999. See also Cipriani, *supra* note 3.

106 Palomba, Federico, "The Instrumental Use of Juveniles in Criminal Activities," in UN Centre for Human Rights et al., *Children in Trouble: UN Expert Group Meeting*, report of the "UN Expert Group Meeting: Children and Juveniles in Detention: Application of Human Rights Standards, Vienna, 30 October to 4 November 1994," Vienna, Austrian Federal Ministry for Youth and Family, 1995.

107 See, inter alia, the Convention concerning the Prohibition and Immediate Action for the Elimination of the Worst Forms of Child Labour (ILO No. 182), 38 I.L.M. 1207, adopted 17 Jun 1999.

108 Integrated Regional Information Network, *Pakistan: Focus on Boys Behind Bars*, UN Office for the Coordination of Humanitarian Affairs, 10 Sept 2001. In general, see Cipriani, *supra* note 3.

them that the packages are drug shipments. If deliveries go through successfully, the traffickers have cheap couriers available for future deliveries. In such cases, *doli incapax* provisions theoretically apply to children between 7 and 12 years. However, if police officers arrest children, traffickers bribe the officers to ensure that their own crimes are ignored, and children are held responsible. Across Pakistan, there are roughly 5000 children in jail, and one expert estimated that the most common charge against them is drug carrying—even for children as young as 8.[109] Another type of instrumentalization is also prevalent—revenge killings—such that almost 20 per cent of children in one prison are awaiting trial on murder charges. More common in rural areas, family members order children to carry out such revenge, usually for previous family killings.

Related challenges have emerged in other countries. In Colombia, traffickers exploited young children to carry out drug-related murders; rather than focus on the adult perpetrators, police officers complained they had no authority to take action against such children.[110] Hong Kong also faced reports of drug-traffickers' exploitation of young children, and resisted MACR increases for fears that such instrumentalization would expand.[111] Concerns for criminal exploitation of children beneath MACRs also directly impacted proposed amendments in countries such as Thailand, the Philippines, and South Africa. In relation to Pakistani revenge killings, parts of Europe suffer a similar form of violence and exploitation—parents ordering boys below MACRs to carry out "honour killings" of their own female family members.[112]

Also in Europe, adults trafficked Romanian children to German cities for pick-pocketing, burglary, and prostitution rings.[113] In particular, traffickers targeted disadvantaged children who were younger than Germany's MACR of 14, placing large groups of them together in closely guarded apartments in Germany. Children's attempts to escape led to threats, beatings, rape, and torture. The governments of Germany and Romania responded with an expedited 36-hour repatriation program for all Romanian children separated from their parents, and the overall number of trafficked children declined as a result. However, deported children often returned to the streets in Romania or to families that had originally

---

109   *Ibid.*; and Society for the Protection of the Rights of the Child, *supra* note 11.

110   Griswold, Eliza, "The 14-Year-Old Hit Man," *New York Times Magazine*, 28 Apr 2002.

111   Law Reform Commission of Hong Kong, *Report on the Age of Criminal Responsibility in Hong Kong*, Wanchai, 2000. In general, see Cipriani, *supra* note 3.

112   Council of Europe Committee of Ministers, *788 Meeting of the Ministers' Deputies: 13 March 2002: Steering committee for equality between women and men (CDEG) Explanatory memorandum*, CM(2002)17 Addendum, 8 Feb 2002.

113   Gittrich, Thomas, "Overview on the Situation of Unaccompanied Minors in Germany – Examples of Good Practice in Reception," in *Final Report from Conference on Separated and Trafficked Children in the Baltic Sea Region*, Vilnius, September 1416, 2003. International Organization for Migration, *Trafficking in Unaccompanied Minors for Sexual Exploitation in the European Union*, Brussels, 2001.

sold them to traffickers, with limited follow-up measures to ensure their protection against repeated trafficking.

Finally, in Tanzania, cases of burglary and theft involving at least three suspects usually include one child suspect between 7 and 13.[114] Adult criminals use children, referred to as "vipanya" (i.e., mice), to enter homes through windows or other tight spaces. The children then open doors from the inside for the adults to enter and burglarize the homes. If the burglary attempt is discovered, children are usually caught alone while the adult masterminds are able to run away. One court's statistics show that almost 40 per cent of adults' criminal offenses involved such instrumental use of children.

Courts' Disregard for MACRs, and Extrajudicial Acts Against Children

In some countries, judges fail to consistently apply domestic MACR provisions, or extrajudicial acts are carried out against alleged child offenders. These phenomena often share a key element—a greater willingness to overlook the law for the sake of retribution when it comes to alleged child offenders. At times, the results are also almost identical: children younger than MACRs are deprived of their liberty, or much worse, and children's rights and the rule of law are subverted.

The most egregious cases involve Iran and the sentencing and imposition of the death penalty against children younger than Iran's MACR at the time of alleged crimes. Beyond the question of the MACR, international law categorically prohibits—as a peremptory norm—the imposition of the death penalty against any person younger than 18 years at the time of alleged crimes.[115] Among other violations of this prohibition, and despite Iran's own MACR of 15 lunar years (i.e., 14 years and 7 months), authorities hanged Makwan Mouladzadeh in December 2007 for crimes he allegedly committed when he was 13 years old. Three men alleged in 2006 that Mouladzadeh had raped them as boys seven years earlier, but they subsequently withdrew their accusations, and Mouladzadeh retracted his own confession as false and coerced by police intimidation.[116] Mouladzadeh's hanging also defied a stay of execution and order for further judicial review by the head of Iran's judiciary, after his determination that the original conviction was contrary

---

114   Legal and Human Rights Centre, *The State of Juvenile Justice In Tanzania: A Fact-Finding Report on Legal and Practical Considerations*, Dar-Es-Salaam, 2003. Tanzania's MACR is 10, with *doli incapax* tests for children between 10 and 12. In Zanzibar, it is 12, with *doli incapax* tests between 12 and 14.

115   Human Rights Committee, *General Comment No. 24: Issues relating to reservations made upon ratification or accession to the Covenant or the Optional Protocols thereto, or in relation to declarations under article 41 of the Covenant*, CCPR/C/21/Rev.1/Add.6, 4 Nov 1994, par. 8. See also CRC Art. 37(a).

116   Human Rights Watch, *Iran: Revoke Death Sentence in Juvenile Case*, Washington, 3 Nov 2007.

to *shari'a*.[117] In other cases, Ahmad Nourzahi received a death sentence for crimes committed when he was apparently 12, and three other boys received sentences and/or were executed for crimes committed when 14 years old (i.e., potentially below the MACR).[118]

Several countries and regions provide other examples of limited application of MACR-related laws. At times, such as in Kosovo and Uganda, courts simply hold children criminally responsible for their acts even if they are younger than the MACR. In remediating the same problem, Bangladesh's Supreme Court effectively ordered officials to apply MACR and *doli incapax* provisions retroactively, and to release children either too young or immature to bear criminal responsibility.[119] In Tanzania, one high-profile case involved a 9-year-old boy who was charged and convicted of raping a 5-year-old girl, despite being younger than the MACR.[120] He was given a sentence of life in prison, although this decision was subsequently annulled.

In contrast to courts' disregard for MACRs, extrajudicial actions are carried out against young children by law enforcement officials as well as through private vigilante justice.[121] These are often related to the belief that legal state responses to children are inadequate—thus the taking of the law into one's own hands. Children younger than MACRs are at particular risk because many countries fail to offer any substantive response to their otherwise illegal acts, fueling impressions that young children are unaccountable. Consequently, as in Jamaica, police lock up children 9 and 10 years old—well below the MACR of 12—even for long periods and in the same cells as adults.[122] Related problems transpire in countries such as Afghanistan and Nigeria. In Israel, the armed forces often arrest Palestinian children younger than the Israeli MACR of 12 years—in defiance of Military Orders—and have apparently tortured and sexually abused at least one such child in prison.[123]

---

117 *Id.*, *Iran: Prevent Execution of Juvenile Offender*, New York, 5 Dec 2007.

118 Amnesty International, *Iran: The last executioner of children*, London, 2007. Child Rights Information Network, *IRAN: Appeal to spare the lives of youths*, Geneva, 8 Jul 2008.

119 World Organisation Against Torture, *Rights of the Child in Bangladesh: Report on the implementation of the Convention on the Rights of the Child in relation to Children in Conflict with the Law by Bangladesh*, Geneva, 2003.

120 Legal and Human Rights Centre, *supra* note 114. Tanzania's MACR is 10, with *doli incapax* tests for children between 10 and 12. In Zanzibar, it is 12, with *doli incapax* tests for children between 12 and 14.

121 In general, see Cipriani, *supra* note 3.

122 UN Economic and Social Council: Commission on Human Rights, *Question of the Human Rights of All Persons Subjected to Any Form of Detention or Imprisonment, in Particular: Torture and Other Cruel, Inhuman or Degrading Treatment or Punishment: Report of the Special Rapporteur, Mr. Nigel S. Rodley, submitted pursuant to Commission on Human Rights resolution 1995/37, E/CN.4/1996/35*, 9 Jan 1996, par. 94.

123 Office of the Special Representative of the Secretary-General for Children and Armed Conflict, *Report: Visit of the Special Representative for Children & Armed Conflict*

Instead, vigilante justice against young children is a significant problem in countries including Mozambique and Tanzania, where private citizens often apprehend children used in burglary attempts or suspected in robberies.[124] In Tanzania, mob justice is apparently a common response against children younger than MACRs, including group beatings that are sometimes fatal.

Conclusion

A wide range of practical challenges complicate and undermine MACR implementation in countries around the world: no proof of age and unreliable age estimates; problematic responses or no response to children younger than MACRs who come into conflict with the law; low MACRs that lead to prosecution of children who are unable to participate effectively in their own defense; *doli incapax* and similar presumptions that are ignored or applied inconsistently and discriminatorily; adults' instrumental use of young children in criminal activities; and both judicial disregard for MACRs and extra-judicial acts against children younger than MACRs. Children's rights principles, as well as the rule of law and efficient public policy in general, call for these problems to be addressed and resolved. Debates on juvenile justice and MACR provisions provide a fitting opportunity for such action, and indeed, they must take full account of at least these potential problems in order to achieve coherent reform.

Higher MACR levels are closely related to many of these problems. For example, where children do not widely possess reliable proof of age, age estimates in later adolescence may be increasingly difficult as children's physical appearances approximate adults', and false age claims may increase. If governments do not provide credible, systematic, and appropriate responses to children younger than MACRs who come into conflict with the law—whose numbers accrue in step with MACR increases—pressures grow to intervene inappropriately and/or to roll back MACRs for criminal law responses. In these circumstances, state interventions that skirt and violate children's rights are a clear threat, as are extrajudicial treatment and vigilante justice. Indeed, juvenile justice history is marked by problematic state interventions, and current research shows that such risks continue, for example in many juvenile justice systems influenced by Soviet law. Higher MACRs may also open the door to further instrumental use of young children in criminal activities.

---

to the Middle East: Lebanon, Israel and occupied Palestinian territory, 9–20 April 2007, 2007. Special Committee to Investigate Israeli Practices Affecting the Human Rights of the Palestinian People and Other Arabs of the Occupied Territories, *Report*, A/62/336, 24 Sept 2007, par. 66.

124 Legal and Human Rights Centre, *supra* note 114. Committee on the Rights of the Child, *Initial report of States parties due in 1996: Mozambique*, CRC/C/41/Add.11, 14 May 2001.

The question of appropriate state responses to young children in conflict with the law deserves special attention. As this study argues in Chapter 2, a holistic children's rights perspective calls for states to hold all children accountable for their actions at developmentally appropriate levels, and in appropriate ways, carefully heeding international juvenile justice standards. This is true both above and below the MACR, which is the substantive and symbolic limit to how children may legally be held accountable. Beneath its age threshold, among other factors, responses must be non-criminal, non-punitive, and with only the very rarest of exceptions, non-custodial. Research roughly supports this view and coincides with the international consensus that 12 years is the lowest acceptable MACR. Studies show that the most effective responses to children 12 and younger preclude arrest, deprivation of liberty, and related legal sanctions. Moreover, the absence of effective responses to young children's delinquency is related to their development over time into serious, chronic, and violent offenders. What may be the two most common responses to children younger than MACRs who come into conflict with the law—punitive-oriented measures and no coordinated response at all—are probably the most counterproductive responses possible. At the same time that they violate children's rights, they lead to worse delinquency problems over time, which are then consistently more difficult and expensive to address.

The challenge highlighted in this chapter that is most sensitive to low MACRs is ensuring children's effective participation at trial, a central right in international juvenile justice standards. Low MACRs may systematically expose to criminal trials children who cannot normatively be expected to participate effectively in them; who cannot readily improve or learn to participate effectively; and who are unlikely to be screened out of criminal trials when they do not participate effectively. Although a complex matter, the best starting point in this context may be MACRs at the lowest age where the majority of children are capable of effective participation. Future national level and comparative research on necessary competencies, explicitly under the international standards for children's effective participation, could make an important contribution as such. Broadly related research in the United States suggests that the ages of 11–13 years are critical in children's development of competencies specifically under US standards.

In the end, the assorted challenges highlighted in this chapter probably affect every country in some way, regardless of MACR age level or juvenile justice approach. As seen in Chapter 3, obligations under the Convention on the Rights of the Child pertain to all of these issues, and thus it would seem that virtually every country has a responsibility to take action on continuing problems. Where implementation efforts fail to address them, the MACR tends to become less of a crucial milestone in juvenile justice, and more of a misleading claim about children's rights.

Chapter 7
Making MACRs Work for Children's Rights

The minimum age of criminal responsibility (MACR) is the lowest age upon which children may potentially be judged delinquent or held liable in juvenile justice for infringements of a given country's penal laws. It also marks a country's commitment to respond to younger children in conflict with the law only in ways that are non-punitive and that reflect the absence of criminal responsibility. Despite this inherent significance, MACRs themselves may indicate very little in practice about the protection of children's rights. Making MACRs work for children's rights depends, to a large extent, upon broader national efforts towards full implementation of all children's rights, including through effective juvenile justice and child protection systems that fully respect such rights. Within this larger framework, MACRs are an important turning point that needs to be carefully addressed, but only in close consideration of the implications for children both younger and older than their threshold.

At the same time, the basic legitimacy of legal systems necessitates the establishment of MACRs—as a minimum requirement for the certainty of law and the moral condemnation transmitted by criminal punishments. Moreover, as per obligations under the Convention on the Rights of the Child (CRC) for all but two countries of the world, and apparently as a general principle of international law applicable to all countries, every country faces a legal obligation to establish an MACR. Depending on the country, such obligations may be enforceable before national, regional, and/or international judicial bodies. In addition, broad international guidance advises countries—sometimes with the weight of additional legal obligations—on how they should establish and apply their MACR provisions.

By way of conclusion, and drawing from the findings of the present study, this chapter delineates the key considerations for establishing and implementing MACRs in ways that support the rights of children.

Defining a More Meaningful MACR

Although it may appear to be fairly straightforward, the MACR is not just a question of setting and applying an age limit. In the context of children, criminal responsibility must be understood in relation to associated procedures, measures, and conditions, as well as the justifications for them, both in law and in practice. This is true for children younger and older than MACRs, in adult and juvenile criminal law, and in civil law in the context of welfare, care, and protection. MACRs are important legal milestones, but the ages at which they are set, and the nominal justifications for those age levels, are often less revealing than what transpires in practice.

As such, it is insufficient to limit the MACR's description to simply the lowest age at which children may potentially be held criminally responsible. The emerging international consensus understands that the MACR must provide one clear legal standard that is applicable throughout the territories of respective countries, and that is equally applicable to all children within them, enforced uniformly without any form of discrimination. It precludes secondary and multiple ages of criminal responsibility, such as *doli incapax* and similar provisions, and multiple age limits according to type or supposed seriousness of offense. In contrast, pursuant to international human rights and juvenile justice standards, it presumes that the minimum age for responsibility in adult criminal court (i.e., the minimum age for penal majority) is 18 years or higher.

The international consensus further holds that children younger than MACRs at the time of alleged offenses cannot be formally charged or subjected to penal law procedures or responses, in either juvenile or adult criminal justice systems. Such children cannot be treated in any criminalized manner either, in the context of any system whatsoever, including by detention in police custody or other forms of detention. Instead, special protective measures may be taken in their best interests, either through non-penal judicial proceedings or without resorting to judicial proceedings at all. Important rights apply in all protective proceedings, and legal safeguards must ensure that procedures and treatment are fair. In particular, additional rights related to the deprivation of liberty apply in those exceptionally rare cases where special protective measures may deprive the liberty of children younger than MACRs.

It is not always clear, however, how national practices should be held up against this broader understanding of the MACR. This is particularly true in the case of special protective measures applied to children younger than MACRs, since many countries' measures lie ambiguously between protection and punishment. Classic criminal law definitions of punishment provide an additional reference point to assess what measures may indicate de facto criminal responsibility.[1] Punishment generally includes all unpleasant sanctions that are justified predominantly as retribution for offending conduct, or as prevention of further offending conduct. More precisely, criminal punishments are legally sanctioned measures linked to some past offense that are primarily intended to punish the offender or ensure public safety. As such, even where rehabilitation, reform, and therapeutic measures are ordered based on past conduct or offenses, and are intended to prevent future conduct or offenses, they remain criminal punishments.

These various facets of punishment and the MACR's meaning provide the foundation for an objective basis against which national MACRs should be assessed. Practices or provisions that contradict the MACR's definition should be

---

1 Packer, Herbert L., *The Limits of the Criminal Sanction*, Stanford, Stanford University Press, 1968.

rectified. If they are indicative of punishment, and thus responsibility, they should be rejected as unacceptable for children younger than MACRs. Proper remedies should be pursued.

Competent national authorities bear primary responsibility for ensuring such conformity with the contextual MACR definition described in this section. Other bodies are also critical, including national courts and independent human rights institutions; regional and international judicial bodies; regional and international human rights monitoring bodies; and national, regional, and international non-governmental organizations (NGOs). As a starting point, they should examine formal legal and policy provisions; actual state responses to children younger and older than nominal MACRs, and respective indications of the rationales behind them; the function of children's conduct to those responses; and whether or not treatment justifications are reflected in practice and are generally expected to be beneficial. In addition, comprehensive data on state responses, lawful or otherwise, should be scrutinized for children both younger and older than MACRs.[2]

MACR Provisions: Establishment, Implementation, and Monitoring

The enactment of MACRs is a highly political and revealing moment in the constant struggle to define childhood. Across juvenile justice history, that struggle has been broadly driven in terms of welfare and justice approaches, which are founded upon drastically different accounts of children's competence, rights, criminal responsibility, and therefore MACRs. Both approaches bring conceptual flaws with important and far-reaching practical consequences for children. International children's rights also carry a set of ideas about children and childhood, but within a viable and enduring framework that addresses and mediates welfare-justice tensions. Its account of children's criminal responsibility is colored by a range of procedural and substantive considerations for children both above and below the MACR, with the multi-faceted concept of children's evolving capacities lying at the center. This section discusses several of these aspects in their consequences for establishing, implementing, and monitoring MACRs.

A Question of Age?

In very specific terms of establishing an MACR age level, academic evidence to date is not sufficiently compelling to recommend one optimal age limit for all countries. Nonetheless, this study does find a number of important indicators that

---

[2] For example, data disaggregated by at least the following: age; gender; region; rural/urban area; national, social, and ethnic origin; reason, nature, duration, setting, and periodicity of review of intervention; all cases of deprivation of liberty for any period of time, including arrest; and number of places where children are deprived of their liberty, the number of spaces available, and ratio of caregivers to children.

point to 12–13 years as the MACR age levels most amenable to children's rights. First, the international consensus is that MACRs should be set at 12 years or higher. Likewise, the current median age for MACRs worldwide is 12 years, an important practical consideration in terms of receptivity to change and long-term age-level stability. Although conducted only in North America, the most comprehensive delinquency research available demonstrates that for children 12 and younger, the most effective responses are strictly non-punitive and treatment-oriented, and are based in homes or schools. When implemented correctly, certain model programs consistently reduce short-term and long-term problem behavior and offending, and are perfectly consonant with the rights of children younger than MACRs. In contrast, arrest, deprivation of liberty, and other punitive-oriented responses to children 12 and younger are generally ineffective, and in fact typically worsen behavior and delinquency problems over time.

Children's ability to participate effectively in trials is another crucial consideration in establishing MACR age levels. Low MACRs systematically expose younger children to criminal trials when it may not be possible for them to participate effectively in their own defense, and courts may not be able to identify all such children and refer them to appropriate welfare or protection procedures. From this perspective, the best approach may be to set MACRs at the age where children can, more likely than not, participate effectively in their own defense at trial. Future comparative and national-level research on the international standards' definition of effective participation might identify the ages by which children typically gain necessary competencies. Research on broadly related legal standards in the United States suggests that the ages of 11–13 years are critical for children's development in such competencies, although these findings cannot be extrapolated directly to other countries.

Progressively higher age levels for MACRs pose a wide range of difficulties for respecting children's rights, at both theoretical and practical levels. The general international consensus that MACRs should not be set lower than 12 already reflects relevant protective-oriented arguments, thus it is implicit that lower MACRs are irreconcilable with children's rights. Even though some authorities support setting MACRs at age levels significantly higher than 12—still driven largely by protective arguments—such levels create other challenges.

The interrelated nature of children's rights dictates that this protective thrust be balanced with other relevant principles, but isolated arguments for significantly higher MACRs fail to do so. For example, they inherently depict children as less competent and less responsible, and this characterization is irreconcilable with arguments for greater participation of such children, for increasing consideration of their views, and indeed for the exercise of their rights on their own behalf.

The principle of evolving capacities calls for children's competencies to be faithfully acknowledged, respected, and fostered, and for both liberty rights and responsibilities to accrue as children become capable of exercising their own rights. Part of this process for children is to increasingly see the consequences of their choices at developmentally appropriate levels, in a gradual transition towards full adult rights and responsibilities. Juvenile justice systems are a compatible and valuable part of this developmental path, and both responsibility and criminal responsibility play important roles therein. The protective aspect of evolving capacities, for example to protect children from responsibilities for which they are not prepared, is indeed important. Nevertheless, delaying criminal responsibility in the name of such protection, by pushing MACRs increasingly higher, encroaches upon other rights of children. The procedural and substantive rules of international juvenile justice standards better address the recurring problems of juvenile justice that generally prompt such protective concerns. Implementation of these standards is the challenging yet sustainable solution that respects all children's rights.

In contrast, increasing MACRs beyond 12–13 years in hopes of avoiding the problems of juvenile justice seems neither sustainable nor likely to respect children's rights in practice. Relatively high MACRs often play into simplistic notions of children as innocent or evil, victim or perpetrator. These notions cannot realistically expect to claim all persons younger than 18 as "innocent," and some older children will be exposed to the possibility of criminal responsibility. At a minimum, harsh rhetoric and policies will likely be directed against them. Moreover, isolated violent crimes by younger children can quickly turn this logic against its protective intentions, leading to intense public and political pressures for retribution against the "evil" children committing them, as well as inestimable setbacks for the broader rights agenda.

The push to raise MACRs also lends itself in practice to wide and problematic state intervention against younger children, such as in former *situación irregular* systems of Latin America, some welfare-oriented juvenile justice systems, and apparently in many systems influenced by Soviet law. The difficulty of providing strictly non-punitive measures to relatively older groups of adolescents increases, and tends to conflict with public pressure for accountability, leading at times to extrajudicial treatment and vigilante justice. Other problems loom larger as the MACR grows higher. Where children do not widely possess reliable proof of age, age estimation may become increasingly difficult as more children in conflict with the law lie near its limit. Without significantly more effective efforts to stop child exploitation, instrumental use of young children in criminal activities may also increase.

Age Means Little without Implementation and Monitoring

As suggested above, MACRs lower than 12 are held to be incompatible with children's rights, at the same time that MACRs beyond 12–13 years grow increasingly contradictory to children's rights. Nonetheless, simply setting MACRs at 12 or 13 years is insufficient. Age levels themselves cannot be separated from policies for children younger and older than respective MACRs, and MACRs will not effectively serve their intended function unless such policies are carefully coordinated. This section highlights some minimum considerations that need to be simultaneously addressed.

The foundation is full national implementation of children's rights and international juvenile justice standards. Quite simply, the realization of children's social, economic, civil, and political rights in particular decreases the need for subsequent interventions of all types, as does continuous and comprehensive delinquency prevention efforts for all children. These proactive steps directly decrease later pressures for punitive policies against young children and other practices contrary to children's rights. In general, such work requires implementation and monitoring across social, economic, legal, political, institutional, policy, and other spheres—synchronizing systems that may not traditionally see themselves as relevant—and it explicitly encourages a structural-institutional understanding of children and delinquency. This forces a fundamental rethinking of the conventional understanding of delinquency prevention. It shifts to a larger base of roles and responsibilities; an earlier start on prevention programs for all children; and a focus on specific model programs that are non-punitive, and home- and school-based, which prevent youth crime in the short- and long-term. It also requires universal birth registration, plus age verification systems and policies that conform to the latest international guidance.

Children's rights principles also guide actions at the level of individual children, and these include developmentally appropriate responses to all children in conflict with the law, both above and below MACRs. First, for children younger than MACRs, procedures and responses must reflect the absence of criminal responsibility both in name and in substance. Similar to universal prevention programs, the proven-effective model intervention programs for younger children's disruptive, aggressive, and/or delinquent behavior are all treatment-oriented, non-custodial, and non-punitive. That is, they are generally acceptable in the absence of criminal responsibility. Options that generally contradict the absence of responsibility, such as punitive measures, legal sanctions, and the deprivation of liberty, may tend to worsen such behavior over time. Likewise, simply ignoring children's early disruptive behavior and offending is linked to continued and more serious offending over time. Worsening delinquency problems are not only more difficult and more expensive to address, but also lead to pressures to decrease MACRs. Youth policy should take young children and their actions seriously, and consistently respond to them through developmentally-appropriate model programs.

For children who have reached MACRs, there exists the possibility of criminal responsibility. This neither means nor suggests, however, that all children beginning at the MACR and in conflict with the law should face criminal proceedings or be found criminally responsible. Such children should indeed see developmentally appropriate responses to their actions, but children's rights encourage the route of alternative procedures plus a wide variety of disposition options, rather than formal criminal proceedings and sanctions. The same model intervention programs for younger children—which are consistently non-custodial, non-punitive, and treatment-oriented—are also the most effective responses to older children's problem behavior and delinquent acts. These can generally be provided through diversion alternatives such as restorative justice, community conferencing, and traditional justice systems, assuming children's authentic consent and full respect for their rights.[3] Importantly, international children's rights also dictate that the deprivation of liberty only be used in exceptional cases, as a disposition of last resort, and only for the minimum necessary period. Punitive sanctions and the deprivation of liberty are usually just as ineffective or harmful for older children as they are for younger children.

This structure supporting the MACR—national implementation of all children's rights, universal delinquency prevention for all children, and appropriate responses to children respectively younger and older than the MACR—also needs the public's buy-in to keep the MACR stable and effective over time. As part of larger obligations and efforts to make the CRC's principles and provisions "widely known, by appropriate and active means, to adults and children alike," proactive national debates should be fostered to encourage understanding of children's rights in juvenile justice.[4] Such efforts include constructive engagement with the media, public education and awareness campaigns, as well as training for relevant public officials. This communicates a vision of childhood that resists reduction of the debate into terms of good and evil children, instead promoting respect and dignity for all children, and that encourages appropriate responses to all children. Such messages underscore the common societal role and responsibility for implementing children's rights, as well as the benefits to be reaped for all of society. When embedded within a broader acceptance of such discourses, the MACR more successfully marks and holds the line between non-responsibility and criminal responsibility in juvenile justice.

All the same, the presence of serious MACR-related challenges in probably every country of the world underscores the importance of careful monitoring of implementation efforts. Children's rights and juvenile justice monitoring need to scrutinize potential MACR problems, such as those related to age estimates; inconsistent or problematic responses to children younger than MACRs; effective participation at trial; instrumental use of children for criminal activities; as well as widening public misconceptions about juvenile justice. Laws, policies, and programs should be adjusted accordingly where signs of challenges emerge. Such monitoring and adjustment are primarily the task of national authorities with responsibility for children's rights implementation under the CRC. Their work should be both complemented and held accountable by bodies such as independent human rights institutions, national and international NGOs, and national, regional, and international judicial and treaty monitoring bodies.

The MACR is indeed a crucial marker in childhood, but this age limit alone cannot end the rights violations that often surround it in practice. Making MACRs work for children's rights requires a broader approach and more holistic efforts, but the rights of children call for nothing less.

---

3   See Van Bueren, Geraldine, "A Curious Case of Isolationism: America and International Child Criminal Justice," 18 *Quinnipiac Law Review* 451, 1999.

4   Art. 42, CRC.

Annex 1

United Nations Convention on the Rights of the Child (Adopted by UN General Assembly Resolution 44/25 of 20 November 1989, and entered into force 2 September 1990)

Preamble

The States Parties to the present Convention,

Considering that, in accordance with the principles proclaimed in the Charter of the United Nations, recognition of the inherent dignity and of the equal and inalienable rights of all members of the human family is the foundation of freedom, justice and peace in the world,

Bearing in mind that the peoples of the United Nations have, in the Charter, reaffirmed their faith in fundamental human rights and in the dignity and worth of the human person, and have determined to promote social progress and better standards of life in larger freedom,

Recognizing that the United Nations has, in the Universal Declaration of Human Rights and in the International Covenants on Human Rights, proclaimed and agreed that everyone is entitled to all the rights and freedoms set forth therein, without distinction of any kind, such as race, colour, sex, language, religion, political or other opinion, national or social origin, property, birth or other status,

Recalling that, in the Universal Declaration of Human Rights, the United Nations has proclaimed that childhood is entitled to special care and assistance,

Convinced that the family, as the fundamental group of society and the natural environment for the growth and well-being of all its members and particularly children, should be afforded the necessary protection and assistance so that it can fully assume its responsibilities within the community,

Recognizing that the child, for the full and harmonious development of his or her personality, should grow up in a family environment, in an atmosphere of happiness, love and understanding,

Considering that the child should be fully prepared to live an individual life in society, and brought up in the spirit of the ideals proclaimed in the Charter of the United Nations, and in particular in the spirit of peace, dignity, tolerance, freedom, equality and solidarity,

Bearing in mind that the need to extend particular care to the child has been stated in the Geneva Declaration of the Rights of the Child of 1924 and in the Declaration of the Rights of the Child adopted by the General Assembly on 20 November 1959 and recognized in the Universal Declaration of Human Rights, in the International Covenant on Civil and Political Rights (in particular in articles 23 and 24), in the International Covenant on Economic, Social and Cultural Rights (in particular in article 10) and in the statutes and relevant instruments of specialized agencies and international organizations concerned with the welfare of children,

Bearing in mind that, as indicated in the Declaration of the Rights of the Child, "the child, by reason of his physical and mental immaturity, needs special safeguards and care, including appropriate legal protection, before as well as after birth",

Recalling the provisions of the Declaration on Social and Legal Principles relating to the Protection and Welfare of Children, with Special Reference to Foster Placement and Adoption Nationally and Internationally; the United Nations Standard Minimum Rules for the Administration of Juvenile Justice (The Beijing Rules); and the Declaration on the Protection of Women and Children in Emergency and Armed Conflict,

Recognizing that, in all countries in the world, there are children living in exceptionally difficult conditions, and that such children need special consideration,

Taking due account of the importance of the traditions and cultural values of each people for the protection and harmonious development of the child,

Recognizing the importance of international co-operation for improving the living conditions of children in every country, in particular in the developing countries,

Have agreed as follows:

PART I

Article 1

For the purposes of the present Convention, a child means every human being below the age of eighteen years unless under the law applicable to the child, majority is attained earlier.

Article 2

1. States Parties shall respect and ensure the rights set forth in the present Convention to each child within their jurisdiction without discrimination of any kind, irrespective of the child's or his or her parent's or legal guardian's race, colour, sex, language, religion, political or other opinion, national, ethnic or social origin, property, disability, birth or other status.

2. States Parties shall take all appropriate measures to ensure that the child is protected against all forms of discrimination or punishment on the basis of the status, activities, expressed opinions, or beliefs of the child's parents, legal guardians, or family members.

Article 3

1. In all actions concerning children, whether undertaken by public or private social welfare institutions, courts of law, administrative authorities or legislative bodies, the best interests of the child shall be a primary consideration.
2. States Parties undertake to ensure the child such protection and care as is necessary for his or her well-being, taking into account the rights and duties of his or her parents, legal guardians, or other individuals legally responsible for him or her, and, to this end, shall take all appropriate legislative and administrative measures.
3. States Parties shall ensure that the institutions, services and facilities responsible for the care or protection of children shall conform with the standards established by competent authorities, particularly in the areas of safety, health, in the number and suitability of their staff, as well as competent supervision.

Article 4

States Parties shall undertake all appropriate legislative, administrative, and other measures for the implementation of the rights recognized in the present Convention. With regard to economic, social and cultural rights, States Parties shall undertake such measures to the maximum extent of their available resources and, where needed, within the framework of international co-operation.

Article 5

States Parties shall respect the responsibilities, rights and duties of parents or, where applicable, the members of the extended family or community as provided for by local custom, legal guardians or other persons legally responsible for the child, to provide, in a manner consistent with the evolving capacities of the child, appropriate direction and guidance in the exercise by the child of the rights recognized in the present Convention.

Article 6

1. States Parties recognize that every child has the inherent right to life.
2. States Parties shall ensure to the maximum extent possible the survival and development of the child.

Article 7

1. The child shall be registered immediately after birth and shall have the right from birth to a name, the right to acquire a nationality and. as far as possible, the right to know and be cared for by his or her parents.
2. States Parties shall ensure the implementation of these rights in accordance with their national law and their obligations under the relevant international instruments in this field, in particular where the child would otherwise be stateless.

Article 8

1. States Parties undertake to respect the right of the child to preserve his or her identity, including nationality, name and family relations as recognized by law without unlawful interference.
2. Where a child is illegally deprived of some or all of the elements of his or her identity, States Parties shall provide appropriate assistance and protection, with a view to re-establishing speedily his or her identity.

Article 9

1. States Parties shall ensure that a child shall not be separated from his or her parents against their will, except when competent authorities subject to judicial review determine, in accordance with applicable law and procedures, that such separation is necessary for the best interests of the child. Such determination may be necessary in a particular case such as one involving abuse or neglect of the child by the parents, or one where the parents are living separately and a decision must be made as to the child's place of residence.
2. In any proceedings pursuant to paragraph 1 of the present article, all interested parties shall be given an opportunity to participate in the proceedings and make their views known.
3. States Parties shall respect the right of the child who is separated from one or both parents to maintain personal relations and direct contact with both parents on a regular basis, except if it is contrary to the child's best interests.
4. Where such separation results from any action initiated by a State Party, such as the detention, imprisonment, exile, deportation or death (including death arising from any cause while the person is in the custody of the State) of one or both parents or of the child, that State Party shall, upon request, provide the parents, the child or, if appropriate, another member of the family with the essential information concerning the whereabouts of the absent member(s) of the family unless the provision of the information would be detrimental to the well-being of the child. States Parties shall further ensure that the submission of such a request shall of itself entail no adverse consequences for the person(s) concerned.

Article 10

1. In accordance with the obligation of States Parties under article 9, paragraph 1, applications by a child or his or her parents to enter or leave a State Party for the purpose of family reunification shall be dealt with by States Parties in a positive, humane and expeditious manner. States Parties shall further ensure that the submission of such a request shall entail no adverse consequences for the applicants and for the members of their family.
2. A child whose parents reside in different States shall have the right to maintain on a regular basis, save in exceptional circumstances personal relations and direct contacts with both parents. Towards that end and in accordance with the obligation of States Parties under article 9, paragraph 1, States Parties shall respect the right of the child and his or her parents to leave any country, including their own, and to enter their own country. The right to leave any country shall be subject only to such restrictions as are prescribed by law and which are necessary to protect the national security, public order (*ordre public*), public health or morals or the rights and freedoms of others and are consistent with the other rights recognized in the present Convention.

Article 11

1. States Parties shall take measures to combat the illicit transfer and non-return of children abroad.
2. To this end, States Parties shall promote the conclusion of bilateral or multilateral agreements or accession to existing agreements.

Article 12

1. States Parties shall assure to the child who is capable of forming his or her own views the right to express those views freely in all matters affecting the child, the views of the child being given due weight in accordance with the age and maturity of the child.
2. For this purpose, the child shall in particular be provided the opportunity to be heard in any judicial and administrative proceedings affecting the child, either directly, or through a representative or an appropriate body, in a manner consistent with the procedural rules of national law.

Article 13

1. The child shall have the right to freedom of expression; this right shall include freedom to seek, receive and impart information and ideas of all kinds, regardless of frontiers, either orally, in writing or in print, in the form of art, or through any other media of the child's choice.

2. The exercise of this right may be subject to certain restrictions, but these shall only be such as are provided by law and are necessary:

   a. For respect of the rights or reputations of others; or
   b. For the protection of national security or of public order (*ordre public*), or of public health or morals.

Article 14

1. States Parties shall respect the right of the child to freedom of thought, conscience and religion.
2. States Parties shall respect the rights and duties of the parents and, when applicable, legal guardians, to provide direction to the child in the exercise of his or her right in a manner consistent with the evolving capacities of the child.
3. Freedom to manifest one's religion or beliefs may be subject only to such limitations as are prescribed by law and are necessary to protect public safety, order, health or morals, or the fundamental rights and freedoms of others.

Article 15

1. States Parties recognize the rights of the child to freedom of association and to freedom of peaceful assembly.
2. No restrictions may be placed on the exercise of these rights other than those imposed in conformity with the law and which are necessary in a democratic society in the interests of national security or public safety, public order (*ordre public*), the protection of public health or morals or the protection of the rights and freedoms of others.

Article 16

1. No child shall be subjected to arbitrary or unlawful interference with his or her privacy, family, home or correspondence, nor to unlawful attacks on his or her honour and reputation.
2. The child has the right to the protection of the law against such interference or attacks.

Article 17

States Parties recognize the important function performed by the mass media and shall ensure that the child has access to information and material from a diversity of national and international sources, especially those aimed at the promotion of his or her social, spiritual and moral well-being and physical and mental health. To this end, States Parties shall:

a. Encourage the mass media to disseminate information and material of social and cultural benefit to the child and in accordance with the spirit of article 29;
b. Encourage international co-operation in the production, exchange and dissemination of such information and material from a diversity of cultural, national and international sources;
c. Encourage the production and dissemination of children's books;
d. Encourage the mass media to have particular regard to the linguistic needs of the child who belongs to a minority group or who is indigenous;
e. Encourage the development of appropriate guidelines for the protection of the child from information and material injurious to his or her well-being, bearing in mind the provisions of articles 13 and 18.

Article 18

1. States Parties shall use their best efforts to ensure recognition of the principle that both parents have common responsibilities for the upbringing and development of the child. Parents or, as the case may be, legal guardians, have the primary responsibility for the upbringing and development of the child. The best interests of the child will be their basic concern.
2. For the purpose of guaranteeing and promoting the rights set forth in the present Convention, States Parties shall render appropriate assistance to parents and legal guardians in the performance of their child-rearing responsibilities and shall ensure the development of institutions, facilities and services for the care of children.
3. States Parties shall take all appropriate measures to ensure that children of working parents have the right to benefit from child-care services and facilities for which they are eligible.

Article 19

1. States Parties shall take all appropriate legislative, administrative, social and educational measures to protect the child from all forms of physical or mental violence, injury or abuse, neglect or negligent treatment, maltreatment or exploitation, including sexual abuse, while in the care of parent(s), legal guardian(s) or any other person who has the care of the child.
2. Such protective measures should, as appropriate, include effective procedures for the establishment of social programmes to provide necessary support for the child and for those who have the care of the child, as well as for other forms of prevention and for identification, reporting, referral, investigation, treatment and follow-up of instances of child maltreatment described heretofore, and, as appropriate, for judicial involvement.

Article 20

1. A child temporarily or permanently deprived of his or her family environment, or in whose own best interests cannot be allowed to remain in that environment, shall be entitled to special protection and assistance provided by the State.
2. States Parties shall in accordance with their national laws ensure alternative care for such a child.
3. Such care could include, *inter alia*, foster placement, *kafalah* of Islamic law, adoption or if necessary placement in suitable institutions for the care of children. When considering solutions, due regard shall be paid to the desirability of continuity in a child's upbringing and to the child's ethnic, religious, cultural and linguistic background.

Article 21

States Parties that recognize and/or permit the system of adoption shall ensure that the best interests of the child shall be the paramount consideration and they shall:

a. Ensure that the adoption of a child is authorized only by competent authorities who determine, in accordance with applicable law and procedures and on the basis of all pertinent and reliable information, that the adoption is permissible in view of the child's status concerning parents, relatives and legal guardians and that, if required, the persons concerned have given their informed consent to the adoption on the basis of such counselling as may be necessary;
b. Recognize that inter-country adoption may be considered as an alternative means of child's care, if the child cannot be placed in a foster or an adoptive family or cannot in any suitable manner be cared for in the child's country of origin;
c. Ensure that the child concerned by inter-country adoption enjoys safeguards and standards equivalent to those existing in the case of national adoption;
d. Take all appropriate measures to ensure that, in inter-country adoption, the placement does not result in improper financial gain for those involved in it;
e. Promote, where appropriate, the objectives of the present article by concluding bilateral or multilateral arrangements or agreements, and endeavour, within this framework, to ensure that the placement of the child in another country is carried out by competent authorities or organs.

Article 22

1. States Parties shall take appropriate measures to ensure that a child who is seeking refugee status or who is considered a refugee in accordance with applicable international or domestic law and procedures shall, whether unaccompanied or accompanied by his or her parents or by any other person, receive appropriate protection and humanitarian assistance in the enjoyment of

applicable rights set forth in the present Convention and in other international human rights or humanitarian instruments to which the said States are Parties.
2. For this purpose, States Parties shall provide, as they consider appropriate, co-operation in any efforts by the United Nations and other competent intergovernmental organizations or non-governmental organizations co-operating with the United Nations to protect and assist such a child and to trace the parents or other members of the family of any refugee child in order to obtain information necessary for reunification with his or her family. In cases where no parents or other members of the family can be found, the child shall be accorded the same protection as any other child permanently or temporarily deprived of his or her family environment for any reason, as set forth in the present Convention.

Article 23

1. States Parties recognize that a mentally or physically disabled child should enjoy a full and decent life, in conditions which ensure dignity, promote self-reliance and facilitate the child's active participation in the community.
2. States Parties recognize the right of the disabled child to special care and shall encourage and ensure the extension, subject to available resources, to the eligible child and those responsible for his or her care, of assistance for which application is made and which is appropriate to the child's condition and to the circumstances of the parents or others caring for the child.
3. Recognizing the special needs of a disabled child, assistance extended in accordance with paragraph 2 of the present article shall be provided free of charge, whenever possible, taking into account the financial resources of the parents or others caring for the child, and shall be designed to ensure that the disabled child has effective access to and receives education, training, health care services, rehabilitation services, preparation for employment and recreation opportunities in a manner conducive to the child's achieving the fullest possible social integration and individual development, including his or her cultural and spiritual development
4. States Parties shall promote, in the spirit of international cooperation, the exchange of appropriate information in the field of preventive health care and of medical, psychological and functional treatment of disabled children, including dissemination of and access to information concerning methods of rehabilitation, education and vocational services, with the aim of enabling States Parties to improve their capabilities and skills and to widen their experience in these areas. In this regard, particular account shall be taken of the needs of developing countries.

Article 24

1. States Parties recognize the right of the child to the enjoyment of the highest attainable standard of health and to facilities for the treatment of illness and rehabilitation of health. States Parties shall strive to ensure that no child is deprived of his or her right of access to such health care services.
2. States Parties shall pursue full implementation of this right and, in particular, shall take appropriate measures:

    a. To diminish infant and child mortality;
    b. To ensure the provision of necessary medical assistance and health care to all children with emphasis on the development of primary health care;
    c. To combat disease and malnutrition, including within the framework of primary health care, through, *inter alia*, the application of readily available technology and through the provision of adequate nutritious foods and clean drinking-water, taking into consideration the dangers and risks of environmental pollution;
    d. To ensure appropriate pre-natal and post-natal health care for mothers;
    e. To ensure that all segments of society, in particular parents and children, are informed, have access to education and are supported in the use of basic knowledge of child health and nutrition, the advantages of breastfeeding, hygiene and environmental sanitation and the prevention of accidents;
    f. To develop preventive health care, guidance for parents and family planning education and services.

3. States Parties shall take all effective and appropriate measures with a view to abolishing traditional practices prejudicial to the health of children.
4. States Parties undertake to promote and encourage international co-operation with a view to achieving progressively the full realization of the right recognized in the present article. In this regard, particular account shall be taken of the needs of developing countries.

Article 25

States Parties recognize the right of a child who has been placed by the competent authorities for the purposes of care, protection or treatment of his or her physical or mental health, to a periodic review of the treatment provided to the child and all other circumstances relevant to his or her placement.

Article 26

1. States Parties shall recognize for every child the right to benefit from social security, including social insurance, and shall take the necessary measures to achieve the full realization of this right in accordance with their national law.

2. The benefits should, where appropriate, be granted, taking into account the resources and the circumstances of the child and persons having responsibility for the maintenance of the child, as well as any other consideration relevant to an application for benefits made by or on behalf of the child.

Article 27

1. States Parties recognize the right of every child to a standard of living adequate for the child's physical, mental, spiritual, moral and social development.
2. The parent(s) or others responsible for the child have the primary responsibility to secure, within their abilities and financial capacities, the conditions of living necessary for the child's development.
3. States Parties, in accordance with national conditions and within their means, shall take appropriate measures to assist parents and others responsible for the child to implement this right and shall in case of need provide material assistance and support programmes, particularly with regard to nutrition, clothing and housing.
4. States Parties shall take all appropriate measures to secure the recovery of maintenance for the child from the parents or other persons having financial responsibility for the child, both within the State Party and from abroad. In particular, where the person having financial responsibility for the child lives in a State different from that of the child, States Parties shall promote the accession to international agreements or the conclusion of such agreements, as well as the making of other appropriate arrangements.

Article 28

1. States Parties recognize the right of the child to education, and with a view to achieving this right progressively and on the basis of equal opportunity, they shall, in particular:

   a. Make primary education compulsory and available free to all;
   b. Encourage the development of different forms of secondary education, including general and vocational education, make them available and accessible to every child, and take appropriate measures such as the introduction of free education and offering financial assistance in case of need;
   c. Make higher education accessible to all on the basis of capacity by every appropriate means;
   d. Make educational and vocational information and guidance available and accessible to all children;
   e. Take measures to encourage regular attendance at schools and the reduction of drop-out rates.

2. States Parties shall take all appropriate measures to ensure that school discipline is administered in a manner consistent with the child's human dignity and in conformity with the present Convention.
3. States Parties shall promote and encourage international cooperation in matters relating to education, in particular with a view to contributing to the elimination of ignorance and illiteracy throughout the world and facilitating access to scientific and technical knowledge and modern teaching methods. In this regard, particular account shall be taken of the needs of developing countries.

Article 29

1. States Parties agree that the education of the child shall be directed to:

   a. The development of the child's personality, talents and mental and physical abilities to their fullest potential;
   b. The development of respect for human rights and fundamental freedoms, and for the principles enshrined in the Charter of the United Nations;
   c. The development of respect for the child's parents, his or her own cultural identity, language and values, for the national values of the country in which the child is living, the country from which he or she may originate, and for civilizations different from his or her own;
   d. The preparation of the child for responsible life in a free society, in the spirit of understanding, peace, tolerance, equality of sexes, and friendship among all peoples, ethnic, national and religious groups and persons of indigenous origin;
   e. The development of respect for the natural environment.

2. No part of the present article or article 28 shall be construed so as to interfere with the liberty of individuals and bodies to establish and direct educational institutions, subject always to the observance of the principle set forth in paragraph 1 of the present article and to the requirements that the education given in such institutions shall conform to such minimum standards as may be laid down by the State.

Article 30

In those States in which ethnic, religious or linguistic minorities or persons of indigenous origin exist, a child belonging to such a minority or who is indigenous shall not be denied the right, in community with other members of his or her group, to enjoy his or her own culture, to profess and practise his or her own religion, or to use his or her own language.

Article 31

1. States Parties recognize the right of the child to rest and leisure, to engage in play and recreational activities appropriate to the age of the child and to participate freely in cultural life and the arts.
2. States Parties shall respect and promote the right of the child to participate fully in cultural and artistic life and shall encourage the provision of appropriate and equal opportunities for cultural, artistic, recreational and leisure activity.

Article 32

1. States Parties recognize the right of the child to be protected from economic exploitation and from performing any work that is likely to be hazardous or to interfere with the child's education, or to be harmful to the child's health or physical, mental, spiritual, moral or social development.
2. States Parties shall take legislative, administrative, social and educational measures to ensure the implementation of the present article. To this end, and having regard to the relevant provisions of other international instruments, States Parties shall in particular:

    a. Provide for a minimum age or minimum ages for admission to employment;
    b. Provide for appropriate regulation of the hours and conditions of employment;
    c. Provide for appropriate penalties or other sanctions to ensure the effective enforcement of the present article.

Article 33

States Parties shall take all appropriate measures, including legislative, administrative, social and educational measures, to protect children from the illicit use of narcotic drugs and psychotropic substances as defined in the relevant international treaties, and to prevent the use of children in the illicit production and trafficking of such substances.

Article 34

States Parties undertake to protect the child from all forms of sexual exploitation and sexual abuse. For these purposes, States Parties shall in particular take all appropriate national, bilateral and multilateral measures to prevent:

a. The inducement or coercion of a child to engage in any unlawful sexual activity;
b. The exploitative use of children in prostitution or other unlawful sexual practices;
c. The exploitative use of children in pornographic performances and materials.

Article 35

States Parties shall take all appropriate national, bilateral and multilateral measures to prevent the abduction of, the sale of or traffic in children for any purpose or in any form.

Article 36

States Parties shall protect the child against all other forms of exploitation prejudicial to any aspects of the child's welfare.

Article 37

States Parties shall ensure that:

a. No child shall be subjected to torture or other cruel, inhuman or degrading treatment or punishment. Neither capital punishment nor life imprisonment without possibility of release shall be imposed for offences committed by persons below eighteen years of age;
b. No child shall be deprived of his or her liberty unlawfully or arbitrarily. The arrest, detention or imprisonment of a child shall be in conformity with the law and shall be used only as a measure of last resort and for the shortest appropriate period of time;
c. Every child deprived of liberty shall be treated with humanity and respect for the inherent dignity of the human person, and in a manner which takes into account the needs of persons of his or her age. In particular, every child deprived of liberty shall be separated from adults unless it is considered in the child's best interest not to do so and shall have the right to maintain contact with his or her family through correspondence and visits, save in exceptional circumstances;
d. Every child deprived of his or her liberty shall have the right to prompt access to legal and other appropriate assistance, as well as the right to challenge the legality of the deprivation of his or her liberty before a court or other competent, independent and impartial authority, and to a prompt decision on any such action.

Article 38

1. States Parties undertake to respect and to ensure respect for rules of international humanitarian law applicable to them in armed conflicts which are relevant to the child.
2. States Parties shall take all feasible measures to ensure that persons who have not attained the age of fifteen years do not take a direct part in hostilities.
3. States Parties shall refrain from recruiting any person who has not attained the age of fifteen years into their armed forces. In recruiting among those persons who

have attained the age of fifteen years but who have not attained the age of eighteen years, States Parties shall endeavour to give priority to those who are oldest.
4. In accordance with their obligations under international humanitarian law to protect the civilian population in armed conflicts, States Parties shall take all feasible measures to ensure protection and care of children who are affected by an armed conflict.

Article 39

States Parties shall take all appropriate measures to promote physical and psychological recovery and social reintegration of a child victim of: any form of neglect, exploitation, or abuse; torture or any other form of cruel, inhuman or degrading treatment or punishment; or armed conflicts. Such recovery and reintegration shall take place in an environment which fosters the health, self-respect and dignity of the child.

Article 40

1. States Parties recognize the right of every child alleged as, accused of, or recognized as having infringed the penal law to be treated in a manner consistent with the promotion of the child's sense of dignity and worth, which reinforces the child's respect for the human rights and fundamental freedoms of others and which takes into account the child's age and the desirability of promoting the child's reintegration and the child's assuming a constructive role in society.
2. To this end, and having regard to the relevant provisions of international instruments, States Parties shall, in particular, ensure that:

    a. No child shall be alleged as, be accused of, or recognized as having infringed the penal law by reason of acts or omissions that were not prohibited by national or international law at the time they were committed;
    b. Every child alleged as or accused of having infringed the penal law has at least the following guarantees:

        i. To be presumed innocent until proven guilty according to law;
        ii. To be informed promptly and directly of the charges against him or her, and, if appropriate, through his or her parents or legal guardians, and to have legal or other appropriate assistance in the preparation and presentation of his or her defence;
        iii. To have the matter determined without delay by a competent, independent and impartial authority or judicial body in a fair hearing according to law, in the presence of legal or other appropriate assistance and, unless it is considered not to be in the best interest of the child, in particular, taking into account his or her age or situation, his or her parents or legal guardians;

iv. Not to be compelled to give testimony or to confess guilt; to examine or have examined adverse witnesses and to obtain the participation and examination of witnesses on his or her behalf under conditions of equality;
v. If considered to have infringed the penal law, to have this decision and any measures imposed in consequence thereof reviewed by a higher competent, independent and impartial authority or judicial body according to law;
vi. To have the free assistance of an interpreter if the child cannot understand or speak the language used;
vii. To have his or her privacy fully respected at all stages of the proceedings.

3. States Parties shall seek to promote the establishment of laws, procedures, authorities and institutions specifically applicable to children alleged as, accused of, or recognized as having infringed the penal law, and, in particular:

   a. The establishment of a minimum age below which children shall be presumed not to have the capacity to infringe the penal law;
   b. Whenever appropriate and desirable, measures for dealing with such children without resorting to judicial proceedings, providing that human rights and legal safeguards are fully respected.

4. A variety of dispositions, such as care, guidance and supervision orders; counselling; probation; foster care; education and vocational training programmes and other alternatives to institutional care shall be available to ensure that children are dealt with in a manner appropriate to their well-being and proportionate both to their circumstances and the offence.

Article 41

Nothing in the present Convention shall affect any provisions which are more conducive to the realization of the rights of the child and which may be contained in:

a. The law of a State party; or
b. International law in force for that State.

PART II

Article 42

States Parties undertake to make the principles and provisions of the Convention widely known, by appropriate and active means, to adults and children alike.

Article 43

1. For the purpose of examining the progress made by States Parties in achieving the realization of the obligations undertaken in the present Convention, there shall be established a Committee on the Rights of the Child, which shall carry out the functions hereinafter provided.
2. The Committee shall consist of eighteen experts of high moral standing and recognized competence in the field covered by this Convention. The members of the Committee shall be elected by States Parties from among their nationals and shall serve in their personal capacity, consideration being given to equitable geographical distribution, as well as to the principal legal systems.
3. The members of the Committee shall be elected by secret ballot from a list of persons nominated by States Parties. Each State Party may nominate one person from among its own nationals.
4. The initial election to the Committee shall be held no later than six months after the date of the entry into force of the present Convention and thereafter every second year. At least four months before the date of each election, the Secretary-General of the United Nations shall address a letter to States Parties inviting them to submit their nominations within two months. The Secretary-General shall subsequently prepare a list in alphabetical order of all persons thus nominated, indicating States Parties which have nominated them, and shall submit it to the States Parties to the present Convention.
5. The elections shall be held at meetings of States Parties convened by the Secretary-General at United Nations Headquarters. At those meetings, for which two thirds of States Parties shall constitute a quorum, the persons elected to the Committee shall be those who obtain the largest number of votes and an absolute majority of the votes of the representatives of States Parties present and voting.
6. The members of the Committee shall be elected for a term of four years. They shall be eligible for re-election if renominated. The term of five of the members elected at the first election shall expire at the end of two years; immediately after the first election, the names of these five members shall be chosen by lot by the Chairman of the meeting.
7. If a member of the Committee dies or resigns or declares that for any other cause he or she can no longer perform the duties of the Committee, the State Party which nominated the member shall appoint another expert from among its nationals to serve for the remainder of the term, subject to the approval of the Committee.
8. The Committee shall establish its own rules of procedure.
9. The Committee shall elect its officers for a period of two years.
10. The meetings of the Committee shall normally be held at United Nations Headquarters or at any other convenient place as determined by the Committee. The Committee shall normally meet annually. The duration of the meetings of the Committee shall be determined, and reviewed, if necessary, by a meeting

of the States Parties to the present Convention, subject to the approval of the General Assembly.
11. The Secretary-General of the United Nations shall provide the necessary staff and facilities for the effective performance of the functions of the Committee under the present Convention.
12. With the approval of the General Assembly, the members of the Committee established under the present Convention shall receive emoluments from United Nations resources on such terms and conditions as the Assembly may decide.

Article 44

1. States Parties undertake to submit to the Committee, through the Secretary-General of the United Nations, reports on the measures they have adopted which give effect to the rights recognized herein and on the progress made on the enjoyment of those rights

    a. Within two years of the entry into force of the Convention for the State Party concerned;
    b. Thereafter every five years.

2. Reports made under the present article shall indicate factors and difficulties, if any, affecting the degree of fulfilment of the obligations under the present Convention. Reports shall also contain sufficient information to provide the Committee with a comprehensive understanding of the implementation of the Convention in the country concerned.
3. A State Party which has submitted a comprehensive initial report to the Committee need not, in its subsequent reports submitted in accordance with paragraph 1 (b) of the present article, repeat basic information previously provided.
4. The Committee may request from States Parties further information relevant to the implementation of the Convention.
5. The Committee shall submit to the General Assembly, through the Economic and Social Council, every two years, reports on its activities.
6. States Parties shall make their reports widely available to the public in their own countries.

Article 45

In order to foster the effective implementation of the Convention and to encourage international co-operation in the field covered by the Convention:

a. The specialized agencies, the United Nations Children's Fund, and other United Nations organs shall be entitled to be represented at the consideration of the implementation of such provisions of the present Convention as fall within the scope of their mandate. The Committee may invite the specialized agencies, the United Nations Children's Fund and other competent bodies as it may consider appropriate to provide expert advice on the implementation of the Convention in areas falling within the scope of their respective mandates. The Committee may invite the specialized agencies, the United Nations Children's Fund, and other United Nations organs to submit reports on the implementation of the Convention in areas falling within the scope of their activities;

b. The Committee shall transmit, as it may consider appropriate, to the specialized agencies, the United Nations Children's Fund and other competent bodies, any reports from States Parties that contain a request, or indicate a need, for technical advice or assistance, along with the Committee's observations and suggestions, if any, on these requests or indications;

c. The Committee may recommend to the General Assembly to request the Secretary-General to undertake on its behalf studies on specific issues relating to the rights of the child;

d. The Committee may make suggestions and general recommendations based on information received pursuant to articles 44 and 45 of the present Convention. Such suggestions and general recommendations shall be transmitted to any State Party concerned and reported to the General Assembly, together with comments, if any, from States Parties.

PART III

Article 46

The present Convention shall be open for signature by all States.

Article 47

The present Convention is subject to ratification. Instruments of ratification shall be deposited with the Secretary-General of the United Nations.

Article 48

The present Convention shall remain open for accession by any State. The instruments of accession shall be deposited with the Secretary-General of the United Nations.

Article 49

1. The present Convention shall enter into force on the thirtieth day following the date of deposit with the Secretary-General of the United Nations of the twentieth instrument of ratification or accession.

2. For each State ratifying or acceding to the Convention after the deposit of the twentieth instrument of ratification or accession, the Convention shall enter into force on the thirtieth day after the deposit by such State of its instrument of ratification or accession.

Article 50

1. Any State Party may propose an amendment and file it with the Secretary-General of the United Nations. The Secretary-General shall thereupon communicate the proposed amendment to States Parties, with a request that they indicate whether they favour a conference of States Parties for the purpose of considering and voting upon the proposals. In the event that, within four months from the date of such communication, at least one third of the States Parties favour such a conference, the Secretary-General shall convene the conference under the auspices of the United Nations. Any amendment adopted by a majority of States Parties present and voting at the conference shall be submitted to the General Assembly for approval.
2. An amendment adopted in accordance with paragraph 1 of the present article shall enter into force when it has been approved by the General Assembly of the United Nations and accepted by a two-thirds majority of States Parties.
3. When an amendment enters into force, it shall be binding on those States Parties which have accepted it, other States Parties still being bound by the provisions of the present Convention and any earlier amendments which they have accepted.

Article 51

1. The Secretary-General of the United Nations shall receive and circulate to all States the text of reservations made by States at the time of ratification or accession.
2. A reservation incompatible with the object and purpose of the present Convention shall not be permitted.
3. Reservations may be withdrawn at any time by notification to that effect addressed to the Secretary-General of the United Nations, who shall then inform all States. Such notification shall take effect on the date on which it is received by the Secretary-General

Article 52

A State Party may denounce the present Convention by written notification to the Secretary-General of the United Nations. Denunciation becomes effective one year after the date of receipt of the notification by the Secretary-General.

Article 53

The Secretary-General of the United Nations is designated as the depositary of the present Convention.

Article 54

The original of the present Convention, of which the Arabic, Chinese, English, French, Russian and Spanish texts are equally authentic, shall be deposited with the Secretary-General of the United Nations. In witness thereof the undersigned plenipotentiaries, being duly authorized thereto by their respective Governments, have signed the present Convention.

Annex 2
Worldwide MACR Provisions and Statutory Sources by Country

Country	MACR	ACR specific crimes	*Doli incapax* test	MACR source statute
Afghanistan	12	–	–	Juvenile Code, 2005, Art. 5(1).[1] A person who has not completed the age of 12 is not criminally responsible.
Albania	14	16	–	Criminal Code, as of 2001, Art. 12.[2] A person bears criminal responsibility if, at the time he or she commits an offence, has reached the age of fourteen. A person who commits a criminal contravention bears responsibility at the age of sixteen.
Algeria	13[3]	–	–	Criminal Code, Art. 49.[4]
Andorra	12	–	–	Llei qualificada de la jurisdicció de menors, de modificació parcial del Codi penal i de la Llei qualificada de la Justícia, 1999, Art. 3 … . El menor de 12 anys és inimputable. Les accions en reclamació dels danys i perjudicis derivats d'una infracció penal comesa per un menor de 12 anys han de ser resoltes davant la jurisdicció civil ordinària.
Angola	12	–	–	Lei N.º 9/96 Sobre O Julgado de Menores, 1996, Art. 12 and 16. Art. 12: Compete ao Julgado de Menores: … b) aplicar medidas de prevenção criminal aos menores com idade compreendida entre os 12 e os 16 anos de idade, exclusivé. Art. 16: As medidas de prevenção criminal são aplicáveis aos menores que pratiquem factos tipificados na lei como delitos.
Antigua and Barbuda	8	–	–	Juvenile Act, 1951, Sect. 3. It shall be conclusively presumed that no child under the age of eight years can be guilty of any offence.

1   Unofficial translation provided by UNICEF Afghanistan.
2   Translation by Alibali, Agron, Albanian Legal Information Initiative, Chicago-Kent College of Law, Illinois Institute of Technology, pbosnia.kentlaw.edu/resources/legal/albania/crim_code.htm.
3   While the Criminal Code stipulates that "Only protective or re-education measures may be applied to a minor aged under 13," such measures apparently include placement in any of roughly 30 specialized re-education centers administered by the Ministry of Justice. Nearly 2000 children in conflict with the law between the ages of 8 and 13 were deprived of their liberty in these centers in 2005. See Committee on the Rights of the Child, *Second periodic reports of States parties due in 2000: Algeria*, CRC/C/93/Add.7, 3 Mar 2005, par. 332; and *Id.*, *Compte rendu analytique de la 1057e séance*, CRC/C/SR.1057, 20 Sept 2005, par. 91.
4   *Id.*, *Second periodic reports of States parties due in 2000: Algeria*, CRC/C/93/Add.7, 3 Mar 2005, par. 332.

Country	MACR	ACR specific crimes	*Doli incapax* test	MACR source statute
Argentina	16[5]	18	–	Ley 22.278, Régimen Penal de la Minoridad, as of 1983, Arts. 1–2.[6] Art. 1: No es punible el menor que no haya cumplido dieciséis años de edad. Tampoco lo es el que no haya cumplido dieciocho años, respecto de delitos de acción privada o reprimidos con pena privativa de la libertad que no exceda de dos años, con multa o con inhabilitación… . Art. 2: Es punible el menor de dieciséis a dieciocho años de edad que incurriere en delito que no fuera de los enunciados en el artículo primero … .
Armenia	14	16	–	Criminal Code, 2003, Arts. 24(1–2).[7] Art. 24 (1): The person who reached the age of 16 before the committal of the crime is subject to criminal liability. (2): The persons who reached the age of 14 before the committal of the crime are subject to criminal liability for murder (Articles 104–109), for inflicting willful severe or medium damage to health (Articles 112–116), for kidnapping people (Article 131), for rape (Article 138), for violent sexual actions (Article 139), for banditry (Article 179), for theft (Article 177), for robbery (Article 176), for extortion (Article 182), getting hold of a car or other means of transportation without the intention of appropriation (Article 183), for destruction or damage of property in aggravating circumstances (Article 185, parts 2 and 3), for theft or extortion of weapons, ammunition or explosives (Article 238), for theft or extortion of narcotic drugs or psychotropic substances (Article 269), for damaging the means of transportation or communication lines (Article 246), for hooliganism (Article 258).
Australia	10	–	10–14	Source depends on jurisdiction.[8] Commonwealth: Crimes Act 1914, s4M, and

5   The 2005 *Ley de protección integral de los derechos de las niñas, niños y adolescentes* explicitly abrogates the 1919 Agote law, which was the basis for Argentina's *situación irregular* policy of, in effect, discretionary deprivation of liberty of children of any age. The 2005 law would also seem to annul provisions in this spirit in the 1980 *Ley 22.278, Régimen Penal de la Minoridad*. However, final analysis may hinge upon pending legislation on juvenile criminal responsibility.

6   Art. 1: "No punishment may be imposed on any person under the age of 16 years. Nor may any punishment be imposed on a person under the age of 18 years for a privately actionable offence, an offence carrying a custodial sentence of not more than two years, or an offence punishable by a fine or disqualification … ." Art. 2: "Punishment may be imposed on a person between the ages of 16 and 18 years who has committed an offence other than the ones specified in article 1 … ." Committee on the Rights of the Child, *Periodic reports of States parties due in 1998: Argentina*, CRC/C/70/Add.10, 26 Feb 2002, par. 615.

7   Unofficial translation by the American Bar Association, Central European and Eurasian Law Initiative. See www.internews.am/legislation/index.asp.

8   Australian Institute of Criminology, *Young People and Crime: Table 1: Ages of criminal responsibility by Australian jurisdiction (as at 12 July 2005)*, www.aic.gov.au/research/jjustice/definition.html.

Annex 2: Worldwide MACR Provisions and Statutory Sources by Country 189

Country	MACR	ACR specific crimes	*Doli incapax* test	MACR source statute
				Criminal Code Act 1995, s7.1; *doli incapax*: Crimes Act 1914, s4N, and Criminal Code Act 1995, s7.2. Australian Capital Territory: Criminal Code 2002, s25; *doli incapax*: Criminal Code 2002, s26. Northern Territory: Criminal Code Act, as in force 2005, s38(1); *doli incapax*: Criminal Code Act, as in force 2005, s38(2). New South Wales: Children (Criminal Proceedings) Act 1987, s5; *doli incapax*: common law. Victoria: Children and Young Persons Act 1989, s127; *doli incapax*: common law. South Australia: Young Offenders Act 1993, s5; *doli incapax*: common law. Western Australia: Criminal Code Act Compilation Act 1913, s29. Queensland: Criminal Code Act 1899, s29(1); *doli incapax*: Criminal Code Act 1899, s29(2). Tasmania: Criminal Code Act 1924, s18(1); *doli incapax*: Criminal Code Act 1924, s18(2).
Austria	14	16	–	Jugendgerichtsgesetz, 1988, §1(1–2) and 4. §1: Im Sinne dieses Bundesgesetzes ist 1. Unmündiger: wer das vierzehnte Lebensjahr noch nicht vollendet hat; 2. Jugendlicher: wer das vierzehnte, aber noch nicht das neunzehnte Lebensjahr vollendet hat. §4: (1) Unmündige, die eine mit Strafe bedrohte Handlung begehen, sind nicht strafbar. (2) Ein Jugendlicher, der eine mit Strafe bedrohte Handlung begeht, ist nicht strafbar, wenn 1. er aus bestimmten Gründen noch nicht reif genug ist, das Unrecht der Tat einzusehen oder nach dieser Einsicht zu handeln, 2. er vor Vollendung des sechzehnten Lebensjahres ein Vergehen begeht, ihn kein schweres Verschulden trifft und nicht aus besonderen Gründen die Anwendung des Jugendstrafrechts geboten ist, um den Jugendlichen von strafbaren Handlungen abzuhalten, oder 3. die Voraussetzungen des § 42 StGB vorliegen.
Azerbaijan	14[9]	16	–	Criminal Code, Art. 20 (1–2).[10] (1) The person who has reached age of 16, to time of committing a crime shall be subjected to the criminal liability. (2) The persons who have reached the age of 14, to time of committing a crime, shall be subjected to the criminal

9 Under the 2002 Law on "Commission on minors and the protection of the rights of the children," administrative commissions may consider the cases of all children younger than 14 years of age suspected of having committed crimes, and they may impose disciplinary measures on such children including confinement in "special correction schools." See Azerbaijan NGO Alliance for Children's Rights, *Juvenile Justice in Azerbaijan: NGO Alternative Report on Situation of Juvenile Justice System in Azerbaijan within the period of 1998–2005*, Baku, 2005; and Committee on the Rights of the Child, *Second periodic reports of States parties due in 1999: Azerbaijan*, CRC/C/83/Add.13, 7 Apr 2005, pars. 436–444.

10 Unofficial translation by the Organization for Security and Co-operation in Europe, Office for Democratic Institutions and Human Rights, www.legislationline.org.

Country	MACR	ACR specific crimes	Doli incapax test	MACR source statute
				liability for deliberate murder, deliberate causing of heavy or less heavy harm to health, kidnapping of the person, rape, violent actions of sexual nature, theft, robbery, extortion, illegal occupation of the automobile or other vehicle without the purpose of plunder, deliberate destruction or damage of property under aggravating circumstances, terrorism, capture of the hostage, hooliganism under aggravating circumstances, plunder or extortion of fire-arms, ammunition, explosives and explosives, plunder or extortion of narcotics or psychotropic substances, reduction unsuitability of vehicles or means of communication.
Bahamas	7	–	7–12	Penal Code, Ch. 84 of the 2001 Statute Law of the Bahamas, Sect. 91(1–2). (1) Nothing is an offence which is done by a person under seven years of age. (2) Nothing is an offence which is done by a person of or above seven and under twelve years of age, who has not attained sufficient maturity of understanding to judge of the nature and consequences of his conduct in the matter in respect of which he is accused.
Bahrain	0[11]	–	–	–
Bangladesh	9	–	9–12	Penal Code, as of 2004, Sect. 82–83. Sect. 82: Nothing is an offense which is done by a child under nine years of age. Sect. 83: Nothing is an offense which is done by a child above nine years of age and under twelve, who has not attained sufficient maturity of understanding to judge of the nature and consequences of his conduct on that occasion.
Barbados	11	–	–	Juvenile Offenders Act, as of 1998, Sect. 7. Sections 8 and 9 shall not render punishable for an offence any child who is not, in the opinion of the court, above the age of 11 years and of sufficient capacity to commit crime.
Belarus	14	16	–	Criminal Code, as of 1 May 1994, Art. 10.[12] Criminal responsibility shall be applied to persons who had reached the age of sixteen before they committed a crime. Persons who have committed a crime at the age of between fourteen and sixteen shall be liable to criminal responsibility only for killing, encroachment upon the life of a militiaman, people's guard or other person, no less than for encroachment

11   Bahrain has held that its 1976 Penal Code, Article 32, establishes an MACR of 15 years, and that Juveniles Act No. 17 of 1976 provides non-criminal reform and protection responses to younger children. In reality, 15 years is the age of penal majority, and there is no lower age limit to what are clearly punitive responses, "such as detention in social welfare centres for up to 10 years for felonies (e.g. article 12 of the 1976 Juvenile Law)." The Committee on the Rights of the Child observed that there is no MACR. See *Concluding observations: Bahrain*, CRC/C/15/Add.175, 7 Feb 2002, par. 47; and *Initial reports of States parties due in 1994: Bahrain*, CRC/C/11/Add. 24, 23 Jul 2001.

12   Translation by SoftInform Engineering Information Company, Ltd., *JurInform Information System on Belarusian Legislation*, www.belarus.net/softinfo/lowcatal.htm.

Annex 2: Worldwide MACR Provisions and Statutory Sources by Country   191

Country	MACR	ACR specific crimes	*Doli incapax* test	MACR source statute
				upon the life of their close relations, deliberate infliction of bodily injuries which have caused derangement of health, rape, robbery, robbery, stealing of property in especially grand amounts, distortion, theft, persistent or especially persistent hooliganism, deliberate destruction or damage of property which has entailed grave consequences, stealing of firearms, ammunitions or explosives, stealing of narcotic substances, as well as for deliberate committing of actions which may cause a crash of a train … .
Belgium	12	–	–	Loi relative à la protection de la jeunesse, à la prise en charge des mineurs ayant commis un fait qualifié infraction et à la réparation du dommage causé par ce fait, as of 2006, Arts. 36(4°), 37(§1), 37(§2)(1er)(1°-3°), 37(§2)(2), 37(§ 2quater)(1er)(1°), and 37(§ 2quater)(3). Art. 36(4°): Le tribunal de la jeunesse connaît: … 4° des réquisitions du ministère public à l'égard des personnes poursuivies du chef d'un fait qualifié infraction, commis avant l'âge de dix-huit ans accomplis. Art. 37(§1): Le tribunal de la jeunesse peut ordonner à l'égard des personnes qui lui sont déférées, des mesures de garde, de préservation et d'éducation… . Art. 37(§2)(1er)(1°-3°): Il peut, le cas échéant, de façon cumulative: 1° réprimander les intéressés et, sauf en ce qui concerne ceux qui ont atteint l'âge de dix-huit ans, les laisser ou les rendre aux personnes qui en assurent l'hébergement, en enjoignant à ces dernières, le cas échéant, de mieux les surveiller ou les éduquer à l'avenir; 2° les soumettre à la surveillance du service social compétent; 3° les soumettre à un accompagnement éducatif intensif et à un encadrement individualisé d'un éducateur référent dépendant du service désigné par les communautés ou d'une personne physique répondant aux conditions fixées par les communautés… . Art. 37(§2)(2): Seules les mesures visées à l'alinéa 1er, 1°, 2° et 3°, peuvent être ordonnées à l'égard des personnes de moins de douze ans … . Art. 37(§ 2quater)(1er)(1°): § 2quater. Le tribunal ne peut ordonner la mesure de placement en institution communautaire publique de protection de la jeunesse visée au § 2, alinéa 1er, 8°, en régime éducatif ouvert, qu'à l'égard des personnes qui ont douze ans ou plus et qui: 1° soit, ont commis un fait qualifié infraction qui, s'il avait été commis par une personne majeure, aurait été de nature à entraîner, au sens du Code pénal ou des lois particulières, une peine d'emprisonnement correctionnel principal de trois ans ou une peine plus lourde… . Art. 37(§ 2quater)(3): Sans préjudice des conditions énumérées à

Country	MACR	ACR specific crimes	*Doli incapax* test	MACR source statute
				l'alinéa 2, le tribunal peut ordonner la mesure de placement en institution communautaire publique de protection de la jeunesse visée au § 2, alinéa 1er, 8°, en régime éducatif fermé, à l'égard d'une personne âgée de douze à quatorze ans, qui a gravement porté atteinte à la vie ou à la santé d'une personne et dont le comportement est particulièrement dangereux.
Belize	9	–	9–12	Criminal Code, as of 2000, Sect. 25. (1) Nothing is a crime which is done by a person under nine years of age. (2) Nothing is a crime which is done by a person of nine and under twelve years of age who has not attained sufficient maturity of understanding to judge of the nature and consequences of his conduct in the matter in respect of which he is accused.
Benin	13	–	–	l'Ordonnance 69–23 du 10 juillet 1969 relative au jugement des infractions commises par les mineurs de moins de 18 ans, Art. 23.[13]
Bhutan	10	–	–	Penal Code, 2004, §114. If the defendant is a child of 10 years and below, he shall not be held liable for any offence committed by him.
Bolivia	12	–	–	Código del Niño, Niña y Adolescente, 1999, Art. 223. Las niñas y niños que no hubieren cumplido los doce años de edad, están exentos de responsabilidad social quedando a salvo la responsabilidad civil, la cual será demandada ante los tribunales competentes … .
Bosnia and Herzegovina	14	–	–	Criminal Code, 2003, Art. 8.[14] Criminal legislation of Bosnia and Herzegovina shall not be applied to a child who, at the time of perpetrating a criminal offence, had not reached fourteen years of age.
Botswana	8	12	8–14	Penal Code, Sect. 13.[15]
Brazil	12	–	–	Estatuto da Criança e do Adolescente, 1990, Arts. 2 and 105. Art. 2: Considera-se criança, para os efeitos desta Lei, a pessoa até doze anos de idade incompletos, e adolescente aquela entre doze e dezoito anos de idade. Art. 105: Ao ato infracional praticado por criança corresponderão as medidas previstas no art. 101 [Medidas Específicas de Proteção].
Brunei Darussalam	7	–	7–12	Penal Code, Sects. 82–83.[16]

13 Sodjiedo Hounton, Rita-Félicité, "La Justice pour mineurs au Bénin: protection juridique et judiciaire de l'enfant au Bénin," in *Nouvelle Tribune Internationale des droits de l'enfant*, nos. 8–9, Défense des Enfants International – Belgique, September 2005.

14 Office of the High Representative Legal Department, www.ohr.int/ohr-dept/legal.

15 Committee on the Rights of the Child, *Initial reports of States parties due in 1997: Botswana*, CRC/C/51/ADD.9, 27 Feb 2004, par. 86. Boys younger than 12 years of age are presumed to be incapable of having "carnal knowledge."

16 *Id.*, *Initial reports of States parties due in 1998: Brunei Darussalam*, CRC/C/61/Add.5, 13 Mar 2003, par. 292.

Annex 2: Worldwide MACR Provisions and Statutory Sources by Country 193

Country	MACR	ACR specific crimes	*Doli incapax* test	MACR source statute
Bulgaria	14[17]	–	14–18	Penal Code, as of 2002, Arts. 31(2).[18] A juvenile who has accomplished 14 years of age but who has not accomplished 18 years of age shall be criminally responsible if he could have realised the quality and the importance of the act and handle his conduct.
Burkina Faso	13[19]	–	13–18	Penal Code, 1996, Art. 74.[20]
Burundi	13	–	–	Décret-loi n°1/6 du 4 avril 1981 portant réforme du code pénal, Art. 14. Les infractions commises par les mineurs de moins de treize ans ne donnent lieu qu'à des réparations civiles.
Cambodia	0	–	–	–
Cameroon	10	–	–	Code Pénal, Art. 80(1).[21] Le mineur de dix ans n'est pas pénalement responsable.
Canada	12	–	–	Criminal Code, as of 1985, Sect. 13. No person shall be convicted of an offence in respect of an act or omission on his part while that person was under the age of twelve years.
Cape Verde	16	–	–	–[22]
Central African Republic	13	–	–	Penal Code, Art. 49.[23]
Chad	13	–	–	Loi N° 007/PR/99 Portant procédure de poursuites et jugement des infractions commises par les mineurs de treize (13) à moins de Dix huit (18) ans, 1999, Art. 22. Le mineur de 13 ans ne pourra être soumis, si la prévention est établie contre lui, qu'à des mesures de tutelle, de surveillance ou d'éducation prévues au Chapitre V de la

17 Art. 32(2) of the Penal Code allows corrective measures, as defined under the Juvenile Delinquency Law, to be applied against children under 14 who have committed socially dangerous acts. Commissions for Prevention of Juvenile Delinquency may administratively order such measures, including deprivation of liberty in Social-pedagogic boarding schools for children as young as 7, and in Correctional boarding schools for children as young as 8. See, e.g., Bulgarian Helsinki Committee, *Memorandum of the Bulgarian Helsinki Committee*, Sofia, 17 Oct 2005; and National Statistical Institute of the Republic of Bulgaria, *Anti-Social Acts of Minor and Juvenile Persons in 2005*, 31 Mar 2006, www.nsi.bg/index_e.htm.

18 Translation by the Organization for Security and Co-operation in Europe, Office for Democratic Institutions and Human Rights, www.legislationline.org.

19 Although children younger than 13 are technically not criminally responsible, Act No. 19/61 of 9 May 1961 on juvenile offenders and children at risk does not prevent their deprivation of liberty by law enforcement officials: "Act No. 19/61 does not regulate the police phase of the deprivation of liberty … . Consequently, minors under the age of 13 who are presumed not to be responsible for their actions may be held in police custody … ." Committee on the Rights of the Child, *Initial reports of States parties due in 1997: Burkina Faso*, CRC/C/65/Add.18, 13 Feb 2002, par. 440.

20 *Ibid.*, pars. 417 and 424.

21 Défense des Enfants International – Section Cameroun, *Journées d'étude sur les enfants en conflit avec la loi et les enfants en difficulté au Cameroun: Rapport Général, 30–31 août et 1er septembre 1993, Yaoundé*, 1993.

22 Committee on the Rights of the Child, *Periodic reports due in 1994: Cape Verde*, CRC/C/11/Add.23, 9 Jan 2001, par. 59.

23 *Id., Initial reports of States parties due in 1994: Central African Republic*, CRC/C/11/Add.18, 18 Nov 1998, par. 7.

Country	MACR	ACR specific crimes	*Doli incapax* test	MACR source statute
				présente loi. Aucune condamnation pénale ne pourra être prononcée contre lui.
Chile	14	16	–	Ley N° 20.084 que establece un sistema de responsabilidad penal de los adolescentes por infracciones a la ley penal, as of 2007, Arts. 1 and 3. Art. 1: … . Tratándose de faltas, sólo serán responsables en conformidad con la presente ley los adolescentes mayores de dieciséis años … . Art. 3: La presente ley se aplicará a quienes al momento en que se hubiere dado principio de ejecución del delito sean mayores de catorce y menores de dieciocho años … .
China	14[24]	16	–	Criminal Code, 1997, Art. 17.[25]
	Hong Kong: 10	–	10–14	Hong Kong Special Administrative Region (SAR): Juvenile Offenders Ordinance, as of 2003, Sect. 3, and common law (*doli incapax* presumption).
	Macao: 12	–	–	Macao SAR: Decree-Law 65/99/M, 1999, Art. 6(1).
Colombia	14	–	–	Código de la Infancia y la Adolescencia, 2006, Art. 142.[26] Art. 142: … las personas menores de catorce (14) años, no serán juzgadas ni declaradas responsables penalmente, privadas de libertad, bajo denuncia o sindicación de haber cometido una conducta punible … .
Comoros	13; or 14–15 or physical maturity (boys) or marriage (girls)[27]	–	–	Criminal Code and Islamic law.

24 The *laodong jiaoyang* system is one of the administrative detention systems used to punish most minor offences without official charge, trial, or judicial review. A patchwork regulatory framework apparently restricts its use to children 13 and older, although in the past children as young as 11 were detained. Deprivation of liberty is currently possible for up to 4 years total, based in large part upon the discretion of public security officials. Re-education is formally justified as a child protection measure of assistance for reintegration into society, yet the UN Special Rapporteur on Torture has considered the system a form of inhuman and degrading treatment or punishment. See, inter alia, Committee of Experts on the Application of Conventions and Recommendations, *Individual Observation concerning Worst Forms of Child Labour Convention, 1999 (No. 182): China*, 2007; Trevaskes, Susan, "Severe and Swift Justice in China," 47 *British Journal of Criminology* 23, 2007; and UN Commission on Human Rights, *Report of the Special Rapporteur on torture and other cruel, inhuman or degrading treatment or punishment, Manfred Nowak: Mission to China*, E/CN.4/2006/6/Add.6, 10 Mar 2006.

25 Zhou, Mi, and Shizhou Wang, "China," 2001, in Fijnaut, Cyrillus, and Frankk Verbruggen, eds, "Criminal Law," in Blanpain, Roger, ed., *International Encyclopaedia of Laws*, The Hague, Kluwer Law International, 2004.

26 Provisions on criminal responsibility in the *Código de la Infancia y la Adolescencia* progressively enter into force by judicial district between 2007 and 2009, substituting *situación irregular* provisions under the *Código del Menor, Decreto 2739 del 27 noviembre 1989*.

27 Comoros has indicated that, as stipulated in the Criminal Code, its MACR is 13 years. However, the Criminal Code and Islamic law are both legally recognized sources, and there are no

Country	MACR	ACR specific crimes	*Doli incapax* test	MACR source statute
Congo (Republic of the)	13[28]	–	–	Code de procédure pénale, 1963, Art. 686. 1o Le tribunal pour enfants et la cour criminelle des mineurs … . (2o:) [peuvent,] lorsque les circonstances et la personnalité du délinquant leur paraissent l'exiger, prononcer à l'égard du mineur âgé de plus de treize ans une condamnation pénale … .
Costa Rica	12	–	–	Ley de Justicia Penal Juvenil, 1996, Art. 6. Los actos cometidos por un menor de doce años de edad, que constituyan delito o contravención, no serán objeto de esta ley; la responsabilidad civil quedará a salvo y se ejercerá ante los tribunales jurisdiccionales competentes … .
Côte d'Ivoire	10	–	–	Code pénal, 1981, Art. 116. Les faits commis par un mineur de 10 ans ne sont pas susceptibles de qualification et de poursuites pénales … .
Croatia	14	–	–	Criminal Code, Art. 10, and Juvenile Courts Act, 1997, Art. 2.[29]
Cuba	0[30]	–	–	Decreto– Ley No. 64 del Sistema para la Atención a Menores con Trastornos de Conducta del 30 de diciembre de 1982.
Cyprus	10	12	10–12	Criminal Code, as of 1999, Cap. 154, Sect. 14.[31]
Czech Republic	15	–	–	Law on the Responsibility of Youth for Criminal Acts and on Justice in Juvenile Matters, 2003.[32]

fixed age limits under Muslim law. Physical maturity or the age of 14–15 years confers criminal responsibility on boys, while marriage at any age confers criminal responsibility upon girls. Committee on the Rights of the Child, *Initial reports of States parties due in 1995: Comoros (Additional Info from State Party)*, CRC/C/28/Add.13, 7 Oct 1998, pars. 52, 79, and 141–142.

28 Although apparently classified as protection, assistance, and education measures, children younger than 13 may be declared guilty, held in remand institutions, and placed in "a suitable educational or professional training establishment, or any public or private institution providing care for children, or in an appropriate boarding school for offenders of school age." See *Id.*, *Initial reports of States parties due in 1999: Congo*, CRC/C/COG/1, 20 Feb 2006, pars. 428–430.

29 Cvjetko, Bo_ica, "Croatia: Criminal Responsibility of Minors in the Republic of Croatia," 75 *International Review of Penal Law (Revue internationale de droit pénal)* 263, 2004.

30 Cuba claims its MACR is 16, but this limit is actually the age of penal majority as stipulated in Penal Code Art. 16(2). The main juvenile justice legislation, *Decreto-Ley No. 64 del Sistema para la Atención a Menores con Trastornos de Conducta del 30 de diciembre de 1982*, does not contain any minimum age for its application. Under this system, relevant children are seen as offenders in conflict with the law, and administrative "prevention and social welfare commissions" may order their deprivation of liberty indefinitely in specialized re-education centers. See, inter alia, Committee on the Rights of the Child, *Initial reports of States parties due in 1993: Cuba*, CRC/C/8/Add.30, 15 Feb 1996; Romero, Lidia, and Luis Gómez, *La Política Cubana de Juventud Entre 1995 y 1999: Principales Características (La Experiencia del Pradjal en Cuba)*, La Habana, Centro de Estudios Sobre la Juventud, 2000; and Zaragoza Ramírez, Alina, and Bárbara Mirabent Garay, "Administración de justicia de menores: un desafío a la contemporaneidad," *Cubalex: Revista Electrónica de Estudios Jurídicos*, no. 9, July–September 1999.

31 Government of Cyprus, *Second Periodic Report: Implementation of the Convention on the Rights of the Child: Answers to Questionnaire Dated 7 February 2003 CRC/C/Q/CYP/2*, 9 Apr 2003, at 66–67. Boys younger than 12 are presumed to be incapable of having "carnal knowledge."

32 Válková, Helena, *New Juvenile Justice Law in the Czech Republic*, presented at the Conference of the European Society of Criminology, Amsterdam, 25–28 August 2004.

Country	MACR	ACR specific crimes	*Doli incapax* test	MACR source statute
Democratic People's Republic of Korea	14	–	–	Criminal Procedure Law, Art. 53.[33]
Democratic Republic of the Congo	0	–	–	–[34]
Denmark	15[35]	–	–	Criminal Code, Sect. 15.[36]
Djibouti	13	–	–	Code pénal.[37]
Dominica	12	–	–	Children and Young Persons Act, 1970, Sect. 3.[38] It shall be conclusively presumed that no child under the age of twelve years can be guilty of an offence.
Dominican Republic	13	–	–	Código para el Sistema de Protección de los Derechos Fundamentales de Niños, Niñas y Adolescentes, 2003, Art. 223 … . Los niños y niñas menores de trece (13) años, en ningún caso, son responsables penalmente, por tanto no pueden ser detenidos, ni privados de su libertad, ni sancionados por autoridad alguna.
Ecuador	12	–	–	Código de la Niñez y Adolescencia, 2003, Arts. 4 and 307. Art. 4: Niño o niña es la persona que no ha cumplido doce años de edad… . Art. 307: Los niños y niñas son absolutamente inimputables y tampoco son responsables; por tanto, no están sujetos ni al juzgamiento ni a las medidas socio-educativas contempladas en este Código … .
Egypt	7	–	–	Children's Code, 1996, Art. 94.[39]
El Salvador	12	–	–	Ley Penal Juvenil, as of 2006, Art. 2 … . Los menores que no hubieren cumplido doce años

33   Democratic People's Republic of Korea, *The 3rd and 4th Periodic Reports of the Democratic People's Republic of Korea on the Implementation of the Convention on the Rights of the Child*, Pyongyang, 2007.

34   Otshudiin, Henri Wembolua, "L'anachronisme du Décret du 6 décembre 1950 sur l'enfance délinquante: cas du flou sur la majorité pénale en R.D.C.," in *Nouvelle Tribune Internationale des droits de l'enfant*, nos. 10–11, Défense des Enfants International – Belgique, December 2005.

35   The Administration of Justice Act (as of 2004), part 75b, grants police the authority to detain suspects as young as 12 years of age in waiting rooms, holding cells, etc. Detention may be extended for up to 24 hours, and solitary confinement is permitted for up to six hours. Police may also conduct wiretaps, surveillance, searches, and seizures against such children. See Committee on the Rights of the Child, *Written Replies by the Government of Denmark Concerning the List of Issues (CRC/C/Q/DNK/3)*, CRC/C/RESP/91, 19 Aug 2005; and National Council for Children, *Report to the UN Committee on the Rights of the Child: Supplementary report to Denmark's 3rd periodic report*, Copenhagen, 2005.

36   Langsted, Lars Bo, Peter Garde, and Vagn Greve, "Denmark," 2003, in Fijnaut, Cyrillus, and Frankk Verbruggen, eds, "Criminal Law," in Blanpain, Roger, ed., *International Encyclopaedia of Laws*, The Hague, Kluwer Law International, 2004.

37   République de Djibouti, *Rapport périodique portant sur la mise en œuvre de la Convention relative aux droits de l'enfant*, CRC/C/DJI, April 2007, at 19.

38   Committee on the Rights of the Child, *Initial reports of States parties due in 1993: Dominica*, CRC/C/8/ADD.48, 15 Oct 2003, par. 69.

39   *Id.*, *Periodic reports of States parties due in 1997: Egypt*, CRC/C/65/Add.9, 11 Nov 1999, pars. 50 and 189–90.

Annex 2: Worldwide MACR Provisions and Statutory Sources by Country   197

Country	MACR	ACR specific crimes	*Doli incapax* test	MACR source statute
				de edad y presenten una conducta antisocial no estarán sujetos a este régimen jurídico especial, ni al común; están exentos de responsabilidad ....
Equatorial Guinea	16	–	–	–[40]
Eritrea	12	–	–	Transitional Penal Code, Art. 52.[41] Provision of this code shall not apply to children not having attained the age of 12 years. Such children are not deemed to be responsible for their acts under the law ....
Estonia	7	–	–	Juvenile Sanctions Act, as of 2004, §1(1)–(2) and §2. §1(1) This Act provides sanctions applicable to minors and the competence of juvenile committees. §1(2) This Act applies to a minor: 1) who, at less than 14 years of age, commits an unlawful act corresponding to the necessary elements of a criminal offence prescribed by the Penal Code; 2) who, at less than 14 years of age, commits an unlawful act corresponding to the necessary elements of a misdemeanour prescribed by the Penal Code or another Act .... §2 For the purposes of this Act, a minor is a person between seven and eighteen years of age.
Ethiopia	9	–	–	Penal Code, 2004.[42]
Fiji	10	12	10–12	Penal Code, as of 2005, Sect. 14. (1) A person under the age of ten years is not criminally responsible for any act or omission. (2) A person under the age of twelve years is not criminally responsible for an act or omission, unless it is proved that at the time of doing the act or making the omission he had capacity to know that he ought not to do the act or make the omission. (3) A male person under the age of twelve years is presumed to be incapable of having carnal knowledge.
Finland	15	–	–	Penal Code, as of 2003, Ch. 3, Sect. 4(1).[43] Conditions for criminal liability are that the offender had reached the age of fifteen years at the time of the act and is criminally responsible.
France	0[44]	–	0–18	Code Pénal, as of 2005, Art. 122–8. Les mineurs capables de discernement sont pénalement responsables des crimes, délits ou contraventions dont ils ont été reconnus coupables ....

40 *Id.*, *Compte rendu analytique de la 990e séance: Equatorial Guinea*, CRC/C/SR.990, 31 Jan 2005, par. 18.

41 UNICEF Eritrea, correspondence with author, May 2002.

42 Committee on the Rights of the Child, *Summary record of the 1162nd meeting (Chamber B): Ethiopia*, CRC/C/SR.1162, 21 Sept 2006, par. 49.

43 Unofficial translation by the Ministry of Justice, Finland.

44 All children deemed capable of discernment and found to have committed illegal acts are considered criminally responsible. The measures that such children may face vary according to their ages, as stipulated in the *Ordonnance relative à l'enfance délinquante* (as of March 2007). Adjudicated children of all ages are subject to "mesures de protection, d'assistance, de surveillance et d'éducation"

Country	MACR	ACR specific crimes	*Doli incapax* test	MACR source statute
Gabon	13	–	–	Penal Code, Art. 56.[45]
Gambia	12	–	–	Children's Act, 2005, Sect. 209.[46] The minimum age of criminal responsibility is twelve years.
Georgia	12	14	–	Criminal Code, as of 2007, Art. 33.[47]
Germany	14	–	14–18	Jugendgerichtsgesetz (Youth Court Act), 1953, §1 and 3. §1: (1) Dieses Gesetz gilt, wenn ein Jugendlicher oder ein Heranwachsender eine Verfehlung begeht, die nach den allgemeinen Vorschriften mit Strafe bedroht ist. (2) Jugendlicher ist, wer zur Zeit der Tat vierzehn, aber noch nicht achtzehn, Heranwachsender, wer zur Zeit der Tat achtzehn, aber noch nicht einundzwanzig Jahre alt ist. Jugendgerichtsgesetz §3:[48] Ein Jugendlicher ist strafrechtlich verantwortlich, wenn er zur Zeit der Tat nach seiner sittlichen und geistigen Entwicklung reif genug ist, das Unrecht der Tat einzusehen und nach dieser Einsicht zu handeln ….
Ghana	12	–	–	Criminal Code, as of 1998.[49]
Greece	13[50]	–	–	Penal Code, as of 2003, Arts. 121, 126–127.
Grenada	7	–	7–12	Criminal Code, Sect. 50 (1)–(2).[51]

(see, inter alia, Arts. 1–2). "Sanctions éducatives," which in certain cases deprive children of their liberty, are applicable to children ages 10 and older (Art. 15-1). "Peines," which also in certain cases deprive children of their liberty, are applicable to children 13 and older (Arts. 20-2 to 20-9).

45   Committee on the Rights of the Child, *Initial reports of States parties due in 1996: Gabon*, CRC/C/41/Add.10, 13 Jul 2001, par. 76.

46   Saine, Marie, *Protecting the Rights of Children in Trouble with the Law: A Case Study of South Africa and the Gambia*, thesis, Pretoria, University of Pretoria, 2005.

47   Amendments in 2007 were intended to enter into force on 1 Jul 2008. These apply the pre-existing limit of 14 years for most crimes, but create a lower MACR of 12 for premeditated murder, including under aggravated circumstances, intentional damage to health, rape, most types of robbery, assault, and possession of a knife. Georgia has claimed that incomplete facilities arrangements will prevent the amendments from entering into force for the foreseeable future. Committee on the Rights of the Child, *Written Replies by the Government of Georgia to the List of Issues*, CRC/C/GEO/Q/3/Add.1, 20 May 2008, par. 48. Georgia, *Additional Information on the Implementation of the Convention on the Rights of the Child in Respect of the Third Periodic Report of Georgia*, circa May 2008.

48   "A young person is criminally responsible if at the time of the act he was mature enough, due to his moral and mental development, to understand the wrongfulness of the act and to act according to this understanding … ." English translation by Crofts, Thomas, *The Criminal Responsibility of Children and Young Persons: A Comparison of English and German Law*, Aldershot (England), Ashgate, 2002, at 134.

49   Committee on the Rights of the Child, *Second periodic reports of States parties due in 1997: Ghana*, CRC/C/65/ADD.34, 14 Jul 2005, par. 49.

50   The Penal Code formally assigns criminal responsibility at age 13. However, juvenile courts have jurisdiction over children ages 8 and older in conflict with the law (Penal Code, Arts. 121 and 126), and may order rehabilitation and therapeutic measures (Arts. 122–123, respectively) for children that may deprive them of their liberty. See, inter alia, World Organisation Against Torture et al., *State Violence in Greece: An Alternative Report to the UN Committee Against Torture 33rd Session*, Athens, 2004.

51   Committee on the Rights of the Child, *Initial reports of States parties due in 1992: Grenada*, CRC/C/3/Add.55, 28 Nov 1997, pars. 39 and 170.

Annex 2: Worldwide MACR Provisions and Statutory Sources by Country 199

Country	MACR	ACR specific crimes	*Doli incapax* test	MACR source statute
Guatemala	13	–	–	Ley de protección integral de la niñez y adolescencia, 2003, Art. 138. Los actos cometidos por un menor de trece años de edad, que constituyan delito o falta no serán objeto de este título, la responsabilidad civil quedará a salvo y se ejercerá ante los tribunales jurisdiccionales competentes ... .
Guinea	13	–	–	Code pénal, 1998, Art. 64.[52] Les faits commis par un mineur de dix ans ne sont pas susceptibles de qualification et de poursuites pénales. Le mineur de treize ans bénéficie de droit, en cas de culpabilité, de l'excuse absolutoire de minorité. Les mineurs de dix à treize ans ne peuvent faire l'objet que de mesures de protection, d'assistance, de surveillance et d'éducation ... .
Guinea-Bissau	16	–	–	Penal Code, Arts. 10 and 12.[53]
Guyana	10	–	–	Juvenile Offenders Act, as of 1972, Sect. 3. It shall be conclusively presumed that no child under the age of ten years can be guilty of an offence.
Haiti	13	–	–	Code pénal, 1961, Art. 51.[54] Lorsque les circonstances de la cause et la personnalité du prévenu ou de l'accusé de plus de 13 ans exigent une condamnation pénale, le jugement sera prononcé ainsi qu'il suit ... .
Honduras	12	–	–	Código de la Niñez y de la Adolescencia, 1996, Art. 180. Los niños ... sólo podrá deducírseles la responsabilidad prevista en este Código por las acciones u omisiones ilícitas que realicen. Lo dispuesto en el presente Título únicamente se aplicará a los niños mayores de doce (12) años de edad que cometan una infracción o falta. Los niños menores de doce (12) años no delinquen ... .
Hungary	14	–	–	Criminal Code, 1978, Sect. 23.[55] The person who has not yet completed his fourteenth year when perpetrating an act, shall not be punishable.
Iceland	15	–	–	General Penal Code, as of 1 March 2004, Art. 14.[56] A person shall not be punished on account of an act committed before he or she attained the age of 15 years.

52 Toure N'fa, Ousmane, and Fanta Oulen Bakary Camara, "Guinée," in Lachat, Michel, ed., *Séminaire de formation en justice des mineurs pour magistrats et autres acteurs en justice juvénile de l'Afrique francophone: Séminaire de Ouagadougou du 29 novembre au 3 décembre 2004: Working report*, Agence Intergouvernementale de la Francophonie, 2005, at 165.

53 Committee on the Rights of the Child, *Initial reports of States parties due in 1992: Guinea-Bissau*, CRC/C/3/Add.63, 26 Jul 2001, par. 136.

54 Unofficial version compiled by the Canadian Ministry of Justice, www.oas.org/juridico/mla/fr/hti.

55 Translation by the Trier Academy of European Law, www.era.int/domains/corpus-juris/public/texts/legal_text.htm.

56 Official translation of the Icelandic Ministry of Justice and Ecclesiastical Affairs.

Country	MACR	ACR specific crimes	*Doli incapax* test	MACR source statute
India	7	–	7–12	Penal Code, 1860, Sects. 82–82. Sect. 82: Nothing is an offence which is done by a child under seven years of age. Sect. 83: Nothing is an offence which is done by a child above seven years of age and under twelve, who has not attained sufficient maturity of understanding to judge of the nature and consequences of his conduct on that occasion.
Indonesia	8	–	–	Juvenile Court Act, 1997, Art. 5.[57]
Iran (Islamic Republic of)	9/15[58]	–	–	Islamic Penal Code, 1991, Art. 49, and Civil Code, as of 1982, Art. 1210, Note 1. Penal Code: Les enfants, en cas de la commission d'une infraction, ne sont pas pénalement responsables … .[59] Civil Code: the age of majority for boys is fifteen lunar years and for girls nine lunar years.[60]
Iraq	9	–	–	Juvenile Welfare Act No. 76, 1983.[61]
Ireland	10	12	–	Children Act 2001, as of 2006, Sect. 52(1–2). (1) Subject to subsection (2), a child under 12 years of age shall not be charged with an offence. (2) Subsection (1) does not apply to a child aged 10 or 11 years who is charged with murder, manslaughter, rape, rape under section 4 of the Criminal Law (Rape) (Amendment) Act 1990 or aggravated sexual assault.
Israel	12 OPT[62]: 9	– –	– –	Penal Law, 1996, Sect. 34F, and OPT Child Law, 2005, Arts. 67–69.[63] Penal Law: A person is not criminally responsible for an act done by him before he has completed his twelfth year.[64]
Italy	14	–	14–18	Codice Penale, as of 1999, Arts. 97–98. Art. 97: Non è imputabile chi, nel momento in cui ha commesso il fatto, non aveva compiuto i

57 Committee on the Rights of the Child, *Second periodic reports of States parties due in 1997: Indonesia*, CRC/C/65/Add.23, 7 Jul 2003, par. 472.

58 The MACR is 9 lunar years (8 years and 9 months) for girls and 15 lunar years (14 years and 7 months) for boys.

59 Islamic Penal Code Art. 49, Note 1, defines "enfant" as anyone not having passed the age of "religious puberty" (*Bolug - é - sharii*), which is in turn defined by Civil Code Art. 1210, Note 1, as 15 lunar years for boys and 9 lunar years for girls. See Ardebili, Mohammad-Ali, and Ali-Hossein Nadjafi, "Iran: La responsabilité pénale des mineurs en droit iranien," 75 *International Review of Penal Law (Revue internationale de droit pénal)* 401, 2004.

60 Translation by Alavi & Associates, www.alaviandassociates.com.

61 Committee on the Rights of the Child, *Summary record of the 483rd meeting: Iraq*, CRC/C/SR.483, 30 Sept 1998, pars. 47–48; and UNICEF Middle East and North Africa Regional Office, "Juvenile Justice," in *Middle East and North Africa Child Protection Profile*, unpublished draft, Amman, 2001.

62 Occupied Palestinian Territory.

63 Musleh, Dahab, and Katherine Taylor, *Child Protection in the Occupied Palestinian Territory: A National Position Paper*, Secretariat of the National Plan of Action for Palestinian Children, El Shurafeh, 2005; and UNICEF Middle East and North Africa Regional Office, *UN Study on Violence against Children: Regional Report: Middle East and North Africa Region*, draft, Amman, June 2005.

64 Unofficial English translation. "Penal Law--Draft Proposal and New Code," 30 *Israel Law Review* 5, 1996, reproduced by Buffalo Criminal Law Center, State University of New York at Buffalo School of Law, wings.buffalo.edu/law/bclc/israeli.htm.

Country	MACR	ACR specific crimes	*Doli incapax* test	MACR source statute
				quattordici anni. Art. 98: È imputabile chi, nel momento in cui ha commesso il fatto, aveva compiuto i quattordici anni, ma non ancora i diciotto, se aveva capacità d'intendere e di volere ….
Jamaica	12	–	–	Child Care and Protection Act, 2004, Sect. 63. It shall be conclusively presumed that no child under the age of twelve years can be guilty of any offence.
Japan	11[65]	–	–	Juvenile Law, as of May 2007.[66]
Jordan	7	–	–	Juveniles Act, as of 2002, Art. 36.[67] Criminal proceedings shall not be instituted in respect of an offence committed by a person who was under seven years of age at the time the offence was committed.
Kazakhstan	14[68]	16	–	Criminal Code, as of 2004, Art. 15.[69] (1) A person shall be subject to criminal liability who reached sixteen years of age by the time of the commission of a given crime. (2) Persons, who reached fourteen years of age by the time of the commission of a crime, shall be subject to criminal liability for murder (Article 96), deliberate causation of serious damage to health (Article 103), deliberate causation of medium gravity damage to health under aggravated circumstances (Article 104, the second part), rape (Article 120), forcible acts of a sexual

65 May 2007 amendments to the Juvenile Law allow Family Courts to order their most severe disposition against children as young as 11 in conflict with the law – commitment to Juvenile Training Schools, which are supervised by the Ministry of Justice Correction Bureau. Previously, the minimum age for such placements was generally 14 years. Under the amendments, such children may also be subject to police questioning, searches, and seizures. The age limit of 14 years is also frequently cited because it is the lowest possible age for waiver to adult criminal court for certain serious crimes (Penal Code Art. 41). See, inter alia, Ito, Masami, "Diet lowers incarceration age to 'about 12'," *The Japan Times*, 26 May 2007; Jin, Guang-Xu, "Japan: The Criminal Responsibility of Minors in the Japanese Legal System," 75 *International Review of Penal Law (Revue internationale de droit pénal)* 409, 2004; and "Juvenile crime wave prompts Justice Ministry crackdown," *The Japan Times*, 25 Aug 2004.

66 Ito, *ibid*.

67 Committee on the Rights of the Child, *Third periodic report of States parties due in 2003: Jordan*, CRC/C/JOR/3, 2 Mar 2006, par. 53.

68 Criminal Code Art. 15 (Commentary) notes courts' authority, under certain conditions, to apply coercive measures of correctional education to children 11 and older. This signifies placement for up to three years in special educational institutions, which are reorganized correctional colonies (i.e., juvenile prisons). Also, Centers of temporary isolation, adaptation and rehabilitation may admit children younger than the MACR who have committed acts harmful to the public. See, e.g., Children's Fund of Kazakhstan et al., *Alternative Report of Non-Governmental Organizations of Kazakhstan with Commentaries to the Initial Report of the Government of Kazakhstan*, Almaty, 2002; Committee on the Rights of the Child, *Second and third periodic reports of States parties due in 2006: Kazakhstan*, CRC/C/KAZ/3, 23 Aug 2006, pars. 28 and 458–466; and Kazakhstan NGOs' Working Group "On Protection of Children's Rights," *Alternative Report of Non-Governmental Organizations with the Comments to the Second and Third Reports of the Government of the Republic of Kazakhstan*, Almaty, 2006.

69 Translation by the Organization for Security and Co-operation in Europe, Office for Democratic Institutions and Human Rights, www.legislationline.org.

Country	MACR	ACR specific crimes	Doli incapax test	MACR source statute
				character (Article 121), kidnapping (Article 125), theft (Article 175), robbery (Article 178), brigandage (Article 179), extortion (Article 181), illegal occupation of an automobile or other transport vehicle without the purpose of theft under aggravated circumstances (Article 185, the second, third, and fourth parts), deliberate destruction or damage to property under aggravating circumstances (Article 187, the second and third parts), terrorism (Article 233), capture of a hostage (Article 234), deliberately false notice of an act of terrorism (Article 242), theft or extortion of arms, ammunition, explosive materials, and explosion devices (Article 255), hooliganism under aggravating circumstances (Article 257, the second and third parts), vandalism (Article 258), theft or extortion of drugs or psychotropic substances (Article 260), desecration of the bodies of the deceased and places of burial under aggravated circumstances (Article 275, the second part), and deliberate spoilage of transport vehicles or communications ways (Article 299). (3) If a minor reached the age stipulated in the first and second parts of this Article, but during the commission of a lesser or medium gravity crime, due to lagging behind in psychical development which is not associated with a mental disorder, could not be fully aware of the actual character or public danger of his acts (omission of acts), or could not guide them, then he shall not be subject to criminal liability.
Kenya	8	12	8–12	Penal Code, s. 14(1–2).[70]
Kiribati	10	12	10–14	Penal Code, as of 1999, Sect. 14. (1) A person under the age of 10 years is not criminally responsible for any act or omission. (2) A person under the age of 14 years is not criminally responsible for an act or omission, unless it is proved that at the time of doing the act or making the omission be had capacity to know that he ought not to do the act or make the omission. (3) A male person under the age of 12 years is presumed to be incapable of having sexual intercourse.
Kuwait	7	–	–	Penal Code, 1960, Art. 18.[71] Any one who, at the time of committing an offence, was under 7 years of age shall not be liable to criminal prosecution.

70 Situma, Francis D.P., "Kenya," 1999, in Fijnaut, Cyrillus, and Frankk Verbruggen, eds, "Criminal Law," in Blanpain, Roger, ed., *International Encyclopaedia of Laws*, The Hague, Kluwer Law International, 2004. Boys younger than 12 are assumed incapable of having "carnal knowledge," but may be convicted of indecent assault if proved to have known the act was morally wrong.

71 Committee on the Rights of the Child, *Initial reports of States parties due in 1993: Kuwait*, CRC/C/8/Add.35, 9 Dec 1996, par. 22.

Annex 2: Worldwide MACR Provisions and Statutory Sources by Country   203

Country	MACR	ACR specific crimes	*Doli incapax* test	MACR source statute
Kyrgyzstan	14[72]	16	–	Criminal Code, 1998, Art. 18.[73] (1) The person is subject to the criminal responsibility if at the moment of committing a crime he has reached the age of 16. (2) The person who has reached 14 years is subject to criminal responsibility in case of murder; deliberate "painful and more painful crimes"; kidnapping; rape; violent sexual actions; theft; rustler (cattle stealing); robbery; stealing property in a large quantity; extortion; car-stealing; deliberate arson; terrorism; capture of a hostage; hooliganism; vandalism; stealing or extortion with fire-arms; illegal drugs: producing possession, distribution and selling; stealing or extortion for drugs.
Lao People's Democratic Republic	15[74]	–	–	Penal Code, Art. 17.[75]
Latvia	14	–	–	Criminal Law, as of 2004, Sect. 11.[76] A natural person may be held criminally liable who, on the day of the commission of a criminal offence, has attained fourteen years of age. A juvenile, that is, a person who has not attained fourteen years of age, may not be held criminally liable.
Lebanon	7	–	–	Law No. 422 for the Protection of Juveniles in Conflict with the Law or at Risk, 2002, Art. 3.[77]
Lesotho	7	–	7–14	Common law.[78]
Liberia	7	–	–	Juvenile Court Procedural Code, 1972, Sect. 11.11.[79]
Libyan Arab Jamahiriya	7[80]	–	–	Penal Code, Arts. 80 and 150–151.

72 Administrative bodies (Commissions on Minors' Affairs) have jurisdiction over children younger than 14 who are in conflict with the law. They may place children from the age of 11 in "special correctional schools" for 1 to 5 years, in effect depriving them of their liberty. See Meuwese, Stan, ed., *KIDS BEHIND BARS: A study on children in conflict with the law*, Amsterdam, Defence for Children International The Netherlands, 2003; and Youth Human Rights Group, *Alternative NGO Report to the UN Committee on the Rights of the Child*, Bishkek, 2004.

73 Meuwese, *ibid*.

74 Special measures are applied under the Penal Code against children at least as young as 12, including deprivation of liberty in custodial re-education institutions. See Committee on the Rights of the Child, *Initial reports of States parties due in 1993: Lao People's Democratic Republic*, CRC/C/8/Add.32, 24 Jan 1996, pars. 161 and 166; and UNICEF East Asia and Pacific Regional Office, *Overview of Juvenile Justice in East Asia and the Pacific Region*, Bangkok, 2001.

75 Committee on the Rights of the Child, *ibid.*, pars. 43 and 161.

76 Translation by the Translation and Terminology Centre, www.ttc.lv, 2004.

77 Committee on the Rights of the Child, *Third periodic reports of States parties due in 2003: Lebanon*, CRC/C/129/Add.7, 25 Oct 2005, pars. 500 and 502.

78 *Id.*, *Initial reports of States parties due in 1994: Lesotho*, CRC/C/11/Add.20, 20 Jul 1998, par. 26.

79 American Bar Association Africa Law Initiative and UNICEF, *Assessment of the Liberian Juvenile Justice System*, Monrovia, 2006, at 21.

80 Although Libya generally maintains that its MACR is 14 years, relevant Penal Code articles provide that children between 7 and 14 who are proven culpable of acts classified as misdemeanours or felonies may be the subject of preventive measures, which include commitment for a period of less

Country	MACR	ACR specific crimes	*Doli incapax* test	MACR source statute
Liechtenstein	14	–	–	Jugendgerichtsgesetz (Juvenile Court Act), 1988, §2(1–2). In diesem Gesetz werden genannt: 1. Personen, die zwar das vierzehnte, aber noch nicht das achtzehnte Lebensjahr vollendet haben: Jugendliche. 2. mit gerichtlicher Strafe bedrohte Handlungen und Unterlassungen, die von Jugendlichen begangen werden: Jugendstraftaten.
Lithuania	14	16	–	Criminal Code, 2003, Art. 13.[81]
Luxembourg	0[82]	–	–	Loi relative à la protection de la Jeunesse, as of 1995, Arts. 1(4) and 4. Art. 1(4): Le tribunal de la jeunesse prend à l'égard des mineurs qui comparaissent devant lui des mesures de garde, d'éducation et de préservation. Il peut selon les circonstances: … les placer dans un établissement de rééducation de l'Etat. Art. (4): Si le mineur a commis un fait qualifié crime punissable de la réclusion, le tribunal de la jeunesse peut, s'il prend l'une des mesures prévues aux articles 1er, 5 et 6, prolonger cette mesure au-delà de sa majorité pour un terme qui ne peut dépasser sa vingt-cinquième année ….
Madagascar	13	–	13–18	Ordonnance 62-038 du 19 septembre 1962 sur la protection de l'enfance, Arts. 35, 44, and 46. Art. 35: Si la prévention est établie à l'égard d'un mineur de treize ans, le tribunal pour enfants ne pourra prendre à son encontre qu'une simple mesure éducative : remise aux parents, au tuteur, à la personne qui en avait la garde ou à une personne digne de confiance. Art. 44: Si l'accusé a plus de treize ans et moins de seize ans et si son irresponsabilité pénale est admise, la cour criminelle des mineurs prononcera les mesures éducatives …. Art. 46: Si l'accusé a plus de seize ans et moins de dix-huit ans, les dispositions des deux articles précédents seront applicables ….
Malawi	7	12	7–12	Penal Code, Sect. 14.[83]

than one year to a juvenile education and guidance centre. See, inter alia, Committee on the Rights of the Child, *Second periodic reports of States parties due in 2000: Libyan Arab Jamahiriya*, CRC/C/93/Add.1, 19 Sept 2002, pars. 29–30 and 76.

81   *Id.*, *Second periodic reports of States parties due in 1999: Lithuania*, CRC/C/83/Add.14, 15 Jul 2005, par. 533.

82   In essence, Luxembourg holds that 16 years is its MACR and minimum age for penal majority (*Loi relative à la protection de la Jeunesse*, Art. 32), and that only protection measures of care, therapy, and education are available for younger children. However, several juvenile court measures indicate a penal-correctional response to children's actions without any lower age limit. These may deprive children of their liberty, and in some cases, solitary confinement may be ordered for up to 10 consecutive days as a disciplinary sanction. See, e.g., *Id.*, *Concluding observations of the Committee on the Rights of the Child: Luxembourg*, CRC/C/15/Add.250, 31 Mar 2005.

83   Committee on the Rights of the Child, *Initial reports of States parties due in 1993: Malawi*, CRC/C/8/Add.43, 26 Jun 2001, par. 56. The Penal Code also holds that boys younger than 12 are presumed incapable of having "carnal knowledge."

Annex 2: Worldwide MACR Provisions and Statutory Sources by Country   205

Country	MACR	ACR specific crimes	*Doli incapax* test	MACR source statute
Malaysia	0[84]	puberty/10/13	10–12	Essential (Security Cases) Regulations, 1975, Sect. 3,[85] Syariah Criminal Offences (Federal Territories) Act, 1997, Sects. 2(1) and 51,[86] Syariah Criminal Procedure (Federal Territories) Act, 1997, Sect. 2(1), Evidence Act, 1950, Sect. 113,[87] and Penal Code, Sects. 82–83.[88] Essential (Security Cases) Regulations Sect. 3: Where a person is accused or charged with a security offence, he shall, regardless of his age, be dealt with and tried in accordance with the provisions of these Regulations and the Orders made thereunder, and the Juvenile Courts Act 1947 shall not apply to such a person. Syariah Criminal Offences (Federal Territories) Act Sect. 2(1): In this Act, unless the context otherwise requires … "*baligh*" means having attained the age of puberty according to Islamic Law. Sect. 51: Nothing is an offence which is done by a child who is not *baligh*. Syariah Criminal Procedure (Federal Territories) Act Sect. 2(1): In this Act, unless the context otherwise requires … "youthful offender" means an offender above the age of ten and below the age of sixteen years.[89] Evidence Act, 1950, Sect. 113: It shall be an irrebuttable presumption of law that a boy under the age of thirteen years is incapable of committing rape. Penal Code Sect. 82: Nothing is an offence which is done by a child under ten years of age. Sect. 83: Nothing is an offence which is done by a child above ten years of age and under twelve, who has not attained sufficient maturity of understanding to judge of the nature and consequence of his conduct on that occasion.
Maldives	puberty[90]	10/15	–	Regulation on Conducting Trials, Investigations and Sentencing Fairly for Offences Committed

84   Among explanations on various provisions regarding children and responsibility, Malaysia has suggested that Penal Code Section 82 establishes an MACR of 10 years. Other provisions clearly set a lower age threshold. *Id., Initial report of States parties due in 1997: Malaysia*, CRC/C/MYS/1, 22 Dec 2006, par. 131(f).

85   Hussin, Nasimah, *Juvenile Delinquencies in Malaysia: Legal Provisions and Prospects for Reforms*, paper presented at 4th World Congress on Family Law and Children's Rights, Cape Town, South Africa, 20–23 March 2005, at footnote 16.

86   Respective state laws reproduce these provisions as well as that of Sect. 1(2)(b), which holds that the act only applies "to persons professing the religion of Islam." See Committee on the Rights of the Child, *Initial report of States parties due in 1997: Malaysia*, CRC/C/MYS/1, 22 Dec 2006, par. 131(h–i).

87   Hussin, *supra* note 85, at 9.

88   Law Reform Commission of Hong Kong, *Report on the Age of Criminal Responsibility in Hong Kong*, Wanchai, 2000.

89   This provision apparently signifies that children are assumed to bear criminal responsibility, regardless of physical signs of puberty, upon attaining the age of 10 years. See Committee on the Rights of the Child, *supra* note 83, par. 131(i).

90   Maldives has described its MACR as 10 years under Art. 4(a) of the Regulation on Conducting Trials, Investigations and Sentencing Fairly for Offences Committed by Minors. However, this same

206   *Children's Rights and the Minimum Age of Criminal Responsibility*

Country	MACR	ACR specific crimes	*Doli incapax* test	MACR source statute
				by Minors, 2006, Arts. 4–6. Art. 4: (a) Any child up to age of 10 years shall not be held criminally liable for any offence. (b) However, if the child of the age referred to in Clause 4 (a) has attained physical maturity [*baligh*'], the child shall bear criminal liability amongst the offences stated in Clause 5 (a) and (b) for which *hadh*' is prescribed in *Sharia*'. Art. 5: A minor from attainment of 10 years of age till completion of 15 years of age shall be liable to bear criminal responsibility only if the minor commits an offence specified below. (a) Amongst the offences for which *hadh*' is prescribed in Islam; (1) Apostasy. (2) Revolution against the state. (3) Fornication. (4) Fallaciously accusing a person of fornication. (5) Consumption of alcohol. (b) Unlawful intentional killing of human beings, other offences relating to homicide and participation therein. (c) All offences related to drugs. Art. 6: Children from attainment of 15 years of age till 18 years of age shall bear criminal liability in respect of all offences committed by them.
Mali	13	–	13–18	Code de protection de l'enfant, 2002, Art. 98. L'enfant âgé de moins de treize ans est présumé irréfragablement n'avoir pas la capacité d'enfreindre la loi pénale, cette présomption devient réfragable pour les enfants âgés de plus de treize ans et de moins de dix-huit ans … . Lorsque le prévenu ou l'accusé aura plus de 13 ans et moins de 18 ans, il sera relaxé ou acquitté s'il est décidé qu'il a agi sans discernement. Dans les cas prévus aux alinéas précédents, le mineur sera remis à ses parents ou à une institution d'éducation spécialisée publique ou privée pour le temps que le jugement détermine et qui, toutefois, ne pourra excéder l'âge de ses 18 ans.
Malta	9	–	9–14	Criminal Code, as of 2004, Art. 35(1–2). (1) Minors under nine years of age shall be exempt from criminal responsibility for any act or omission. (2) Minors under fourteen years of age shall likewise be exempt from criminal responsibility for any act or omission done without mischievous discretion.
Marshall Islands	0[91]	–	–	Revised Code, 2004, Title 26 Sects. 303(2–3) and 307. Sect. 303(2–3): As used in this Chapter … (2) 'child' means any natural person

Regulation attributes criminal responsibility upon puberty, without consideration for age, for certain offences. *Id.*, *Second and third periodic reports of States parties due in 1998 and 2003: Maldives*, CRC/C/MDV/3, 10 Apr 2006.

91   Marshall Islands describes its MACR as 10 years according to Criminal Code Section 107. However, juvenile delinquency statutes establish procedures to adjudicate children as delinquent, without any lower age limit, and to order their deprivation of liberty as a consequence. The Committee on the Rights of the Child observed that there is no MACR. *Id.*, *Concluding observations: Marshall*

Annex 2: Worldwide MACR Provisions and Statutory Sources by Country 207

Country	MACR	ACR specific crimes	*Doli incapax* test	MACR source statute
				under the age of eighteen (18) years; and (3) 'delinquent child' includes any child: (a) who violates any law of the Republic ... ; (b) who does not subject himself to the reasonable control of his parents, teachers, guardian, or custodian, by reason of being wayward or habitually disobedient; (c) who is a habitual truant from home or school; or (d) who deports himself so as to injure or endanger the morals or health of himself or others. Sect. 307: A person adjudged to be a delinquent child may be confined in such place, under such conditions, and for such period as the court deems the best interests of the child require, not exceeding the period for which he might have been confined if he were not treated as a "juvenile offender" under this Chapter.
Mauritania	7	–	–	Ordonnance n°2005–015 portant protection pénale de l'enfant, Art. 2. L'enfant âgé de moins de sept ans est présumé irréfragablement n'avoir pas la capacité d'enfreindre la loi pénale, cette présomption devient réfragable pour les enfants âgés de sept ans révolus ... .
Mauritius	0[92]	–	–	Criminal Code, Sects. 44–45.
Mexico	12	–	–	Constitución Política de los Estados Unidos Mexicanos, as of 2006, Art. 18 ... . La Federación, los Estados y el Distrito Federal establecerán, en el ámbito de sus respectivas competencias, un sistema integral de justicia que será aplicable a quienes se atribuya la realización de una conducta tipificada como delito por las leyes penales y tengan entre doce años cumplidos y menos de dieciocho años de edad ... . Las personas menores de doce años que hayan realizado una conducta prevista como delito en la ley, solo serán sujetos a rehabilitación y asistencia social ... .
Micronesia (Federated States of)	0[93]	–	–	Laws of the Federated States of Micronesia, as of 1999, Title 12 §1102 and 1105. §1102: As used in this Title, "delinquent child" includes

Islands, CRC/C/MHL/CO/2, 2 Feb 2007; and *Id.*, *Initial reports of States parties due in 1995: Marshall Islands*, CRC/C/28/Add.12, 18 Nov 1998.

92 Children younger than 14 that the court deems not capable of discernment, apparently without any lower age limit at all, may be sent under certain circumstances to a correctional institution until their eighteenth birthdays. The court may place children deemed capable of discernment, again without any lower age limit, in a correctional institution. See *Id.*, *Second periodic reports of States parties due in 1997: Mauritius*, CRC/C/65/ADD.35, 19 Jul 2005, pars. 125 and 477–478.

93 Micronesia has suggested that 16 is the MACR and the minimum age for penal majority under the Laws of the Federated States of Micronesia (Title 12 §1101, and in parallel provisions of respective state codes). However, juvenile delinquency statutes establish procedures to adjudicate children as delinquent, without any lower age limit, and to order their deprivation of liberty as a consequence. The Committee on the Rights of the Child observed that there is no clearly defined MACR. *Id.*, *Concluding observations: Micronesia (Federated States of)*, CRC/C/15/Add.86, 4 Feb 1998; and *Id.*, *Initial reports of States parties due in 1995: Micronesia (Federated States of)*, CRC/C/28/Add.5, 17 Jun 1996.

Country	MACR	ACR specific crimes	*Doli incapax* test	MACR source statute
				any child: (1) who violates any Trust Territory or district law ... or (2) who does not subject himself to the reasonable control of his parents, teachers, guardian, or custodian, by reason of being wayward or habitually disobedient; or (3) who is a habitual truant from home or school; or (4) who deports himself so as to injure or endanger the morals or health of himself or others. §1105: A person adjudged to be a delinquent child may be confined in such place, under such conditions, and for such period as the court deems the best interests of the child require, not exceeding the period for which he might have been confined if he were not treated as a juvenile offender under this Chapter.
Moldova	14	16	–	Criminal Code, 2002, Art. 21(1).[94] Subject to criminal responsibility are liable natural persons who, at the moment of perpetrating grave, major or exceptionally grave offenses have reached the age of 14 years as well as persons who at the moment of perpetration minor or less grave offenses have reached the age of 16 years ... .
Monaco	13	–	–	Criminal Code.[95]
Mongolia	14	16	–	Criminal Code, as of 2002, Arts. 21(1)–(2).[96] Art. 21(1): Persons who have attained 16 years of age at the time of committing a crime shall be subject to criminal liability. Art. 21(2): Persons of 14 to 16 years of age shall be subject to criminal liability for homicide (Article 91), deliberate infliction of a severe bodily injury (Article 96), rape (Article 126), theft in aggravating circumstances (Article 145), misappropriation (Article 146), robbery (Article 147), deliberate destruction or damage of property (Article 153) and hooliganism in aggravating circumstances (Arts. 181.2 and 181.3).
Montenegro	14	–	–	Criminal Code, as of 2004, Art. 80.[97] Criminal sanctions can not be applied to a juvenile who at the time of the commission of a criminal offence was under the age of 14 fourteen years (a child).
Morocco	12	–	–	Penal Code, Art. 138.[98]
Mozambique	0[99]	–	–	Statute of Legal Aid to Minors, Art. 16.

94   Translation by Transparency International – Moldova, www.transparency.md/laws.htm.
95   Committee on the Rights of the Child, *Initial reports of States parties due in 1995: Monaco*, CRC/C/28/Add.15, 17 Jul 2000, par. 37.
96   UN High Commissioner for Refugees, posted by European Country of Origin Information Network, www.ecoi.net.
97   Translation by the Organization for Security and Co-operation in Europe, Office for Democratic Institutions and Human Rights, www.legislationline.org.
98   Committee on the Rights of the Child, *Second periodic reports of States parties due in 2000: Morocco*, CRC/C/93/Add.3, 12 Feb 2003, par. 160.
99   Mozambique has alternatively suggested that its MACR is 10 years (Penal Code Art. 43) or 16 years (Penal Code Art. 42), stating in particular that children younger than 16 may only face

Annex 2: Worldwide MACR Provisions and Statutory Sources by Country   209

Country	MACR	ACR specific crimes	*Doli incapax* test	MACR source statute
Myanmar	7	–	7–12	Child Law, 1993, Art. 28. (a) Nothing is an offence which is done by a child under 7 years of age; (b) Nothing is an offence which is done by a child above 7 years of age and under 12 who has not attained sufficient maturity of understanding to judge of the nature and consequences of his conduct on that occasion.
Namibia	7	–	7–14	Common law.[100]
Nauru	0[101]	–	–	Criminal Justice Act.
Nepal	0[102]	10	–	Terrorist and Disruptive Activities (Control and Punishment) Ordinance, 2004, and Children's Act, 1992, Art. 11(1). Children's Act Art. 11(1): If the Child below the age of 10 years commits an at which is an offence under law, he shall not be liable to any type of punishment.
Netherlands	12[103]	–	–	Wetboek van Strafrecht (Penal Code), as of 2005, Art. 77a.[104] Ten aanzien van degene die ten tijde van het begaan van een strafbaar feit de leeftijd van twaalf jaren doch nog niet die van achttien jaren heeft bereikt, zijn de artikelen 9, eerste lid, 10 tot en met 22a, 24c, 37 tot en met 38i, 44 en 57 tot en met 62 niet van toepassing. In de plaats daarvan treden de bijzondere bepalingen vervat in de artikelen 77d tot en met 77gg.

punishment vis-à-vis protection, assistance, or educational measures, without deprivation of liberty. Instead, 16 years appears to be the age of penal majority, while younger children fall under the jurisdiction of the Juvenile Court as stipulated in the Statute of Legal Aid to Minors. Art. 16 of this Statute allows corrective measures, including measures of deprivation of liberty, to be ordered for children who have committed acts deemed crimes or misdemeanours in the penal law. See *Id.*, *Initial reports of States parties due in 1996: Mozambique*, CRC/C/41/Add.11, 14 May 2001.

100   Zimba, R.F., and E. Zimba, *Review of the compliance of Namibian domestic legislation to the Convention on the Rights of the Child*, Windhoek, UNICEF and the Ministry of Women Affairs and Child Welfare, 2004.

101   Children ages 14 and older are held criminally responsible in adult court, although the court also has the discretion to try younger children accused of murder. In general, children under the age of 14 are considered minors and their criminal responsibility is decided on a case-by-case basis without any lower age limit. Russell Kun, Principal Legal Adviser, Department of Justice, telephone interview with author, 19 Sept 2002.

102   Nepal has noted its MACR as 10 years according to Children's Act Art. 11, but the Terrorist and Disruptive Activities (Control and Punishment) Ordinance applies to children of all ages for certain offences. Committee on the Rights of the Child, *Second periodic report of States parties due in 1997: Nepal*, CRC/C/65/Add.30, 3 Dec 2004. UNICEF Regional Office for South Asia, *Juvenile Justice in South Asia: Improving Protection for Children in Conflict with the Law*, Kathmandu, 2006.

103   Police officers may arrest children younger than 12 and interrogate them at police stations for up to six hours. Some authors have described these and related measures as effective criminal responsibility at age 10. Detrick, Sharon, et al., *Violence against Children in Conflict with the Law: A Study on Indicators and Data Collection in Belgium, England and Wales, France and the Netherlands*, Amsterdam, Defence for Children International – The Netherlands, 2008. Uit Beijerse, Jolande, and Rene van Swaaningen, "The Netherlands: Penal Welfarism and Risk Management," in Muncie, John, and Barry Goldson, eds, *Comparative Youth Justice*, London, Sage, 2006.

104   "Articles 9, section 1, 10–22a, 24c, 37–38i, 44 and 57–62 are not applicable to a person who had reached the age of twelve, but was not yet eighteen years of age, at the time the criminal offense was committed. The special provisions laid down in articles 77d–77gg apply in lieu thereof."

Country	MACR	ACR specific crimes	*Doli incapax* test	MACR source statute
New Zealand	10	14	10–14	Children, Young Persons, and their Families Act, as of 2004, Arts. 2(1) and 272(2), and Crimes Act, as of 2006, Arts. 21(1) and 22(1). Children, Young Persons, and their Families Act, Art. 2(1): … . "Young person" means a boy or girl of or over the age of 14 years but under 17 years … . Art. 272(2): Where any child who is of or over the age of 10 years is charged with murder or manslaughter … the provisions of this Act … shall apply accordingly as if that child were a young person. Crimes Act, Art. 21(1): No person shall be convicted of an offence by reason of any act done or omitted by him when under the age of 10 years. Art. 22(1): No person shall be convicted of an offence by reason of any act done or omitted by him when of the age of 10 but under the age of 14 years, unless he knew either that the act or omission was wrong or that it was contrary to law.
Nicaragua	13	–	–	Código de la Niñez y la Adolescencia, 1998, Art. 95. La Justicia Penal Especial del Adolescente … se aplicará a los Adolescentes que tuvieren 13 años cumplidos y que sean menores de 18 años al momento de la comisión de un hecho tipificado como delito o falta … . Las niñas y niños que no hubieren cumplido los trece años de edad, no serán sujetos a la Justicia Penal Especial del Adolescente, están exentos de responsabilidad penal, quedando a salvo la responsabilidad civil … . Se prohibe aplicarles, por ningún motivo cualquier medida que implique privación de libertad.
Niger	13	–	13–18	Penal Code, Art. 45.[105]
Nigeria	Northern States: 7	–	7–12	Northern States: Penal Code, Art. 50.[107]
	Southern States: 7	12	7–12	Southern States: Criminal Code, Art. 30.[108]
	various States: puberty[106]	7	–	Bauchi, Borno, Gombe, Jigawa, Kaduna, Kano, Katsina, Kebbi, Niger, Sokoto, Yobe, and

English translation: "The Dutch Penal Code," *The American Series of Foreign Penal Codes*, Littleton (Colorado), Fred B. Rothman & Co., 1997.

105   Committee on the Rights of the Child, *Initial reports of States parties due in 1992: Niger*, CRC/C/3/Add.29/Rev.1, 17 Oct 2001, par. 38.

106   Among many conflicting statements, Nigeria has cited various ages as the MACRs under state laws. However, twelve states' *shari'a* criminal laws assign criminal responsibility upon puberty, without regard to age per se, for adultery or fornication; rape; sodomy; incest; lesbianism; bestiality; acts of gross indecency; and false accusation of adultery or fornication. For other crimes, children are potentially responsible at 7 years of age. See, e.g., *Id.*, *Initial reports of States parties due in 1993: Nigeria*, CRC/C/8/Add.26, 21 Aug 1995; and Nigerian Federal Ministry of Women Affairs, *Convention on the Rights of the Child: Second Country Periodic Report*, CRC/C/70/Add.24/Rev.2, Abuja, 2004.

107   World Organisation Against Torture and the Centre for Law Enforcement Education, *Rights of the Child in Nigeria: Report on the implementation of the Convention on the Rights of the Child by Nigeria*, Geneva, 2004, at 9.

108   Boys younger than 12 are "presumed to be incapable of having carnal knowledge."

Country	MACR	ACR specific crimes	*Doli incapax* test	MACR source statute
				Zamfara States:[109] Zamfara State Sharia Criminal Procedure Code law of 2000, No. 1, Vol. 4, Sect. 237,[110] and Zamfara State of Nigeria Shari'ah Penal Code Law, Sects. 47, 71, and 126–141.[111]
Norway	15	–	–	General Civil Penal Code, as of 1994, §46. No person may be punished for any act committed before reaching 15 years of age.
Oman	9	–	–	Penal Code, 1974, Art. 104. Any person having not completed nine years of age when committing a crime shall not be penally prosecuted … .
Pakistan	0[112]	7	7–12	Penal Code, Sects. 82–83,[113] the 1979 Hudood Ordinances,[114] and the Anti-Terrorism Act, as of 2002.[115] Penal Code Sect. 82: Nothing is an offence which is done by a child under seven years of age. Sect. 83: Nothing is an offence which is done by a child above seven years of age and under twelve, who has not attained sufficient maturity of understanding to judge of the nature and consequences of his conduct on that occasion.
Palau	10	–	10–14	National (Legal) Code, Title 17.106.[116]
Panama	14	–	–	Ley No. 40 del Régimen Especial de Responsabilidad Penal para la Adolescencia, 1999, Art. 8. Las personas menores de edad que no hayan cumplido los catorce años, no son responsables penalmente por las infracciones a la ley penal en que hubieren podido incurrir … .
Papua New Guinea	7[117]	14	7–14	Criminal Code, as of 1993, Art. 30. (1) A person under the age of seven years is not criminally responsible for any act or omission.

109   In 2000–01, these 12 states adopted *shari'a* criminal law in virtually identical statutes based upon the Zamfara State laws. In theory, these laws apply in the respective jurisdictions to all Muslims and others who voluntarily consent to their regime (see *Shari'ah* Penal Code Law, Introduction (C)).

110   Nigerian Federal Ministry of Women Affairs, *supra* note 106 at 29.

111   See www.zamfaraonline.com/sharia/introduction.html.

112   Pakistan cites its MACR as 7 years according to Penal Code Sect. 82. However, various other legal provisions set no minimum age for responsibility for certain offences. Committee on the Rights of the Child, *Second periodic reports of States parties due in 1997: Pakistan*, CRC/C/65/Add.21, 11 Apr 2003.

113   Amnesty International, *Pakistan: Denial of basic rights for child prisoners*, London, 2003.

114   The 1979 *Hudood* Ordinances hold all Pakistanis criminally responsible—regardless of age—for specific offenses such as rape, adultery, the use of alcohol and drugs, theft, armed robbery, and slander.

115   Children of all ages are subject to arrest and trial, as well as the death penalty, under this Act's provisions. See UNICEF Regional Office for South Asia, *Juvenile Justice in South Asia: Improving Protection for Children in Conflict with the Law*, Kathmandu, 2006.

116   Committee on the Rights of the Child, *Initial reports of States parties due in 1997: Palau*, CRC/C/51/Add.3, 23 Mar 2000, par. 234.

117   Besides the Criminal Code's MACR provisions, the 1961 Child Welfare Act (as of 1990) allows the Children's Court to deprive the liberty of child offenders of any age (see, inter alia, Arts. 32(2)(a)(ii) and 41(1)(b)(iii)).

Country	MACR	ACR specific crimes	*Doli incapax* test	MACR source statute
				(2) A person under the age of 14 years is not criminally responsible for an act or omission, unless it is proved that at the time of doing the act or making the omission he had capacity to know that he ought not to do the act or make the omission. (3) A male person under the age of 14 years is presumed to be incapable of having carnal knowledge, but this presumption is rebuttable.
Paraguay	14	–	–	Ley Nº 1.702/01, as of 2003, Art. 1, and Código de la Niñez y la Adolescencia, 2001, Art. 194. Ley Nº 1.702/01, Art. 1: ... Adolescente: toda persona humana desde los catorce años hasta los diecisiete años de edad ... . Código de la Niñez y la Adolescencia, Art. 194: La responsabilidad penal se adquiere con la adolescencia ... .
Peru	14	–	–	Código de los Niños y Adolescentes, as of 2007, Art. IV ... . En caso de infracción a la ley penal, el niño y el adolescente menor de catorce (14) años será sujeto de medidas de protección y el adolescente mayor de catorce (14) años de medidas socio-educativas.
Philippines	15[118]	–	15–18	Juvenile Justice and Welfare Act of 2006, Sect. 6. A child fifteen (15) years of age or under at the time of the commission of the offense shall be exempt from criminal liability ... . A child above fifteen (15) years but below eighteen (18) years of age shall likewise be exempt from criminal liability and be subjected to an intervention program, unless he/she has acted with discernment, in which case, such child shall be subjected to the appropriate proceedings in accordance with this Act ... .
Poland	0[119]	–	–	Law of 26 October 1982 on Procedure in Cases Involving Juveniles.
Portugal	12	–	–	Lei Tutelar Educativa, 1999, Art. 1. A prática, por menor com idade compreendida entre os 12 e os 16 anos, de facto qualificado pela lei como crime dá lugar à aplicação de medida tutelar educativa em conformidade com as disposições da presente lei.
Qatar	7	–	7–18	Penal Code.[120] 1. There shall be no criminal responsibility for any act perpetrated by a

118 The MACR is technically 15 years and one day. See Bayoran, Gilbert, "56 minors to be cleared of criminal liability soon," *The Visayan Daily Star*, Bacolod City (Philippines), 23 May 2006, www.visayandailystar.com/2006/May/23.

119 In response to evidence of any child's "demoralization," which includes his or her commission of an offense, courts may order educative, protective, and therapeutic measures. In some cases, these measures signify the deprivation of liberty for indeterminate periods of time. See, inter alia, Committee on the Rights of the Child, *Periodic reports of States parties due in 1998: Poland*, CRC/C/70/Add.12, 6 Feb 2002, par. 360; and Stando-Kawecka, Barbara, *The Juvenile Justice System in Poland*, presented at the Conference of the European Society of Criminology, Amsterdam, 25–28 August 2004.

120 Committee on the Rights of the Child, *Initial reports of States parties due in 1997: Qatar*, CRC/C/51/Add.5, 11 Jan 2001, pars. 21 and 28. Penal Code Article numbers not cited.

Annex 2: Worldwide MACR Provisions and Statutory Sources by Country   213

Country	MACR	ACR specific crimes	*Doli incapax* test	MACR source statute
				minor under seven years of age; 2. If the minor is over seven but under 18 years of age, he shall not be held criminally responsible unless he is sufficiently mature in awareness to judge the nature or consequences of the act which he perpetrates.
Republic of Korea	14[121]	–	–	The Criminal Procedure Act, Art. 9, and the Criminal Act.[122]
Romania	14	–	14–16	Criminal Code, 2004, Art. 113.[123] (1) A minor under the age of 14 shall not be criminally liable. (2) A minor aged from 14 to 16 shall be criminally liable, only if it is proven that he/she committed the act in discernment. (3) A minor over the age of 16 shall be criminally liable within the framework of the system of sanctions applicable to minors.
Russian Federation	14[124]	16	–	Criminal Code, as of 2004, Art. 20(1–2).[125] 1. A person who, before the commission of a crime, has attained the age of 16 years shall be subject to criminal responsibility. 2. Persons who, before the commission of a crime, have attained the age of 14 years shall be subject to criminal liability for homicide (Article 105), intentional infliction of grave bodily injury causing a impairment of health (Article 111), intentional infliction of bodily injury of average gravity (Article 112), kidnapping (Article 126), rape (Article 131), forcible sexual actions (Article 132), theft (Article 158), robbery (Article 161), brigandism (Article 162), racketeering (Article 163), unlawful occupancy of a car or any other transport vehicle without theft (Article 166), intentional destruction or damage of property under aggravating circumstances (the second part of Article 167), terrorism (Article 205),

121   Children 12 and older accused of committing criminal offences, or deemed likely to do so and also beyond parental control, are handled as juvenile protection cases. Such children are not subject to sentences in juvenile prisons, as children 14 and older are, but they may face protection dispositions that include placement in child welfare institutions, juvenile protection institutions, and juvenile training schools or reformatories. See, inter alia, Republic of Korea, *The Juvenile Protection Education Institution*, www.jschool.go.kr/HP/JSC80/jsc_01/jsc_1020.jsp.

122   Committee on the Rights of the Child, *Periodic reports of States parties due in 1998: Republic of Korea*, CRC/C/70/Add.14, 26 Jun 2002, pars. 36 and 196.

123   Unofficial translation by Organization for Security and Co-operation in Europe, Office for Democratic Institutions and Human Rights, www.legislationline.org.

124   The 1999 law on "The Bases of the System of Preventing/Combating Homelessness and Juvenile Offenses" allows for the placement of children younger than the MACR in centers for the temporary confinement of juvenile delinquents, via a judicial sentence or judge's order in response to "socially dangerous acts." Although placement is limited to 30 days, there were 54,800 such placements in 1999, 30,000 in 2000, and 24,400 in 2001. See Committee on the Rights of the Child, *Third periodic reports of States parties due in 2001, Russian Federation*, CRC/C/125/Add.5, 15 Nov 2004, par. 323; and Stoecker, Sally W., "Homelessness and criminal exploitation of Russian minors: Realities, resources, and legal remedies," *Demokratizatsiya*, Spring 2001.

125   Translation by www.russian-criminal-code.com.

Country	MACR	ACR specific crimes	*Doli incapax* test	MACR source statute
				seizure of a hostage (Art. 206), making deliberately false report about an act of terrorism (Art. 207), hooliganism under aggravating circumstances (the second and third parts of Art. 213), vandalism (Art. 214), theft or possession of firearms, ammunition, explosives, and explosion devices (Art. 226), theft or possession of narcotics or psychotropic substances (Art. 229), the destruction of transport vehicles or ways of communication (Art. 267).
Rwanda	14	–	–	Penal Code, Art. 77.[126] When the perpetrator or accomplice of a crime or an offence was over 14 and less than 18 years of age at the time of the offence, the penalties shall be as follows if he is liable to a criminal sentence … .
Saint Kitts and Nevis	8	–	–	Juvenile Act, Sect. 3.[127] It shall be conclusively presumed that no child under the age of eight years can be guilty of any offence.
Saint Lucia	12	–	–	The Children and Young Person's Act of 1972, Section 3.[128]
St Vincent and the Grenadines	8	–	–	Juveniles Act, cap. 168, sect. 3, and the Criminal Code, cap. 124, sect. 12.[129]
Samoa	8	–	8–14	Crimes Ordinance 1961, Sects. 11–12. Sect. 11: No person shall be convicted of an offence by reason of any act done or omitted by him when under the age of 8 years. Sect. 12: No person shall be convicted of an offence by reason of any act done or omitted by him when of the age of 8 but under the age of 14 years, unless the jury by whom he was tried, or the Court before whom he is charged having jurisdiction to deal with the charge summarily, is of the opinion that he knew such act or omission was wrong.
San Marino	12	–	12–18	Codice penale, Art. 10. Non è imputabile chi ha un'età inferiore agli anni dodici. Per i minori che abbiano superato gli anni dodici ma non i diciotto, il giudice, ove accerti la capacità d'intendere e di volere, applica la pena con una diminuzione … .
Sao Tome and Principe	16[130]	–	–	Criminal Code, Art. 42, and Statute on judicial assistance for minors (Decree No. 417/71), Arts. 15–16.[131]

126 Committee on the Rights of the Child, *Second periodic reports of States parties due in 1998: Rwanda*, CRC/C/70/Add.22, 8 Oct 2003, par. 92.

127 *Id.*, *Initial reports of States parties due in 1992: Saint Kitts and Nevis*, CRC/C/3/Add.51, 5 May 1997, par. 16.

128 Prof. Hazel Thompson-Ahye, Eugene Dupuch Law School, Bahamas, correspondence with author, July 2005.

129 Committee on the Rights of the Child, *Initial reports of States parties due in 1995: Saint Vincent and the Grenadines*, CRC/C/28/Add.18, 10 Oct 2001, par. 34.

130 Under the Statute on judicial assistance for minors, children younger than 16 who have committed acts deemed offences or crimes are only subject to protection, assistance, or education measures ordered by juvenile courts. Such measures may involve the deprivation of liberty, as in the case of placement in educational institutions and private educational establishments, although these do not appear to be used in practice. See, inter alia, *Id.*, *Initial reports of States parties due in 1993: Sao Tome and Principe*, CRC/C/8/Add.49, 1 Dec 2003, pars. 103, 107, and 109.

131 *Ibid.*, pars. 103 and 111.

Annex 2: Worldwide MACR Provisions and Statutory Sources by Country 215

Country	MACR	ACR specific crimes	*Doli incapax* test	MACR source statute
Saudi Arabia	puberty[132]	7 or 12[133]	–	–
Senegal	13	–	–	Code pénal, as of 2000, Art. 52. Si … il est décidé qu'un mineur âgé de plus de treize ans doit faire l'objet d'une condamnation pénale, les peines seront prononcées ainsi qu'il suit … .
Serbia	14	–	–	Criminal Code, 2005, Art. 4(3).[134] A criminal sanction may not be imposed on a person who has not turned fourteen at the time of the commission of an offence … .
Seychelles	7	12	7–12	Penal Code, Sect. 15.[135] A person under the age of seven years is not criminally responsible for any act or omission. A person under the age of 12 years is not criminally responsible for an act or omission, unless it is proved that at the time of doing the act or making the omission he had capacity to know that he ought not to do the act or make the omission. A male person under the age of twelve years is presumed to be incapable of having carnal knowledge.
Sierra Leone	14	–	–	Child Right Act, 2007, Art. 70. In any judicial proceeding in Sierra Leone, a child shall not be held to be criminally responsible for his actions if he is below the age of fourteen years.
Singapore	7	–	7–12	Penal Code, as of 1998, Arts. 82–83. Art. 82: Nothing is an offence which is done by a child under 7 years of age. Art. 83: Nothing is an offence which is done by a child above 7 years of age and under 12, who has not attained sufficient maturity of understanding to judge of the nature and consequence of his conduct on that occasion.
Slovakia	14	–	14–15	Penal Code, 2005, §94–96.[136]
Slovenia	14[137]	–	–	Criminal Code, 1995, Art. 71.[138] Criminal sanctions shall not be applied against minors

132   Children who have reached puberty may face the death penalty for crimes including adultery, apostasy, "corruption on earth," drug trafficking, sabotage, (political) rebellion, murder during armed robbery, murder, and manslaughter, as well as for actions within the broad category allowing courts' discretionary punishment (*ta'zīr*). In addition, judges may consider physical characteristics of puberty at the time of trial or upon sentencing, rather than considering children's ages at the time of alleged offenses, and may exercise significant discretion over which physical characteristics to assess. Human Rights Watch, *Adults Before Their Time: Children in Saudi Arabia's Criminal Justice System*, New York, 2008.

133   At least until recent years, the age of criminal responsibility for crimes besides capital offenses was 7 years. Government statements/policies regarding an intended or approved increase to 12 years are largely inconsistent, and in either case may only apply to boys. *Ibid.* Committee on the Rights of the Child, *Initial reports of States parties due in 1998: Saudi Arabia*, CRC/C/61/Add.2, 29 Mar 2000, par. 55.

134   Translated by OSCE Mission to Serbia and Montenegro, Organization for Security and Co-operation in Europe, www.legislationline.org.

135   National Council for Children, Seychelles, correspondence with author, September 2002.

136   Committee on the Rights of the Child, *Second periodic reports of States parties due in 1999: Slovakia*, CRC/C/SVK/2, 21 Sept 2006, pars. 49–50.

137   Despite the nominal MACR of 14, welfare agencies called "Social Work Centers" have the authority to commit younger children to juvenile institutions, which are substantially equivalent to educational institution placements for older children in criminal cases. See Filipcic, Katja, "Slovenia: Dealing with Juvenile Delinquents in Slovenia," 75 *International Review of Penal Law* (*Revue internationale de droit pénal*) 493, 2004.

138   *Ibid.*, at 498.

Country	MACR	ACR specific crimes	Doli incapax test	MACR source statute
				who were under the age of fourteen at the time a criminal offence was committed (children).
Solomon Islands	0[139]	–	–	Juvenile Offenders Act, as of 1996, Sects. 2 and 16(i–j). Sect. 2: ... "child" means a person who is ... under the age of fourteen years; ... "young person" means a person who is ... fourteen years of age or upwards and under the age of eighteen years. Sect. 16(i–j): Where a child or young person charged with any offence is tried by any court, and the court is satisfied of his guilt the court ... may deal with the case in any of the following manners or combination thereof, namely— ... (i) by committing the offender to custody in a place of detention; or (j) where the offender is a young person, by sentencing him to imprisonment ... .
Somalia	0[140]	–	–	–
South Africa	7	–	7–14	Common law.[141]
Spain	14	–	–	Ley Orgánica 5/2000, de 12 de enero, reguladora de la responsabilidad penal de los menores, as of 2006, Arts. 1(1) and 3. Art. 1(1): Esta Ley se aplicará para exigir la responsabilidad de las personas mayores de catorce años y menores de dieciocho por la comisión de hechos tipificados como delitos o faltas en el Código Penal o las leyes penales especiales. Art. 3: Cuando el autor de los hechos mencionados en los artículos anteriores sea menor de catorce años, no se le exigirá responsabilidad ... .
Sri Lanka	8	–	8–12	Penal Code, as of 1980, Sects. 75–76. Sect. 75: Nothing is an offence which is done by a child under eight years of age. Sect. 76: Nothing is an offence which is done by a child above eight years of age and under twelve, who has not attained sufficient maturity of understanding to judge of the nature and consequence of his conduct on that occasion.

139   Solomon Islands has indicated that Penal Code Section 14 sets the MACR at 8 years. However, the Juvenile Offenders Act does not set any lower age limit for holding children guilty of offences and depriving them of their liberty as a consequence. Committee on the Rights of the Child, *Initial reports of States parties due in 1997: Solomon Islands*, CRC/C/51/Add.6, 12 Jul 2002.

140   Although overlapping customary/traditional law, Islamic law, and codified criminal law all contain relevant standards, there is no effective MACR. In customary/traditional law, the MACR is understood to be 15 years. Islamic law grants judges the authority to decide on the dangerous character of juvenile delinquents under the age of 15, and to order them to periods of up to three months in reformatory facilities. Under the Penal Code, article 59 nominally sets an MACR of 14 years, yet article 177 details circumstances under which judges may commit younger children who have committed offences to reformatories for 2 years or more. UNICEF Somalia, "Juvenile Justice in Post-Conflict Situations: Somalia," unpublished draft presented at the conference *Juvenile Justice in Post-Conflict Situations*, UNICEF Innocenti Research Centre, Florence, May 2001.

141   Milton, J.R.L., S.E. van der Merwe, and D. van Zyl Smit, "Republic of South Africa," 1994, in Fijnaut, Cyrillus, and Frankk Verbruggen, eds, "Criminal Law," in Blanpain, Roger, ed., *International Encyclopaedia of Laws*, The Hague, Kluwer Law International, 2004.

Annex 2: Worldwide MACR Provisions and Statutory Sources by Country   217

Country	MACR	ACR specific crimes	*Doli incapax* test	MACR source statute
Sudan	0[142]	7 15/18 /puberty	–	Criminal Law Act (Penal Code) of 1991, Arts. 3, 9, 27(2), and 47, and Narcotic Drugs and Psycho-tropic Substances Act of 1994, Arts. 15 and 20.
Suriname	10	–	–	Code of Criminal Procedure, Art. 56, Par. 1.[143]
Swaziland	7	–	7–14	Common law.[144]
Sweden	15	–	–	Penal Code, as of 2004, Sect. 6. No sanction shall be imposed upon a person for a crime committed before attaining the age of fifteen.
Switzerland	10	–	–	Loi fédérale régissant la condition pénale des mineurs, 2003, Art. 3(1). La présente loi s'applique à quiconque commet un acte punissable entre 10 et 18 ans.
Syrian Arab Republic	10	–	–	Juveniles Act No. 18 of 1974, as of 2003, Arts. 2 and 30.[145]
Tajikistan	14[146]	16	–	Criminal Code, Art. 23.[147] (1) A person who has attained the age of 16 years old by the time of committing a crime is liable to criminal responsibility. (2) Persons reached the age of 14 years old by the time of committing a crime are liable to criminal liability for homicide (Article 104), intentional major bodily injury (Article 110), intentional minor bodily injury (Article 111), kidnapping (Article 130), rape (Article 138), forcible act of sexual character (Article 139), terrorism (Article 179), capture of hostage (Article 181), theft of weapons,

142   Regardless of Sudan's various claims, Criminal Code Articles 3 and 9 only nominally limit criminal responsibility to children 15 or older who have attained puberty, and to adults 18 or older. Article 47 allows courts to order children 7 and older who have committed offenses to correctional institutions for 2–5 years, and there is no minimum age limit at all for offences including alcohol or drug handling or consumption, and sexual relations outside of marriage. Moreover, under certain circumstances, Article 27(2) allows capital punishment for children ages 7 to 18 who commit murder, *hadd* offences, or offences subject to *qasas*. Committee on the Rights of the Child, *Initial reports of States parties due in 1992: Sudan*, CRC/C/3/Add.3, 16 Dec 1992, par. 33. *Id.*, *Periodic reports of States parties due in 1997: Sudan*, CRC/C/65/Add.17, 6 Dec 2001, pars. 40–41, 52, and 347.

143   *Id.*, *Initial reports of States parties due in 1995: Suriname*, CRC/C/28/Add.11, 23 Sept 1998, par. 18.

144   *Id.*, *Initial report of States parties due in 1997: Swaziland*, CRC/C/SWZ/1, 16 Feb 2006, par. 456.

145   Human Rights Committee, *Consideration of reports submitted by States parties under article 40 of the Covenant, Third periodic report: Syria*, CCPR/C/SYR/2004/3, 19 Oct 2004, pars. 126, 250–251, and 384.

146   Under Order n° 178 of the President of the Republic of Tajikistan, of 23 Feb 1995 (Regulations on the Commission on Minors), administrative Commissions consider the cases of children younger than 14 suspected of having committed criminal acts. There is no minimum age limit to Commissions' mandate in this respect, and they may apply punishments including the deprivation of liberty for children apparently as young as 7. There are indications that even younger children, contrary to Regulations, have been deprived of their liberty. See, e.g., World Organisation Against Torture, *Human Rights Violations in Tajikistan: Alternative Report to the UN Committee Against Torture 37th Session*, Geneva, 2006.

147   Unofficial translation by the Organization for Security and Co-operation in Europe, Office for Democratic Institutions and Human Rights, www.legislationline.org.

Country	MACR	ACR specific crimes	*Doli incapax* test	MACR source statute
				ammunition and explosives (Article 199), illegal trafficking of narcotics (Article 200), theft of drugs and precursors (Article 202), illegal cultivating of plants containing narcotic substances (Article 204), destruction of transport or ways of communication (Article 214), hooliganism under aggravating circumstances (Article 237, p.2 and 3), larceny (Article 244), robbery (Article 248), extortion (Article 250), robbery with extreme violence (249), hi-jacking of a vehicle or other means of transportation without the purpose of stealing (Article 252), intentional damaging or destruction of property under aggravating circumstances (Article 255). (3) In separate cases provided for by the Special Part of the Code only persons reached more than 16 years old are liable to criminal liability.
Thailand	7	–	–	Penal Code, Sect. 73.[148] A child below 7 years of age, who commits a criminal offence, is not liable to punishment.
The former Yugoslav Republic of Macedonia	14	–	–	Criminal Code, as of 2004, Art. 71.[149] Criminal sanctions may not be applied against a juvenile who at the time of perpetration of the crime has not reached fourteen years (child).
Timor-Leste	12	–	–	United Nations Transitional Administration in East Timor Regulation 2000/30 on Transitional Rules of Criminal Procedure, as of 2001, Sect. 45.1 … . A minor under 12 years of age shall be deemed incapable of committing a crime and shall not be subjected to criminal proceedings … .
Togo	13	–	–	Code de Procédure Pénale, 1983, Arts. 455. Les mineurs de treize ans sont pénalement irresponsables … .
Tonga	7	–	7–12	Criminal Offences Act, as of 2005, Sect. 16. (1) Nothing shall be deemed an offence which is done by a person under 7 years of age. (2) Nothing shall be deemed an offence which is done by a person of or above 7 and under 12 years of age unless in the opinion of the Court or jury such person had attained sufficient maturity of understanding to be aware of the nature and consequences of his conduct in regard to the act of which he is accused.
Trinidad and Tobago	7	–	10–14	Common law.[150]
Tunisia	13	–	13–15	Code de la Protection de l'Enfant, 1995, Art. 68. L'enfant âgé de moins de treize ans est présumé irréfragablement n'avoir pas la

---

148 Committee on the Rights of the Child, *Initial reports of States parties due in 1994: Thailand*, CRC/C/11/Add.13, 30 Sept 1996, par. 82.

149 Translation by the Organization for Security and Co-operation in Europe, Office for Democratic Institutions and Human Rights, www.legislationline.org.

150 Committee on the Rights of the Child, *Second periodic reports of States parties due in 1999: Trinidad and Tobago*, CRC/C/83/Add.12, 15 Nov 2004, pars. 248–250.

Annex 2: Worldwide MACR Provisions and Statutory Sources by Country

Country	MACR	ACR specific crimes	*Doli incapax* test	MACR source statute
				capacité d'enfreindre la loi pénale, cette Présomption devient réfragable pour les enfants âgés de treize à quinze ans révolus.
Turkey	12[151]	–	12–15	Criminal Code, 2004, Art. 31(1–2).[152] (1) The children having not attained the full age of twelve on the commission date of the offense, may not have criminal responsibility. Besides, no criminal prosecution may be commenced against such persons ... (2) In case a person who attained the age of twelve but not yet completed the age of fifteen on the commission date of the offense does not have the ability to perceive the legal meaning and consequences of the offense, or to control his actions, he may not have criminal responsibility for such behavior ... .
Turkmenistan	14	16	–	Criminal Code, 1998, Art. 21.[153]
Tuvalu	10	12	10–14	Penal Code, as of 1978, Sect. 14. (1) A person under the age of 10 years is not criminally age responsible for any act or omission. (2) A person under the age of 14 years is not criminally responsible for an act or omission, unless it is proved that at the time of doing the act or making the omission he had capacity to know that he ought not to do the act or make the omission. (3) A male person under the age of 12 years is presumed to be incapable of having sexual intercourse.
Uganda	12	–	–	Children's Statute, 1996, Sect. 89.[154] The minimum age of criminal responsibility shall be twelve years.
Ukraine	14[155]	16	–	Criminal Code, 2001, Art. 22.[156] 1. Persons who have reached the age of 16 years before the

151 Under the Criminal Code, children younger than 12—as well as children between 12 and 15 deemed unable to perceive the legal meaning and consequences of their offences or as lacking the ability to control their actions—may face security measures/precautions. Furthermore, under the 2005 Juvenile Protection Law, any child in conflict with the law and deemed not criminally responsible may face "protective and supportive measures" that include deprivation of liberty in educational, governmental, and private care institutions. There is no lower age limit to the application of such measures, they may be imposed through a child's eighteenth birthday, and judges are not required to hold hearings before ordering them. See, inter alia, Arts. 3(1)(a)(2), 5(1)(b-c), 7(6), 11(1) and 13(1).

152 Unofficial translation by the Organization for Security and Co-operation in Europe, Office for Democratic Institutions and Human Rights, www.legislationline.org.

153 Committee on the Rights of the Child, *Initial reports of States parties due in 1995: Turkmenistan*, CRC/C/TKM/1, 5 Dec 2005, pars. 54 and 194.

154 Foundation for Human Rights Initiative, *The Human Rights Reporter 1998*, Kampala, 1999, Note 59.

155 Criminal Code Chapter XV on "Specific Features of Criminal Liability and Punishment of Minors" casts doubt upon the effective MACR. Art. 97(2) states that "A court shall also apply compulsory reformation measures ... to a person, who committed a socially dangerous act ... before he/she attained the age of criminal liability." Such measures include "placing a minor in a special educational and correctional institution for children and teenagers until the minor's complete correction but for a term not exceeding three years" (Art. 105(2)). Translation by the Organization for Security and Co-operation in Europe, Office for Democratic Institutions and Human Rights, www.legislationline.org.

156 *Ibid.* (Translation).

Country	MACR	ACR specific crimes	*Doli incapax* test	MACR source statute
				commission of a criminal offense shall be criminally liable. 2. Persons who have committed criminal offenses at the age of 14 to 16 years shall be criminally liable only for a murder (Articles 115–117), attempted killing of a statesperson or public figure, a law enforcement officer, a member of a civilian peace-keeping or border-guard unit, or a serviceman, judge, assessor or juror, in connection with their activity related to the administration of justice, a defense attorney or agent of any person in connection with their activity related to legal assistance, or a foreign representative (Articles 112, 348, 379, 400 and 443), intended grievous bodily injury (Article 121, paragraph 3 of Articles 345, 346, 350, 377 and 398), intended bodily injury of medium gravity (Article 122, paragraph 2 of Articles 345, 346, 350, 377 and 398), sabotage (Article 113), gangsterism (Article 257), act of terrorism (Article 258), hostage taking (Articles 147 and 348), rape (Article 152), violent unnatural satisfaction of sexual desire (Article 153), theft (sections 185, paragraph 1 of Articles 262 and 308), robbery (Articles 186, 262 and 308), brigandage (Article 187, paragraph 3 of Articles 262 and 308), extortion (Article 189, 262 and 308), willful destruction or endamagement of property (paragraph 2 of Articles 194, 347, 352 and 378, paragraphs 2 and 3 of Article 399), endamagement of communication routes and means of transportation (Article 277), theft or seizure of railroad rolling stock, air-, sea- or river-craft (Article 278), misappropriation of transportation (paragraph 2 and 3 of Article 289), and hooliganism (Article 296).
United Arab Emirates	7	–	7-n/a	Federal Act No. 9 of 1976, Art. 6.[157] Criminal proceedings shall not be brought against a juvenile delinquent under seven years of age ....
United Kingdom of Great Britain and Northern Ireland	England, Wales: 10	–	–	England and Wales: Children and Young Persons Act, as of 1988, Sect. 50.
	Northern Ireland: 10	–	–	Northern Ireland: The Criminal Justice (Children) (Northern Ireland) Order, 1998, Sect. 3.
	Scotland: 8	–	–	Scotland: Criminal Procedure (Scotland) Act, 1995, Sect. 41.
	Others: vary 8–10	varies	varies	Other jurisdictions (Overseas Territories and Crown Dependencies)[158]: Anguilla (MACR 10, *doli incapax* 10–14); Bermuda (MACR 8, *doli*

157 Committee on the Rights of the Child, *Initial reports of States parties due in 1999: United Arab Emirates*, CRC/C/78/Add.2, 24 Oct 2001, par. 97.

158 Provisions from the Bailiwick of Guernsey, the Bailiwick of Jersey, and Gibraltar are not listed. See UK Government, *The Consolidated 3rd and 4th Periodic Report to UN Committee on the Rights of the Child: United Kingdom Overseas Territories and Crown Dependencies: Summary*

Country	MACR	ACR specific crimes	*Doli incapax* test	MACR source statute
				incapax 8–14); British Virgin Islands (MACR 10, ACR Other Crimes 12, *doli incapax* 10–14); Cayman Islands (MACR 10, *doli incapax* 10–14); Falkland Islands (MACR 10, *doli incapax* 10–14); Isle of Man (MACR 10); Montserrat (MACR 10, *doli incapax* 10–14); Pitcairn (MACR 10); St. Helena and its dependencies (MACR 10, *doli incapax* 10–14); Turks and Caicos Islands (MACR 8).
United Republic of Tanzania	10	–	10–12	Penal Code, as of 1998, Sect. 15.[159] (1) A person under the age of ten years is not criminally responsible for any act or omission. (2) A person under the age of twelve years is not criminally responsible for an act or omission, unless it is proved that at the time of doing the act or making the omission he had capacity to know that he ought not to do the act or make the omission.
	Zanzibar: 12	–	12–14	Act 11 of 1986.[160]
United States of America[161]	CA, NJ,[162]	– –	CA[164]: 0–14 –	CA: Penal Code, as of 2006, §26. –
	PA,	PA: 10	–	PA: Consolidated Statutes, as of 2006, Title 42 §6302 and §6355(e).
	VT, and others: 0[163]	VT: 10	–	VT: Statutes, as of 2006, Title 33 §5502(a)(1)(A) and (C).

Reports, CRC/C/GBR/4, July 2007, pars. 8, 17, 247(a), 299, 333(a-b), 390(a-b), 426 (a-b), and 459(c). Committee on the Rights of the Child, *Initial reports of States parties due in 1996: Overseas Dependent Territories and Crown Dependencies of the United Kingdom of Great Britain and Northern Ireland*, CRC/C/41/Add.7, 22 Feb 2000, pars. 62(a) and 136(a). *Id.*, *Initial reports of States parties due in 1996: Overseas Dependent Territories and Crown Dependencies of the United Kingdom of Great Britain and Northern Ireland*, CRC/C/41/Add.9, 29 May 2000, pars. 26 and 146. The British Virgin Islands presume boys younger than 12 incapable of having "carnal knowledge."

159   Mashamba, J. Clement, *Basic Elements and Principles to be Incorporated in New Children Statute in Tanzania*, National Network of Organisations Working with Children in Tanzania, Dar es Salaam, 2003.

160   Committee on the Rights of the Child, *Initial reports of States parties due in 1993: United Republic of Tanzania*, CRC/C/8/Add.14/Rev.1, 25 Sept 2000, par. 96.

161   Juvenile justice is principally regulated and administered under respective state law. The states, plus the District of Columbia, and their respective abbreviations are the following: Alabama-AL, Alaska-AK, Arizona-AZ, Arkansas-AR, California-CA, Colorado-CO, Connecticut-CT, Delaware-DE, District of Columbia-DC, Florida-FL, Georgia-GA, Hawaii-HI, Idaho-ID, Illinois-IL, Indiana-IN, Iowa-IA, Kansas-KS, Kentucky-KY, Louisiana-LA, Maine-ME, Maryland-MD, Massachusetts-MA, Michigan-MI, Minnesota-MN, Mississippi-MS, Missouri-MO, Montana-MT, Nebraska-NE, Nevada-NV, New Hampshire-NH, New Jersey-NJ, New Mexico-NM, New York-NY, North Carolina-NC, North Dakota-ND, Ohio-OH, Oklahoma-OK, Oregon-OR, Pennsylvania-PA, Rhode Island-RI, South Carolina-SC, South Dakota-SD, Tennessee-TN, Texas-TX, Utah-UT, Vermont-VT, Virginia-VA, Washington-WA, West Virginia-WV, Wisconsin-WI, and Wyoming-WY.

162   New Jersey jurisprudence, exemplified in two juvenile sex offender cases, arguably upholds the availability of the common law *doli incapax* presumption in juvenile court delinquency proceedings (see State of New Jersey in the Interest of J.P.F., 845 A.2d 173 (2004); In the Matter of Registrant J.G., 777 A.2d 891 (2001); and Carter, Andrew M., "Age Matters: The Case for a Constitutionalized Infancy

Country	MACR	ACR specific crimes	*Doli incapax* test	MACR source statute
	NC: 6	–	–	NC: General Statutes, as of 2006, §7B-1501(7).
	MD, MA, NY: 7	–	–	MD: Code, as of 2006, § 3-8A-05(d). MA: General Laws, as of 2006, §119–52. NY: Family Court Act, as of, §301.2(1).
	AZ, WA: 8	–	– WA: 8–12	AZ: Revised Statutes, as of 2006, Sects. 8–201(11) and 8–201(13)(a)(iv). WA: Revised Code, as of 2006, §9A.04.050.
	AR, CO, KS, LA, MN, MS, SD, TX, WI: 10	–	–	AR: Code, as of 2006, Sect. 9-27-306(a)(1)(A)(i). CO: Revised Statutes, as of 2006, Sect. 18-1-801. KS: Revised Statutes, as of 2006, Sects. 38-2302(i) and 38-2302(n). LA: Children's Code, as of 2006, Art. 804(3). MN: Statutes, as of 2006, Sect. 260C.007(6)(12). MS: Code, as of 2006, §43-21-105(i). SD: Codified Laws, as of 2006, §26-8C-2. TX: Family Code, as of 2006, §51.02(2)(A). WI: Revised Statutes, as of 2006, §938.02(3m).
Uruguay	13	–	–	Código de la Niñez y la Adolescencia, 2004, Art. 74 ... . Sólo puede ser sometido a proceso especial, regulado por este Código, el adolescente mayor de trece y menor de dieciocho años de edad, imputado de infracción a la ley penal ... .

Defense," 54 *Kansas Law Review* 687, 2006). However, neither decision attempts to reconcile such availability with the provision, referring to the Code of Criminal Justice chapter on sex offenses, that "No actor shall be presumed to be incapable of committing a crime under this chapter because of age ... ." (New Jersey Statutes §2C:14-5(b)). One lower court in another juvenile sex offender case interpreted this provision as a "clear statutory disavowal of the old common law three-tiered rule." (State of New Jersey in the Interest of C.P. & R.D., 514 A.2d 850, 854 (1986)).

163 In statutory and/or case law, these states either have no minimum age for adjudicating children delinquent in juvenile court proceedings, or have no minimum age for original adult criminal court jurisdiction. In addition, the federal government has no minimum age limit to adjudicating children delinquent; federal law enforcement officials arrest approximately 400 children per year, but cases may be transferred under certain conditions to state courts. "Others" include AL, AK, CT, DE, DC, FL, GA, HI, ID, IL, IN, IA, KY, ME, MI, MO, MT, NE, NV, NH, NM, ND, OH, OK, OR, RI, SC, TN, UT, VA, WV, and WY. See, inter alia, King, Melanie, and Linda Szymanski, "National Overviews," *State Juvenile Justice Profiles*, Pittsburgh, National Center for Juvenile Justice, 2006, www.ncjj.org/stateprofiles; and Snyder, Howard N., and Melissa Sickmund, *Juvenile Offenders and Victims: 2006 National Report*, Washington, DC, United States Department of Justice, Office of Juvenile Justice and Delinquency Prevention, 2006.

164 This table notes the two states—California and Washington—where some type of *doli incapax* test is currently available in juvenile delinquency proceedings (see also footnote 162 regarding New Jersey). Case law in roughly 20 other states upholds the common law *doli incapax* provisions only in adult criminal courts, without necessarily barring delinquency proceedings in juvenile courts. Although such provisions are theoretically applicable to all relevant children in adult courts, *doli incapax* has generally fallen into disuse, and respective case law is typically dated. See Carter, *supra* note 162; Thomas, Tim A., *Annotation: Defense of Infancy in Juvenile Delinquency Proceedings*, 83 ALR4th 1135, 1991 and August 2002 Supplement; and King and Szymanski, *ibid.*

Annex 2: Worldwide MACR Provisions and Statutory Sources by Country

Country	MACR	ACR specific crimes	*Doli incapax* test	MACR source statute
Uzbekistan	13[165]	14/16	–	Criminal Code, 1994, Art. 17.[166] Sane individuals aged sixteen years or above at the moment of commission of a crime, shall be subject to liability. Individuals aged thirteen years or above at the moment of commission of a crime, shall be subject to liability only for intentional aggravated killing (Paragraph 2 of Article 97). Individuals aged fourteen years or above at the moment of commission of a crime, shall be subject to liability for the crimes envisaged by Paragraph 1 of Article 97, Articles 98, 104–106, 118, 119, 137, 164–166, and 169, Paragraphs 2 and 3 of Article 173, Articles 220, 222, 247, 252, 263, 267, and 271, Paragraphs 2 and 3 of Article 277 of this Code … .
Vanuatu	10	–	10–14	Penal Code, as of 1988, Sect. 17(1). No child under the age of 10 years shall be capable of committing any criminal offence. A child of 10 years of age or over but under 14 years of age shall be presumed to be incapable of committing a criminal offence unless it is proved by evidence that he was able to distinguish between right and wrong and that he did so with respect to the offence with which he is charged.
Venezuela (Bolivarian Republic of)	12	–	–	Ley Orgánica para la protección del niño y del adolescente, 1998, Arts. 2 and 528. Art. 2: … . Se entiende por adolescente toda persona con doce años o más y menos de dieciocho años de edad … . Art. 528: El adolescente que incurra en la comisión de hechos punibles responde por el hecho en la medida de su culpabilidad, de forma diferenciada del adulto … .
Viet Nam	14[167]	16	–	Penal Code, 1999, Art. 12.[168] Art. 12: 1. Toute personne âgée de seize ans accomplis est pénalement responsable de toute infraction. 2. Toute personne âgée de quatorze ans accomplis et de moins de seize ans est pénalement responsable des infractions très graves commises de manière intentionnelle ou des infractions extrêmement graves.

165 Regional and municipal Commissions on Minors' Affairs have primary responsibility, subject to public prosecutor supervision, for responding to children younger than 13 in conflict with the law. Commissions may return such children to parental supervision or send them to children's institutions for at least three years. See Danish Centre for Human Rights and UNICEF, *Juvenile Justice in Uzbekistan: Assessment 2000*, Copenhagen, 2001; and World Organisation Against Torture, *Rights of the Child in Uzbekistan*, Geneva, 2006.

166 Translation by the Organization for Security and Co-operation in Europe, Office for Democratic Institutions and Human Rights, www.legislationline.org.

167 Under the administrative procedures of Government Decree No. 33/CP of 1997, Art. 1, and the Ordinance on Sanctions against Administrative Violations, 2002, Art. 5(1)(a), children from age 12 who commit Penal Code violations are subject to placement in reform schools for 6 months to 2 years. See Human Rights Watch, *"Children of the Dust": Abuse of Hanoi Street Children in Detention*, New York, 2006; and Committee on the Rights of the Child, *Periodic reports of States parties due in 1997: Viet Nam*, CRC/C/65/Add.20, 5 Jul 2002, pars. 114(b) and 232(a).

168 Translation by la Maison du droit vietnamo-française, www.maisondudroit.org.

Country	MACR	ACR specific crimes	*Doli incapax* test	MACR source statute
Yemen	7	–	–	Penal Code.[169]
Zambia	8	12	8–12	Penal Code, as of 1995, Art. 14. (1) A person under the age of eight years is not criminally responsible for any act or omission. (2) A person under the age of twelve years is not criminally responsible for an act or omission, unless it is proved that at the time of doing the act or making the omission he had capacity to know that he ought not to do the act or make the omission. (3) A male person under the age of twelve years is presumed to be incapable of having carnal knowledge.
Zimbabwe	7	12	7–14	–[170]

169 Committee on the Rights of the Child, *Second periodic reports of States parties due in 1998: Yemen*, CRC/C/70/Add.1, 23 Jul 1998, par. 6.

170 Geltoe, Geoffrey, "Zimbabwe," 2000, in Fijnaut, Cyrillus, and Frankk Verbruggen, eds, "Criminal Law," in Blanpain, Roger, ed., *International Encyclopaedia of Laws*, The Hague, Kluwer Law International, 2004. Boys younger than 12 are irrebuttably presumed to be incapable of sexual intercourse, and cannot be guilty of rape or incest as principal offenders.

Index

Additional Protocol I to the Geneva Conventions 44–9, 51–2, 55, 68, 126
adult criminal court, *See* minimum age of penal majority
Afghanistan 82, 84, 90, *98*, *112*, 154, *187*
Africa 65, 82, 88–9, 109, 139, 149
African Charter on the Rights and Welfare of the Child 65
age
    at time of offense, trial, or sentencing 57, 64, 68, *108*, 132, 158
    estimation methods 57–8, 90, 131–6, 155, 161–3
    proof of, and birth registration 57–8, 64, 68, 75, 131–6, 155, 161–3
ages of criminal responsibility,
    multiple 59–60, 64, 68, 85–6, 97, 109–10, 123–4, 128, 158
    by jurisdiction 60, 64, 68, 109–10, 158
    by offense 59–60, 64, 68, 85–6, 97, 109–10, 123, 128, 158
    See also doli incapax
Albania 86, *98*, 109, *187*
Algeria *98*, 137, *187*
almshouses 5
American Convention on Human Rights 43–4
Andorra *98*, *112*, *187*
Angola *98*, *187*
Antigua and Barbuda *98*, *187*
anti-terrorism laws, MACRs in 59–60, 64, 68
apprenticeships 5
Argentina 8, 49, *98*, 110, *112*, *188*
armed conflict xv, 44–5, 47–8
Armenia *98*, 109, *188*
arrest 22, 49, 57, 118, 120, 132–3, 138, 140, 151–2, 154, 156, 160
Asia 82, 84, 88, 132, 149

Australia 59, *98*, *112*, 117, 149, 151, *188*
Austria *98*, 110, 134, *189*
Azerbaijan 87, *98*, 109, 138, *189*

Bahamas *98*, *190*
Bahrain 63, *98*, *108*, *112*, 127, 137, *190*
Bangladesh *98*, *112*, 120, 132, 149, 154, *190*
Barbados *98*, *112*, *190*
Beijing Rules, *See* United Nations Standard Minimum Rules for the Administration of Juvenile Justice
Belarus *98*, 109, *190*
Belgium 7–8, 96, *98*, *191*
Belize *98*, *112*, *192*
Benin *98*, *192*
best interests of the child 20–27, 30, 37, 43, 57, 61, 64, 68, 81, 158
Bhutan *98*, *112*, 128, *192*
birth registration, *See* age
Blair, Tony 116
Bolivia *98*, *112*, *192*
boot camps 138
    See also deprivation of liberty
Bosnia and Herzegovina 87, *98*, 192
Botswana *98*, 110, *192*
Brazil 45–7, *98*, *112*, 121, *192*
Brown, Gordon 117
Brunei Darussalam *98*, *192*
Bulgaria 86–7, *98*, 138, *193*
Bulger case 66–7, 114–17
Burkina Faso 99, 137, *193*
Burundi 49, 99, *112*, *193*

Cambodia 99, *108*, *112*, 127, *193*
Cameroon 99, *193*
Canada 6, 10, 46, 99, 114, 121, 140–41, 143–4, *193*
canon law 75
Cape Verde 99, *193*
capital punishment 45, 80, 153–4

CAT, *See* Convention against Torture and Other Cruel, Inhuman or Degrading Treatment or Punishment
centers, *See* institutions
Central African Republic 99, *193*
Chad 99, *193*
chargeability 43–4
Chicago, Illinois, USA 6
child labor 5, 87, 137–8, 151
child trafficking 151–3
childhood, construction of 1–8, 11–17, 25, 38–9, 89, 91, 113–25, 128–30, 159–61, 163
   binary portrayals of children 7–8, 13–17, 25, 38–9, 113–25, 129–30, 161, 163
children in need of protection as distinct from children in conflict with the law 63
children's rights
   concern for structural and individual perspectives 36–9, 162–3
   indivisibility of 24–5, 129–30, 160
   value of approach xiii–xiv, 159
Chile 99, 110, *112*, *194*
China 86–7, 99, 109, *112*, 113, 137–8, 152, *194*
Colombia 99, *112*, 152, *194*
Committee on the Rights of the Child xiii–xiv, 20, 23, 26–8, 32, 37, 41, 50–51, 56–64, 67–8, 94, 97, 110–11, 120, 129, 132, 134–5, 137–8, 144
   General Comment on "Children's rights in juvenile justice" xiv, 56–64
   guidance on children younger than MACRs 57, 60–64, 94, 137–8
common law
   English 13, 55–6, 74–6, 88, 90–91, 109–10, 117–18, 120, 148–50
   Roman-Dutch 150
community conferencing 162
Comoros 82–3, 99, *108*, 127, *194*
competence, children's xv, 1–4, 7–8, 10–14, 16–17, 25, 27–36, 38, 43–4, 47, 53, 55, 57, 69, 72, 75, 78–9, 85, 88, 127, 143–8, 150, 156, 159–61
   adjudicative, *See* effective participation at trial, children's right to

Congo (Republic of the) 99, 137, *195*
consistency, principle of 4, 30–31
Convention against Torture and Other Cruel, Inhuman or Degrading Treatment or Punishment (CAT) 49
Convention for the Protection of Human Rights and Fundamental Freedoms (European Convention on Human Rights) 28–9, 66
Convention on the Rights of the Child (CRC) ix–xi, xiii–xiv, 3–4, 16, 19–37, 41, 44, 50, 52–66, 68, 91, 93, 109 111–13, 124, 127–9, 147, 156–7, 163
   definition of children 3–4
   full text 165–85
   general principles 20–21, 26
Costa Rica 99, *112*, *195*
Côte d'Ivoire 99, *195*
Council of Europe 66
CRC, *See* Convention on the Rights of the Child
criminal court, *See* minimum age of penal majority
criminal punishment, Packer's definition of 94–6, 129, 136–7, 158
Croatia 65, 87, *100*, *195*
Cuba 87, *100*, *108*, 127, 138, *195*
culpability of children, lesser xv, 34
   See also mitigation
customary law systems 71, 87–90
Cyprus *100*, 110, *112*, *195*
Czech Republic 63, 87, *100*, *112*, 124, *195*

data collection and analysis 24, 140–41, 159
death penalty 45, 80, 153–4
delinquency
   effective prevention and intervention programs 21, 35–6, 142–4, 156, 160, 162–3
   ineffective responses to 35, 138–9, 156, 160, 163
   trends in the development of 140–44, 156, 162
Democratic People's Republic of Korea 87, *100*, *196*
Democratic Republic of the Congo *100*, *108*, 127, *196*

Denmark *100*, *196*
deprivation of liberty ix–x, xiv, 20, 22–4, 34, 36–7, 60, 62–64, 66, 68–9, 87, 113–14, 123, 136–8, 153, 156, 158, 160, 162–3
   counterproductive effects of 138–9, 156, 160, 163
   definition of 22
   international juvenile justice standards' restrictions on 22–4, 36–7, 62–4, 68–9, 162–3
   See also institutions
desert theory 9–10
developmental research 113–14, 144–8, 156, 160
discernment 7, 33, 43, 47, 50, 66, 71, 74, 76, 78, 84–5, 91, 113–15, 122, 125, 137, 148, 150
discrimination 8, 59–60, 64, 68, 82–3, 90, 121, 124, 131–2, 141, 149–50, 155, 158
   See also non-discrimination, principle of
diversion ix–x, 34, 58, 162–3
Djibouti *100*, *196*
doli incapax 42–4, 53, 56, 59, 64, 68, 72–6, 91, 97, 110, 114–15, 117–18, 128, 131, 146–50, 152, 154–5, 158
   historical development 72–6, 91, 117–18, 148
   international guidance 42–4, 53, 56, 59, 64, 68, 158
   undermining of 148–50
Dominica *100*, *196*
Dominican Republic *100*, *112*, *196*
drug trafficking 151–2
due process rights x, 6, 9–10, 20, 24–6, 51, 62–3, 69

Ecuador *100*, *112*, *196*
effective participation at trial, children's rights to 7, 20, 26–9, 32, 38, 67, 115, 128, 131, 144–8, 156, 160, 163
   See also views of the child, respect for the
Egypt *100*, *196*
El Salvador *100*, *112*, *196*
emergency laws, MACRs in 59–60, 64, 68
Equatorial Guinea *100*, *197*
Eritrea *100*, *197*
Estonia 87, *100*, *197*
Ethiopia 89, *100*, 133, *197*
Europe 6, 10, 65–7, 71, 73–4, 77, 85, 87–8, 90, 117, 134, 151–2
   Central and Eastern 84
   Scandinavia 109
European Committee of Social Rights 65
European Convention on Human Rights, *See* Convention for the Protection of Human Rights and Fundamental Freedoms
European Court of Human Rights 28, 66–7, 69, 128
European Social Charter 65–6
evolving capacities of the child 20, 29–36, 38–9, 53, 159–61
extradition xv
extrajudicial actions against children 153–5, 161

fair trial, right to and aspects of 9, 27–9, 38, 62, 144, 148
   See also due process rights; effective participation at trial, children's right to
Fiji *100*, 110, *197*
Finland 65, *100*, 120, *197*
France 63, 74–7, 85, 88, 91, *100*, *108*–9, *112*, 122–3, 125–7, 137, 148, *197*
   influence on MACR history 74–7, 85, 88, 91, 109, 148, 150
free will 10, 12–16

Gabon *100*, *198*
Gambia *100*, *112*, *198*
general principle of international law 47–9, 67–8, 93, 126–8, 130, 157
Geneva Conventions 44–9, 51–2, 55, 68, 126
Georgia 86, *100*, 109, *112*, 123–4, *198*
Germany 3, 65, *100*, 114, 121, 150, 152, *198*
Ghana *100*, *112*, 117, *198*
Greece 65, *101*, 137, *198*
Greek philosophy 71
Grenada *101*, *198*
Guatemala 63, *101*, *112*, *199*

Guinea 101, 199
Guinea-Bissau 101, 199
Guyana 101, 199

Haiti 101, 199
Honduras 101, 112, 121, 199
human rights, in general 12, 19, 24, 53, 83, 125, 158–9, 163
    indivisibility of 24–5, 129–30
Human Rights Committee 42–3
Hungary 65, 87, 101, 199

ICCPR, *See* International Covenant on Civil and Political Rights
Iceland 65, 101, 199
ICESCR, *See* International Covenant on Economic, Social and Cultural Rights
ICRC, *See* International Committee of the Red Cross
impunity 123, 154
imputability, *See* chargeability
In re Gault 9
In re Winship 9
India 101, 200
Indonesia 101, 112, 128, 200
industrial revolution 5
institutions, nominally for care, welfare, protection, education, reform, rehabilitation, training, etc. x, 5, 8, 61–4, 87, 122, 136–9
    See also deprivation of liberty
instrumental use of children for criminal activities 131, 151–3, 155, 161, 163
Inter-American Commission on Human Rights 43–4
Inter-American Court of Human Rights 43–4
International Committee of the Red Cross (ICRC) 44–5
International Covenant on Civil and Political Rights (ICCPR) 41–3, 52
International Covenant on Economic, Social and Cultural Rights (ICESCR) 21, 43
international juvenile justice standards xiii, 19–39, 69, 124–5, 142, 146–7, 156, 158, 160–62

intervention programs, *See* delinquency, effective prevention and intervention programs
Iran 82, 84, 101, 153–4, 200
Iraq 101, 200
Ireland 101, 110, 112, 200
Islamic law 52, 71, 76–84, 87, 89–91, 94, 127
    compatibility with children's rights 82–4, 127
    criminal responsibility in classic 77–9, 91
    ta'dīb 78-81
    See also religious law systems
Israel 101, 109, 154, 200
Italy 47, 65, 101, 151, 200

jail, *See* deprivation of liberty
Jamaica 101, 154, 201
Japan 46, 101, 112, 121–2, 125–6, 201
Jordan 101, 112, 201
just deserts theory 9–10
justice approach 1, 4, 8–17, 19, 24–6, 28, 37–9, 51, 63, 90, 116, 128, 159
juvenile delinquency, *See* delinquency
juvenile justice
    history 1, 4–10, 16
    international standards, *See* international juvenile justice standards

Kazakhstan 87, 101, 109, 138, 201
Kent v. United States 9
Kenya 89, 101, 110, 112, 137, 149, 202
Kiribati 102, 110, 202
Kosovo 154
Kuwait 102, 202
Kyrgyzstan 87, 102, 109, 138, 203

Lansdown, Gerison 29, 31
Laos 87, 102, 138, 203
Latin America 6, 8, 60, 63, 109, 113, 120, 128, 132, 161
    See also situación irregular
Latvia 65, 102, 203
law enforcement, *See* police
Lebanon 93, 102, 112, 203
Lesotho 89, 102, 112, 203

Liberia 61, *102*, *203*
liberty rights 1–4, 6–7, 11, 17, 30–33, 38, 59, 160
Libya 82, *102*, 137, *203*
Liechtenstein *102*, *204*
life and maximum survival and development, children's right to 30
limitations of the present study xv, 97
Lithuania 65, *102*, 109, *204*
Luxembourg *102*, *108*, 127, 137, *204*

Macedonia 87, *106*, *218*
MACR (minimum age of criminal responsibility)
  convergence of international guidance 67–8, 158
  definition xiii, 55–7, 157–9
  distinction from the minimum age of penal majority xiii, 93, 158
  distribution of age levels worldwide *108*–9
  establishment, implementation, and monitoring 159–63
  general principle of international law regarding 47–9, 67–8, 93, 126–8, 130, 157
  governments' accounts xiv, 93–7, 127–9
  provisions and statutory sources by country 187–*224*
  responses to children younger than x, 20–24, 60–64, 68–70, 87, 90, 93–7, 136–44, 155–63
  summary of related provisions by country 98–*108*
  summary of trends since 1989 111–12
  See also ages of criminal responsibility, multiple
Madagascar 62, *102*, *204*
Malawi *102*, 110, *112*, *204*
Malaysia 82, *102*, *108*, 110, 127, *205*
Maldives 82, 84, *102*, *108*, 110, *112*, 127, *205*
Mali *102*, *206*
Malta *102*, *206*
Marshall Islands *102*, *108*, 127, *206*
mass media
  constructive role of 124–5, 163
  sensationalism over youth crime 66, 114–19, 121–5, 129

Mauritania *103*, *207*
Mauritius *103*, *108*, 127, *207*
Merkel, Angela 121
methodology of the present study 97
Mexico 58, *103*, *112*, 113, *207*
Micronesia *103*, *108*, 127, *207*
military conflict xv, 44–5, 47–8
minimum age of criminal responsibility, *See* MACR
minimum age of penal majority xiii, 41, 45, 64, 68, 74, 93, 113, 122, 128, 138, 158
mitigation xv, 11, 71–4, 96
  See also culpability of children, lesser
Moldova *103*, 109, *208*
Monaco *103*, *208*
Mongolia 86, *103*, 109, *208*
Montenegro 87, *103*, *208*
moral agency 10–11, 13, 16, 30, 32–3, 39, 50, 53, 71–2, 91, 146
moral blame 11, 14–15, 17, 37, 39, 95–6, 115–16, 157
moral panic 115–16, 125
moral responsibility 10–11, 13–17, 32–3, 50, 53, 71–2, 146
Morocco *103*, *208*
Mozambique *103*, *108*, 127, 155, *208*
Myanmar *103*, 150, *209*

Namibia *103*, *112*, 150, *209*
Nauru *103*, 109, 127, *209*
Nepal 60, 89, *103*, 109–10, *112*, 127, 135, *209*
Netherlands 65, *103*, 120, *209*
New Zealand *104*, 110, 120, 141, *210*
NGOs, *See* non-governmental organizations
Nicaragua *104*, *112*, 121, *210*
Niger *104*, 150, *210*
Nigeria 60, 62, 82–3, *104*, 109–10, 127, 133, 154, *210*
non-discrimination, principle of 60, 64, 68, 82–3, 158
  See also discrimination
non-governmental organizations (NGOs) 70, 159, 163
North America 5, 160
Norway 65, *104*, *211*

Oman 84, *104*, *112*, 133, *211*

Packer, Herbert L. 94–7, 129, 136
Pakistan 81–3, *104*, 109–10, 127, 150–52, *211*
Palau *104*, *211*
Panama *104*, *112*, *211*
Papua New Guinea *104*, 110, 137, *211*
Paraguay *104*, *112*, *212*
parens patriae 5–7, 9, 25
parents and legal guardians 3, 5–6, 16, 21–4, 26, 29, 120, 133, 140, 143–4, 152
    responsibility for children's acts 120
participation, *See* effective participation at trial, children's right to
pauper laws 4–6
penal majority, minimum age of, *See* minimum age of penal majority
penal minority, minimum age of, *See* MACR
peremptory norm of international law 153
Peru *104*, *112*, *212*
Peters, Rudolph 79
Philippines *104*, *112*, 113, 125, 132, 152, *212*
Poland 61, 86–7, *104*, 109, 127, 138, *212*
police 120–21, 123, 133, 143, 149, 152–3
    custody, cells, stations, etc. 49, 61, 64, 68, 154, 158
politics
    in defining criminal responsibility 15–16
    in redefining childhood 4, 15–16, 114, 116–17, 121–2, 124–5, 159, 161
    political exploitation of childhood 37, 114, 116–17, 121–5, 129, 161
Portugal *104*, *112*, 128, *212*
positivism 6, 9
predicting future offenders, difficulties in 140–41
prevention programs, *See* delinquency, effective prevention and intervention programs
prison, *See* deprivation of liberty
protection rights 1–3, 6, 17, 25, 30–31, 33, 38, 59
puberty 60, 88, 110, 127
    in Islamic law 78–9, 81–4, 91, 127
    in Roman law 71–3, 91

public opinion and perceptions of youth crime 14–16, 36–7, 66, 96, 155, 161, 163
punishment
    cruel, inhuman, or degrading, *See* torture and other cruel, inhuman, or degrading treatment or punishment
    Packer's definition of 94–6, 158
    See also criminal punishment, Packer's definition of

Qatar 82, *104*, *212*

re-education through labor 87, 137–8
reformatories, *See* institutions
refugee law xv
rehabilitation, Packer's definition of 95–6, 158
reintegration, principle of 36–8, 130
religious law systems 87–90
    See also Islamic law
Republic of Korea 62, *104*, 137, *213*
responsibility, construction of 15–16
restorative justice 36, 162
Roman law 71–5, 77, 90–91, 148
Romania 65, 86–7, *104*, 152–3, *213*
Russian Federation 86–7, *104*, 109, 138, 151, *213*
    See also Soviet law
Rwanda *105*, *214*

Saint Kitts and Nevis *105*, *214*
Saint Lucia *105*, *214*
Saint Vincent and the Grenadines *105*, *214*
Samoa 89, *105*, *112*, *214*
San Marino *105*, *214*
Sao Tome and Principe *105*, 137, *214*
Sarkozy, Nicolas 123
Saudi Arabia 82, *105*, 109–10, *112*, 127, *215*
Scandinavia 109
scared straight programs 138
schools 20–22, 37–8, 118, 120, 123, 140–44, 160, 162
    law enforcement presence and measures in 120, 123
    prevention and intervention programs in 142–4, 160, 162
    See also institutions

Schüler-Springorum, Horst 51–2
Senegal 63, *105*, *215*
Serbia 87, *105*, *215*
serious crimes, MACRs for nominally, *See* ages of criminal responsibility, multiple
Seychelles *105*, 110, *215*
shari'a 52, 90, 154
   See also Islamic law
Sierra Leone 89, *105*, *112*, *215*
Singapore *105*, *215*
situación irregular 8, 44, 49, 60, 63, 94, 111, 113, 121, 128, 161
   See also Latin America
Slovakia 65, 87, *105*, *112*, 124, *215*
Slovenia 87, *105*, 138, *215*
SNAP Under 12 Outreach Project 143–4
social control 5, 9, 12, 14–15, 17
social responsibility 14–17, 36–9, 91, 116, 163
social welfare approach, *See* welfare approach
Solomon Islands *105*, 109, 127, *216*
Somalia 19, 41, 49, 82–3, 89, *105*, 109, 127, *216*
South Africa 89, *106*, *112*, 117, 150, 152, *216*
Soviet law
   influence on MACR history 76–7, 84–7, 90–91, 109
   problematic responses in countries influenced by 87, 90, 94, 137–8, 155, 161
Spain 65, *106*, *112*, *216*
Sri Lanka 43, *106*, 133, 150, *216*
statistics, *See* data collection and analysis
status offenses xiv
street children 49, 133, 149
Sudan 60, 82–3, *106*, 109–10, 127, *217*
Suriname *106*, *112*, *217*
Swaziland *106*, *112*, *217*
Sweden 65, *106*, 141, *217*
Switzerland 44, *106*, *112*, 120, 139, *217*
Syria *106*, *112*, 113, *217*

Tajikistan 87, *106*, 109, 138, *217*
Tanenhaus, David S. 6
Tanzania *107*, 109, *112*, 132, 153–5, *221*

terrorism laws, MACRs in 59–60, 64, 68
Thailand *106*, *112*, 152, *218*
Timor-Leste *106*, *112*, *218*
Togo *106*, *218*
Tonga *106*, *218*
Toronto, Canada 143–4
torture and other cruel, inhuman, or degrading treatment or punishment 49, 66–7, 120, 136, 138, 154
traditional law systems 87–90, 163
treatment, Packer's definition of 95–6, 129
tribal law systems 87–90
Trinidad and Tobago *106*, *218*
Tunisia *106*, *218*
Turkey 65–6, *106*, 137, *219*
Turkmenistan *106*, 109, *219*
Tuvalu *106*, 110, *219*

Uganda *106*, *112*, 117, 154, *219*
Ukraine 87, *107*, 109, 138, *219*
unaccompanied children 135, 152–3
UNICEF (United Nations Children's Fund) 54, 83, 113
United Arab Emirates 82, *107*, *220*
United Kingdom of Great Britain and Northern Ireland 4–5, 28–9, 71, *107*, 109–10, *112*, 113, 139, 141, *220*
   Bulger case 66–7, 114–17, 120–21, 125
   influence on MACR history 74–7, 88, 90–91, 109–10, 148
   problems with *doli incapax* in the past 148–9
   See also common law
United Nations Centre for Social Development and Humanitarian Affairs 51, 54, 56
United Nations General Assembly 19, 53, 111
United Nations Guidelines for the Prevention of Juvenile Delinquency 21
United Nations High Commissioner for Refugees 135
United Nations Rules for the Protection of Juveniles Deprived of their Liberty 22

United Nations Special Rapporteur on
    Torture 138
United Nations Standard Minimum Rules
    for the Administration of Juvenile
    Justice (Beijing Rules) ix–x, 26–7,
    32–3, 44, 50–56, 58, 66–7, 69, 145
United States of America 19, 41, 49, *107*,
    109–10, 127, 140–41, *221*
  adjudicative competence, 145–7, 156,
    160
    See also effective participation at
        trial, children's right to
  and juvenile justice history 5–6, 9–10
  MACR and juvenile justice
    trends 117–21, 123, 126
United States Supreme Court 9–10, 51, 118
Universal Declaration of Human
    Rights 19, 29

Uruguay 46, *108*, *112*, 120, *222*
Uzbekistan 86–7, *108*, 109, 138, *223*

Vanuatu *108*, *223*
Venezuela *108*, *112*, *223*
Viet Nam 86–7, *108*, 110, 138, *223*
views of the child, respect for the 20,
    26–7, 30, 38, 147, 160
vigilante justice against children 154–5, 161

welfare approach 1, 4–10, 15–17, 19, 22,
    24–5, 28, 37–8, 51, 63, 90, 94, 96,
    114, 118, 122, 128–9, 159, 161

Yemen 82, 89, *108*, *224*

Zambia *108*, 110, *224*
Zimbabwe *108*, 110, *224*

Advances in Criminology

Full series list

Hate on the Net:
Extremist Sites, Neo-fascism On-line,
Electronic Jihad
Antonio Roversi

Decisions to Imprison:
Court Decision-Making Inside
and Outside the Law
Rasmus H. Wandall

The Policing of Transnational Protest
*Edited by Donatella della Porta,
Abby Peterson and Herbert Reiter*

Migration, Culture Conflict, Crime
and Terrorism
*Edited by Joshua D. Freilich and
Rob T. Guerette*

Re-Thinking the Political Economy
of Punishment:
Perspectives on Post-Fordism
and Penal Politics
Alessandro De Giorgi

Deleuze and Environmental Damage:
Violence of the Text
Mark Halsey

Globalization and Regulatory Character:
Regulatory Reform after the Kader Toy
Factory Fire
Fiona Haines

Family Violence and Police Response:
Learning From Research, Policy and
Practice in European Countries
*Edited by Wilma Smeenk and
Marijke Malsch*

Crime and Culture:
An Historical Perspective
*Edited by Amy Gilman Srebnick and
René Lévy*

Power, Discourse and Resistance:
A Genealogy of the Strangeways Prison
Riot
Eamonn Carrabine

Hard Lessons:
Reflections on Governance and Crime
Control in Late Modernity
Richard Hil and Gordon Tait

Becoming Delinquent: British and
European Youth, 1650–1950
Edited by Pamela Cox and Heather Shore

Migration, Culture Conflict and Crime
*Edited by Joshua D. Freilich, Graeme
Newman, S. Giora Shoham and
Moshe Addad*

Critique and Radical Discourses on Crime
George Pavlich

Contrasting Criminal Justice:
Getting from Here to There
Edited by David Nelken

Integrating a Victim Perspective within
Criminal Justice:
International Debates
Edited by Adam Crawford and Jo Goodey

Blood in the Bank:
Social and Legal Aspects of Death at Work
Gary Slapper

Engendering Resistance: Agency and
Power in Women's Prisons
Mary Bosworth

Governable Places:
Readings on Governmentality and Crime
Control
Edited by Russell Smandych